'Race', Ethnicity and Racism in Sports Coaching

In recent years there has been a steady increase in the racial and ethnic diversity of the playing workforce in many sports around the world. However, there has been a minimal throughput of racial and ethnic minorities into coaching and leadership positions. This book brings together leading researchers from around the world to examine key questions around 'race', ethnicity and racism in sports coaching.

The book focuses specifically on the ways in which 'race', ethnicity and racism operate, and how they are experienced and addressed (or not) within the socio-cultural sphere of sports coaching. Theoretically informed and empirically grounded, it examines macro- (societal), meso- (organisational), and micro- (individual) level barriers to racial and ethnic diversity as well as the positive action initiatives designed to help overcome them. Featuring multi-disciplinary perspectives, the book is arranged into three thematic sections, addressing the central topics of representation and racialised barriers in sports coaching; racialised identities, diversity and intersectionality in sports coaching; and formalised racial equality interventions in sports coaching.

Including case studies from across North America, Europe and Australasia, *'Race', Ethnicity and Racism in Sports Coaching* is essential reading for students, academics and practitioners with a critical interest in the sociology of sport, sport coaching, sport management, sport development, and 'race' and ethnicity studies.

Steven Bradbury is Lecturer in Sport, Equality and Diversity at the School of Sport, Exercise and Health Sciences, Loughborough University, UK. His research interests focus on 'race', ethnicity and racisms and the effectiveness of measures designed to address racialised inequalities in the playing, coaching and leadership tiers of amateur and professional football and other sports. He has been actively involved with anti-racism campaigns in football in the UK and Europe as a researcher and activist for over 25 years.

Jim Lusted is Student Experience Manager at The Open University, UK and Associate Lecturer at University of Northampton, UK. He has been researching inequalities in sport for over 15 years, focusing on the formation and implementation of equality policies in recreational sport. He has held several voluntary roles in sport including Chair of Kick It Out's Grassroots Guidance Group and is Vice-Chair of the Northamptonshire Football Association's Inclusion Advisory Group.

Jacco van Sterkenburg is Associate Professor at the Erasmus Research Centre for Media Communication and Culture, Erasmus University Rotterdam, the Netherlands. He is also a Visiting Research Fellow at the Mulier Institute – Dutch Centre for Social Science Research in Sport, the Netherlands. His research focuses on discourses surrounding race/ethnicity and whiteness in multi-ethnic society, with a particular focus on the case of sports, sports media, and sport management and leadership.

Routledge Critical Perspectives on Equality and Social Justice in Sport and Leisure

Series editors:
Kevin Hylton, Leeds Beckett University, UK
Jonathan Long, Leeds Beckett University, UK

This series presents important new critical studies that explore and explain issues relating to social justice and equality in sport and leisure. Addressing current debates and examining key concepts such as inclusion and exclusion, (anti) oppression, neo-liberalism, resistance, merit(ocracy), and sport for all, the series aims to be a key location for scholars, students and policy makers interested in these topics.

Innovative and interrogative, the series will explore central themes and issues in critical sport and leisure studies, including: theory development, methodologies and intersectionality; policy and politics; 'race', ethnicity, gender, class, sexuality, disability; communities and migration; ethics and morals; and media and new technologies. Inclusive and transdisciplinary, it aims to showcase high quality work from leading and emerging scholars working in sport and leisure studies, sport development, sport coaching and PE, policy, events and health studies, and areas of sport science that consider the same concerns.

Available in this series:

Sport, Leisure and Social Justice
Edited by Jonathan Long, Thomas Fletcher and Beccy Watson

Youth Sport, Migration and Culture
Two Football Teams and the Changing Face of Ireland
Max Mauro

'Race', Youth Sport, Physical Activity and Health
Global Perspectives
Edited by Symeon Dagkas, Laura Azzarito and Kevin Hylton

'Race', Ethnicity and Racism in Sports Coaching
Edited by Steven Bradbury, Jim Lusted and Jacco van Sterkenburg

'Race', Ethnicity and Racism in Sports Coaching

Edited by
Steven Bradbury, Jim Lusted and Jacco van Sterkenburg

LONDON AND NEW YORK

First published 2021
by Routledge
2 Park Square, Milton Park, Abingdon, Oxon OX14 4RN

and by Routledge
52 Vanderbilt Avenue, New York, NY 10017

Routledge is an imprint of the Taylor & Francis Group, an informa business

© 2021 selection and editorial matter, Steven Bradbury, Jim Lusted and Jacco van Sterkenburg; individual chapters, the contributors

The right of Steven Bradbury, Jim Lusted and Jacco van Sterkenburg to be identified as the authors of the editorial material, and of the authors for their individual chapters, has been asserted in accordance with sections 77 and 78 of the Copyright, Designs and Patents Act 1988.

With the exception of Chapter 3, no part of this book may be reprinted or reproduced or utilised in any form or by any electronic, mechanical, or other means, now known or hereafter invented, including photocopying and recording, or in any information storage or retrieval system, without permission in writing from the publishers.

Chapter 1 of this book is available for free in PDF format as Open Access from the individual product page at www.routledge.com. It has been made available under a Creative Commons Attribution-Non Commercial-No Derivatives 4.0 license.

Trademark notice: Product or corporate names may be trademarks or registered trademarks, and are used only for identification and explanation without intent to infringe.

British Library Cataloguing-in-Publication Data
A catalogue record for this book is available from the British Library

Library of Congress Cataloging-in-Publication Data
A catalog record has been requested for this book

ISBN: 978-0-367-42669-9 (hbk)
ISBN: 978-0-367-85428-7 (ebk)

Typeset in Goudy
by Taylor & Francis Books

Contents

List of contributors	x
Acknowledgements	xiv
Introduction	xv
STEVEN BRADBURY, JIM LUSTED AND JACCO VAN STERKENBURG	

PART I
Representation and racialised barriers in sports coaching   1

1 The under-representation of racial minorities in coaching and leadership positions in the United States   3
GEORGE B. CUNNINGHAM

2 'Fit for doing but not fit for organising': Racisms, stereotypes and networks in coaching in professional football in Europe   22
STEVEN BRADBURY

3 Is there a glass ceiling or can racial and ethnic barriers be overcome?: a study on leadership positions in professional Belgian football among African coaches   43
CHRIS HEIM, JORIS CORTHOUTS AND JEROEN SCHEERDER

4 Race, ethnicity, whiteness and mediated stereotypes in football coaching: the Dutch context   59
JACCO VAN STERKENBURG

5 British Asian football coaches: exploring the barriers and advocating action in English football   78
DANIEL KILVINGTON

PART II
Racialised identities, diversity and intersectionality in sports coaching   95

6 Finding the 'natural': talent identification and racialisation in sports coaching and selection practices in Australia   97
   BRENT MCDONALD AND RAMÓN SPAAIJ

7 From freedom to oppression?: a Freirean perspective on coaching and indigenous players' journeys to the NRL and AFL   112
   RICHARD LIGHT AND JOHN EVANS

8 Black women, intersectionality and sport coaching   128
   ALEXANDRA J. RANKIN-WRIGHT AND KEVIN HYLTON

9 Beyond the Xs and Os: the representation of black college coaches   143
   JOYCE OLUSHOLA-OGUNRINDE AND AKILAH R. CARTER-FRANCIQUE

10 Transnational coaches: a critical exploration of intersections of race/ethnicity and gender   160
   ANNELIES KNOPPERS AND DONNA DE HAAN

PART III
Formalised racial equality interventions in sports coaching   177

11 When the law won't work: the US National Football League's extra-judicial approach to addressing employment discrimination in coaching   179
   N. JEREMI DURU

12 The EFL voluntary code of recruitment: using reflexive regulation to increase the racial diversity of professional football coaching in England   196
   SOPHIE COWELL

13 Game changer or empty promise?: the EFL mandatory code of coach recruitment in men's professional football youth academies in England   211
   DOMINIC CONRICODE AND STEVEN BRADBURY

PART IV
Conclusions 233

14 Priorities for researching 'race', ethnicity and racism in sports coaching and recommendations for future practice 235
JIM LUSTED, STEVEN BRADBURY AND JACCO VAN STERKENBURG

Index 254

Contributors

Steven Bradbury is Lecturer in Sport, Equality and Diversity at the School of Sport, Exercise and Health Sciences, Loughborough University, UK. His research interests focus on 'race', ethnicity and racisms and the effectiveness of measures designed to address racialised inequalities in the playing, coaching and leadership tiers of amateur and professional football and other sports. He has been actively involved with anti-racism campaigns in football in the UK and Europe as a researcher and activist for over 25 years.

Akilah R. Carter-Francique is an Associate Professor at San Jose State University (SJSU) in the Department of African American Studies. She also serves as the Executive Director for the Institute for the Study of Sport, Society, and Social Change (ISSSSC) at SJSU. Her scholarly endeavours and field of focus encompasses issues of diversity, social movements, and the dynamics of social change and development with an emphasis on race and gender sporting experiences.

George B. Cunningham is a Professor and Sr. Assistant Provost for Graduate and Professional Studies at Texas A&M University. His research focus is on diversity and inclusion in sport and physical activity. He has published over 200 peer-reviewed journal articles and book chapters; has authored an award-winning book (Diversity in Sport Organizations); and has co-edited an award-winning book (Routledge Handbook of Theory in Sport Management). He is a member of the National Academy of Kinesiology.

Dominic Conricode is a doctoral researcher at the School of Sport, Exercise and Health Sciences, Loughborough University, UK. His research examines the representation and experiences of Black, Asian and Minority Ethnic (BAME) coaches in professional football, and the efficacy of positive action measures designed to address racialised inequities in the professional coaching industry.

Joris Corthouts is a scientific researcher within the Policy in Sports & Physical Activity Research Group within the Department of Movement Sciences at the KU Leuven, Belgium. Currently, he prepares a PhD thesis as part of the Flemish Policy Research Centre on Sports 2017–2022. His research focuses on sociological aspects of organisational innovation within the non-profit sports sector.

Sophie Cowell is a researcher for the Forum for Research into Equality and Diversity, that sits within the University of Chester Law School, UK. Her research interests focus on Discrimination Law and its application within sport. She is studying for a PhD considering the use of positive action to increase the representation of Black, Asian and Minority Ethnic football coaches.

Donna de Haan is a Principal Lecturer at the Hague University of Applied Sciences in the Netherlands. Her teaching and research expertise lie in the field of inclusion and diversity associated with issues of participation, coaching, leadership and governance in sport. Her work has been published in numerous peer-reviewed journals including Sports Coaching Review, the International Review for the Sociology of Sport, and she has been awarded grants for her work on gender equity from the International Olympic Committee, UEFA and Erasmus.

N. Jeremi Duru is a Professor of Law at American University's Washington College of Law. He studies all aspects of sports law, with a focus on race, gender and disability discrimination in the sports industry. He is the author of Advancing the Ball: Race, Reformation, and the Quest for Equal Coaching Opportunity in the NFL.

John Evans is Professor of Indigenous Health Education in the school of Sport and Exercise Science in the Faculty of Health at the University of Technology Sydney. He has a research background in sport pedagogy, Indigenous sport pedagogy and Indigenous education.

Chris Heim is a scientific researcher within the Policy in Sports & Physical Activity Research Group in the Department of Movement Sciences at the KU Leuven, Belgium. His main research lies in sport sociology, sport anthropology and sport management. His main focus is on investigating the issue of racism in football in Belgium, along with examining corporate social responsibility (CSR) as a tool to promote social inclusion and to tackle discrimination in sport.

Kevin Hylton is Emeritus Professor of Equality and Diversity in Sport, Leisure and Education, Leeds Beckett University, UK. Kevin's research is world-leading in regard to race research in sport and education. Kevin authored 'Race' and Sport: Critical Race Theory and Contesting 'Race' and Sport: Shaming the Colour Line. Kevin is Visiting Professor at the

University of South Wales and was formerly Head of the Research Centre for Diversity, Equity and Inclusion at Leeds Beckett University.

Daniel Kilvington is a Senior Lecturer in Media, Communication, Cultures at Leeds Beckett University, UK. His research interests focus on 'race' and racism within sport and new media contexts. He is the founder of the annual Sport and Discrimination Conference series and the BAME inclusion initiative, Creating and Developing Coaches.

Annelies Knoppers is Professor (emerita) at the Utrecht School of Governance, Utrecht University, Netherlands. Her research and publications have focused on the often invisible processes that may hamper the practice and implementation of diversity in coaching, sport administration and boards of directors. She was a senior editor of the Sociology of Sport Journal and is currently a member of the editorial board of Sport Management Review. She has been awarded grants directed towards changing current gendered practices in sport by the Dutch Organization for Scientific Research and the International Olympic Committee and has chaired research and dissertation committees at national and international levels.

Richard Light is Professor of Sport Pedagogy at the University of Canterbury, New Zealand and has held positions in Australia, the UK and France. He has a strong research profile in sport pedagogy with an emphasis on situating learning, coaching and teaching in larger cultural and institutional contexts and has recently extended this programme of research to focus on Indigenous sport in Australia, New Zealand and Fiji.

Jim Lusted is Student Experience Manager at The Open University, UK and Associate Lecturer at University of Northampton, UK. He has been researching inequalities in sport for over 15 years, focusing on the formation and implementation of equality policies in recreational sport. He has held several voluntary roles in sport including Chair of Kick It Out's Grassroots Guidance Group and is Vice-Chair of the Northamptonshire Football Association's Inclusion Advisory Group.

Brent McDonald is a senior lecturer in the sociology of sport at Victoria University. His research focuses on sport in the post-colonial context and racialisation. In particular he examines the return of biological notions of race and the ways in which these ideas enter popular discourse.

Joyce Olushola-Ogunrinde is an Assistant Professor of Health and Human Performance at the University of Houston, USA. Her research interests focus on uncovering the cultural meanings associated with sport for African American communities and redefining those meanings more emically to create sport programmes that can be leveraged to redress health, social and economic disparities. In this way, she seeks to redefine sport, and consequently, its utility in our society.

Alexandra J. Rankin-Wright is an award-winning researcher, whose work is recognised nationally and internationally within the area of 'race' and gender equity and issues of diversity and inclusion related to sports coaching. AJ is an Assistant Professor at Durham University, having previously worked as a researcher at Leeds Beckett University and for the International Council for Coach Education.

Jeroen Scheerder is professor of sport policy and sport sociology in the Department of Movement Sciences (KU Leuven) where he heads the Policy in Sports & Physical Activity Research Group. He is promotor-coordinator of the Flemish Policy Research Centre on Sports and was president of the European Association for Sociology of Sport (2014–2016). His research focuses on political and sociological aspects of sport and physical activity. He is co-founder of both the European MEASURE and POLIS Research Networks that focus on sport participation and sport policy/sport politics respectively.

Ramón Spaaij is a Professor at Victoria University in Melbourne, Australia, and Special Chair of Sociology of Sport in the Department of Sociology at the University of Amsterdam. Ramón's research focuses on questions of social cohesion, conflict and social change. He has two established fields of research that address these questions: the sociology of sport and the sociology of terrorism. His work has contributed to contemporary academic and public debates on sport's relationship to diversity, social inclusion, community development and violence.

Jacco van Sterkenburg is Associate Professor at the Erasmus Research Centre for Media Communication and Culture, Erasmus University Rotterdam, the Netherlands. He is also a Visiting Research Fellow at the Mulier Institute – Dutch Centre for Social Science Research in Sport, the Netherlands. His research focuses on discourses surrounding race/ethnicity and whiteness in multi-ethnic society, with a particular focus on the case of sports, sports media, and sport management and leadership.

Acknowledgements

Firstly, we would like to thank the scholars featured in this volume for their individual and collaborative efforts in producing high-quality chapters and for their powerful and insightful contributions in this respect. We are greatly appreciative of your receptiveness, patience and professionalism in engaging with the editorial process, particularly against the backdrop of broader institutional pressures in academia.

Secondly, we would like to thank the research participants drawn from a range of dominant and marginalised ethnicities whose perceptions and experiences feature prominently within many of the chapters in this volume. We are particularly appreciative of those who have been willing to share and reflect on often difficult and challenging personal experiences of racisms and other intersectional forms of discrimination in the sports coaching context.

Thirdly, we would like to thank the Routledge commissioning, editorial and production team for their efforts in enabling the completion of this volume, in particular; Simon Whitmore and Rebecca Connor. We would also like to thank the Routledge Critical Perspectives on Equality and Social Justice in Sport and Leisure Series Editors, Professor Kevin Hylton and Professor Jonathon Long, whose intellectual support and guidance was also greatly appreciated.

Finally, we would like to thank our respective families and friends for your love, patience and understanding throughout the completion of this volume. Without you, much less is possible.

Introduction

Steven Bradbury, Jim Lusted and Jacco van Sterkenburg

'Race', ethnicity and racism in sports coaching: the broader context

The social and cultural arena of sport is often held up in popular public and mediated discourse as an increasingly post-racial, meritocratic and egalitarian space where 'race' no longer matters and where racial inequalities are a thing of the past (Carrington, 2010; Hartmann, 2000; Van Sterkenburg et al., 2019). Such assumptions draw heavily on the increased incidence of sport performers from diverse racial, ethnic and cultural backgrounds, whose participation in the playing tiers of some sports in many Western countries has become comparable to or exceeded national racial population demographics (Bradbury et al, 2011; Lapchick, 2017; Watson et al., 2017). These successful sporting endeavours are often posited as evidence of the inherent inclusivity of sport and its assumed capacity to offer opportunities for advancement for minoritised[1] groups in ways which might be denied in other areas of social and public life. However, these powerful (and powerfully dominant) neo-liberalist narratives arguably promulgate the apolitical, meritocratic and integrative myth of sporting modernity and overplay the extent to which access to and experiences of sport are free from wider social, cultural and economic limits and pressures. Such majoritarian stories and related '*melting pot idealism*' (Hylton, 2012: 30) also arguably underplay the extent and ways in which the development, organisation and practice of sport is informed by a series of historically inscribed and deeply racialised power relations which are reflective of and reflect back on the societies in which they take place (Andrews, 2002). More recently, however, an emerging discourse – led by high-profile minoritised sporting figures – has begun to problematise this de-racialised sporting idealism. This quote from Chris Hughton, arguably the most successful black football manager in England, illustrates such a position:

> When I started my pathway, black players were often considered to be good wingers, good players, but not captain or management material. It

has changed since then, which is pleasing, but we still have so far to go. We [BAME managers] don't want tokenism, but there needs to be a transitional period that allows us an opportunity. The culture has to change to allow good, worthy coaches to be associated with big clubs and big organisations.

(quoted in Banerjee, 2018)

This more critical view of the role of 'race' in shaping sporting opportunities is also slowly being taken up among political and policy circles too, with recognition of an institutionalised basis of racism in sport – exemplified in a policy recommendation from the European Commission against Racism and Intolerance (ECRI):

> Sport can be a powerful tool for promoting social cohesion and important values, such as fair play, mutual respect and tolerance. But sometimes it is also an area in which racism and racial discrimination can thrive……There is persuasive evidence that racism and racial discrimination in sport goes beyond the individual or collective behaviour of fans or isolated cases of racist gestures and remarks made, for example, by athletes, coaches or club managers. In fact, institutional racism is also at work in the field of sport.
>
> (COE/ECRI, 2008)

From this more critical perspective, sport can be understood less as a natural harbinger of meritocracy and equitable 'race' relations, and more as a distinctly 'racial formation' (Omi & Winant 2002) wherein a series of hierarchical racialised structures, ideologies and practices have been created, maintained and contested over time (Ansari, 2004; Carrington, 2010).

This is evident in the ways in which a multiplicity of individual, institutional and structural racisms impinge upon and are generated in and through the organisation and practice of sports – as implied by the quotes above from Chris Hughton and ECRI. This happens both in explicit ways and in subtle and less visible forms. The multi-dimensional and multi-levelled character of these racisms, and related forms of racialised discrimination, has also impacted in shaping the opportunities, experiences and outcomes of different minoritised groups in different ways across a range of intersectional indices and national contexts and with respect to different tiers of sport. In this respect, as Hylton & Lawrence (2016: 2742) have argued:

> *Off field social rituals, the historical legacy of racial inequalities, failures in practice and policy and racialised intolerance converge to create conditions, across various sports, whereby white, able bodied, middle class, heterosexual men are disproportionately advantaged to obtain and maintain status as players, coaches and administrators.*

Whilst over the last 40 years there has steadily developed a relatively extensive body of academic work examining the complex and shifting relationship between 'race', ethnicity and sport, much of this academic inquiry has focused on issues pertaining to the racialised identities and experiences of minoritised athletes. In contrast, much less scholarly attention has been paid to the under-researched field of racial diversity and sports coaching. Where empirical research of this kind has been undertaken it has been conducted in a fairly isolated way and has been largely limited in its focus to professional and college sports in the US and more recently to professional football and amateur sports contexts in England and Europe. This relatively disparate but overlapping body of scholarly work has been published sporadically in peer-reviewed journals, as stand-alone book chapters within edited collections, or referred to more generally in monographs which focus on issues of 'race', ethnicity and sport, or socio-cultural aspects of sport more broadly (e.g., Hassan & Acton, 2018; Hylton, 2009, 2018; Kilvington & Price, 2017; Lavoi, 2016; Ratna & Farooq Samie, 2018). As a result, this field of study has tended to feel marginalised from and peripheral to the more central empirical and analytical concerns of 'race' and sport scholars and of scholars examining broader equality and diversity issues in sports coaching.

Nonetheless, where research of this kind has been undertaken, it has alluded to the general under-representation of coaches from minoritised backgrounds and patterns of occupational segregation in the coaching workforce across a range of national and sporting contexts (Braddock et al., 2012; Bradbury et al., 2018; Cunningham, 2010,; Day, 2015; Norman et al., 2014; Lapchick, 2017). A number of scholars have argued these representational disparities are underscored by a series of embedded racialised barriers at the macro (societal), meso (organisational) and micro (individual) level. For example, at the meso level, they have identified monocultural processes and cultures within sports organisations and have alluded to the ways in which practices of unconscious racial bias and the operation of racially closed networks-based approaches to coach recruitment have sustained patterns of 'homologous reproduction' within the coaching workforce (Bradbury et al., 2018; Branham, 2008; Cunningham, 2010; Regan & Feagin, 2017; Sagas & Cunningham, 2005; Sartore & Cunningham, 2006; Singer et al., 2010). Also, at the micro level, they have drawn attention to the often inequitable interactional spaces of voluntary and professional sports coaching environments where the existence and application of racialised microaggressions, incivility and stereotyping has problematised the actions and behaviours of some minoritised coaches (and players) (Cunningham et al., 2012; Gearity & Henderson Metzger,2017; Jowett & Frost, 2007; King, 2004; Khomutova, 2016; Zhang, 2017). Whilst scholarly work in this field has focused primarily on men's sports, recent studies have also extended theoretical and empirical analysis to identify and examine the intersectional experiences of racism amongst minoritised women. In particular, these studies have alluded to the double marginalisation of minoritised women from and within sports coaching contexts across a range of professional, educational and more recreational sports settings (Abney, 2007; Borland & Bruening, 2010; Bruening, 2005; Carter-Francique & Olushola, 2016; Rankin-Wright et al., 2016, 2017, 2018). Taken together, this work has drawn attention to the myriad processes and practices of racialised (and gendered) access and treatment discrimination in sports coaching, and the deleterious impacts of these constraints in limiting the pace and scope of career progression for minoritised coaches across a range of national and sporting contexts. Further, the relative permanence of these racialised inequities in sports coaching (and the mixed success of measures designed to address them) is argued by some scholars to be underscored by the normative relational and definitional power of hegemonic whiteness (and masculinity) embedded within the senior decision-making tiers of sports organisations (Bradbury et al., 2018; Hylton, 2018; Rankin-Wright et al., 2017). These racialised (and gendered) power relations have arguably enabled institutional and intersectional forms of racism to be effortlessly reproduced and perpetuated, and for the dominant hegemonic structures and cultures which underpin them to have remained unchallenged and unchanged over time. As a result, many highly qualified and appropriately experienced minoritised coaches have remained excluded from or have been positioned as 'outsiders within' the culturally narrow occupational marketplace of sports coaching.

About the book

This book is the first comprehensive collection of academic work focusing specifically on issues of 'race', ethnicity and racism in sports coaching, and aims to provide a timely and insightful scholarly contribution to this relatively marginalised field of study in one volume. It also has a significant degree of topicality, in the context of recent popular, mediated and academic debates around the lack of racial diversity in the sports coaching workforce, and growing calls for the implementation of positive action measures such as the US National Football League (NFL) 'Rooney Rule' to redress this racialised imbalance across a range of national and sporting contexts[2]. The book also has a particular relevance for scholars and practitioners with an interest in examining the relationship between racial diversity and operational effectiveness in the sports coaching workplace, and with particular respect to supporting the vocational development and career progression of minoritised coaches and players within these settings.

The book has an international scope and includes contributions from authors from six countries (United States, Australia, New Zealand, England, Belgium, Netherlands) across three continents (North America,

Australasia, Europe). Whilst some of these authors discuss issues of racial diversity and sports coaching at a transnational and continental level, in other cases they focus on the experiences of minoritised coaches within specific national boundaries. The book also has a strongly multi-disciplinary focus and includes contributions from authors working within a range of academic disciplines, including; the sociology of sport, sport pedagogy, sport psychology, sport management and critical legal and media studies. As a result, the authors draw on and apply a range of distinct but overlapping theoretical and conceptual approaches in their analysis, including; Critical Race Theory, Cultural Studies, Social Dominance Theory, Post Structuralism, Black Feminism, Intersectionality, Critical Pedagogy, and Multi-Level Models of analysis.

The authors featured in this collection also draw on a range of quantitative and more qualitative methodologies to provide a series of highly original empirical findings which allude to the levels of representation and racialised experiences of minoritised coaches and the broader national political and sport policy landscapes within which they take place. Central to these methodological approaches is the concerted efforts of some authors to access, foreground and critically reflect on the experientially informed narratives of research participants drawn from dominant and marginalised ethnicities, in order to present a holistic and culturally considered account of processes, events and outcomes. Such approaches also provide an important mechanism through which to illuminate the voices and render visible the historically subjugated testimonies of diverse minoritised groups whose experiences have traditionally been excluded from dominant master narratives on the realities and impacts of 'race' and racism across a range of societal and sporting contexts (Solórzano & Yosso, 2002; Hylton, 2005). In this respect, the authors in this collection have been encouraged by the editorial team to exercise an epistemologically and culturally reflexive approach to the presentation and analysis of research findings, and to explicitly acknowledge the ways in which their own racialised and gendered identities and social, cultural and political positionality have impacted on the research process. This is especially important given the diverse positions of research participants and authors and the commonalities and specificities of their experiences across a range of national and sporting contexts. It is important that we as editors also reflect on our own social, cultural and political positionality as three White Western European males each working in the distinctly middle-class arena of academia in our respective countries of origin. In particular, in relation to the privileged space our own professional, racialised, gendered and classed identities imbue with respect to reporting on rather than being subject to the myriad racisms and racialised inequalities discussed in this collection. As a result, throughout the editorial process and in relation to the production of our own chapters we have sought to reflect on the ways in which such positioning might impact on the process of meaning making and knowledge production. In doing so, we argue that a theoretically informed and lived engagement with the practice of critical and cultural reflexivity is a useful epistemological tool through which to better consider the self and the self in relation to others (Fletcher, 2014; Fletcher & Hylton, 2017; Frankenberg, 2004; Van Sterkenburg, 2011). In particular, it has enabled us to broaden the diversity of discourses we draw upon to help make sense of and better represent emergent experiential narratives in a more culturally considered and balanced way. Such an approach squares firmly with our scholarly commitment to make visible, challenge and disrupt dominant forms of normative White privilege and to engage in work which contributes to transformational social justice at a sporting and societal level.

The authors featured in this collection are drawn from a relatively diverse but not fully representative range of racial, ethnic, cultural and gender backgrounds: 11 are White men, four are White women, three are minoritised men, and two are minoritised women. The demographic make-up of these authors is to some extent reflective of the comparative under-representation of minoritised and women scholars in the White male dominated field of sports studies more broadly and the study of 'race', ethnicity and sport more specifically. This 'diversity shortfall' is also replicated in the small but developing field of study into racial diversity in sports coaching, especially in the countries which have formed the analytical foci of this book. The inclusion of authors in this collection (as with edited collections more broadly) is to some extent also informed by a set of more practical considerations. In particular, the existing research priorities, availability and willingness of authors to proactively respond to calls for contributions and to deliver chapters on the topic under review in a timely fashion. In this latter respect, it is hoped that the scholarly contributions which do feature in this collection will act as an intellectual stimulus to scholars from a diverse range of backgrounds to extend empirical and critical analysis in this important field of study in the future and in ways which both supplement and challenge the work featured herein.

Thematic overview of the book

This book features a variety of focused, overlapping and complementary contributions which each has as its primary focus an examination of the ways in which 'race', ethnicity and racism operate and are experienced within the socio-cultural sphere of sports coaching. In each case, the authors begin by outlining their own theoretical and methodological positioning before drawing on relevant empirical data to offer an academically substantive account of the issues under review. The authors also provide some clarification and justification for the use of their preferred terminological classification to describe minoritised and majority populations. See the earlier endnote in this chapter for our justification of the use of the term 'minoritised' in both the Introduction and concluding chapter of this collection. The authors (and editorial team) remain cognisant that categorisations of this kind which seek to capture the commonalities and specificities of diverse racial and ethnic identities and their varied and overlapping experiences remain conceptually limited and subject to contestation. This task is made more difficult in the context of the myriad racial, ethnic and cultural diversity of populations referred to in this collection and the distinct national and sporting contexts in which their experiences have been 'played out'. As a result, the conceptually preferred terminologies utilised by authors can be understood to be reflective of both dominant academic discourses and the everyday nomenclature of research participants at specific temporal moments, and to have significant practical utility for the international readership of this collection in identifying commonalities and differences in experiences and outcomes across distinct socio-cultural and spatial boundaries. Finally, the authors each provide some contextually considered and culturally relevant policy-based and practical recommendations for action for key stakeholders with respect to addressing racialised inequities in sports coaching. These nationally and culturally specific recommendations will be developed further in a more holistic way by the editors in the concluding chapter.

The chapters featured in this collection are presented in the following thematic way across three key sections; (i) Representation and racialised barriers in sports coaching, (ii) Racialised identities, diversity and intersectionality in sports coaching, and (iii) Formalised racial equality interventions in sports coaching.

(i) Representation and racialised barriers in sports coaching

Chapter 1 is written by **George B. Cunningham** and provides a useful overarching multi-level analysis of the key factors which have impacted in maintaining the comparative under-representation of racial minorities in coaching and leadership positions in US sports. In doing so, the chapter draws on the author's own extensive work and a range of related studies in the field to identify and examine a series of racialised barriers at the macro (societal), meso (organisational), and micro (individual) level of sports coaching. This opening chapter has particular relevance and transferability in outlining in a broad way many of the issues examined in a more contextually focused and qualitatively detailed way by other authors featured in this collection. For example, **Chapters 2, 3, 4** and **5** extend Cunningham's focus and analysis to the study of 'race', ethnicity and racism in coaching in professional football in Europe. In each case, the authors identify similarly low levels of representation of minoritised coaches across a range of national contexts. **Chapter 2** is written by **Steven Bradbury** and draws on more than 60 interviews with key football stakeholders in 15 countries and elite level minoritised coaches in England, France and the Netherlands. The author identifies a series of key constraining factors which have limited opportunities for the career progression of minoritised coaches from a diverse range of racial, ethnic and cultural backgrounds across the transition from playing to coaching in professional football. In particular, the author alludes to the existence and application of racisms and racial stereotypes and the reliance on networks-based approaches to coach recruitment as primary factors underpinning ongoing racialised inequities in the senior echelons of the professional game in Europe. **Chapter 3** is written by **Chris Heim, Joris Corthouts and Jeroen Scheerder** and provides an original and insightful statistical analysis of the representation of North African, Sub-Saharan African and other 'visible' minoritised coaches in professional football in Belgium. The authors locate these empirical findings within the broader context of the interconnection between 'race', ethnicity and football in Belgian society, and draw on Social Dominance Theory to argue that the under-representation of minoritised coaches is underscored and preserved by a series of hierarchy enhancing legitimising myths at a societal and sporting level. **Chapter 4** is written by **Jacco van Sterkenburg** and also provides original empirical data pertaining to the under-representation and lack of throughput of minoritised coaches into the elite tiers of professional football in the Netherlands. The author also draws on the experiential narratives and sometimes contrasting perceptions of ten minoritised coaches from a diverse range of racial, ethnic and cultural backgrounds to identify and examine some key explanatory factors in this respect. In doing so, the author alludes to implicit mechanisms of racial and ethnic inclusion and exclusion, the inclusivity and exclusivity of networks, the role of stereotypes and lack of minoritised coach role models, and the operation of whiteness and pressures on minoritised coaches to 'play down' oppositional racial and ethnic identities in the Dutch professional football context. **Chapter 5** is written by **Daniel Kilvington** and extends his extensive prior work with British Asian players to examine the racialised experiences of British Asian coaches in professional and amateur football in England. Drawing on interview data with four British Asian coaches, Kilvington alludes to the existence of overt and inferential racisms, cultural and body stereotypes, racially closed networks, and a lack of British Asian coach role models as key factors which have contributed to and sustained the extended marginalisation of British Asian coaches beyond that of other (Black) minoritised groups with stronger prior playing capital in English football. The qualitative contributions of Kilvington (Chapter 5), Van Sterkenburg (Chapter 4) and Bradbury (Chapter 2) are each informed by and draw on the key methodological and theoretical tenets of Critical Race Theory. In particular, as a means through which to foreground and 'make heard' the marginalised voices of minoritised coaches and to locate these experiential narratives within a theoretical framework which centralises 'race' and racism in its analysis, critiques notions of meritocracy, objectivity and race neutrality, and recognises and seeks to disrupt the normative power of hegemonic whiteness in societal and sporting contexts.

(ii) Racialised identities, diversity and intersectionality in sports coaching

Chapters 6 and **7** shift attention to the relationship between racial diversity and practices of sports coaching in Australian contexts and with particular respect to the experiences and impacts on players from newly settled and indigenous backgrounds. **Chapter 6** is written by **Brent McDonald** and **Ramón Spaaij** and draws attention to discourses of racialisation embedded in processes of talent identification and selection practices in professional sports coaching contexts in Australia. In particular, the authors allude to the residual embeddedness of pseudo-scientific ideas and practices which draw 'unproblematically' on notions of biological reductionism and 'race logic' to inform the targeted recruitment of 'natural athletes' from (some, but not other) minoritised backgrounds. In doing so, the authors draw on Critical Race Theory to argue that the resultant recolonisation of racialised bodies is informed by patterns of White privilege within sports science and sports coaching contexts and that its effects are apparent at the organisational, inter-personal and embodied level of sports. **Chapter 7** is written by **Richard Light** and **John Evans** and draws on extensive life history interviews with 16 indigenous Australian athletes to identify and examine their experiential journeys from local community sport to playing and being coached at a professional level in Australian Rugby League and Australian Rules Football. The authors draw on the theoretical framework of critical pedagogy and the work of Paolo Freire to argue that the early youthful experiences of these players in relation to 'learning' these games were markedly different from their adolescent and adult experiences within more formalised and regulated sports coaching contexts. The authors conclude that dominant 'banking' approaches to sports coaching objectify and dehumanise learners and learning and can have particular implications for Aboriginal players in underplaying the role of sport as an important form of Aboriginal cultural practice and in limiting opportunities for freedom of physical and cultural expression. **Chapters 8, 9** and **10** explore issues of identity construction and negotiation across key intersectional indices of 'race', ethnicity and gender. **Chapter 8** is written by **Alexandra J. Rankin-Wright** and **Kevin Hylton** and begins by drawing attention to the dominance of White masculine discourses within sports related research and the consequent silencing of the voices and experiences of black women. Drawing on key tenets of Critical Race Theory and Black Feminism the authors argue for the need for a stronger intersectional analysis of 'race', ethnicity and gender within sports coaching research which supplements and challenges previously established epistemologies, methodologies and theoretical perspectives. In doing so, the authors also draw on the experiential narratives of black women coaches in the UK to examine and elucidate the complexities of their intersectional experiences of inclusion and exclusion and double marginalisation in grassroots and professional sports coaching contexts. **Chapter 9** is written by **Joyce Olushola-Ogunrinde** and **Akilah Carter-Francique** and extends discussion of the intersections of 'race', ethnicity and gender in sports coaching to intercollegiate sports in the US. In particular, the authors draw on key tenets of Critical Race Theory and Crenshaw's Intersectionality framework to identify and analyse the structural, representational and political challenges experienced by Black women and men coaches in these settings. In doing so, the authors provide significant insights into the ways in which gendered and racialised processes of access and treatment discrimination have impacted on shaping the career pathways and experiences of Black women and men coaches in subtly different and overlapping ways. **Chapter 10** is written by **Annelies Knoppers** and **Donna de Haan** and explores how the employment of transnational coaches in sports might contribute to intersectional social processes which disrupt, challenge and reinforce dominant ideologies of race, ethnicity and gender in host countries. The authors draw on poststructuralist theory to argue that social fields such as sports coaching are both socially constructed and constituted by dominant discourses of whiteness, heteronormativity and masculinity which privilege the notion of White male expertise and marginalise other gendered and racialised identities. The authors also review the strengths and limitations of existing scholarly work examining the experiences of and discourses around transnational coaches, before outlining how new and alternative theoretical and conceptual approaches which prioritise an examination of power, intersectionality and translocational positionality might enrich scholarship in this field.

(iii) Formalised racial equality interventions in sports coaching

Chapters 11, 12 and **13** outline and evaluate the legislative development, operational effectiveness and measurable impacts of positive action interventions designed to address racialised inequalities in sports coaching. **Chapter 11** is written by **N. Jeremi Duru** and begins by identifying racialised inequities in the coaching tiers of the US NFL at the turn of the 21st century, before examining the inadequacies of the legal system in failing to address the disparate treatment of and disparate impacts on coaches of colour in these settings. The author then provides an insightful account of the development and effectuation of the 'Rooney Rule' as an alternative extra-legal solution designed to ensure a diverse candidate slate and increase the likelihood of selection and recruitment of coaches of colour in the NFL. The author concludes by alluding to the diversity gains engendered by the 'Rooney Rule' and its potential and realised effectiveness as a creative non-legal formula for selection and recruitment for other sporting and non-sporting organisations. **Chapter 12** is written by **Sophie Cowell** and extends Duru's legal analysis to examine the development and implementation of the English Football League (EFL) *Voluntary* Code of Coach Recruitment, which requires professional clubs to interview at least one Black, Asian and Minority Ethnic (BAME) candidate for emergent coaching positions at first team level. The author argues that the legislative development of the 'code' can be understood as a form of reflexive regulation which allows employers to engage in permissive positive actions as defined by the 2010 UK Equality Act in order to redress historical representational disadvantages across a range of social fields, including in sports coaching. However, the author continues that the lack of appropriate consultation, monitoring, or financial sanctions for non-compliance has meant that the operational implementation of the 'code' has remained piecemeal and that its effectiveness in increasing the representation of BAME coaches has been limited. **Chapter 13** is written by **Dominic Conricode** and **Steven Bradbury** and draws on survey data and interviews with 35 youth academy managers, key stakeholders, and BAME coaches to examine the implementation of the EFL *mandatory* code of coach recruitment which is focused at the youth academy level of professional football clubs in England. In doing so, they allude to the extent and ways in which the operational implementation and effectiveness of the 'code' has been enabled or constrained by the *'race-conscious'* or *'race-neutral'* attitudinal approaches of key decision-making personnel at club youth academies to issues of equality and diversity management. In doing so, the authors draw on Critical Race Theory to argue that liberalism alone is not enough to address deeply embedded forms of institutional racism and that colour-blind ideologies tend to sustain rather than redress patterns of racialised disadvantage in sports coaching and other societal settings.

The final concluding chapter **(Chapter 14)** is written by the editorial team of **Jim Lusted, Steven Bradbury** and **Jacco van Sterkenburg** and begins by outlining some potential priorities for future research into the field of 'race' ethnicity and racism in sports coaching. In doing so, they draw on the work of Cunningham to call for a multi-level analysis in proposing future research which considers the complex interplay between the macro (societal), meso (organisational) and micro (individual) level of racialised relations in sports coaching. The authors also draw together the key recommendations from the chapters in this collection to outline some prospective priorities for addressing racialised inequalities and establishing a more diverse and equitable environment in sports coaching. In doing so, they call on key stakeholders in sports to develop and implement a multi-level and holistic approach, incorporating; robust policy interventions, education and training programmes, and enhanced opportunities for networking and the development of social capital amongst minoritised sports coaches.

Notes

1 The term 'minoritised' is used in this chapter to reflect an understanding of 'minority status' as a socially constructed process (rather than as an entity) which takes place in specific social, economic and political contexts over time and which has resulted in 'minoritised groups' having less power or representation compared to other (White) groups in society. A further discussion of terminology used by authors across the book is provided in the thematic overview section of this chapter.
2 The 'Rooney Rule' is a 'consideration forcing' mechanism of coach recruitment which was first implemented at the policy level by the US National Football League (NFL) in 2003. It mandates that all NFL clubs interview at least one minority candidate upon the vacancy of a head coach position or be subject to a significant monetary fine. The development, implementation and effectiveness of the 'Rooney Rule' is discussed in detail by Duru in Chapter 11 of this collection, and its applicability to a range of other national and sporting contexts is elaborated on further by a range of authors throughout this collection.

References

Abney, R. (2007) African American women in intercollegiate coaching and athletic administration: Unequal access. In Brooks, D. & Althouse, R. (eds) *Diversity and Social Justice in College Sports.* pp. 51–76.

Andrews, D. (2002) Coming to terms with cultural studies. *Journal of Sport and Social Issues*, 26(1), 110–117.

Ansari, H. (2004) Introduction: Racialization and sport. *Patterns of Prejudice*, 38(3), 209–212.

Banerjee, R. (2018) Chris Hughton: 'BAME managers don't want tokenism, we want an opportunity'. Why the Brighton manager is much more than one of the nicest men in football. New Statesman (08/03/18) available at: https://www.newstatesman.com/politics/sport/2018/03/chris-hughton-bame-managers-don-t-want-tokenism-we-want-opportunity.

Borland, J. F. & Bruening, J. E. (2010) Navigating barriers: A qualitative examination of the under-representation of Black females as head coaches in collegiate basketball. *Sport Management Review*, 13, 407–420.

Bradbury, S., Amara, M., Garcia, B. & Bairner, A. (2011) *Representation and Structural Discrimination in Football in Europe: The Case of Minorities and Women.* Loughborough University and the FARE Network.

Bradbury, S., Van Sterkenburg, J. & Mignon, P. (2018) The under-representation and experiences of elite level minority coaches in professional football in England, France and the Netherlands. *International Review of the Sociology of Sport*, 53 (3), 313–334.

Braddock, J., Smith, E. & Dawkins, M. (2012) Race and pathways to power in the National Football League. *American Behavioural Scientist*, 56(5), 711–727.

Branham, D. (2008) Taking advantage of an untapped pool: Assessing the success of African American head coaches in the National Football League. *The Review of Black Political Economy*, 35(4), 129–146.

Bruening, J. E. (2005) Gender and racial analysis in sport: Are all the women White and all the Blacks men? *Quest*, 57, 20.

Carrington, B. (2010) *Race, Sport and Politics: The Sporting Black Diaspora*. London: Sage.

Carter-Francique, A. R. & Olushola, J. (2016) Women coaches of color: Examining the effects of intersectionality. In Lavoi, N. (ed.) *Women in Sports Coaching*. Oxon: Routledge.

Council of Europe: European Commission against Racism and Intolerance (COE/ECRI) (2008) ECRI General Policy Recommendation No.12 on Combating racism and racial discrimination in the field of sport.

Cunningham, G. B. (2010) Understanding the under-representation of African American coaches: A multilevel perspective. *Sport Management Review*, 13(4), 395–406.

Cunningham, G. B., Miner, K. & McDonald, J. (2012) Being different and suffering the consequences: The influence of head coach-player dissimilarity on experienced incivility. *International Review for the Sociology of Sport*, 48(6) 689–705.

Day, J. C. (2015) Transitions to the top: Race, segregation, and promotions to executive positions in the college football coaching profession. *Work and Occupations*, 42(4), 408–446.

Fletcher, T. (2014) Does he look like a Paki? An exploration of whiteness, positionality and reflexivity in inter racial sports research. *Qualitative Research in Sport, Exercise and Health*, 6(2), 244–260.

Fletcher, T. & Hylton, K. (2017) 'Race', whiteness and sport. In Nauright, J. and Wiggins, D. (eds) *Routledge Handbook of Sport, Race and Ethnicity*. Routledge. pp. 87–106.

Frankenberg, R. (2004) On unsteady ground: Crafting and engaging in the critical study of whiteness. In Bulmer, M. & Solomos, J. (eds) *Researching Race and Racism*. London: Routledge. pp. 104–118.

Gearity, B. & Henderson Metzger, L. (2017) Intersectionality, micro-aggressions and micro-affirmations: Towards a cultural praxis of sports coaching. *Sociology of Sport Journal*, 34(2), 160–175.

Hartmann, D. (2000) Rethinking the relationships between sport and race in American culture: Golden ghettos and contested terrain. *Sociology of Sport Journal*, 17(3), 229–253.

Hassan, D. & Acton, C. (2018) *Sport and Contested Identities*. London: Routledge.

Hylton, K. (2005) 'Race', sport and leisure: Lessons from critical race theory. *Leisure Studies*, 24(1), 81–98.

Hylton, K. (2009) *Race and Sport: Critical Race Theory*. London and New York: Routledge.

Hylton, K. (2012) Talk the talk, walk the walk: Defining critical race theory in research. *Race Ethnicity and Education*, 15(1), 23–41.

Hylton, K. (2018) *Contesting 'Race' and Sport*. London: Routledge.

Hylton, K. & Lawrence, S. (2016) 'For your ears only!' Donald Sterling and backstage racism in sport. *Ethnic and Racial Studies*, 39(15), 2740–2757.

Jowett, S. & Frost, T. (2007) Race/Ethnicity in the all-male coach-athlete relationship: Black footballers' narratives. *International Journal of Sport and Exercise Psychology*, 5 (3), 255–269.

Khomutova, A. (2016) Basketball coaches' experiences in working with multicultural teams: Central and Northern European perspectives. *Sport in Society*, 19 (7), 861–876.
Kilvington, D. & Price, J. (2017) *Sport and Discrimination*. Routledge.
King, C. (2004) 'Race' and cultural identity: Playing the race game inside football. *Leisure Studies*, 23(1), 19–13.
Lapchick, R. (2017) *The 2017 Racial and Gender Report Card*. Institute of Diversity and Ethics. University of Central Florida.
Lavoi, N. (2016) *Women in Sports Coaching*. Routledge.
Norman, L., North, J., Hylton, K., Flintoff, A. & Rankin, A. (2014) Sporting experiences and coaching aspirations among Black and Minority Ethnic (BME) groups. Sports Coach UK and Leeds Metropolitan University.
Omi, M. & Winant, H. (2002) Racial formation. In Essed, P. & Goldberg, D. (eds) *Race Critical Theories*. Oxford: Blackwell.
Rankin-Wright, A. J., Hylton, K. & Norman, L. (2016) Off-colour landscape: Framing race equality in sport coaching. *Sociology of Sport Journal*, 33(4), 357–368.
Rankin-Wright, A. J., Hylton, K. & Norman, L. (2017) The policy and provision landscape for racial and gender equality in sport coaching. In Long, J., Fletcher, T., Watson, B. (eds) *Sport, Leisure and Social Justice*. London: Routledge. pp. 194–208.
Rankin-Wright, A. J. & Norman, L. (2018) Sport coaching and the inclusion of Black women in the United Kingdom. In Ratna, A. & Farooq Samie, S. (eds) *Race, Gender and Sport: The Politics of Ethnic 'Other' Girls and Women*. Routledge.
Ratna, A. & Farooq Samie, S. (eds) (2018) *Race, Gender and Sport: The Politics of Ethnic 'Other' Girls and Women*. Routledge.
Regan, M. & Feagin, J. (2017) College sport leadership: Systemic employment barriers. In Kilvington, D. & Price, J. (eds) *Sport and Discrimination*. Routledge. pp. 15–31.
Sagas, M. & Cunningham, G. B. (2005) Racial differences in the career success of assistant football coaches: The role of discrimination, human capital, and social capital. *Journal of Applied Social Psychology*, 35(4), 773–797.
Sartore, M. L. & Cunningham, G. B. (2006) Stereotypes, race, and coaching. *Journal of African American Studies*, 10(2), 69–83.
Singer, J., Harrison, K. & Buksten, S. (2010) A critical race analysis of the hiring process for head coaches in NCAA college football. *Journal of Intercollegiate Sport*, 3(2), 270–296.
Solórzano, D. G. & Yosso, T. J. (2002) Critical race methodology: Counter-storytelling as an analytical framework for education research. *Qualitative Inquiry*, 8(1), 23–44.
Van Sterkenburg, J. (2011) *Race, Ethnicity and the Sport Media*. Amsterdam: Amsterdam University Press/Pallas Publications.
Van Sterkenburg, J., Peeters, R. & Van Amsterdam, N. (2019) Everyday racism and constructions of racial/ethnic difference in and through football talk. *European Journal of Cultural Studies*, 22(2), 195–212.
Watson, G., Palmer, F. & Ryan, G. (2017) Aotearoa/New Zealand. In Nauright, J. and Wiggins, D. (eds) *Routledge Handbook of Sport, Race and Ethnicity*. Routledge. pp. 131–145.
Zhang, L. (2017) A fair game? Racial bias and repeated interaction between NBA coaches and players. *Administrative Science Quarterly*, 62(4), 603–625.

Part I

Representation and racialised barriers in sports coaching

Chapter 1

The under-representation of racial minorities in coaching and leadership positions in the United States

George B. Cunningham

Introduction

Racial minorities[1] in the US have a history of facing stereotypes, prejudice, and discrimination—a pattern that continues today. The result is differential access to quality education (Carter et al., 2017), health disparities (Edberg et al., 2017), limited housing opportunities (Sadler & Lafreniere, 2017), and high rates of incarceration (Peffley et al., 2017), among other ills. Add to this list limited opportunities for meaningful work or the chance to assume leadership positions. The following statistic perhaps best illustrates the pervasiveness of bias in the American workplace: there have only been 15 African American chief executive officers in the entire history of the Fortune 500 (McGirt, 2016). Thus, even though racial minorities make up about 39 percent of the US population—a figure demographers expect to grow to 55.7 percent by 2060 (Vespa et al., 2018)—their access and opportunities to work pale in comparison to those of Whites. This is the case for leadership positions and access to work in general, where unemployment rates for racial minorities is higher than for Whites.

The sport world tells a different story, though the ending is the same. In Figure 1.1, I show the representation of players, assistant coaches, and head coaches across various North American leagues. With the exception of Major League Baseball, the proportion of racial minorities players far outpaces that of racial minority assistant coaches or head coaches. Among National Collegiate Athletic Association (NCAA) women's basketball programs, racial minorities are nearly 4 times more likely to be players than they are to serve as a head coach. This pattern, which is evident among most professional and collegiate sport leagues, signals that racial minorities have opportunities on the court or field, but not in leadership roles. The trend persists despite the fact that most coaches were former players (Cunningham & Sagas, 2002), and players represent the most viable pool of potential assistant coaches (Everhart & Chelladurai, 1998).

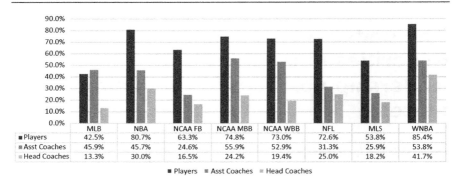

Figure 1.1 Representation of Racial Minority Coaches and Players in US Sport Organizations

Notes. Data for professional leagues from 2017 season. Data from NCAA for 2016–2017 season. Data gathered from The Institute for Diversity and Ethics in Sport (www.tidesport.org) and NCAA Sport Sponsorship, Participation, and Demographics Research (http://web1.ncaa.org/rgdSearch/exec/main). MLB = Major League Baseball. NBA = National Basketball Association. NCAA = National Collegiate Athletic Association. FB = American football. MBB = Men's basketball. WBB = Women's basketball. NFL = National Football League. MLS = Major League Soccer. WNBA = Women's National Basketball Association.

As shown in Figure 1.1, as the prestige and power of the coaching position increases, the proportion of racial minorities decreases. In Major League Baseball, for example, racial minorities are 3.5 times more likely to hold an assistant coach position, relative to serving as manager (head coach). This pattern is the same for every sport league considered in Figure 1.1. Even among NCAA men's basketball teams, which has the highest proportion of racial minority assistant coaches (55.9 percent), racial minorities are only half as likely to be a head coach (24.2 percent). Other researchers have shown that, among assistant coaches of American football teams, Whites are most likely to hold the highest paying and more powerful roles (coordinators), while racial minorities are more likely to hold more peripheral roles (Cunningham & Bopp, 2010).

Coaching is not the only occupation where racial minorities face access discrimination. In Figure 1.2, I show the proportion of racial minorities in administrative roles across North American sport leagues. Unlike coaching, where former players are the most viable potential pool of applicants, sport organization leaders need not have previous playing experience to secure a position. As such, the proportion of racial minorities in the US population (39.1 percent; Vespa et al., 2018) serves as an apt point of comparison. The data show that in every league, Whites occupy a greater proportion of top administrative roles than their proportion in the US population would predict. With Major League Baseball, racial minorities are about a third less likely to hold an administrative position than would their proportion in the US population predict.

The aforementioned data point to evidence of what Greenhaus et al. (1990) refer to as access discrimination, or the limited access to positions, careers, or

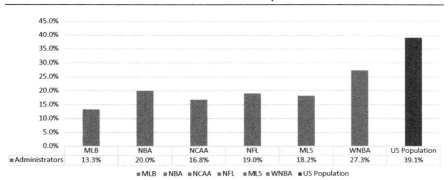

Figure 1.2 Representation of Racial Minorities in Administrative Roles in US Sport Organizations

Notes. Data for professional leagues from 2017 season. Data from NCAA for 2016–2017 season. Data gathered from The Institute for Diversity and Ethics in Sport (www.tidesport.org) and NCAA Sport Sponsorship, Participation, and Demographics Research (http://web1.ncaa.org/rgdSearch/exec/main). MLB = Major League Baseball. NBA = National Basketball Association. NCAA = National Collegiate Athletic Association. NFL = National Football League. MLS = Major League Soccer. WNBA = Women's National Basketball Association.

academic tracks among members of a social group. Discrimination can also take the form of treatment discrimination, whereby members of a social group receive fewer opportunities and are treated poorer than they would otherwise deserve based on their work performance (Greenhaus et al., 1990). Treatment discrimination can take many forms, including differences in pay, quality of work, opportunities for promotion, professional development, and the like. For instance, data from the US Census Bureau show that most racial minorities earn but a fraction of what Whites do, and the differences are particularly striking among racial minority women (Kochhar & Cilluffo, 2018). Asians earn, on average, more than Whites, but this group also has the within-group income inequality (Kochhar & Cilluffo, 2018).

A number of researchers have pointed to evidence of treatment discrimination in the sport world. For instance, Bradbury et al. (2018) conducted a qualitative study of 40 racial minority soccer coaches in England, the Netherlands, and France. The coaches relayed a number of instances of treatment discrimination, including (a) poor experiences in coaching education, incidences of ostracism and racism, and (b) feelings of exclusion from important social networks. In other cases, decision makers hold African Americans to a higher standard than Whites, and these expectations affect dismissal rates (Madden, 2004; Madden & Ruther, 2009). Coaches and people working in sport are not the only ones affected by treatment discrimination: racial minority athletes expect to encounter discrimination if they become coaches (Kamphoff & Gill, 2008)—something ostensibly due to their observation of those working in sport now.

Collectively, the research evidence suggests racial minorities face discrimination in the US, in general, and in sport, specifically. The resultant question is: why? In the following space, I draw from my previous work (Cunningham, 2010, 2012, 2019) to offer a multilevel explanation. Multilevel models make explicit the societal (macro-level), organizational and group influences (meso-level), and individual factors (micro-level) that can shape access to and experiences in sport. When scholars and practitioners fail to consider factors at multiple levels of analysis, they necessarily take for granted elements that could influence the phenomenon of interest (Dixon & Cunningham, 2006).

Multilevel model explaining the under-representation of racial minorities in sport

Macro-level factors

Macro-level factors are those operating at the societal level of analysis. In the current model, I focus on institutional racism, political climate, and stakeholder expectations.

Institutional racism

From a critical race theory perspective, racism is embedded deeply in society—it is endemic (Hylton, 2009). Theorists argue that racism is enmeshed within the cultural fabric of society, intertwined with prevailing norms and values (see Cobb & Russell, 2015). From this perspective, major societal institutions, including educational systems, religious institutions, the legal system, and sport, among others, are tinged with racist ideals. As a result, Whites enjoy privilege, power, and status within these institutions, and the cultural arrangements are such that the ideals and norms perpetuate the status quo—that is, racial minorities' subjugation.

These principles are applicable to the business sector (Feagin, 2006) and people who work in sport and physical activity (Hylton, 2012). Feagin for instance, critiqued capitalism in the US, suggesting that it *"has been, from the beginning, a whitecrafted and white oriented economic system imbedded in white-made business laws"* (Feagin 2006: 198). Similar critiques are applicable for sport organizations in the US—entities steeped in the capitalistic model. That is, sport organizations are largely White owned and operated, are situated within a capitalist economic model, and frequently operate in ways that privilege those in power (i.e., Whites) while subjugating others (i.e., racial minorities). Further, when activities and practices are institutionalized, they become solidified and resistant to change. New members into that system are socialized to consider the practices as legitimate (Washington & Patterson, 2011); consequently, the activities, beliefs, and policies that privilege some groups over others become perpetuated. When it comes to institutional racism, systems and arrangements of oppression remain, hurting racial minorities' opportunities and experiences in the sport context.

Political climate

The political climate can also affect access and opportunities. Political attitudes and policies can affect a number of sport and physical activity outcomes, including funding for people to be active (Harris & Adams, 2016; Nassif & Amara, 2015) and resources to reduce the incidence of health disparities (Bourgois et al., 2017). The political climate can also influence diversity-related activities and people's attitudes toward them. Examples include attitudes toward affirmative action (Sidanius et al., 1996), efforts aimed to promote social justice (Leath & Chavous, 2017), and educational opportunities (Hess & McAvoy, 2014), among others.

The political climate can influence sport organizations and employment decisions through the enactment of employment laws. A number of major laws aimed at enhancing opportunities and ending employment discrimination in the US (e.g., Civil Rights Act of 1964, Voting Rights Act of 1965) were passed in the 1960s under the Democratic leadership of Lyndon Johnson. The president worked closely with civil rights leaders, including Martin Luther King, Jr., to craft the laws. In addition to influencing the type of laws passed, the political climate influences the enforcement of diversity laws. Marshall (2005), for example, showed that liberal political leadership more stringently administers diversity-related laws and fair labor practices, relative to when conservatives are in office (see also Cunningham & Benavides-Espinoza, 2008). This scholarship provides evidence for the notion that racial minorities' access to jobs and their experiences in those roles can be influenced by the political climate in the region or country.

Stakeholder expectations

According to Clarkson (1995), stakeholders are constituents who have an interest or stake in the organization. They can be internal to the sport organization, such as players, coaches, and administrators, or external to it, including donors, fans, former students, and so on. Depending on the stakeholder management approach decision makers adopt, stakeholder input has the potential to shape organizational processes and outcomes.

In intercollegiate athletic departments in the US, alumni and donors—the majority of whom are White—provide financial support to the institutions. The support is considerable, to the tune of 14 percent of the budget for major athletic programs (Fulks, 2014), resulting in an average of $8.7 million annually. Given their considerable financial support, these stakeholders have tremendous influence on the operations of the athletic department, including who is hired and who is not. In many cases, the hiring decisions focus, at least in part, on coaches with whom the financial stakeholders can identify. Michael Rosenberg (2004) of the *Detroit Free Press* noted:

> It is largely about money. It is about a face to show the alumni, especially the ones with big wallets. College coaches don't just coach; they

are, in many ways, the public faces of their schools. And if the big donors don't like a coach because of his weight/accent/skin color, schools will stay away.

Noted racial activist Richard Lapchick drew similar conclusions:

> I have had discussions with people in searches for coaches and athletic directors that the final decision was made to hire a White male because they were afraid their alumni, who also happen to be strong boosters of the football program, would not contribute nearly as much or as readily to an African American athletic director or football coach.
>
> (as cited in Wong, 2002: 1)

The quotations illustrate that financial supporters of athletic departments, most of whom are White men, want to identify with key decision makers and athletic coaches. Further, racial similarity among the coach, alumni, and boosters can help spur perceptions of fit and identification among the parties involved (Stewart & Garcia-Prieto Sol, 2008). On the other hand, the lack of fit among athletic administrators and coaches, and the financial stakeholders, can affect hiring decisions. The end result is a preference for Whites and men (see also Cunningham & Sagas, 2005; Sartore & Cunningham, 2006).

Meso-level factors

Meso-level factors are those operating at the organizational or intergroup levels. These include bias in decision making, organizational culture, and diversity policies.

Bias in decision making

Bias takes three forms (Cuddy et al., 2008). First are stereotypes, which are in the cognitive domain and represent *"the traits that we view as characteristic of social groups, or individual members of those groups, and particularly those that differentiate groups from each other"* (Stangor, 2009: 2). Prejudice, which is in the attitudinal or affective domain, is the second form of bias and reflects a differential evaluation of a person or social group based on group membership (Brewer, 2007; Crandall et al., 2002). Finally, discrimination is in the behavioral domain and *"comes about only when we deny to individuals or groups equality of treatment"* (Allport, 1954: 51). Each can influence the under-representation of racial minorities in coaching and leadership positions. As I discussed access and treatment discrimination in previous sections, I focus the current discussion on stereotypes and prejudice.

Social psychologists have shown that people frequently develop stereotypes about typical leaders and who should hold these roles (Lord & Maher, 1991).

These cognitions help to shape who decision makers consider a good fit for the position. In some cases, the leadership stereotypes are racialized (Rosette et al., 2008), and in the US, this means that Whites are privileged in the decision-making process. Consider, for example, that people consistently see Whites in key leadership roles. This pattern holds for chief executives, presidents, athletic directors, and other leaders. As a result, people are socialized to link cognitively leadership with being White. Consistent with this perspective, Rosette et al. (2008) found that people considered being White as a prototype for business leaders, though they did not hold the same associations for employees holding other roles in the organization. The conditioning also meant that study participants considered Whites as more effective leaders than racial minorities. This linkage was especially strong when organizational success was attributed to the leader.

Borland & Bruening (2010) observed as much in sport, too. They conducted interviews with African American women who coached in the NCAA. The interviewees noted that stereotypes limited their career advancement, as decision makers saw the coaches as best suited for recruiting roles instead of leading a team. Sartore & Cunningham (2006) zconducted an experimental study and observed that people relied on sport-related and racial stereotypes when making coaching hiring recommendations. Welty Peachey et al. (2015) also noted the prevalence of stereotypes in their review of the leadership literature. The authors wrote, *"as a result of the dominant influence of White, able-bodied, heterosexual men in sport leadership, women and other minority groups are negatively affected by stereotypes of what is deemed acceptable sport leadership at all levels of the leadership process"* (Welty Peachey, 2015: 581). The data in Figures 1.1 and 1.2 offer strong support for these contentions.

Prejudice represents the second dimension of bias, and researchers have shown that it can negatively influence the quality of work people experience. For example, Jones et al. (2017) conducted a large-scale study to understand the influence of racism on people's work. The authors found that this form of prejudice was associated with felt discrimination and bias in performance appraisals, among other outcomes. More implicit forms of racism can also impact people's work; implicit racism is associated with help provided to others (Pearson et al., 2009).

The sport world is not immune from racism's effects. Cunningham et al. (2006) conducted a study of NCAA assistant football and men's basketball coaches, asking about their experiences in the sport and career expectations. Racial minorities in the study indicated that racism limited their opportunities in the field. The pattern was especially strong among football coaches. Football is also a sport where Whites hold most of the powerful assistant positions (Cunningham & Bopp, 2010) and head coaching roles (see Figure 1.1).

Organizational culture

Another meso-level factor that can affect racial minorities' opportunities and experiences is the culture of the workplace. According to Schein (2004), organizational culture represents *"a pattern of shared basic assumptions ... that has worked well enough to be considered valid and, therefore, to be taught to new members as the correct ways to perceive, think, and feel in relation to those problems"* (Schein, 2004: 17). The culture of a sport organization sends a signal as to what is important, who has power, and who can be successful. Organizational cultures of inclusion are those where all employees have the chance to thrive, irrespective of their personal demographics (Doherty & Chelladurai, 1999; Fink & Pastore, 1999). In these cultures, people can express identities important to them, including their racial identity, and they also feel a sense of connection to the organization (Shore et al., 2011).

Illustrative of organizational culture's importance, McKay et al. (2007) conducted a study of thousands of managers in the US. They asked the participants about the diversity culture at their work and their workplace attitudes. As expected, a pro-diversity workplace culture was associated with stronger commitment and lower turnover intentions, and the patterns were especially strong for African Americans. Importantly though, the significant patterns held for all employees, signaling that an inclusive environment benefits all in the workplace. In a similar analysis, McKay et al. (2008) found that a pro-diversity culture also helped employee performance. As with the previous study, the findings were significant for all races but were especially strong among African Americans.

If pro-diversity workplace cultures are beneficial for employees and especially racial minorities, the opposite is also the case: cultures of similarity hurt employee workplace connection and performance. Bradbury (2013) argued as much in his analysis of the under-representation of soccer coaches in Europe. He argued that *"the 'invisible centrality of whiteness' embedded within the senior organizational tiers of the game"* (Bradbury, 2013: 299) served to restrict the progression of racial minorities in the sport (see also Rankin-Wright et al., 2016). Other researchers have shown that the detriments of exclusive cultures hurt those outside the organization, too, including potential job applicants (Lee & Cunningham, 2015) and racial minority consumers (Santucci et al., 2014).

As a final note on organizational culture, there is evidence that an inclusive culture can enhance organizational performance, especially when coupled with a diverse workforce. Cunningham (2009a) collected data from US athletic departments, asking them about their organizational culture, characteristics of the workforce, and other workplace characteristics. He found that an inclusive culture interacted with racial diversity of the staff to predict objective measures of performance (wins and losses of athletic teams). These findings are consistent with other studies showing that inclusiveness, when coupled with employee diversity, is associated with a variety of desired work outcomes (Cunningham, 2011a, 2011b, 2015; Cunningham & Melton, 2014; Singer & Cunningham, 2012).

Organizational policies

In some respects, organizational policies are subsumed under the larger umbrella of organizational culture. However, there is also evidence that inclusive-focused policies can have a unique effect on the attraction and retention of racial minorities in coaching and leadership positions. Examples include when sport organizations enact policies related to hiring, promotions, performance appraisals, and professional development that potentially influence the experiences and opportunities of racial minorities.

One of the more famous diversity-related policies in the US is the National Football League's (NFL) Rooney Rule. The league had a history of poor representation of racial minorities in coaching positions, so in 2003, enacted the Rooney Rule. The policy requires teams to interview at least one racial minority when it is hiring a new head coach. The NFL recently expanded the policy to also include senior-level administrative positions. DuBois (2015) empirically analyzed the effects of the policy to examine whether it impacted racial diversity in the league. She identified naturally occurring control conditions in the way of college football teams, as the NCAA does not have such policies in place. In doing so, she was able to rule out potential societal or industry changes that could have influenced the hiring rates; that is, if societal changes alone explained the changes in hiring, their influence would occur in both settings. On the other hand, if the Rooney Rule was the key driver of change, then greater diversity gains would occur in the NFL than in the NCAA. DuBois' analyses showed that the Rooney Rule did, in fact, positively influence the proportion of racial minority coaches. Relative to the comparisons, racial minorities were 19–21 percent more likely to fill a head coaching position in the NFL after the Rooney Rule went into effect. Recognizing the potential of hiring-focused diversity policies and the effectiveness of the Rooney Rule, in 2018, the English Football Association started using a similar approach for the selection of national team coaches and administrators (English Soccer, 2018).

Micro-level factors

Finally, micro-level factors are those specific to the individual. Importantly, a focus on the individual does not equate to a "blame the victim" approach, as some diversity scholars have suggested in other contexts (Knoppers, 1987). Rather, the micro-level examination is consistent with multilevel modeling (see also McLeroy et al., 1988; Kozlowski & Klein, 2000) and recognizes that meso- and macro-level factors can influence the individual. As an example, Assari et al. (2017) found that experiences with discrimination (a meso-level factor) negatively affected African Americans' health (a micro-level factor) even a decade later, and the pattern was especially strong for men. In the sports world, researchers have shown that intercollegiate athletes are aware of the racism deeply rooted in coaching (a macro-level factor) and adjust their expectations for the coaching profession accordingly (a micro-level factor; Cunningham, 2003; Cunningham & Singer, 2010; Kamphoff & Gill, 2008). Thus, differences between (say) racial minorities and Whites in their attitudes or behaviors is not due to innate differences between the social groups but, instead, the result of varying organizational, intergroup, and societal-level influences. In the current chapter, I focus on three micro-level factors: capital investments, personal identity, and self-limiting behaviors.

Capital investments

People make investments in their career, beyond those of the monetary nature. Researchers have generally classified them in two categories: human capital and social capital (Becker, 1993; Coleman, 1986). Human capital investments are related to people's education, experience, the different roles they have held, and so on. Social capital investments include people's social networks. Scholars consider how many people are in the social network, where those connections are, the quality of the connections—all of which can influence access to information, support from others, and career advocacy. In general, as human and social capital investments increase, so too does one's career outcomes.

Capital investments are relevant to the discussion of racial minorities in leadership and coaching positions. One perspective is that racial minorities do not have the capital investments that Whites do, so they do not see valued career returns. However, empirical evidence does not support this position. Cunningham et al. (2001) collected data from a racially diverse sample of assistant coaches of NCAA men's basketball teams. Whites were more likely to have a graduate degree than were African Americans; however, African Americans were more likely to have played the sport they coached at the collegiate level and earned honors for doing so. In fact, African Americans were 68 percent more likely to have playing experience—a human capital investment seen as required for quality assistant coaches (Everhart & Chelladurai, 1998).

In other cases, racial differences in career success might be due to differential returns on capital investments—a position consistent with the notion of treatment discrimination (Ibarra, 1995; Sagas & Cunningham, 2005). A number of researchers have offered empirical support for this position, such that Whites and racial minorities are differentially rewarded for similar investments (Day, 2015, 2018; Day & McDonald, 2010). What's more, there are racial differences in the types of social networks needed to be successful. Same-race networks benefit Whites and the promotions they have in their careers, but racial minorities benefit from mixed-race networks to realize similar career success. These differences might be a function of who is charged with hiring in many US sport organizations: White men. Consequently, racial minorities might benefit from having Whites in their network more than Whites would benefit from having racial minorities in theirs. In addition, there are racial differences in the type of relationships that are more beneficial, as Whites profit from close network ties, while racial minorities benefit from more informal networks. Finally, the location of the contacts matters: African Americans enjoy more career success when they have high-status contacts, while for Whites, the status of the network is immaterial to their career success. The research collectively demonstrates the presence of racial differences in human and social capital returns, as well as different forms of social capital needed to ensure career success.

Personal identity

One's personal identity reflects the *"individuated self—those characteristics that differentiate one individual from others in a social context"* (Brewer, 1991: 476). It represents how people see themselves and is a central part of their core identity (Luhtanen & Crocker, 1992). For example, two Latinas might share a common racial background but differ substantially in the degree to which their race is a part of their personal identity. For one, her race might be a core part of her self-image, shaping her experiences and how she sees the world. For another, her racial identity might be of little importance.

Researchers have shown that personal identities can impact people in many ways. From an individual perspective, when people differ from others in a group on a characteristic that is an important part of their identity, they are likely to have poor work performance (Randel & Jaussi, 2003) and low satisfaction (Cunningham et al., 2008). People with high racial identity are also more likely to report experiences of racism and discrimination (Major et al., 2002).

Recently, researchers have shown that people use various cues to develop impressions of others' racial identity (Kaiser & Pratt-Hyatt, 2009). These dynamics are important when Whites are evaluating racial minority job applicants. Cunningham and colleagues have shown that Whites rate racial minorities who they believe strongly identify with their race more poorly than they do their counterparts with a presumed weak racial identity (Steward & Cunningham, 2015; Vick & Cunningham, in press). The differences are meaningful. In a study of fitness professionals, the ratings differences affected salary recommendations, and over time, these differences would result in a difference of over $39,000. The findings are also applicable to the current discussion of racial minorities in sport, as those who have a strong racial identity—or who are presumed to have one—are likely to face more barriers in securing a coaching or leadership role.

Self-limiting behaviors

Finally, self-limiting behaviors can negatively affect opportunities and experiences of racial minority coaches and leaders. From this perspective, racial minorities are likely to experience stereotypes, prejudice, and discrimination, all of which negatively impact them. Possible outcomes include missed opportunities, negative work feedback, and few opportunities for advancement. Over time, they can come to internalize the bias and negative feedback. When this occurs, they might withdraw from sport as a profession, come to believe that their performance is inferior, or pass on chances for advancement because they believe they do not have a chance to be successful. These are all examples of what researchers call self-limiting behaviors (Ilgen & Youtz, 1986; Sartore, 2006).

A number of researchers have offered evidence of self-limiting behaviors. For example, Wells and Kerwin (2017) collected data from athletic administrators working in the US. The study participants did not vary in their confidence of their abilities, nor did they differ in the career supports they enjoyed. Nevertheless, women and racial minorities anticipated more barriers for advancement than did White men, and consistent with theory, they also expressed fewer intentions to pursue an athletic director position. In other studies, racial minority coaches have consistently reported more barriers to advancement than have Whites (Cunningham & Singer, 2010; Cunningham et al., 2006; Kamphoff & Gill, 2008). Despite these roadblocks, there is little empirical evidence that racial minority assistant coaches are less willing than Whites to pursue a head coaching position.

Though there is equivocal evidence related to pursuing advancement opportunities, researchers have consistently shown racial differences for another form of self-limiting behavior: occupational turnover. Racial differences in occupational turnover are important for a number of reasons, including a lack of racial minority coaches in the profession, relative to Whites. Cunningham et al. (2017) conducted a meta-analysis of empirical research in the area and found that racial minorities were likely to leave coaching sooner than were Whites. The magnitude of the effects was moderate. The authors pointed to a number of contributing factors, including health concerns, family constraints, limited opportunities for advancement, low career satisfaction, and bias experienced.

Conclusions

The purpose of this chapter was to examine the under-representation of racial minorities in coaching and leadership positions in the US. In doing so, I offered evidence that racial minorities largely have access to playing positions, but when it comes to leading the teams or sport organizations, they face access and treatment discrimination. In seeking to explain why this pattern occurs, I drew from multilevel theory to suggest that societal, organizational, interpersonal, and individual factors all contribute to the trend.

The chapter offers theoretical implications. First, theory offers an understanding of how, when, why, and under what conditions phenomena take place (Cunningham, 2013; Cunningham, et al., 2016). The model offered here provides such insights, illustrating how societal-, organizational-, group-, and individual-level factors all influence the under-representation of racial minorities in coaching. I also showed how factors at different levels of analysis can influence one another (Klein et al., 1994; Kozlowski & Klein, 2000).

The model offers practical implications, too. Frequently, managers will attempt to create diversity-related change by targeting a single element in a system (Cunningham, 2009b). However, as the multilevel model presented in this chapter shows, such efforts are likely to lack the success sport managers might desire. Instead, they must tend to the multiple factors under their purview, while also seeking to influence those outside the workplaces. As I have outlined elsewhere (Cunningham, 2019), at the micro level of analysis, inclusive sport organizations (a) seek to increase intergroup contact among players, coaches, and administrators from different backgrounds; and (b) encourage difficult dialogues among people within their sport organization, thereby engaging in discussions that are frequently challenging to have but are nonetheless productive. At the meso level of analysis, sport organizations have (a) leaders that advocate and model inclusion; (b) diversity allies, or people who are not leaders but nevertheless champion inclusion efforts; (c) a strong commitment to diversity and inclusion; (d) educational and professional development activities focused on inclusion; and (e) integration of diversity and inclusion principles throughout the organizational system. Finally, at the macro level of analysis, inclusive sport organizations (a) are frequently set within a broader community that emphasizes inclusion; and (b) are adaptive and responsive to the social-, political-, effectiveness-based pressures calling for more diverse and inclusive workplaces. It is through concerted, systemic efforts that organizational change becomes possible. Given the importance of diversity and inclusion in sport organizations, such efforts are sorely needed.

Note

1 Throughout the chapter, I use the term "racial minority," terminology that is consistent with my previous work in the area (Cunningham, 2019) and with much of the scholarship in the US. The term "minority" refers to "a collection of individuals who share a common characteristic and face discrimination in society because of their membership in that group" (Cunningham 2019: 91). In the US, persons Whites represent the numerical majority and socially privileged group; thus, those individuals who are not White, including African Americans, Asians, Hispanics, Native Americans, and so on, all represent racial minorities.

References

Allport, G. W. (1954). *The nature of prejudice*. Cambridge, MA: Addison-Wesley.
Assari, S., Moazen-Zadeh, E., Caldwell, C. H., & Zimmerman, M. A. (2017). Racial discrimination during adolescence predicts mental health deterioration in adulthood: Gender differences among Blacks. *Frontiers in Public Health*, 5, 104.
Becker, G. S. (1993). *Human capital*. Chicago, IL: University of Chicago Press.
Borland, J. F., & Bruening, J. E. (2010). Navigating barriers: A qualitative examination of the under-representation of Black females as head coaches in collegiate basketball. *Sport Management Review*, 13(4), 407–420.
Bourgois, P., Holmes, S. M., Sue, K., & Quesada, J. (2017). Structural vulnerability: Operationalizing the concept to address health disparities in clinical care. *Academic Medicine: Journal of the Association of American Medical Colleges*, 92(3), 299–307.
Bradbury, S. (2013). Institutional racism, whiteness and the under-representation of minorities in leadership positions in football in Europe. *Soccer & Society*, 14(3), 296–314.
Bradbury, S., Van Sterkenburg, J., & Mignon, P. (2018). The under-representation and experiences of elite level minority coaches in professional football in England, France and the Netherlands. *International Review for the Sociology of Sport*, 53(3), 313–334.
Brewer, M. B. (1991). The social self: On being the same and different at the same time. *Personality and Social Psychology Bulletin*, 17, 475–482.
Brewer, M. B. (2007). The importance of being we: Human nature and intergroup relations. *The American Psychologist*, 62(8), 726–738.
Carter, P. L., Skiba, R., Arredondo, M. I., & Pollock, M. (2017). You can't fix what you don't look at: Acknowledging race in addressing racial discipline disparities. *Urban Education*, 52(2), 207–235.
Clarkson, M. E. (1995). A stakeholder framework for analyzing and evaluating corporate social performance. *Academy of Management Review*, 20(1), 92–117.
Cobb, F., & Russell, N. M. (2015). Meritocracy or complexity: Problematizing racial disparities in mathematics assessment within the context of curricular structures, practices, and discourse. *Journal of Education Policy*, 30(5), 631–649.
Coleman, J. S. (1986). Social theory, social research, and a theory of action. *American Journal of Sociology*, 91, 1309–1335.
Crandall, C. S., Eshleman, A., & O'Brien, L. (2002). Social norms and the expression of prejudice: The struggle for internalization. *Journal of Personality and Social Psychology*, 82, 359–378.
Cuddy, A. J., Fiske, S. T., & Glick, P. (2008). Warmth and competence as universal dimensions of social perception: The stereotype content model and the BIAS map. *Advances in Experimental Social Psychology*, 40, 61–149.
Cunningham, G. B. (2003). Already aware of the glass ceiling: Race-related effects of perceived opportunity on the career choices of college athletes. *Journal of African American Studies*, 7(1), 57–71.
Cunningham, G. B. (2009a). The moderating effect of diversity strategy on the relationship between racial diversity and organizational performance. *Journal of Applied Social Psychology*, 36, 1445–1460.
Cunningham, G. B. (2009b). Understanding the diversity-related change process: A field study. *Journal of Sport Management*, 23, 407–428.

Cunningham, G. B. (2010). Understanding the under-representation of African American coaches: A multilevel perspective. *Sport Management Review*, 13(4), 395–406.

Cunningham, G. B. (2011a). Creative work environments in sport organizations: The influence of sexual orientation diversity and commitment to diversity. *Journal of Homosexuality*, 58, 1041–1057.

Cunningham, G. B. (2011b). The LGBT advantage: Examining the relationship among sexual orientation diversity, diversity strategy, and performance. *Sport Management Review*, 14, 453–461.

Cunningham, G. B. (2012). Occupational segregation of African Americans in intercollegiate athletics administration. *Wake Forest Journal of Law & Policy*, 2, 165–178.

Cunningham, G. B. (2013). Theory and theory development in sport management. *Sport Management Review*, 16, 1–4.

Cunningham, G. B. (2015). Creating and sustaining workplace cultures supportive of LGBT employees in college athletics. *Journal of Sport Management*, 29, 426–442.

Cunningham, G. B. (2019). *Diversity and inclusion in sport organizations: A multilevel perspective* (4th ed.). New York: Routledge.

Cunningham, G. B., & Benavides-Espinoza, C. (2008). A trend analysis of sexual harassment claims: 1992–2006. *Psychological Reports*, 103(3), 779–782.

Cunningham, G. B., & Bopp, T. D. (2010). Race ideology perpetuated: Media representations of newly hired football coaches. *Journal of Sports Media*, 5(1), 1–19.

Cunningham, G. B., & Melton, E. N. (2014). Signals and cues: LGBT inclusive advertising and consumer attraction. *Sport Marketing Quarterly*, 23, 37–46.

Cunningham, G. B., & Sagas, M. (2002). The differential effects of human capital for male and female Division I basketball coaches. *Research Quarterly for Exercise and Sport*, 73(4), 489–495.

Cunningham, G. B., & Sagas, M. (2005). Access discrimination in intercollegiate athletics. *Journal of Sport and Social Issues*, 29(2), 148–163.

Cunningham, G. B., & Singer, J. N. (2010). "You'll face discrimination wherever you go": Student athletes' intentions to enter the coaching profession. *Journal of Applied Social Psychology*, 40(7), 1708–1727.

Cunningham, G. B., Bruening, J. E., & Straub, T. (2006). The underrepresentation of African Americans in NCAA Division IA head coaching positions. *Journal of Sport Management*, 20(3), 387–413.

Cunningham, G. B., Choi, J. H., & Sagas, M. (2008). Personal identity and perceived racial dissimilarity among college athletes. *Group Dynamics: Theory, Research, and Practice*, 12, 167–177.

Cunningham, G. B., Dixon, M. A., Ahn, N. Y., & Anderson, A. J. (2017, September). *Leaving sport: A meta-analysis of racial differences in occupational turnover*. Paper presented at the annual conference for the European Sport Management Association, Bern, Switzerland.

Cunningham, G. B., Fink, J. S., & Doherty, A. J. (2016). Developing theory in sport management. In G. B. Cunningham, J. S. Fink, & A. J. Doherty (Eds.), *Routledge handbook of theory in sport management* (pp. 3–8). London, UK: Routledge.

Cunningham, G. B., Sagas, M., & Ashley, F. B. (2001). Occupational commitment and intent to leave the coaching profession: Differences according to race. *International Review for the Sociology of Sport*, 36(2), 131–148.

Day, J. C. (2015). Transitions to the top: Race, segregation, and promotions to executive positions in the college football coaching profession. *Work and Occupations*, 42(4), 408–446.

Day, J. C. (2018). Climbing the ladder or getting stuck: An optimal matching analysis of racial differences in college football coaches' job-level career patterns. *Research in Social Stratification and Mobility*, 53, 1–15.

Day, J. C., & McDonald, S. (2010). Not so fast, my friend: Social capital and the race disparity in promotions among college football coaches. *Sociological Spectrum*, 30, 138–158.

Dixon, M. A., & Cunningham, G. B. (2006). Data aggregation in multilevel analysis: A review of conceptual and statistical issues. *Measurement in Physical Education and Exercise Science*, 10(2), 85–107.

Doherty, A. J., & Chelladurai, P. (1999). Managing cultural diversity in sport organizations: A theoretical perspective. *Journal of Sport Management*, 13, 280–297.

DuBois, C. (2015). The impact of "soft" affirmative action policies on minority hiring in executive leadership: The case of the NFL's Rooney rule. *American Law and Economics Review*, 18(1), 208–233.

Edberg, M. C., Cleary, S. D., Andrade, E. L., Evans, W. D., Simmons, L. K., & Cubilla-Batista, I. (2017). Applying ecological positive youth development theory to address co-occurring health disparities among immigrant Latino youth. *Health Promotion Practice*, 18(4), 488–496.

English soccer adopts 'Rooney Rule' for national team jobs. (2018, January). *USA Today*. Retrieved online: https://www.usatoday.com/story/sports/soccer/2018/01/09/english-soccer-adopts-rooney-rule-for-national-team-jobs/109290066/.

Everhart, C. B., & Chelladurai, P. (1998). Gender differences in preferences for coaching as an occupation: The role of self-efficacy, valence, and perceived barriers. *Research Quarterly for Exercise and Sport*, 69(2), 188–200.

Feagin, J. R. (2006). *Systemic racism: A theory of oppression*. New York: Routledge.

Fink, J. S., & Pastore, D. L. (1999). Diversity in sport? Utilizing the business literature to devise a comprehensive framework of diversity initiatives. *Quest*, 51, 310–327.

Fulks, D. L. (2014). *Revenues/expenses: 2004–13 NCAA Division I intercollegiate athletics programs report*. Indianapolis, IN: National Collegiate Athletic Association.

Greenhaus, J. H., Parasuraman, S., & Wormley, W. M. (1990). Effects of race on organizational experiences, job performance, evaluations, and career outcomes. *Academy of Management Journal*, 33, 64–86.

Harris, K., & Adams, A. (2016). Power and discourse in the politics of evidence in sport for development. *Sport Management Review*, 19(2), 97–106.

Hess, D. E., & McAvoy, P. (2014). *The political classroom: Evidence and ethics in democratic education*. New York: Routledge.

Hylton, K. (2009). *"Race" and sport: Critical race theory*. New York: Routledge.

Hylton, K. (2012). Talk the talk, walk the walk: Defining critical race theory in research. *Race Ethnicity and Education*, 15(1), 23–41.

Ibarra, H. (1995). Race, opportunity, and diversity of social circles in managerial networks. *Academy of Management Journal*, 38(3), 673–703.

Ilgen, D. R., & Youtz, M. A. (1986). Factors affecting the evaluation and development of minorities in organizations. In K. Bowland & G. Ferris (Eds.), *Research in personnel and human resource management: A research annual* (pp. 307–337). Greenwich, CT: JAI Press.

Jones, K. P., Sabat, I. E., King, E. B., Ahmad, A., McCausland, T. C., & Chen, T. (2017). Isms and schisms: A meta-analysis of the prejudice-discrimination relationship across racism, sexism, and ageism. *Journal of Organizational Behavior*, 38(7), 1076–1110.

Kaiser, C. R., & Pratt-Hyatt, J. S. (2009). Distributing prejudice unequally: Do Whites direct their prejudice toward strongly identified minorities? *Journal of Personality and Social Psychology*, 96(2), 432–445.

Kamphoff, C., & Gill, D. (2008). Collegiate athletes' perceptions of the coaching profession. *International Journal of Sports Science & Coaching*, 3(1), 55–72.

Klein, K. J., Dansereau, F., & Hall, R. J. (1994). Levels issues in theory development, data collection, and analysis. *Academy of Management Review*, 19, 195–229.

Knoppers, A. (1987). Gender and the coaching profession. *Quest*, 39(1), 9–22.

Kochhar, R., & Cilluffo, A. (2018, July). Key findings on the rise in income inequality within America's racial and ethnic groups. *Pew Research Center*. Retrieved online: http://www.pewresearch.org/fact-tank/2018/07/12/key-findings-on-the-rise-in-income-inequality-within-americas-racial-and-ethnic-groups/.

Kozlowski, S. W. J., & Klein, K. J. (2000). A multilevel approach to theory and research in organizations: Contextual, temporal, and emergent processes. In K. J. Klein and S. W. J. Kozlowski (Eds.), *Multilevel theory, research, and methods in organizations: Foundations, extensions, and new directions* (pp. 3–90). San Francisco, CA: Jossey-Bass.

Leath, S., & Chavous, T. (2017). "We really protested": The influence of sociopolitical beliefs, political self-efficacy, and campus racial climate on civic engagement among Black college students attending Predominantly White Institutions. *The Journal of Negro Education*, 86(3), 220–237.

Lee, W., & Cunningham, G. B. (2015). A picture is worth a thousand words: The influence of signaling, organizational reputation, and applicant race on attraction to sport organizations. *International Journal of Sport Management*, 16, 492–506.

Lord, R., & Maher, K. (1991). *Leadership and information processing*. New York: Unwin Hyman.

Luhtanen, R., & Crocker, J. (1992). A collective self-esteem scale: Self-evaluation of one's social identity. *Personality and Social Psychology Bulletin*, 18, 302–318.

Madden, J. F. (2004). Differences in the success of NFL coaches by race, 1990–2002. *Journal of Sports Economics*, 5, 6–19.

Madden, J. F., & Ruther, M. (2009). Reply to: Differences in the success of NFL coaches by race: A different perspective. *Journal of Sports Economics*, 10(5), 543–550.

Major, B., Quinton, W. J., & McCoy, S. K. (2002). Antecedents and consequences of attributions to discrimination: Theoretical and empirical advances. *Advances in Experimental Social Psychology*, 34, 251–330.

Marshall, A. M. (2005). *Confronting sexual harassment: The law and politics of everyday life*. Burlington, VT: Ashgate.

McGirt, E. (2016, January). Why race and culture matter in the c-suite. *Fortune*. Retrieved online: http://fortune.com/black-executives-men-c-suite/.

McKay, P. F., Avery, D. R., & Morris, M. A. (2008). Mean racial-ethnic differences in employee sales performance: The moderating role of diversity climate. *Personnel Psychology*, 61(2), 349–374.

McKay, P. F., Avery, D. R., Tonidandel, S., Morris, M. A., Hernandez, M., & Hebl, M. R. (2007). Racial differences in employee retention: Are diversity climate perceptions the key? *Personnel Psychology*, 60(1), 35–62.

McLeroy, K. R., Bibeau, D., Steckler, A., & Glanz, K. (1988). An ecological perspective on health promotion programs. *Health Education Quarterly*, 15(4), 351–377.

Nassif, N., & Amara, M. (2015). Sport, policy and politics in Lebanon. *International Journal of Sport Policy and Politics*, 7(3), 443–455.

Pearson, A. R., Dovidio, J. F., & Gaertner, S. L. (2009). The nature of contemporary racism: Insights from aversive racism. *Social and Personality Psychology Compass*, 3, 314–338.

Peffley, M., Hurwitz, J., & Mondak, J. (2017). Racial attributions in the justice system and support for punitive crime policies. *American Politics Research*, 45(6), 1032–1058.

Randel, A. E., & Jaussi, K. S. (2003). Functional background identity, diversity, and individual performance in cross-functional teams. *Academy of Management Journal*, 46(6) 763–774.

Rankin-Wright, A. J., Hylton, K., & Norman, L. (2016). Off-colour landscape: Framing race equality in sport coaching. *Sociology of Sport Journal*, 33(4), 357–368.

Rosenberg, M. (2004). Two few: Of 117 football coaches, two are black; it's called institutional racism. *Detroit Free Press*. Accessed November 14, 2005, from http://www.freep.com/cgi-bin/forms/printerfriendly.pl.

Rosette, A. S., Leonardelli, G. J., & Phillips, K. W. (2008). The White standard: Racial bias in leader categorization. *Journal of Applied Psychology*, 93, 758–777.

Sadler, R. C., & Lafreniere, D. J. (2017). Racist housing practices as a precursor to uneven neighborhood change in a post-industrial city. *Housing Studies*, 32(2), 186–208.

Sagas, M., & Cunningham, G. B. (2005). Racial differences in the career success of assistant football coaches: The role of discrimination, human capital, and social capital. *Journal of Applied Social Psychology*, 35(4), 773–797.

Santucci, D. C., Floyd, M. F., Bocarro, J. N., & Henderson, K. A. (2014). Visitor services staff perceptions of strategies to encourage diversity at two urban national parks. *Journal of Park and Recreation Administration*, 32(3), 15–28.

Sartore, M. L. (2006). Categorization, performance appraisals, and self-limiting behavior: The impact on current and future performance. *Journal of Sport Management*, 20(4), 535–553.

Sartore, M. L., & Cunningham, G. B. (2006). Stereotypes, race, and coaching. *Journal of African American Studies*, 10(2), 69–83.

Schein, E. H. (2004). *Organizational culture and leadership* (3rd ed.). San Francisco, CA: Jossey-Bass.

Shore, L. M., Randel, A. E., Chung, B. G., Dean, M. A., Holcombe Ehrhart, K., & Singh, G. (2011). Inclusion and diversity in work groups: A review and model for future research. *Journal of Management*, 37(4), 1262–1289.

Sidanius, J., Pratto, F., & Bobo, L. (1996). Racism, conservatism, affirmative action, and intellectual sophistication: A matter of principled conservatism or group dominance? *Journal of Personality and Social Psychology*, 70(3), 476–490.

Singer, J. N., & Cunningham, G. B. (2012). A case study of the diversity culture of an American university athletic department: Implications for educational stakeholders. *Sport, Education & Society*, 17, 647–669.

Stangor, C. (2009). The study of stereotyping, prejudice, and discrimination within social psychology: A quick history of theory and research. In T. D. Nelson (Ed.), *Handbook of prejudice, stereotyping, and discrimination* (pp. 1–23). New York: Psychology Press.

Steward, A. D., & Cunningham, G. B. (2015). Racial identity and its impact on job applicants. *Journal of Sport Management, 29*, 245–256.

Stewart, M., & Garcia-Prieto Sol, P. (2008). A relational demography model of workgroup identification: Testing the effects of race, race dissimilarity, racial identification, and communication behavior. *Journal of Organizational Behavior, 29*(5), 657–680.

Vespa, J., Armstrong, D. M., & Medina, L. (2018). *Demographic turning points for the United States: Population projections for 2020 to 2060. Current Population Reports, P25–1144.* Washington, DC: US Census Bureau.

Vick, A., & Cunningham, G. B. (in press). Bias against Latina and African American women job applicants: A field experiment. *Sport, Business, Management: An International Journal.*

Washington, M., & Patterson, K. D. W. (2011). Hostile takeover or joint venture: Connections between institutional theory and sport management research. *Sport Management Review, 14*, 1–12.

Welty Peachey, J., Zhou, Y., Damon, Z. J., & Burton, L. J. (2015). Forty years of leadership research in sport management: A review, synthesis, and conceptual framework. *Journal of Sport Management, 29*(5), 570–587.

Wells, J. E., & Kerwin, S. (2017). Intentions to be an athletic director: Racial and gender perspectives. *Journal of Career Development, 44*(2), 127–143.

Wong, E. (2002). The mystery of the missing minority coaches. *New York Times Online.* Retrieved January 15, 2002, from https://www.patrick.af.mil/deomi/Library/ EOReadFile/ Affirmative%20Action/Spring02/The%20Mystery

Chapter 2

'Fit for doing but not fit for organising'

Racisms, stereotypes and networks in coaching in professional football in Europe

Steven Bradbury

Introduction

Over the past 50 years the higher echelons of men's professional sport in the US, Europe and Australasia has become characterised by the increasing racial, ethnic and cultural diversity of its playing workforce. Whilst these patterns of diversity differ markedly across a range of national and sporting contexts and have not encompassed all minoritised[1] groups to the same extent, in some nationally popular sports such as Basketball in the US and Rugby Union in New Zealand the incidence of elite-level minoritised sports performers has become comparable to or exceeded national racial population demographics (Lapchick, 2017; Watson et al., 2017). This is also the case in professional football in some countries in Western Europe such as England, France and the Netherlands where an estimated 30% of all elite-level players are from minoritised backgrounds in comparison to around 15% of the national population (Bradbury et al., 2011, 2014).

However, during this period there has also been a relatively limited throughput and consequent under-representation of minoritised coaches across a range of national and sporting contexts (Cunningham, 2010; Norman et al., 2014; Lapchick, 2017). Further, where there has been a steady incremental growth in the numbers of minoritised coaches in some (mainly US-based) sports such as American Football, these statistical gains seem restricted to peripheral support coach positions with lower levels of formal authority or decision-making powers and where opportunities for upward career mobility remain limited (Braddock et al., 2012; Day & McDonald, 2010; Day, 2015). These patterns of under-representation also seem apparent in professional football in Western Europe. For example, quantitative research undertaken in 2014 indicated that just 3.4% of all senior coaches at 132 elite-level clubs in England, France, Belgium, Germany, Italy, Spain and the Netherlands were from minoritised backgrounds: inclusive of 2.3% of head coaches and 4.5% of assistant coaches (Bradbury et al., 2014). More recent empirical analysis undertaken in Belgium and the Netherlands has indicated that the numerical paucity of minoritised coaches in these countries has remained relatively unchanged in recent years (see Heim et al. and Van Sterkenburg in Chapter 3 and Chapter 4 of this collection respectively). Similarly, in England, research has indicated that over a 25-year period between 1992 to 2017 just 29 minoritised coaches have held head coach positions at all 92 professional clubs, and that between 2014 and 2017 the levels of representation of minoritised groups in head coach, assistant coach and additional first team support coach positions has remained stubbornly low at around 4% in total (LMA, 2017; SPTT, 2017).

A number of academic scholars have understood these representational disparities in sports coaching as being underscored by a series of deeply embedded racialised barriers at the macro (societal), meso (organisational), and micro (individual) level (Branham, 2008; Cunningham, 2010; Rankin-Wright et al., 2016, 2017; Sagas & Cunningham, 2005; Sartore & Cunningham, 2006; Singer et al., 2010). For example, at the macro level, scholars have alluded to constraints engendered by the broader political and legislative climate and the role of powerful internal and external stakeholders in the coach hiring process. At the meso level, they have identified dominant monocultural processes and cultures and the existence of conscious and unconscious bias within the senior decision-making tiers of sports organisations. Further, at the micro level, they have drawn attention to the impact of structural and institutional constraints on inhibiting opportunities for minoritised groups to develop the requisite network capital to engender upward social mobility as coaches (see Cunningham in Chapter 1 of this collection for a multi-level analysis of these racialised constraints).

These practices and experiences of access and treatment discrimination (Cunningham, 2010) seem especially evident in professional football in Western Europe. For example, research undertaken in England, France and the Netherlands has identified some longstanding and unshifting practices of racially inflected institutional closure embedded in mechanisms of coach recruitment at professional clubs. Also, in the differently racialised experiences of minoritised coaches attending coach education courses or working within professional club coaching environments (Bradbury et al., 2014, 2018). This research and similar studies undertaken in an English context have also alluded to the ways in which the existence and expression of overt and culturally coded racisms and stereotypes has engendered deleterious psychological and vocational impacts for minoritised coaches drawn from diverse racial, ethnic and cultural (and religious) backgrounds (Bradbury, 2018; Cashmore & Clelland, 2011; King, 2004: see Kilvington in Chapter 5 of this collection for insights into the UK South Asian experience of football coaching). The work of these scholars has drawn similar conclusions in suggesting that racisms and discrimination of this kind have impacted significantly in constraining the pace and scope of the progression of minoritised groups across the transition from playing to coach education to coach employment in the professional game.

This chapter will build on and extend the prior work of scholars in this field and will offer an original empirical and theoretically grounded contribution to the study of the under-representation and racialised experiences of minoritised coaches in professional football in Europe. More specifically, the chapter will identify and examine some of the key factors which have limited the potential for and realisation of equitable opportunities, experiences and outcomes for minoritised coaches in these football settings. In doing so, the chapter will focus on two inter-related themes. Firstly, the existence of racisms and racial stereotypes in professional football coaching contexts. Secondly, the over-reliance of racially closed networks-based approaches to coach recruitment at professional football clubs. In particular, the chapter will draw attention to the ways in which a series of overt, culturally coded and institutional forms of racisms and discrimination have impacted in negatively shaping the experiences of minoritised coaches from a diverse range of racial, ethnic and cultural backgrounds in football in different ways across different nation states across Europe. Finally, the chapter will contextualise these findings from within a Critical Race Theory (CRT) perspective. In doing so, it will draw clear linkages between ongoing patterns of minoritised coach under-representation, the manifestation of multiple forms of racisms and discrimination, and the underlying normative power of hegemonic Whiteness in the sport. Prior to the presentation and analysis of findings, this chapter will begin by outlining the key tenets of CRT and also offer an extended discussion of some key methodological considerations engendered by conducting research of this kind. In particular, in relation to efforts to foreground the experientially informed voices of research participants from minoritised backgrounds and the often unacknowledged but centrally important issues of Whiteness, reflexivity and positionality and their negotiation within and impact on the research process. It is these theoretical and methodological considerations to which this chapter now turns.

Theoretical framework

The presentation and analysis of findings in this chapter are informed by and draw upon key tenets of CRT. This transdisciplinary and developing theoretical framework provides a useful conceptual and analytical tool-kit with which to examine the increasingly subtle and complex ways in which the conjunctive relationship between racialised structures, ideologies and discourses can engender deleterious impacts for minoritised populations across a range of socio-cultural contexts, including sport (Delgado & Stefancic, 2012; Hylton, 2005, 2010). In the context of this chapter it is argued that CRT does this in three ways. Firstly, in positioning 'race' as the key organising principle of social life alongside other intersecting forms of social oppression such as gender and social class, and in considering racisms to constitute an engrained (rather than aberrational) feature of the everyday lived experiences of minoritised populations across a range of spatial and sporting contexts (Crenshaw et al., 1995; Hylton, 2009; Ladson-Billings,1998; Massao and Fasting, 2010). This is especially apparent in Europe where a range of structural, cultural and political factors have impacted in shaping the parameters of racialised inclusion and exclusion in different ways across nation state boundaries, but where minoritised populations also experience racisms and discrimination in broadly comparable ways (Bradbury et al., 2011).

Secondly, in critiquing dominant liberal ideologies of objectivity, meritocracy and race neutrality which fail to recognise or seek to address the existence and impacts of racisms unless manifest in their most egregious forms (Bonilla-Silva, 2010). From a CRT perspective, these limited conceptualisations overlook the extent and ways in which the operation of everyday routinised racisms and racialised inequalities have become institutionalised and normalised across a range of societal and sporting contexts over time (Delgado & Stefancic, 2012; Hylton, 2009). Further, such perceptions are considered by some scholars to be underscored by a strong adherence to a series of colour-blind ideologies which present a highly individualised and largely deracialised account of upward social mobility as resulting from individual ability and hard work, and which consequently strip the realities of success or failure from the deeply racialised societal and sporting contexts in which they occur (Bimper, 2015; Bonilla-Silva, 2010; Burdsey, 2011).

Thirdly, in drawing scholarly attention to the normativity of Whiteness as a largely unacknowledged and unremarked powerful structural and cultural practice through which hierarchical systems of racial domination have become effortlessly created and reproduced over time (Delgado & Stefancic, 2012; Giroux, 1997). From a CRT perspective, the power of Whiteness as a process lies in its ability to frame the social, cultural and economic advantages of White privilege as the norm, whilst simultaneously precluding any critical inward gaze as to the ways in which membership of dominant (White) social and cultural networks of mutual acquaintance has created and sustained these benefits over time (McIntosh,1990; Essed & Goldberg, 2002). From this powerful hegemonic position, the under-representation of minoritised groups across a range of societal and sporting fields has been framed as resulting from broader socio-historical exclusions or in terms of the negatively perceived properties of minoritised groups, rather than as being shaped and maintained by the unreflexive and unchanging practices of dominant individuals and institutions (Frankenberg,1999; Bradbury et al., 2018).

Study and methods

The findings presented in this chapter are drawn from two separate studies examining the under-representation and racialised experiences of minoritised coaches in professional football in Europe. The first study was funded by the UEFA (Union of European Football Associations)[2] and FARE (Football Against Racism in Europe) Network[3] in 2011 and involved the author conducting semi-structured interviews with 20 sports academics, equality campaigners and senior governance staff at national football federations and UEFA. In 2015 and 2016 the author also conducted seven further interviews with national federation staff and equality campaigners around similar themes. The aims of this study were to examine the perceptions of key stakeholders drawn from a range of culturally diverse and culturally homogeneous national contexts as to the organisational mechanisms which they felt had contributed to the under-representation of minoritised coaches in professional football in Europe. Overall, interviewees were drawn from 14 countries across Europe, including; England, Northern Ireland, Republic of Ireland, France, Germany, Belgium, Norway, Switzerland, Spain, Malta, Poland, Austria, Hungary and the Netherlands. In total, 19 interviewees were White and eight were drawn from (Black-Caribbean and Black-African) minoritised backgrounds. The second study was also funded by the FARE Network and involved the author and two academic colleagues (Patrick Mignon and Jacco Van Sterkenburg) conducting semi-structured interviews with 40 elite-level minoritised coaches in England, France and the Netherlands. The aims of this study were to examine the perceptions and experiences of minoritised coaches in three culturally diverse countries in Western Europe as to the key factors which had impacted on their career transition from playing to coaching in the professional game. These interviewees were drawn from a range of racial, ethnic and cultural backgrounds and included; Black-Caribbean, Black-African, and South Asian in England (15); Black-African, Black-Antillean, and North African in France (15); and Surinamese, Moroccan, Indonesian/Moluccan and Turkish in the Netherlands (10). In all cases, interviews lasted between 60 and 90 minutes and took place at mutually agreed venues such as club training facilities, office spaces, the homes of interviewees, or via telephone or web-based mediums. All interviewees were encouraged to articulate their perceptions and experiences in their own terms of reference and in a safe and supportive discursive space. This collaborative approach to interviewing yielded in-depth and insightful qualitative data and helped to illuminate the topic under review.

Central to the qualitative approach to data collection and analysis featured within this chapter is the strong emphasis and value placed on the occupationally and culturally informed experiential knowledge of the interviewees and strong efforts to position them centrally as the 'primary knowers' within this interactive discourse. From a CRT perspective, this approach is felt to be important as a means to move beyond majoritarian stories and master narratives embedded in some popular and academic discourse as to the extent and impacts of 'race' and racisms on everyday life (Solórzano & Yosso, 2002). In the context of the range of interview data drawn on in this chapter, this approach is especially keen to illuminate the voices and render visible the historically subjugated testimonies of minoritised groups whose lived experiences have traditionally been excluded from – but remain subject to – dominant narratives on the realities and impacts of 'race' and racism in sport (Hylton, 2005). In doing so, the author remains cognisant of the inherent racialised power imbalance embedded in the social distance between his own White identity and that of the minoritised research participants, and the privileged space this imbues in relation to reporting on rather than directly experiencing the racisms and racialised inequalities referred to by minoritised interviewees. In this respect, it is important to recognise that the normativity of Whiteness embedded within the professional football contexts under review cannot be completely separated from those which exist in the research process, and that the author may unconsciously draw on White Western European hegemonic discourses around 'race' and racisms in the reporting and analysis of findings (Frankenberg, 2004; Sin, 2007). However, such influence is rarely definitive in its application and seldom passive in the ways in which it is negotiated within the research process. Further, it has been argued that a theoretically informed and lived engagement with the practice of critical and cultural reflexivity can provide a useful epistemological tool through which to better consider the self and the self in relation to others, and to help to clarify the conceptual particularity of the research and the political positionality of the researcher (Fletcher, 2014; Fletcher & Hylton, 2017). From this perspective, whilst acknowledging the contextual validity of arguments which allude to the importance of 'identity symmetry' within the research process, it is the contention here that beyond the practical difficulties engendered by such an approach the epistemological quest to uncover a singular and 'authentic' racial truth is heavily reliant on a series of problematic essentialist assumptions and homogenising principles. Such approaches tend to overplay the rigidity of insider and outsider binaries and consequently underplay the multifarious and fluid identity constructions of researchers and researched across a range of structural, cultural and gendered intersections (Berry & Clair, 2011; Milner, 2007). This latter assertion is particularly relevant to the findings presented in this chapter, where the myriad diversity of interviewees drawn from dominant and marginalised populations across different nation states has engendered a series of variegated, overlapping and contextually situated narratives with regard to the topic under review. In this respect, this chapter seeks to present an epistemologically reflexive and culturally considered account of the processes, experiences and outcomes of racialised exclusion in professional football coaching contexts across a range of national settings in Europe.

Findings

(i) Racisms and racial stereotypes in professional football coaching contexts

Interviewees in all countries alluded to the historical and continued incidence of racisms and racial stereotyping in professional football in Europe. These ideas, actions and behaviours were felt to be perpetrated by a range of social actors including spectators, players, coaches and club officials and to be geographically and temporally uneven in their manifestation and expression. More overt forms of racisms were felt to be apparent within professional club environments which remain physically and psychologically rooted in racially closed localised cultures within which the advent of minoritised players and coaches has come to represent a form of multi-cultural trespass into prized White cultural spaces (Back et al., 2001). This was felt to be especially evident in some homogenously White countries in Southern, Central and Eastern Europe where the incidence of intentional and orchestrated racisms remain a relatively commonplace feature of the professional football landscape for minoritised players (Doidge, 2017) and where there has also developed some strong cultural oppositions to the recruitment of coaches from minoritised backgrounds. For example:

> *There is clear racial abuse of migrant players in Hungary and the surrounding countries in the East. And there is clear opposition to them playing at all. They would certainly not be accepted as coaches. There is opposition already to [White] migrant coaches, from outside of these countries, from the Balkans especially. But a [Black] migrant coach, an African, it is unthinkable for the fans, and for the owners of the clubs. It just wouldn't happen. They wouldn't allow it.*
>
> (White Interviewee, Equality Campaign, Hungary)

The above (and below) interviewee narratives allude to the strongly interconnected relationship between the organisation and practice of professional football (and other sports more broadly) and the distinctly racialised sociohistorical and contemporary national political contexts in which they take place (Carrington, 2010). This is especially (but not exclusively) the case in some more racially homogeneous countries in Southern, Central and Eastern Europe in which there exists some relatively rigid models of national identity and sporting citizenship (Bradbury, 2013; Bradbury et al., 2011; EU FRA, 2011). Within such settings, the increasingly popular (and populist) political conjunction of nationalistic ideologies, anti-immigrant sentiment and racialised economic protectionism has also been 'played out' at the meso level of professional club team operations, with the effect of consciously limiting the inclusion of minoritised coaches. For example:

I don't think they want to employ minorities as managers because they are worried that they will not be accepted by the squad, and by the other coaching staff. In terms of black managers, it just wouldn't happen, they just wouldn't be accepted by the players or by the spectators, especially in Central and Eastern Europe.

(White Interviewee, Equality Campaign, Poland)

In contrast, whilst interviewees in some Western European countries felt that overt forms of racism and racial closure of this kind in professional coaching contexts had subsided over time, they alluded instead to the incidence of subtle, codified and inferential racisms as a key factor in underscoring the racially inequitable treatment of minoritised coaches. These disguised racisms were felt to be evidenced in the use of racially inappropriate language and behaviours at an interactional level and through the questioning of the social and technical competencies of minoritised coaches by coach educators and senior coaching staff at professional clubs. Whilst these racialised 'micro-aggressions' (Burdsey 2011; Bradbury et al., 2011; EU FRA, 2011) were considered by many interviewees to be unintentional, unconscious and underpinned by a distinct cultural awareness deficit on the part of perpetrators, they were also felt to have accorded less professional value, status and credibility to minoritised coaches. For example:

There are things that are said that have a racial connotation to it, and it's racist, but it's not obvious. It's the way it's put, little comments about your cultural background, how you do things, the way you conduct yourself. Stuff about not being organised, punctuality, being 'laid back' and so on. Even when it's done in a joking way, it still frames you in a certain way, you know, as different, less important.

(Minoritised Interviewee, Coach, England)

Interviewees felt the aforementioned processes of racialised 'othering' and marginalisation were underpinned by a series of historically embedded and misplaced racial stereotypes through which key power brokers have come to equate specific physical and cultural 'performance traits' on the basis of the assumed 'natural' abilities of minoritised sports people. Such stereotypes have had some historical currency in professional football in Europe (and in other sports globally) and have led to the 'stacking' of minoritised players in peripheral match-play positions and the centralisation and allocation of captaincy duties to White players (Maguire, 1988; McCarthy et al., 2003; Van Sterkenburg et al., 2012). Whilst these racialised ideologies have arguably lessened in some sports over time, interviewees felt this had done little to disrupt the residual permanence and reproduction of these ideas in professional football or to have limited their transference from the review of minoritised players to the coaching tiers of the professional game. For example:

> This is due to the cultural stereotype thing. There is the view that they might play, but they are instinctive players, they don't breathe the game and are not educated in tactics and so on. These are old stereotyping prejudices. And if the managers and owners have specific perceptions of ethnic minority players, and treat them differently as players, then of course, the potential for those players to progress onto coaches and managers is limited.
>
> (White Interviewee, National Federation, Netherlands)

In this respect, interviewees drew attention to the tendencies of key power brokers at professional football clubs to draw on and transpose some physical and cultural stereotypical misconceptions of minoritised players to an inferred evaluation of the (assumedly, limited) social and technical capabilities of minoritised coaches. From these hegemonically dominant, but culturally uninformed, perspectives, Arab coaches of North African and Middle Eastern heritage were felt to have been conceptualised as possessing individual 'trickery', 'cunning' and 'guile' as players, but to lack the collectivist team working attributes and leadership qualities perceived to be necessary to excel as elite-level coaches in professional football. Similarly, Black coaches of West African and Caribbean heritage were felt to have been conceptualised as possessing innate 'strength', 'athleticism' and 'instinct' as players, but to lack the requisite 'organisational skills', 'analytical acumen', and 'intellectual capacities' to be considered for coaching appointments in the elite echelons of the professional game. For example:

> Black players are appreciated because they are strong, tall, hard workers. Many [now] play in central and defensive positions, where most of the present coaches have been recruited. But they are seen mainly as executants. They have to be driven. They lack talent to think about the game. They are not seen as leaders. There are exceptions. But I know that they are very suspicious about the ability for them to become a good coach.
>
> (Minoritised Interviewee, Coach, France)

Interviewees also alluded to the related tendencies of key power brokers to problematise the perceived attitudes, behaviours and aspirations of minoritised coaches and to negatively question their professional and cultural 'suitability', 'competence' and 'authority' to manage teams in professional football. This was felt to be the case in Southern, Central and Eastern Europe where the playing workforce tended to be drawn from a relatively narrow cohort of national and culturally homogenous backgrounds *and* at clubs in Western Europe where player demographics were marked much more by their national and cultural diversity. Accordingly, it was felt by some interviewees that minoritised coaches tended to be adversely conceptualised in terms of their perceived racial, ethnic and cultural traits, rather than in relation to their evidential technical and experiential abilities as coaches. Further, such racialised conceptualisations were considered to be rarely extended to the vocational review of comparably qualified or experienced White coaches. For example:

It is the case in many countries, especially France and Belgium, which I know, if you are a minority [coach] then you are monitored more. The decisions you make, the players you sign, the tactic you use, and so on. If you do well, it is because you are a good coach. But if you do not do well, then it is because you are a minority. And so, you are stigmatised in this way.

(White interviewee, UEFA, Switzerland)

Taken together, as a result of the embedded normativity and unremarked definitional power of the stereotypes alluded to above, interviewees felt that key power brokers at professional clubs had come to conceptualise the appointment of minoritised coaches with notions of 'insecurity', 'uncertainty' and 'risk'. This was felt to have informed decisions to overlook or avoid appointing minoritised coaches with whom they had little prior personal or cultural connection, in favour of recruiting White coaches with whom they had greater levels of cultural familiarity and social comfort. Such approaches to recruitment were considered by interviewees to have limited opportunities for minoritised coaches and sustained patterns of 'homologous reproduction' (Sartore & Cunningham, 2006; Cunningham, 2010) within the professional football coaching workforce. For example:

I do believe that what happens a lot of the time is they want to bring in somebody of their own image, and somebody that probably looks like they did at that sort of age and behaves like they did because that's what they feel comfortable with. I suppose it's quite a natural thing to do in some ways, but the problem is it doesn't move things along, and ultimately it denies people who they don't look like them opportunities.

(Minoritised Interviewee, Coach, England)

(ii) Networks-based methods of coach recruitment at professional clubs

Interviewees in all countries alluded to the historical and continued reliance of professional football clubs on informal networks rather than formalised qualifications-based methods of coach recruitment. This was considered to be most apparent in relation to recruitment to first team head coach and assistant coach positions and to be enacted through processes of personal recommendation, sponsored mobility and patronage on the part of key power brokers at clubs. These commonly practiced 'head-hunting' approaches to identifying and appointing senior coaches were felt by interviewees to replicate a series of normative mechanisms for the targeted recruitment of elite-level players and senior operations staff at clubs. Further, they were felt to have limited opportunities for minoritised coaches to submit applications within a 'reasonable time frame' (Singer et al., 2010) and to be considered for interview for emergent coaching positions at clubs. For example:

> *I think football is quite a unique environment or industry where more than any other job, it's a lot about who you know. It's about friends in the game and calling on favours, and the game is a lot like that. You only have to see how managers drag people about with them when they get new jobs, and the backroom staff. So, without a proper recruitment process, advertising, equal opportunities and all of that, it's still about who you know that gets you jobs.*
> (Minoritised Interviewee, National Federation, England)

These operationally closed processes of coach recruitment were felt by interviewees to favour 'known' White coaches drawn from within the dominant (White) social and cultural networks of the football industry, and to militate against minoritised coaches with fewer longstanding and substantive ties to this informally established occupational marketplace. This was felt to be evident in the ways in which key power brokers at professional clubs tended to consciously and/or unconsciously seek out and recruit coaches with similar norms, values and behaviours and from recognisable (White) backgrounds. Such approaches were argued to restrict racially equitable access to the informal means through which to accrue social capital through association (Sagas & Cunningham, 2005) and to consequently sustain the operational and cultural status quo of coaching and governance relations within club settings. For example:

> *It's really the old boys' network. When they look for coaches, they have a criteria of what they are looking for. And on some level, that criteria fit themselves, or how they see themselves. Because they look alike, and think alike, they will agree easily and they see that as a good fit. They think, in quite a narrow way, that this will work well for the club.*
> (White Interviewee, Equality Campaign, Germany)

Interviewees provided a series of insightful accounts of the ways in which access to these dominant (White) social and cultural networks with the power to enable or constrain the career progression of minoritised coaches was negotiated over the football career life course. In doing so, interviewees alluded to some shared and overlapping racialised experiences and outcomes amongst different (and differently) minoritised groups across a range of national contexts. For example, firstly, interviewees alluded to some commonplace perceptions held by key power brokers at clubs that the successful acquisition of key coaching competencies were premised on prior elite-level professional playing experience. This was perceived by some interviewees to have limited coaching opportunities for a range of 'non-black' minoritised groups such as South Asians in the UK, North Africans in France, Moroccans in the Netherlands, and Turkish groups in Germany amongst whom there has (with some exceptions) been a historically limited throughput of players into the elite echelons of the professional game in Europe. In this respect, these groups were felt to have been doubly marginalised by their lack of prior professional playing capital and by their embodied (and negatively assumed) ethnic, cultural (and religious) distinctiveness, at least within the dominant hegemonic conceptualisations of White cultural normativity embedded within professional football coach contexts. For example:

> *One thing is that you need to have been a professional player to be a coach. Not that you can't be a coach without that, but that is how it is. And it has been hard enough for Black players to make that transition. But other minorities, who have not, maybe, played at the highest level, for them the system is notoriously closed.*
> (White Interviewee, UEFA representative, Switzerland)

Secondly, interviewees alluded to the importance of building positive social relationships with White players, coaches and coach educators throughout the duration of their playing careers. Whilst some (mainly Black and Dual-heritage) interviewees in multi-cultural countries such as England reported relatively (but, not exclusively) positively in this respect, in other less integrated countries in Europe it was felt that minoritised groups drawn from a range of diverse backgrounds had often experienced social and cultural marginalisation from the dominant (White) racialised power dynamics within team and coach education settings. This was felt to have positioned some minoritised players and coaches as 'outsiders within' these interactional spaces and to have limited opportunities for them to develop meaningful and supportive longer term relationships with White colleagues, whose own upwardly mobile career trajectories had led them to later assume senior coaching positions at clubs with powers to appoint 'known' coaching support staff over time. For example:

> *Today, you have a coaches' social milieu. They know each other because they played in professional teams, because they were in the same training sessions, and they are all white. They make sure they look after each other because they are all friends. This is what is missing, Black and White or Arab who played together, who are close. They can speak for each other to the Chairmen. They can help each other, like the others do.*
> (Minoritised Interviewee, Coach, France)

Thirdly, interviewees drew attention to the ways in which minoritised players had traditionally been excluded from opportunities to position themselves favourably within some commonly practiced 'captain to coach' pathways at professional clubs. In doing so, they referred to the cumulative impact of the 'stacking' of minoritised players in peripheral match-play positions rather than those deemed central to the strategic management of team performance and the related tendencies of head coaches to confer captaincy duties on centrally positioned White players. This was felt to have limited 'on-pitch' opportunities for minoritised players to formally exhibit a series of key leadership skills and competencies considered by key power brokers within the professional game to be strong indicators of future elite-level coaching potential. For example:

> I think a lot of the time there's a tendency to want someone who's been a captain, who you almost think his next step is going to be coaching or managing. But the problem is how many black players have there been that really fit that bill. I mean, they're few and far between. Partly because they weren't given the opportunities or the responsibility to be the captain in the first place.
> (Minoritised interviewee, Players Union, England)

Relatedly, interviewees noted that the allocation of captaincy positions were also a key mechanism through which players were afforded a series of 'off-pitch' opportunities for extended levels of contact and networking with the 'inner circle' of almost exclusively White power brokers at professional clubs and other key stakeholders in the game. In this respect, the historical absence of minoritised team captains was felt to have limited opportunities for players and aspiring coaches from minoritised backgrounds to enhance their 'profile', 'visibility' and 'favourability' in relation to forthcoming coaching appointments at professional clubs. For example:

> The coaches know you, the players know you, the supporters to a degree know you, but the directors don't know you. Or they just don't think about you at all. Probably the hardest thing is getting through into that echelon of the board room and directors and influence their perceptions. How do you get into those circles? Your playing career only takes you so far, especially if you were never picked to be a captain.
> (Minoritised interviewee, Coach, England)

Taken together, interviewees in all countries felt that the preponderance of dominant networks-based practices of coach recruitment and uneven opportunities for the development of network capital over the professional football life course had resulted in some predictable patterns of racial closure across the European professional football coaching landscape. This was felt to be evidenced in the predominance of White coaches in elite coaching positions and in the frequency with which White coaches (and predominantly White coaching support teams) were also awarded comparable positions at other clubs over the duration of their coaching careers. In contrast, minoritised coaches were felt to have remained peripheral to and excluded from this coaching and managerial merry-go-round and to be awarded lower status coaching positions where such positions were awarded at all. Further, interviewees felt that minoritised coaches experienced additional psychological and vocational pressures to be successful in such positions given the reduced likelihood of being offered 'second chances' to assume comparable positions at other professional clubs over time. For example:

> When they do get the chance, it is just the one chance, and, you know, who does well on the first chance? Nobody. You are still learning. And then it is back to the beginning. Writing for jobs and getting no response. And they see it is different for white coaches. They have more opportunities. They can make mistakes. It is part of their journey. Whereas for the Black coaches, that journey can stop, very quickly.
> (White interviewee, UEFA, Switzerland)

Discussion

This chapter has drawn on the experientially informed and extensive narratives of key organisational stakeholders and minoritised coaches drawn from a range of dominant and marginalised ethnicities in professional football in Europe. In doing so, the findings presented in this chapter have identified a series of ideological and operational constraints which have impacted negatively in limiting the potential for and realisation of equitable opportunities, experiences and outcomes for minoritised coaches across the transition from playing to coaching in the professional game. In the first instance, the findings have drawn attention to the structural and cultural inseparability of the organisation and practice of professional football from the hierarchical racialised societies in which all aspects of its operations take place. In this respect it is both reflective of and reflects back on a series of historically inscribed racialised power relations (Carrington, 2010) and like other sports is '*an arena in which the complex interplay between "race", nation, culture and identity in different social environments is most publicly articulated*' (Ansari, 2004: 209). From a CRT perspective, the professional football coaching contexts under review can also be understood to constitute a series of contextually situated '*racial projects*' within which the dynamic operation of everyday routinised processes of racisms and racialised discrimination has become normalised and institutionalised to the point of invisibility over time (Delgado & Stefancic, 2012; Hylton, 2009). These racisms have differed in their political orientation and individual and organisational forms of expression and have led different (and differently) minoritised coaches to experience varied and overlapping forms of racialised exclusions across different national contexts. They have also engendered the hierarchical occupational structuring of minoritised coaches in such ways as to *'organise [human] resources along racial lines in seemingly "natural" ways'* (Hylton, 2010: 340).

In the second instance, the findings offer a critique to dominant liberal ideologies of objectivity, meritocracy and race neutrality which deny the salience of 'race' and racisms as a key factor in shaping the parameters of inclusion and exclusion of minoritised groups across a range of societal and sporting contexts. The promulgation of these 'colour-blind' ideologies is particularly evident in popular and mediated narratives around professional football in (especially, Western) Europe. Such discourses position the sport as a post-racial and egalitarian space in which minoritised performers are welcomed, included and supported, whilst simultaneously ignoring the extent and ways in which the opportunities for and experiences of minoritised groups are constrained and racialised in different ways across different levels of the sport (Bradbury, 2013; , Hylton, 2018). From a CRT perspective, the professional football coaching contexts under review can be understood to be receptive to and productive of a series of powerful racialised ideologies, narratives and meanings which have enabled the 'unproblematic' signification of human characteristics along distinctly racial, ethnic and cultural lines (Bradbury et al. 2018). This is evident where key power brokers at clubs have drawn on a series of socially constructed stereotypes which have 'othered' and problematised minoritised coaches in terms of their negatively assumed 'racial self' rather than providing a vocationally considered evaluation of their actualised 'professional self'. Such conceptualisations have framed the falsely perceived attributes of minoritised coaches as *'inconsistent with the characteristics believed necessary to successfully fulfil a managerial role'* (Sartore & Cunningham, 2006: 70) and contributed to sustaining their occupational and cultural positioning as outside and excluded from the European professional football coaching marketplace.

In the third instance, the findings allude to the invisibility, centrality and normativity of hegemonic Whiteness in professional football in Europe. From a CRT perspective, Whiteness can be understood as a powerful structural and cultural practice which has engendered and maintained racialised inequalities in societal and sporting contexts and ensured the *'reproduction of dominance rather than subordination, normativity rather than marginality, and privilege rather than disadvantage'* (Frankenberg, 1999: 237). This is especially the case in relation to the professional football coaching contexts under review where the discursive power of Whiteness has conceptualised minoritised coaches as lacking the intellectual, analytical and cerebral capacities to coach teams successfully in the elite-level game. It is also evident in the ways in which the relational power of Whiteness has underpinned the normative operation of networks-based approaches to coach recruitment which sustain the invisible knapsack of White privilege engendered by membership of powerful racialised groupings (McIntosh, 1990). In such circumstances, it is perhaps unsurprising that many appropriately qualified and experienced minoritised coaches have remained beyond the narrowly conceptualised operational preferences and cultural consciousness of key power brokers drawn from within the dominant (White) social and cultural 'old boys' club' of the professional football industry. As a result, there continues to persist some predictable patterns of minoritised coach under-representation in professional football in Europe and where the dominant White hegemonic structures of the senior organisational tiers of the sport have remained largely unchallenged and unchanged over time (Hylton, 2009; Long & Hylton, 2002).

Conclusions and recommendations

In conclusion, any meaningful efforts designed to address the racialised inequities identified in this chapter need to remain cognisant of the symbiotic relationship between the under-representation of minoritised coaches, the existence and expression of multiple forms of racisms and discrimination, and the underlying normative power of hegemonic Whiteness in professional football in Europe. In this respect, it is argued from a CRT perspective that liberalism alone is not enough to address more embedded and institutionalised forms of racisms and racialised discrimination and that professional football clubs need to move beyond the normative application of colour-blind and networks-based approaches to coach recruitment which have sustained rather than redressed racialised inequalities in football coaching. In doing so, professional football clubs, national football federations and UEFA should work collaboratively to implement a holistic package of positive action measures to ensure equality opportunities and experiences and forcefully stimulate conditions under which equality of outcomes are more likely to be realised.

In the first instance, this should include the establishment of clear policy goals and actions in relation to the collection of baseline data, target setting, and the monitoring of progress to increase minoritised coach representation at professional clubs over time. It should also include the development and implementation of a transparent, equitable and regulated approach to coach recruitment which features a strong emphasis on enabling and enforcing professional clubs to adhere to national and European level equalities legislation with regard to employment practices. The introduction of 'consideration forcing' measures of this kind such as the 'Rooney Rule' in the US NFL – which mandates that clubs must interview at least one suitably qualified candidate from a minoritised background for vacant head coaching positions or incur significant financial penalties – has had some success in increasing the representation of minoritised coaches over time (see Duru in Chapter 11 of this collection). The operational and representational success of the 'Rooney Rule' has informed the development of similar mechanisms of coach recruitment in other sports in the US as well as the English Football League Voluntary and Mandatory Codes of Coach Recruitment in professional and youth academy football (see Cowell and Conricode et al. in Chapter 12 and Chapter 13 respectively in this collection). These interventions provide useful models of best equality practice to which professional clubs and national football federations in Europe could aspire, adhere and develop further.

In the second instance, efforts on this score should also include the establishment and delivery of a bespoke programme of educational support activities. Such measures should be designed to encourage and enable key power brokers at professional clubs and national football federations to go beyond the rhetorical and performative, to a much more meaningful and impactful engagement with the aforementioned legislative and operational approaches to coach recruitment. Work of this kind should feature the delivery of nationally relevant cultural diversity training for senior coaching and governance staff at professional clubs. It should pay particular attention to outlining the ways in which overt, culturally coded racisms and more institutional forms of discrimination can work at a conscious and/or unconscious level to constrain the career progression of minoritised coaches. It should also seek to encourage a perceptual shift on the part of key power brokers in professional football towards conceptualising cultural diversity less as a problem to be dealt with and more as a positive individual and organisational resource to be nurtured and developed. Such an approach would be likely to impact positively in enhancing the organisational effectiveness and public profile of professional clubs and enable them to align more explicitly with the increasingly multi-cultural and corporate impulses of the modern game.

Finally, it is the contention here that the legislative and pedagogical positive actions identified above would engender a complementary and constructive shift towards a more operationally transparent, racially equitable and culturally reflexive approach to coach recruitment. In doing so, this would help to dismantle some of the deeply racialised institutional barriers experienced by minoritised coaches across the transition from playing to coaching and offer at least some disruption to the dominant White hegemonic structures embedded within the senior organisational tiers of the sport. The extent and ways in which such measures might be embraced and implemented will to some degree be dependent on the ideological malleability and operational willingness of key power brokers at professional clubs and the national political, sporting and football governance structures within which they are positioned to effectuate meaningful social change. In particular, in moving beyond traditional liberal ideologies of objectivity, meritocracy and race neutrality, towards the adoption of progressive and 'race conscious' approaches to equality and diversity management within which the use of positive action measures form a central strategic pillar. This chapter concludes that the adoption of these latter approaches will be essential in engendering equality of opportunities, experiences and outcomes for minoritised coaches and in ensuring increased and sustained levels of organisational inclusivity and cultural diversity within the professional football coaching landscape in Europe over time.

Notes

1 The term 'minoritised' is used in this chapter to reflect an understanding of 'minority status' as a socially constructed process (rather than as an entity) which takes place in specific social, economic and political contexts over time and which has resulted in 'minoritised groups' having less power or representation compared to other (White) groups in society. In the context of this chapter, the term 'minoritised' is used to refer to racially, ethnically and culturally distinct populations drawn from non-European heritage resident in European countries in which they also make up a numerical minority. This broad conceptualisation includes, first, second and third generation populations drawn from Asia, Africa, Latin America, the Caribbean and the Middle East. It also includes the 'special case' of transcontinental Turkish heritage populations whose ethnic, cultural and religious 'visibility' is arguably heightened in new countries of settlement in Western Europe. This definition is premised on the recognition that 'minority status' is both objectively ascribed (by the dominant society) and subjectively applied (by minoritised groups) as a means of marking out a range of racial, ethnic and cultural (and religious) difference. Whilst these differences can be positively applied as a marker of cultural identity and group solidarity, they are more often applied negatively as a basis for racialised abuse, hostility and discrimination, especially in the social and cultural arena of professional sports. The author remains cognisant that categorisations of this kind which seek to capture the commonalities and specificities of diverse minoritised identities and their varied and overlapping experiences remains conceptually limited and subject to contestation. This task is made more difficult in the context of the myriad diversity of minoritised populations referred to in this chapter. In particular, in relation to differences in terminological classification and everyday nomenclature used to describe minoritised groups across a range of nation states in Europe, including by interviewees drawn from dominant and marginalised ethnicities. As such the author proceeds with some scholarly caution (and no small amount of practical utility) in using the term 'minoritised' in this chapter as a means of identifying and analysing the experiences of 'minoritised' groups within the professional football coaching contexts under review.
2 UEFA (Union of European Football Associations) is the central administrative body for professional football in Europe. It consists of 55 national federation members and organises competitions including the UEFA European Championship (for national teams) and UEFA Champions League (for club teams).
3 The FARE (Football Against Racism in Europe) Network is an organisation set up to challenge racism and other forms of discrimination in Europe. It consists of equality campaign groups and fan activists drawn from around 30 countries and has received backing from UEFA and the European Commission.

References

Ansari, H. (2004) Introduction: Racialization and sport. *Patterns of Prejudice*, 38(3), 209–212.
Back, L., Crabbe, T. & Solomos, J. (2001) *The Changing Face of Football: Racism, Identity and Multiculture in the English Game*. Oxford: Berg.
Berry, K. & Clair, P. (2011) Reflecting on the call to ethnographic reflexivity: A collage of responses to questions of contestation. *Cultural Studies and Critical Methodologies*, 11(2), 199–209.

Bimper, A. (2015) Lifting the veil: Exploring colorblind racism in Black student athlete experiences. *Journal of Sport and Social Issues*, 39(3), 225–243.

Bradbury, S. (2013) Institutional racism, whiteness and the under-representation of minorities in leadership positions in football in Europe. *Soccer and Society*, 14(3), 296–314.

Bradbury, S., Amara, M., Garcia, B. & Bairner, A. (2011) *Representation and Structural Discrimination in Football in Europe: The Case of Minorities and Women*. Loughborough University and the FARE Network.

Bradbury, S., Van Sterkenburg, J. & Mignon, P. (2014) *Cracking the Glass Ceiling? Levels of Representation of 'Visible' Minorities and Women in Leadership and Coaching in Football in Europe and the Experiences of Elite Level 'Visible' Minority Coaches*. Loughborough University and the FARE Network.

Bradbury, S., Van Sterkenburg, J. & Mignon, P. (2018) The under-representation and experiences of elite level minority coaches in professional football in England, France and the Netherlands. *International Review of the Sociology of Sport*, 53(3), 313–334.

Bradbury, S. (2018) The under-representation and racialised experiences of minority coaches in high level coach education in professional football in England. In Hassan, D. & Action, C. (eds.) *Sport and Contested Identities*. London: Routledge. pp. 11–29.

Braddock, J., Smith, E. & Dawkins, M. (2012) Race and pathways to power in the National Football League. *American Behavioural Scientist*, 56(5), 711–727.

Branham, D. (2008) Taking advantage of an untapped pool: Assessing the success of African American head coaches in the National Football League. *The Review of Black Political Economy*, 35(4), 129–146.

Bonilla-Silva, E. (2010) *Racism Without Racists: Colour-blind Racism and the Persistence of Racial Equality in the United States (Third Edition)*. Oxford: Rowman and Littlefield.

Burdsey, D. (2011) That joke isn't funny anymore: Racial microaggressions, colour-blind ideology and the mitigation of racism in English men's first-class cricket. *Sociology of Sport Journal*, 28(3), 261–283.

Carrington, B. (2010) *Race, Sport and Politics: The Sporting Black Diaspora*. London: Sage.

Cashmore, E. & Clelland, J. (2011) Why aren't there more black managers. *Ethnic and Racial Studies*, 34(9), 1594–1607.

Crenshaw, K., Gotanda, N., Peller, G. & Kendall, T. (1995) *Critical Race Theory: The Key Writings That Formed the Movement*. New York: New Press.

Cunningham, G. B. (2010) Understanding the under-representation of African American coaches: A multilevel perspective. *Sport Management Review*, 13(4), 395–406.

Day, J. C. (2015) Transitions to the top: Race, segregation, and promotions to executive positions in the college football coaching profession. *Work and Occupations*, 42(4), 408–446.

Day, J. C. & McDonald, S. (2010) Not so fast, my friend: Social capital and the race disparity in promotions among college football coaches. *Sociological Spectrum*, 30, 138–158.

Delgado, R. & Stefancic, J. (2012) *Critical Race Theory: An Introduction (Second Edition)*. London: NYU Press.

Doidge, M. (2017) Racism and European football. In Nauright, J. and Wiggins, D. (eds.) *Routledge Handbook of Sport, Race and Ethnicity*. Routledge. pp. 174–185.

Essed, P. & Goldberg, D. T. (2002) *Race Critical Theories*. Oxford: Blackwell.

European Union Fundamental Rights Agency (EU FRA) (2011) *Racism, Ethnic Discrimination and Exclusion of Migrants and Minorities in Sport: A Comparative Overview of the Situation in the European Union*.

Fletcher, T. (2014) 'Does he look like a Paki?' An exploration of whiteness, positionality and reflexivity in inter racial sports research. *Qualitative Research in Sport, Exercise and Health*, 6(2), 244–260.

Fletcher, T. & Hylton, K. (2017) 'Race', Whiteness and Sport. In Nauright, J. and Wiggins, D. (eds.) *Routledge Handbook of Sport, Race and Ethnicity*. Routledge. pp. 87–106.

Frankenberg, R. (1999) *Displacing Whiteness*. Durham and London. Duke University Press.

Frankenberg, R. (2004) On unsteady ground: Crafting and engaging in the critical study of whiteness. In Bulmer, M. and Solomos, J. (eds.) *Researching Race and Racism*. London: Routledge. pp. 104–118.

Gearity, B. & Henderson Metzger, L. (2017) Intersectionality, micro-aggressions and micro-affirmations: Towards a cultural praxis of sports coaching. *Sociology of Sport Journal*, 34(2), 160–175.

Giroux, H. (1997) *Pedagogy and the Politics of Hope: Theory, Culture and Schooling: A Critical Reader*. Boulder: Westview.

Hylton, K. (2005) 'Race', sport and leisure: Lessons from critical race theory. *Leisure Studies*, 24(1), 81–98.

Hylton, K. (2009) *Race and Sport: Critical Race Theory*. London and New York: Routledge.

Hylton, K. (2010) How a turn to critical race theory can contribute to our understanding of 'race', racism and anti-racism in sport. *International Review for the Sociology of Sport*, 45(3), 335–354.

Hylton, K. (2018) *Contesting 'Race' and Sport*. London: Routledge.

King, C. (2004) 'Race' and cultural identity: Playing the race game inside football. *Leisure Studies*, 23(1), 19–13.

Ladson-Billings, G. (1998) Just what is critical race theory and what's it doing in a nice field like education? *International Journal of Qualitative Studies in Education*, 11(1), 7–24.

Lapchick, R. (2017) *The 2017 Racial and Gender Report Card*. Institute of Diversity and Ethics. University of Central Florida.

League Managers Association (LMA) (2017) *Black, Asian and Minority Ethnic (BAME) Football Managers*. League Managers Association.

Long, J. & Hylton, K. (2002) Shades of white: An examination of whiteness in sport. *Leisure Studies*, 21(2), 87–103.

Maguire, J. (1988) 'Race' and position assignment in English soccer: A preliminary analysis of ethnicity and sport in Britain. *Sociology of Sport Journal*, 5(1), 257–269.

Massao, P. & Fasting, K. (2010) Race and racism: Experiences of black Norwegian athletes. *International Review for the Sociology of Sport*, 45(2), 147–162.

McCarthy, D., Jones, R. L. & Potrac, P. (2003) Constructing images and interpreting realities: The case of Black soccer players on television. *International Review for the Sociology of Sport*, 38(2), 217–238.

McIntosh, P. (1990) *White Privilege: Unpacking the Invisible Knapsack*. Independent School, Winter, 31–36.

Milner, H. R. (2007) Race, culture, and researcher positionality: Working through dangers seen, unseen, and unforeseen. *Educational Researcher*, 36(7), 388–400.

Norman, L., North, J., Hylton, K., Flintoff, A. & Rankin, A. (2014) *Sporting Experiences and Coaching Aspirations among Black and Minority Ethnic (BME) Groups*. Sports Coach UK and Leeds Metropolitan University.

Rankin-Wright, A. J., Hylton, K. & Norman, L. (2016) Off-colour landscape: Framing race equality in sport coaching. *Sociology of Sport Journal*, 33(4), 357–368.

Rankin-Wright, A. J., Hylton, K. & Norman, L. (2017) The policy and provision landscape for racial and gender equality in sport coaching. In Long, J., Fletcher, T. and Watson, B. (eds.) *Sport, Leisure and Social Justice*. London: Routledge. pp. 194–208.

Sagas, M. & Cunningham, G. B. (2005) Racial differences in the career success of assistant football coaches: The role of discrimination, human capital, and social capital. *Journal of Applied Social Psychology*, 35(4), 773–797.

Sartore, M. L. & Cunningham, G. B. (2006) Stereotypes, race, and coaching. *Journal of African American Studies*, 10(2), 69–83.

Sin, H. S. (2007) Ethnic matching in qualitative research: Reversing the gaze on 'white others' and 'white' as 'other'. *Qualitative Research*, 7(4), 477–499.

Singer, J. N. (2005) Addressing epistemological racism in sport management research. *Journal of Sport Management*, 19(4), 464–479.

Singer, J., Harrison, K. & Buksten, S. (2010) A critical race analysis of the hiring process for head coaches in NCAA college football. *Journal of Intercollegiate Sport*, 3, 270–296.

Solórzano, D. G. & Yosso, T. J. (2002) Critical race methodology: Counter-storytelling as an analytical framework for education research. *Qualitative Inquiry*, 8(1), 23–44.

Sports People's Think Tank (SPTT) (2017) *Levels of BAME Coaches in Professional Football in England: 3rd Annual Follow Report*. Sports People's Think Tank. FARE Network & Loughborough University.

Watson, G., Palmer, F. & Ryan, G. (2017) Aotearoa/New Zealand. In Nauright, J. and Wiggins, D. (eds.) *Routledge Handbook of Sport, Race and Ethnicity*. Routledge. pp. 131–145.

Van Sterkenburg, J., Knoppers, A. & De Leeuw, S. (2012) Constructing racial/ethnic difference in and through Dutch televised soccer commentary. *Journal of Sport and Social Issues*, 36(4), 422–442.

Chapter 3

Is there a glass ceiling or can racial and ethnic barriers be overcome?

A study on leadership positions in professional Belgian football among African coaches

Chris Heim, Joris Corthouts and Jeroen Scheerder

Introduction

Because of a rich history of international migration, Belgium epitomises a state whose current status has been formed by ethnic cross-pollination, and is shaped by the everyday interactions between native Flemish and Walloon people and both persons with a distinct nationality and individuals of foreign origin(s). Its cultural diversity is highlighted by the fact that 1,327,776 (11.7%) of the 11,376,070 total population are foreign nationals, i.e. having a non-Belgian passport. Additionally, 991,031 (8.8%) are of foreign nationality at birth, but have meanwhile acquired the Belgian nationality (Federal Migration Centre, 2018)[1]. It is difficult to fully grasp the context and situation of migration from a national level, because the collection and analysis of data take place both at a federal and at a regional level in Belgium[2]. Flanders, the northern Dutch-speaking region, is the most populous region with 6,552,967 inhabitants, 548,910 of which are foreign nationals[3] (Flemish Government/ Statistics Department, 2017). Furthermore, the southern French-speaking region known as Wallonia is a society consisting of 3,624,377 inhabitants, with roughly 358,190 of Walloon residents being foreign nationals (Walloon Institute of Evaluation, Forecasting & Statistics, 2018). Lastly, the Brussels-Capital Region is one of the most cosmopolitan cities in the world. Illustrating this is the fact that 71.4% of the estimated 1.2 million inhabitants of the Brussels-Capital Region are of foreign origin, which in this context implies that either the current or first nationality of the person is non-Belgian or the first nationality of the father or mother is not Belgian (BRUZZ, 2018).

Despite the advancements that have been made concerning the integration of foreign nationals and those of foreign origin into Belgian society, forms of racial and ethnic oppression both in everyday life and within the political arena are impeding this social development. The latter being particularly evident through the discourse and policies of the right-wing populist party

Vlaams Belang (Billiet & De Witte, 2008). More critically for this study, discriminatory undertones in the labour market have and continue to be a persistent issue in Belgian society (European Network Against Racism, 2018; Flemish Service for Employment and Vocational Training, 2017). For example, in 2017, the Interfederal Centre for Equal Opportunities (UNIA) opened a total of 2,017 cases of situations where people felt they were subjects of discrimination in the workplace, which is a 6% increase from the previous year. Moreover, of those particular cases, 27% concerned discrimination based on one's race and ethnicity, followed by disability (20.7%) and age (15.7%) (Interfederal Centre for Equal Opportunities, 2018).

One particular domain and working industry, the Belgian Pro League (Division 1A/1B; consisting of sixteen and eight football clubs, respectively), has not been immune to acts of racism. For example, micro-level football actors (i.e. players, coaches and supporters) are one group of stakeholders that have established and sustained racial and ethnic divisions in Belgian football. These (groups of) individuals have manifested racial and ethnic discriminatory attitudes and behaviours overtly, whether impulsively or consciously, particularly against those of African origins, which seem to be deployed for the purpose of triumphing over the athlete and/or as a tool to distract and alter the performance of the footballer (Beloy & Van Laeken, 2016; Heim et al., 2018; Kassimeris, 2009; Scheerder, 2006). Indeed, the 2018–2019 Belgian Pro League campaign was occasionally blemished and overshadowed by racist conduct. This was apparent when Paul-Jose M'Poku accused both K.S.C. Lokeren and Club Brugge K.V. supporters of discrimination in consecutive matches, and additionally when R. Charleroi S.C. defender Francis N'Ganaga was a victim of similar abuse in the forms of monkey chants. Discriminatory conduct has also transpired on the sidelines, as coaches have perpetrated and have been victimised by such intolerance. This was the case when Frederik Vanderbiest of K.V. Mechelen, who was ultimately banned for three matches and fined 1,500 euros, racially abused Royal Union Saint-Gilles assistant coach, Abder Ramdane, in a First Division B match (The Guardian, 2018).

Given that it has been confirmed and determined that discrimination is a relevant topic in the specific industry of Belgian professional football by the aforementioned scholars and media outlets, this chapter serves as a starting point to unravel the extent and prevalence of its nature, and therefore as a basis for a prospective, in-depth study. Thus, we extend our examination on the intersection of race, ethnicity and football to the otherwise under-researched subject of institutional/structural racism: '*As a structured system, racism interacts with social institutions, where the discrimination itself shapes and reshapes institutions to reinforce, justify and perpetuate a racial/ethnic hierarchy*' (Williams et al., 2019: 106). While the discrimination on this level can materialise in an overt manner, this chapter approaches institutional/structural racism by addressing the undertones of implicit racial bias. This denotes the partialities that humans do not know they have towards people of different races and ethnicities. Such ideologies are embedded in people's subconsciousness, which is formed and developed through their everyday experiences and interactions in society (Banakou et al., 2016).

Within this context, we scrutinise if and how the Belgian Pro League is an example of how a community, organisation and sub-culture is structured in a way in which a dominant racial and/or ethnic group possesses more social, economic and cultural benefits and value compared to a socially subordinate group, or if (and how) the Belgian Pro League is an organisation that provides equal opportunities to people of all races and ethnicities. More precisely, the question is raised whether the professional Belgian football industry is a cultural agent that implicitly socialises the population to accept 'as true' the superiority of dominant racial/ethnic groups and the inferiority of non-dominant racial/ethnic groups in the form of restricting the access of elite coaching positions, i.e. head coaches and assistant coaches, to those non-white individuals and those of African origins. Or, conversely, is it an arena that mobilises racial and ethnic minority individuals to become socially and vocationally integrated in terms of equally allocating jobs, elite coaching positions, to non-white individuals and those of African origins? This chapter first situates the Social Dominance Theory (SDT) as an appropriate theoretical framework to address this matter because it offers ways of exploring the structuring of a social system along the lines of group-based hierarchies (Sidanius & Pratto, 1999). In order to examine the questions above, this study conceptualises the notions of race and ethnicity, and then proceeds to collect and analyse the racial and ethnic backgrounds of the professional head coaches and assistant coaches juxtaposed to those backgrounds of professional footballers and Belgian societal demographics. To conclude, policy recommendations are put forward that aim to stimulate stakeholders to build on their responsibility to combat all forms of discrimination in the game and beyond where needed.

Theoretical framework

In Belgium, there appears to be a distinct set of preferences on issues of inequality among social groups, or in other words the varying degrees of one's social dominance orientation (Pratto et al., 1994). Social Dominance Theory (SDT), viewing human societies as systems, is a theory of intergroup relations that theorises how socio-structural, ideological, sociological, psychological and institutional factors work together to produce the systematic effects, whether negative or positive for particular racial and ethnic groups (Sidanius et al., 2004). Indeed, according to SDT, any society can be interpreted as group-based hierarchies, in which at least one particular (usually male-dominated) racial, ethnic and/or religious group holds a positive social value and enjoys special privileges, and at least one other group has a negative social value (Pratto et al., 2006). Such societies are formed and preserved through the deployment of legitimising myths, or widely accepted ideologies that can be used as an instrument to help promote and maintain a certain predisposition that endorses discrimination and group inequality. Ethnic prejudice, racial bias, cultural elitism, nationalism and meritocracy are hierarchy-enhancing legitimising myths that promote the degree to which social inequalities exist. Contrarily, civil rights, social integration and anti-racism policies are hierarchy-attenuating legitimising myths that aim to make societies more balanced (Pratto et al., 1994).

In the labour market and within organisations, dominance and racism are created and sustained through the interplay between the (policies from) macro, meso and micro levels (Pratto et al., 2013). All designations of what constitutes a 'level' are arbitrarily based on population size. First, (macro-level) societal features, such as economic and employment activity, can be key indicators of the social norms and status of a particular society. For example, in Belgium, the fact that the gap between the employment rate of Belgians and non-EU citizens amounts to 27.5% is an alarming statistic that corresponds with the characteristics of a hierarchical society (Statbel, 2018). Racial and ethnic oppression can also be detected through the examination of the policies from, as well as the racial/ethnic structure of, the (meso-level) institution, organisation or industry itself. Laying claim to this in Belgium is the fact that policies for integrating first- and even second-generation immigrants into the general labour force are claimed to be insufficient or ineffective (Sustainable Governance Indicators, 2018). Also, in Belgium, research shows that job applications with foreign sounding names have 30% less chance of being invited to a job interview compared to applicants with a similar profile but with a Flemish sounding name (ENAR, 2018). Lastly, discrimination at a (micro-level) individual basis is noticeable through overt racist rhetoric and the detection of subtler attitudes and beliefs of specific individuals. Reflecting this in Belgium is the fact that, according to 22% of 307 delegates of three Belgian trade unions, regular discrimination amongst staff members in their companies was noticed (RTBF, 2016).

Concerning discrimination in football, while all three levels are of critical importance to exhaustively understand how dominant hierarchical societies are generated and preserved, the following section will focus on the meso-level dimension. At this level, racial and ethnic dominance is established and maintained in society through institutional discrimination, particularly in the allotment of basic vocational resources. For instance, public and private institutions tend to prefer members of (racial and ethnic) dominant groups, rather than members of subordinate groups when determining a job candidate (Pratto & Stewart, 2012). From and within this perspective, this study reveals the diversity levels among head and assistant coaches in professional Belgian football in comparison to those of professional football players. By determining the participation level of racial and ethnic minority individuals in football coaching in the form of a census, we can acquire more insight into whether race and ethnicity are aspects that influence the availability and accessibility of employment for certain (racial and ethnic minority) individuals to become elite coaches. We do realise that these statistics alone can reveal only a limited picture of inclusion, albeit an important starting point for the discussion around issues that may prevent certain individuals from obtaining jobs and becoming integrated into society.

The presence and interconnection of race, ethnicity and football in Belgian society

In Belgium, as in many other European countries, the game of football reigns supreme in terms of popularity along with socio-economic value compared to any other sport in the country. With its long-standing history, traced back to the 1860s, the influence of football weaves its way through the social fabric of contemporary Belgian society. The presence of this realm is embraced by many of its cohorts, including but not limited to its 440,107 licensed players who play over 340,000 matches per season on the 8,000 nation-wide football pitches, as well as the 3.8 million people who attended Belgian Pro League matches in the 2016–2017 season (Deloitte, 2018; Helsen et al., 2018; Royal Belgian Football Association, 2018). Further emphasising the impact of football, both from a grassroots and professional viewpoint, the sport acts as a vehicle for intercultural dialogue, and moreover, it facilitates the integration of foreign nationals and those with foreign origins into Belgian society (Heim et al., 2018; Kassimeris, 2009). As mentioned above, while it is a catalyst for economic, social and cultural development, racist ideologies have undermined the game's soft powers. Moving forward, the remainder of this study is dedicated to delving deeper into this subject by illustrating how race and ethnicity operate on the playing field and within the socio-cultural sphere of professional Belgian football coaching.

Methodology

Conceptualising race and ethnicity

Prior to presenting the racial and ethnic backgrounds of professional Belgian footballers and coaches, it is imperative that the terms race and ethnicity are conceptualised. In the 16th century, according to its etymological origins, the word race denoted kinship and group affiliation. It was not until the 17–18th century, during the Age of Enlightenment, when the word race acquired alternative connotations. Throughout this period and into the 19th century, European biologists and philosophers who were keen to classify human beings created the process of *racial categorisation*. This refers to a taxonomy-based system where skin colour, amongst other phenotypic features, was used as the key biological marker to stratify human beings (Richeson & Sommers, 2016). In many cases, this process has been interpreted and manipulated as an organising principle that has resulted in hierarchical societies, stereotyping and racism. Race indeed is an important category in everyday discourse (in terms of skin colour), although it is not a scientifically valid concept. Even though scientific consensus is that the social phenomenon of race does not exist as a biological category among humans (Claire & Denis, 2015), race and human variation do have value in the sense that they function as a categorising principle in everyday life and – as such – also function as a relevant starting point for the investigation into racial injustices in contemporary society. In this study, in line with previous research (Scheerder, 2006), we compartmentalise the racial backgrounds of players and coaches into two distinct categories, e.g. white and non-white.

Ethnicity like race is a concept that has been socially constructed and is constantly evolving. In addition, ethnicity is also frequently used as a categorising principle – e.g. in terms of cultural (group) affiliation. While ethnicity and race are overlapping concepts that are often used interchangeably, they are quite distinct in the sense that ethnicity signifies more of a concentration and linkage towards citizenship and family origins, but not biology like race does (Bhopal, 2004). At the same time, race and ethnicity are often used in a conflated manner in everyday discourse. Also, there appears to be a seemingly perpetual fluidity of ethnicity, more so compared to race. From this point of view, it can be stated that the way in which people ethnically identify themselves has proven to be complex in nature as people may have a connection to multiple ethnicities, at times disconnecting from one and attaching themselves to another, and constantly alternating between these identifications (Adair & Rowe, 2010). For instance, one individual may have a passport from one country, e.g. Belgium, but could also have a parent or grandparent who was born in another country, e.g. Morocco, thus that person has Belgian citizenship and origins that can be traced back to (North) Africa. Another case that could reflect this view is that an individual was born in one country, migrated to another country and was consequently naturalised in the host country. In sum, ethnicity refers to a group of people, usually within particular geographical borders, who hold a common cultural identity that is based on a shared (perceived) history and is expressed and identified through (a) communal language(s), religion(s), food/diet, music, art and sport (Ferriter, 2016). Elaborating on the categorisation of race, in this study, the ethnicity of non-white footballers and coaches is determined by both discovering one's passport (citizenship) and tracing one's family origins (ancestry/bloodline). We then classify the ethnicity of these individuals into clusters on a (sub-)continental basis with a keen focus on those with North African and sub-Saharan African[4] ethnicities, as these individuals are the most visible (non-European) ethnic minorities in Belgium (Myria, 2018). Like the concept of race, we treat ethnicity as Brown & Langer (2010) do in the sense that it can be utilised as a gauge to measure concepts such as diversity and social distance.

Data collection and analysis

The data pertaining to the racial and ethnic backgrounds of players and coaches were collected through the process of content web-based desk-research of the 24 professional football clubs that comprise the Belgian Pro League (i.e. the two highest divisions of Belgian football), along with browsing the 'squad' and 'staff' section of each professional Belgian football club on www.transfermarkt.com. First, the backgrounds of 530 players were revealed. This population consists of players who were included in the squads' selection during the season 2016–2017, regardless of their playing minutes. Regarding coaches, we collected data on the 24 head coaches (T1). Additionally, information of the assistant coaches (e.g. auxiliary and goalkeeper coaches) was gathered. Unlike head coaches, the number of assistant coaches varies from one to three coaches per club, accumulating to 65 assistant coaches.

Results

First, in terms of race, Figure 3.1 illustrates the distribution of white versus non-white players, head coaches and assistant coaches in the Belgian Pro League. A clear difference is noticeable between the racial background of players compared to that of the two (head and assistant) coaching positions. More specifically, 57.2% (or 303 out of 530) of the footballers have a white racial background and 42.8% have a non-white racial background, whereas the proportion of non-white individuals for head and assistant coaches is 8.3% and 9.2%, respectively.

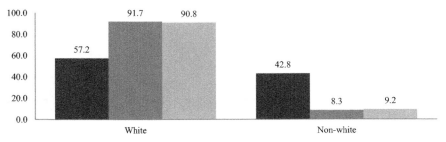

Figure 3.1 Racial backgrounds of players, head coaches and assistant coaches in the Belgian Pro-League
Source: Adapted from Corthouts & Scheerder (2017)

In relation to ethnicity, Figure 3.2 illustrates a breakdown of the ethnicity of the non-white minorities from Figure 3.1 in professional Belgian football. Specifically, Figure 3.2 depicts the constitution of the relative share of all non-white players (42.8%), head coaches (8.3%) and assistant coaches (9.2%) into three identifiable visible minority categories according to their ethnicity, i.e. North African, sub-Saharan and other minorities. These statistics embedded in Figure 3.2 are based on ethnicity as a multitude linkage between one's nationality and family origins. Thus, a non-white individual that has the Belgian first nationality and a North African heritage is included within the North African minority group. From the proportions shown in Figure 3.2, it can be deduced that 24.2% of all players in the Belgian Pro League belong to sub-Saharan minorities, accounting for more than half of all non-white players. In total, only 4.3% of all players in the Belgian Pro League (2016–2017) belong to non-white North African minorities. Other non-white players of, for example, American or Asian heritage, constitute 14.3% of all football players. Another – more balanced – image is noticeable concerning the division of head and assistant coaches. In terms of the former category, we see that the North African minorities as well as the sub-Saharan African minorities represent 4.2% of the total number of head coaches. Additionally, as opposed to the distribution of non-white players, individuals with a North African ethnicity make up a larger proportion of the assistant coaches, in particular 6.2% in comparison with 3.1% of assistant coaches with a sub-Saharan African ethnicity. Both for non-white head and assistant coaches, there is no other visible minority present in the professional Belgian football league, year 2018–2019.

The culturally vibrant playing landscape of professional Belgian football is comprised of various ethnic groups. On a continental basis, those with sub-Saharan African and North African backgrounds combine to make the highest representation of ethnic minorities. However, there is an under-representation of sub-Saharan coaches when compared to players of the same origins,

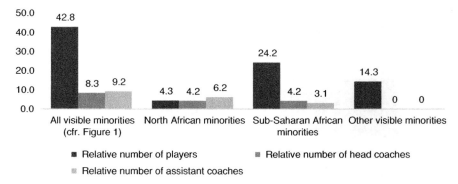

Figure 3.2 Ethnic backgrounds of non-white minority players, head coaches and assistant coaches in the Belgian Pro-League
Source: Adapted from Corthouts & Scheerder (2017)

respectively. Finally, the playing field is shaped by other visible minorities coming from the Americas (mainly South America), Asia and Oceania. These particular backgrounds are not represented within the coaching staff.

Discussion

In today's Belgian football game, Belgians and Europeans constitute the overwhelming majority of the ethnic spectrum of both footballers and coaches, whereas players of, in particular, a sub-Saharan African ethnic background are the most frequently represented ethnic minority group. However, in terms of coaches, this latter demographic is barely visible. Concerning players, the representation of North African and sub-Saharan footballers appears to be a dynamic and ever-growing concept, as over the last six decades, more and more footballers of African origins have launched their football careers in Belgium (Heim et al., 2018).

First, the increases of players with ethnic ties to North Africa could be paralleled to the massive immigration wave during the 1960s when many Moroccans presumably came to Belgium on a temporary basis when the Belgian government passed bilateral immigration agreements. This agreement was primarily for the purpose of bolstering Belgium's precarious mining industry at the time. Eventually a majority settled in the country on a permanent basis, and gradually acquired Belgian citizenship. Nowadays, these naturalised individuals and even those of Moroccan ethnic backgrounds who were born on Belgian soil are still perceived by society as the children of Moroccan migrants. Often this stigma has resulted in that person feeling as a lesser citizen, and caused identity crises, or in other words, 'an illusionary decision concerning what they are with respect to their parents and society' (Odasso, 2016: 82). From a Belgian sub-Saharan African historical perspective, (Darby, 2013:15) states that '*the pace at which football has developed in Africa, both as a European venture and a locally organised pastime, was centrally linked to the nature of Belgian colonial doctrine in the Congo*' with football ironically proving to be an instrument for protest against colonial rule. Today, as a consequence of European colonisation, turmoil and unrest continues to exist throughout sub-Saharan Africa, especially the Democratic Republic of the Congo, it appears that, more than ever, more sub-Saharan Africans are using professional European football as a channel to escape such humanitarian crises. While, indeed, this specific working industry has been successful in reversing ethnic stigmas, and has also provided a plethora of vocational and economic opportunities to footballers of all races and ethnicities, especially those of African origins, from a more critical standpoint, it can be interpreted as an appendage of the economic imperialism of the colonial epoch (Darby, 2013). Certainly, professional Belgian football has had a reputation for its high player turnover rate, as clubs have considered young foreign players as an investment, to be bought cheaply and sold to a top tier European league for a significant profit (Pannenborg, 2012).

Moving forward to the coaching sector, based on the data above, preliminary results suggest that professional Belgian football is, to a certain extent, a social system that is premised on the fundamentals of a hierarchy group-based society where (white) Belgians and Europeans are those with a positive social value both in playing and coaching positions, and those (non-white) individuals of African ethnic backgrounds appear to hold a negative social value in terms of coaching positions. Nevertheless, those with African backgrounds hold a positive social value when it comes to playing opportunities. Such an approach and association with both football and leadership skills may have negative consequences when players want to become a coach after their football career, as it sends a message that specific racial-ethnic groups are targeted solely for playing opportunities, while other racial-ethnic groups are privileged to occupy playing, coaching and executive positions.

This social system seems to be compromised by hierarchy-enhancing legitimising myths in the sense that group-based inequality is created and sustained by directly specifying who is entitled to rights and jobs. Indeed, (white) European men continue to dominate leadership and coaching positions which in turn preserves the status quo of the social status of the coaching sector and reinforces the hegemonic institutionalised ideologies and practices of the white dominant group over non-white people (Kilvington, 2019). Even if there is a proportionate representation of racial/ethnic minority coaches, we could not imply that diversity produces equity. This is because minority workers follow a more restricted pathway to high-level positions where they are limited to formal channels of mobility based on their credentials and skills. Contrarily, whites not only have access to formal channels of mobility but also benefit from the subjective and sometimes biased assessments of their skills and abilities (Day, 2015).

It is with this insight that we posit that the professional Belgian football industry is a cultural agent that implicitly socialises the population to normalise the idea that it is acceptable to view (non-white) people with African ethnicities as inferior to native Belgians and Europeans. In this context, this means that non-white ethnic minorities are perceived incapable of holding leadership positions, while white Europeans continue to hegemonise these roles. However, in order to more precisely determine if this scarcity of racial-ethnic diversity is emblematic of a profounder set of social problems, and to understand the varying degree of social dominance orientation of football stakeholders, a more in-depth study must be executed. Such a qualitative ethnographic study would have to become engaged in discourse analysis pertaining to the rhetoric of the various Belgian football stakeholders. Through this process we can more thoroughly examine the communication of these actors with respect to (institutional) discrimination, stereotypes and racial banter, and better gauge the perceptions of those seeking employment and those in charge of the hiring process, and moreover, the interaction between these groups (Bradbury et al., 2016; Sidanius et al., 2004). All in all, by identifying and understanding the conditions and factors that contribute to the reproduction and the potential spread of racist attitudes and group-based dominance, we can promote a more thorough and active approach against it. In other words, we can enhance the understanding of racism for those whose role will be to identify, report and analyse such phenomena, and in turn, the Belgian football community can then more efficiently create and implement anti-racism and social inclusion and corporate social responsibility (CSR) -related policies.

Policy recommendations

Such CSR-related policies and initiatives have displayed the potential to break down racial and ethnic barriers. For example, at the macro level, the so-called Belgian Football Law ('Voetbalwet/ Loi Foot') is a landmark regulation that provides and clarifies the guidelines and underlying principles for security protocols at football matches. The so-called Football Unit ('Voetbalcel/Cellule Football'), within the Belgian Ministry of Home Affairs, oversees the application of the Football Law by implementing sanctions and advising stakeholders how to handle concrete racist behaviour. However, in this legislation there is no reference to the internal processes of hiring coaches and executives. Thus, it is recommended that legislation is proposed, which expands the parameters of the law, so that it is inclusive of this subject. In this way, a specific unit would be responsible for overseeing the collection of data related to this issue and monitoring it consistently (Bradbury et al., 2014). From a meso-level perspective, the Royal Belgian Football Association (KBVB/URBSFA) has been keen on offering diversity workshops, seminars and conferences on the issues of discrimination and social inclusion (Heim et al., 2018). Also, professional football clubs[5] invest responsibly in social projects that aim to safeguard the cultural richness and enhance the social cohesiveness of Belgian society[6] (Deloitte, 2018). However, there appears to be a shortcoming from both the national football federation and clubs when addressing the topics of institutional/structural racism. It is suggested that the national football association and the respective professional football clubs broaden their educational strategy in a way that focuses on the topics and subjects of this study. Elaborating on this, given that the KBVB/URBSFA has already established social infrastructure, such as the Belgian Football Coaches Association (BFC), it is recommended that this entity first subsidises training courses for (racially and ethnically) marginalised and less privileged individuals, and secondly implements a mentoring/buddy programme. In turn, these programmes would teach management and leadership skills, thus acting as a vehicle for racial and ethnic minorities to access the top tiers of the game (as coaches) in a way that is currently unavailable. Lastly, it is advised that the 'Rooney Rule' is adopted both on a national and club level, where the KBVB/URBSFA and professional Belgian football clubs must interview at least one racial and ethnic minority candidate in case of a vacancy on a managerial level (NFL, 2018).

Conclusions

In the foregoing analysis, the aim was to explore how the social phenomena of race and ethnicity function within the professional Belgian football industry. This was executed through the collection and analysis of the racial and ethnic backgrounds of footballers, head and assistant coaches. Ultimately, when the demographics of coaches were compared to that of professional footballers, individuals with a non-white racial background and people with sub-Saharan African ethnicity appear to be marginalised in terms of their access to the necessary resources and skills to become coaches. Moreover, while the presence of players of (non-white) African ethnicity has flourished over recent decades, it appears that this demographic is struggling to break into the upper echelons of coaching positions. Thus, we posit these (player/athletic) competencies are not transferred to the coaching sector and leadership positions, as individuals from, in particular, sub-Saharan Africa are over-represented on the playing field, but are under-represented on the sidelines and in the executive boxes. While these preliminary results indicate the features of a group-based hierarchical society, these statistics alone cannot fully explain the inequalities that are apparent within the context of coaching positions, and we do not claim to fully understand the mechanisms that are turning this social phenomenon. Nevertheless, this study serves as an open message and a critical starting point to stimulate dialogue and raise awareness that there is a glass ceiling in professional Belgian football, and moreover, racial and ethnic barriers are currently prohibiting African nationals and people of African origins from obtaining coaching and leadership positions.

Notes

1 Of this combined 20.5%, some of the key ethnic identities living in Belgium are the 311,772 Moroccan, 273,350 Italian, 213,619 French, 186,069 Dutch, 155,488 Turkish, 95,801 Polish, 92,746 Romanian, and 60,257 Congolese (Myria, 2018).
2 Also, the sharp contrast amongst each particular region, with regard to their respective socio-historical development, languages, contemporary economic status and political movements requires Belgium to be situated according to its three regions.

3 This is a strong increase from 2005 when there were 297,289 who did not have a Belgian passport.
4 The designation sub-Saharan Africa is commonly used in correspondence with the UN Statistics Division to indicate the whole of Africa except North Africa, which consists of the countries Morocco, Mauritania, Algeria, Arab Democratic Republic of Sahara, Tunisia, Libya and Egypt (United Nations Statistics Division, 2019).
5 22 of 24 clubs have a social inclusion strategy, 16 of 24 clubs have an education strategy, and 15 of 24 have a health strategy (Deloitte, 2018).
6 298 social projects during the 2016–2017 season. Falling under the responsibility of 'Community Manager'; 1.7 million euros budget, 58,000 participants in these projects (Deloitte, 2018).

References

Adair, D. & Rowe, D. (2010). Beyond Boundaries? 'Race', Ethnicity and Identity in Sport. *International Review for the Sociology of Sport*, 45 (3), pp. 251–257.

Agyemang, K. (2014). Toward a Framework of 'Athlete Citizenship' in Professional Sport through Authentic Community Stakeholder Engagement. *Sport, Business and Management*, 4, pp. 26–37.

Banakou, D., Hanumanthu, P., & Slater, M. (2016). Virtual Embodiment of White People in a Black Virtual Body Leads to a Sustained Reduction in Their Implicit Racial Bias. *Journal of Frontiers in Human Neuroscience*, 10, pp. 1–12.

Beloy, P. & Van Laeken, F. (2016). *Vuile zwarte. Racisme in het Belgische voetbal* [Dirty Black. Racism in Belgian Football]. Antwerp: Houtekiet.

Bhopal, R. (2004). Glossary of Terms Relating to Ethnicity and Race. For Reflection and Debate. *Journal of Epidemiology Community Health*, 58 (6), pp. 441–445.

Billiet, J. & De Witte, H. (2008). Everyday Racism as a Predictor of Political Racism in Flemish Belgium. *Journal of Social Issues*, 64 (2), pp. 253–267.

Bradbury, S., Van Sterkenburg, J., & Mignon, P. (2014). The Glass Ceiling in European Football: Levels of Representation of Visible Ethnic Minorities and Women in Leadership Positions, and the Experience of Elite Level Ethnic Minority Coaches [online]. London. The FARE Network. Available at: www.farenet.org/wp-content/uploads/2014/12/The-glass-ceiling-in-football-screen3.pdf.

Bradbury, S., Van Sterkenburg, J., & Mignon, P. (2016). The Under-Representation and Experiences of Elite Level Minority Coaches in Professional Football in England, France and the Netherlands. *International Review for the Sociology of Sport*, 34 (1), pp. 1–22.

Brown, G. & Langer, A. (2010). Conceptualizing and Measuring Ethnicity. *Oxford Development Studies*, 38 (4), pp. 411–436.

BRUZZ (2018). Bewoners van Sint-Joost voor 90 procent van vreemde origine [90% of Residents of Sint-Joost Are of Foreign Origin]. Brussels. Available at: www.bruzz.be/samenleving/bewoners-van-sint-joost-voor-90-procent-van-vreemde-origine-2018-09-14.

Claire, M. & Denis, J. (2015). Sociology of Racism. *The International Encyclopaedia of the Social and Behavioural Sciences*, 19, pp. 857–863.

Common Goal (2019). How Common Goal Works. Available at: https://www.common-goal.org.

Corthouts, J. & Scheerder, J. (2017). *Zwarte voetbalspelers tussen witte lijnen. Sociaal-wetenschappelijk onderzoek naar raciale verschillen in de Belgische eerste voetbalklasse*

[Black football players between white lines. Social research on racial differences in first division Belgian football] (Sport Policy & Management Studies 33). Leuven: KU Leuven/Policy in Sports & Physical Activity Research Group.

Darby, P. (2013). *Africa, Football & FIFA. Politics, Colonialism and Resistance*. 3rd Edition. London: Frank Cass.

Day, J. (2015). Transitions to the Top. Race, Segregation, and Promotions to Executive Positions in the College Football Coaching Profession. *Work & Occupations*, 42 (4), pp. 408–446.

Deloitte (2018). Socio-Economic Impact Assessment of the Pro League on the Belgian Economy. Brussels: Deloitte. Available at: www2.deloitte.com/be/en/pages/strategy-operations/articles/The-socio-economic-impact-of-the-Pro-League-on-the-Belgian-economy.html.

European Network Against Racism (ENAR) (2018). *Racism & Discrimination in Employment in Europe 2013–2017*. [online] Brussels: European Network Against Racism. Available at: www.enar-eu.org/IMG/pdf/20107_shadowreport_2016x2017_long_v8_hr.pdf.

Federal Migration Centre [Myria] (2018). Population and Movements. www.myria.be/files/FR2018-2.pdf.

Ferriter, M. (2016). The Anthropology of Race and Ethnicity in Sport: Unfolding the Map. In J. Nauright & D. Wiggins (Eds.), *Routledge Handbook of Sport, Race and Ethnicity*. Routledge.

Flemish Government/Statistics Department (2017). *Vlaanderen in Cijfers* [Flanders in Numbers]. Brussels: Department of Chancery & Administration/Statistics Flanders.

Flemish Service for Employment and Vocational Training (2017). *Integration Through Work*. Brussels: European Commission. Available at: www.vdab.be/partners/integratie-door-werk.

García, B. & Welford, J. (2015). Supporters and Football Governance, From Customers to Stakeholders. A Literature Review and Agenda for Research. *Sport Management Review*, 18 (4), pp. 517–528.

Groenveld, M. (2009). European Sport Governance, Citizens, and the State. *Public Management Review*, 11 (4), pp. 421–440.

Heim, C., Corthouts, J. & Scheerder, J. (2018). Black Footballers and Coaches Between White Lines. A Multi-Level Analysis of Racism and Anti-Racism Movements in Belgian Football. In T. Busset, R. Besson & B. Fincoeur (Eds.), *En Marge des Grands. Analyse comparée du football belge et suisse*. Bern: Peter Lang, pp. 183–209.

Interfederal Centre for Equal Opportunities and Opposition to Racism (2018). Racism. Available at: www.unia.be/en/articles/more-employment-discrimination-cases-reported-to-unia-in-2017.

Helsen, K., Corthouts, J., Cornelissen, J. & Scheerder, J. (2018). *Een één-twee met Koning Voetbal. Een populaire doe- én kijksport in cijfers* [A one-two dribble with King Football. A popular participatory and spectator sport in figures] (Sport Policy & Management Facts & Figures 51). Leuven: KU Leuven/Policy in Sports & Physical Activity Research Group.

Kassimeris, C. (2009). Football and Prejudice in Belgium and the Netherlands. *Sport in Society*, 12 (10), pp. 1327–1335.

Kilvington, D. (2019). Does English Football Warrant the Rooney Rule? Assessing the Thoughts of British Asian Coaches. *Sport in Society*, 22 (3), pp. 432–448.

NFL (2018). NFL Expands Rooney Rule Requirements to Strengthen Diversity. New York. Available at: www.nfl.com/news/story/0ap3000000999110/article/nfl-expands-rooney-rule-requirements-to-strengthen-diversity.

Odasso, L. (2016). Moroccan Immigration to Europe: Old Legacies and New Ties. In G. Proglio (Ed.), *Decolonising the Mediterranean. European Colonial Heritages in North Africa and the Middle East*. Cambridge Scholar Publishing, pp. 73–90.

Pannenborg, A. (2012). *Big Men Playing Football: Money, Politics, and Foul Play in the African Game* (African Studies Collection 43). Leiden: African Studies Centre.

Pratto, F. & Stewart, A. (2012). Social Dominance Theory. In D.J. Christie (Ed.), *The Encyclopedia of Peace Psychology*. Hoboken: Blackwell.

Pratto, F., Sidanius, J., & Levin, S. (2006). Social Dominance Theory and the Dynamics of Intergroup relations. Taking Stock and Looking Forward. *European Review of Social Psychology*, 17, pp. 217–320.

Pratto, F., Sidanius, J., Stallworth, L., & Malle, B. (1994). Social Dominance Orientation: A Personality Variable Predicting Social and Political Attitudes. *Journal of Personality & Social Psychology*, 67 (4), pp. 741–763.

Pratto, F., Stewart, A., & Zeineddine, F. (2013). When Inequality Fails. Power, Group Dominance, and Societal Change. *Journal of Social and Political Psychology*, 1 (1), pp. 132–160.

Richeson, J. & Sommers, S. (2016). Towards a Social Psychology of Race and Race Relations for the Twenty-First Century. *Annual Review of Psychology*, 67, pp. 439–463.

Royal Belgian Football Association [KBVB/L'URBSFA] (2018). *Voetbal & Diversiteit/ Football & Diversité*. Brussels: The Royal Belgian Football Association.

RTBF (2016). Les Syndicats Publient une Etude. Le Racisme est tres courant au travail [Unions Publish Study. Racism is Very Common at Work]. Brussels. Available at: www.rtbf.be/info/regions/detail_les-syndicats-publient-une-etude-le-racisme-est-tres-courant-au-travail?id=9441326.

Scheerder, J. (2006). Afrika voetbalt in de Lage Landen. Over het relatieve succes van zwarte spelers [Africa plays football in the Low Countries. The relative success of black players]. In P. De Knop, J. Scheerder & B. Vanreusel (Eds.), *Sportsociologie. Het spel en de spelers* [Sociology of sport. The game and its players]. 2nd Edition. Maarssen: Elsevier, pp. 442–455.

Sidanius, J. & Pratto, F. (1999). *Social Dominance: An Intergroup Theory of Social Hierarchy and Oppression*. 2nd Edition. Cambridge: Cambridge University Press.

Sidanius, J., Pratto, F., Van Laar, C., & Levin, S. (2004). Social Dominance Theory. Its Agenda and Method. *Political Psychology*, 25 (6), pp. 845–880.

Statbel. Belgium in Figures. (2018). Unemployment Rate Down to 6,2%. Brussels: Statbel. Available at: https://statbel.fgov.be/en/news/unemployment-rate-down-62.

Sustainable Governance Indicators (2018). *SGI 2018 Survey*. Gutersloh: Sustainable Governance Indicators (SGI). Available at: www.sgi-network.org/2018/.

The Guardian (2018). The Ugly Spectre of Racism in Football on the Rise Across Europe. London. Available at: www.theguardian.com/football/2018/dec/16/racism-on-the-rise-across-europe-football-raheem-sterling-chelsea.

United Nations Statistics Division (2019). Geographic Regions. New York. Available at: https://unstats.un.org/unsd/methodology/m49/.
van Campenhout, G., van Sterkenburg, J., & Oonk, G. (2019). Who Counts as a Migrant Footballer? A Critical Reflection and Alternative Approach to Migrant Football Players on National Teams at the World Cup, 1930–2018. *The International Journal of the History of Sport*, doi:10.1080/09523367.2019.1581769.
Walloon Institute of Evaluation, Forecasting & Statistics (IWEPS) (2018). Population Étrangère [Foreign Population]. Louvain-la-Neuve. Available at: www.iweps.be/indicateur-statistique/population-etrangere/.
Williams, D., Lawrence, J., & Davis, B. (2019). Racism and Health: Evidence and Needed Research. *Annual Review of Public Health*, 40, pp. 105–125.

Chapter 4

Race, ethnicity, whiteness and mediated stereotypes in football coaching
The Dutch context

Jacco van Sterkenburg

Introduction

On 27 November 2016, three panelists in the popular weekly Dutch football TV talk show *Studio Voetbal* [Studio Football] discussed the underrepresentation of minority ethnic[1] coaches in the Dutch highest professional men's football league *de Eredivisie* (https://nos.nl/artikel/2145395-waar-zijn-de-trainers-met-migrantenachtergrond.html). The debate on diversity in coaching lasted for about ten minutes and can be considered unusual as the program usually limits itself to (discussing) the highlights of the matches played during that weekend, with an emphasis on evaluating (men's) teams' and players' performances. Moreover, Dutch football media in general tend to circumvent issues of race and ethnicity and instead focus on individual capacities of players and coaches (Van Sterkenburg et al., 2012). While the studio panelists – who were mainly men of a minority ethnic background – acknowledged the underrepresentation of non-White minority ethnic coaches in the Dutch professional league, it was more difficult for them to find consensus on the possible reasons for this. This is hardly surprising as there is a lack of research data they could possibly draw on, especially for the Dutch context. Only very little research has focused on the number of minority (and majority) ethnic coaches in Dutch professional football and the possible reasons behind the underrepresentation of minority ethnic coaches in football. This chapter is an attempt to address this knowledge gap. The aim of the chapter is to provide a numerical overview of racial/ethnic diversity in elite Dutch football coaching and to discuss the mechanisms that underlie the underrepresentation of minority ethnic coaches in men's professional football.

Dutch context

The point of reference in this chapter is the Dutch context. Dutch society can be characterized as a multi-ethnic society. The Dutch discourse about race and ethnicity is usually framed in terms of a variety of *ethnic* groups rather than in terms of a Black-White racial binary as is quite regular in countries such as the US and the UK. Moreover, as scholars such as Essed & Trienekens (2008) have shown, in the Netherlands the term 'race' is often not mentioned but inherently implicated in the more common everyday discourse on 'ethnicity' that draws on cultural, ethnic and religious references to categorize people. The conflated character of race and ethnicity in everyday discourse becomes evident, for instance, in the fact that a reference to minority ethnic groups usually, in practice, means a reference to *non-White* minority ethnic groups in Dutch discourse. Because of this blending of race and ethnicity in everyday discourse, I often use the terms race and ethnicity in a conflated manner in this chapter ('race/ethnicity'; see also my earlier work, e.g. Van Sterkenburg, 2011; Van Sterkenburg et al., 2019).

According to the Dutch Central Office for Statistics (CBS), the largest minority racial/ethnic groups in the Netherlands are the Moroccan-Dutch, Turkish-Dutch, Surinamese-Dutch and Antillean-Dutch. These minority groups comprise around 7.5% of the entire Dutch population according to official statistics which are based on birthplace of parents (CBS, 2018). According to these statistics, those of Turkish origin constitute the largest minority group (400,367 people) followed by those of Moroccan (391,088), Surinamese (349,978), and Antillean[2] descent (153,469). While the Surinamese and Antillean minority groups came to the Netherlands as a result of the colonial past and the process of decolonization in the 1970s and 80s, the Turkish and Moroccan groups mainly arrived as labor migrants during the 1960s. In the current conjuncture, it is in particular those of Moroccan and Turkish origin who are seen as the racial/ethnic Other in everyday and media discourses in the Netherlands. They are also relatively often lumped together under the overarching label of 'Muslims', with their culture and religion represented as deviant from Dutch majority norms and values (Van Sterkenburg et al., 2012).

Dutch multi-ethnic society is reflected in the Dutch professional football context. In recent years, it is particularly the Dutch players of Surinamese and Moroccan descent such as Virgil van Dijk and Hakim Ziyech who are visible in Dutch and international football clubs, while the Dutch national (men's) team consists of majority White Dutch players as well as Dutch players of Caribbean, African and South-American descent (Vlietstra, 2017, 2019). While the players of Suriname descent have historically constituted an important part of Dutch club football teams and the Dutch national men's team, it is particularly the number of players of Moroccan decent that has increased in recent years. In November 2017, 31 Dutch players of Moroccan descent were active at the highest level in the Dutch football competition – the so-called *Eredivisie* ('Marokkanen in Eredivisie'). In addition, the amount of foreign players that do *not* have Dutch citizenship increased considerably during the last 15 years, from around 13% in the 1995/1996 season to around 36% in the 2008/2009 season (Hack, 2008). In recent years the number of foreign players has more or less stabilized, with a slight decline over the years – from 232 foreign players in the 2010/2011 season to 192 in the 2018/2019 season (Abbink, 2019).

The racial/ethnic diversity of football players on the pitch stands in stark contrast with the racial/ethnic homogeneity in football coaching. Bradbury et al. (2014) concluded that almost all head coach and assistant head coach positions at elite level football clubs in the main European leagues, including the Dutch league, are held by White men. These data were, however, collected some time ago and only included the highest level in the Dutch football competition (*Eredivisie*). The current chapter will present more recent figures thereby including not only the *Eredivisie* but also the two professional levels below the *Eredivisie*, thus including in total the three highest levels of professional men's football in the Netherlands (called *Eredivisie*, *Jupiler League* and *Tweede Divisie*). In total, this includes 56 clubs (18 *Eredivisie*; 20 *Jupiler League*; 18 *Second Division* clubs). The clubs have roughly similar coaching structures dependent on size and resources, including a head coach and one or several assistant coaches.

Theoretical perspectives

In this chapter, as in much of my previous work (e.g. Van Sterkenburg et al., 2019; Van Sterkenburg, 2011), I draw on insights from cultural studies, Critical Race Theory, and whiteness studies to make sense of race/ethnicity in football coaching. A cultural studies perspective is useful as it addresses how meaning making processes related to social dimensions such as race/ethnicity are always mediated by relations of power in which some social groups are constructed as included and the norm (the 'We') while other social groups are being excluded and (re)constructed as the 'Other' (the 'They') (Long & Hylton, 2002). Cultural studies stresses the importance of popular cultural practices like football and football coaching in these meaning making processes. In so doing, cultural studies scholars assume everyone is racially/ethnically positioned (Wekker, 2016) thereby acknowledging the 'racialness' of White as well as Black people. It makes the cultural studies perspective particularly applicable to this project as most people working in professional football coaching and leadership are White males thus rendering a critical reflection on race/ethnicity *including whiteness* useful.

Insights from cultural studies are supplemented with insights from Critical Race Theory (CRT) and whiteness theory which emphasize the centrality of race/ethnicity in everyday discourses and in the (re)constructions of social hierarchies (Hylton, 2009). CRT scholars argue that a critical study of racial dynamics is fundamental in understanding processes of inclusion and exclusion in society and in social domains such as sport. At the same time, CRT scholars point out how a critical study of race and ethnicity has often remained at the periphery of academic attention and has been under-researched in football and football coaching (Rankin-Wright et al., 2016). This is, in a way, surprising since sport, and particularly football as a multi-ethnic practice, acts as a major frame of reference in society for meanings given to race/ethnicity (Bruce, 2004; Carrington, 2011; Ortega & Feagin, 2017). CRT *does* place race at the center of analysis and finds it important to 'give voice' to the experiences of minority racial/ethnic groups in sport, amongst other things those working in positions of leadership and coaching (Bradbury et al., 2018). This chapter, therefore, like various other chapters in this edited collection, prioritizes the experiential knowledge and narratives of minority ethnic football coaches (also Bradbury et al., 2018; Rankin-Wright et al., 2016).

Racial/ethnic positionedness

Acknowledging the centrality of race/ethnicity in meaning making processes also means I will reflect on my own social positionedness as a White, majority ethnic, male scholar. Being part of the majority racial/ethnic group, I find myself in a privileged position in (Dutch) multi-ethnic society. It means, amongst other things, that I have not experienced forms of racial/ethnic discrimination which minority ethnic interviewees in the study have faced (Bradbury et al., 2018). Moreover, earlier research has demonstrated that White people generally have difficulties seeing their own whiteness and White-situated frames of meaning making which are often deeply ingrained in everyday (mediated) discourses, especially regarding issues surrounding race and multi-ethnic society (Ortega & Feagin, 2017). To avoid, as much as possible, that my writing and analysis would overlook relevant meanings in the narratives of the minority ethnic interviewees, I give primacy to insights from CRT and cultural studies which stress the existence of racialized power relations and the importance of self-reflexivity (Frankenberg, 2004; Van Sterkenburg, 2011). It enables me to reflect, as much as I can, on my own White-situated discourses and White privilege while widening at the same time the reservoir of discourses I can draw on when analyzing and interpreting the narratives of the interviewees (Van Sterkenburg, 2011; Van Sterkenburg et al., 2019). As such, I believe that, even though I have, in a way, "appropriated" (Sykes, 1998: 158) the experiences and stories of the coaches, to make them 'fit' for publication, the coaches' narratives, as I will present them here, have much value in that they offer a theoretically informed reflection of their experiences of their progression along the coach employment pathway, within the Dutch context (Bradbury et al., 2014; 2018; Van Sterkenburg et al., 2019).

Method

General design

Findings in this chapter draw on two earlier research projects undertaken with colleagues in the past years (Peeters & Van Sterkenburg, 2017; Bradbury et al., 2014, 2018). The first project was a small-scale quantitative study commissioned by a Dutch non-profit sport organization (*Kennis Centrum Sport – Knowledge Center Sport*) exploring the proportion of minority and majority ethnic coaches in Dutch professional football in the 2016/2017 season (Peeters & Van Sterkenburg, 2017). The other, larger, project was commissioned by the European football association UEFA and the Fare network and was conducted between 2012 and 2014, in cooperation with colleagues from England and France (Steve Bradbury who was project leader, and Patrick Mignon). The qualitative part of this international project used in-depth interviews to gain insights into factors and mechanisms that underlie the underrepresentation of minority ethnic coaches in football. More specifically, in-depth interviews were held with 40 minority ethnic coaches in England, France and the Netherlands to gain insights into how they experienced and reflect on their career pathway into football coaching (Bradbury et al., 2014, 2018). Results from the interviews in these three countries have been published on an aggregate level (Bradbury et al., 2014, 2018). However, due to word limitations, there was relatively little space in those publications to elaborate more in depth on the specific narratives by the Dutch minority ethnic coaches. The present chapter fills this gap and presents findings from the interviews held with the Dutch minority coaches. This allows me to present and discuss more in depth some aspects which were relevant in this particular national context. It also allows me to connect recent quantitative findings regarding the proportion of minority ethnic coaches in the Netherlands (Peeters & Van Sterkenburg, 2017) with explanatory mechanisms that underlie the limited racial/ethnic diversity within the (Dutch) football coaching corps.

Data and sample

Our *quantitative* overview of Dutch coaches with a minority ethnic background was based on desk- and web-based research of available information by the first author (Peeters & Van Sterkenburg, 2017). For this particular chapter, we focus on coaching positions in the three highest levels of the *men's* game, with the period 29 November – 22 December 2016 as the specific reference period for which we collected the data. The focus is on men's football since the contrast between racial/ethnic diversity in playing squads on the one hand and within the coaching tiers of the game on the other, is particularly evident in the men's game (also Peeters & Van

Sterkenburg, 2017). To define 'people of a minority ethnic background' we broadly applied the definition by Bradbury et al. (2014: 9) which means we referred to minority ethnic groups as people from non-European heritage including "*generationally settled and new migrant populations*" drawn from Asia, Africa, the Caribbean, the Middle-East and Latin-America[3]. It also includes the Turkish ethnic population who is often regarded as a visible minority ethnic group in European countries including the Netherlands (Bradbury et al., 2014; Peeters & Van Sterkenburg, 2017).

The *qualitative* findings are based on in-depth interviews with ten Dutch football coaches of a minority racial/ethnic background (Bradbury et al., 2014). These coaches have been interviewed by the author of this chapter and by an assistant researcher within the framework of her internship[4]. The interviews lasted between 1.5 and 2 hours and were held face-to-face across the Netherlands, at a venue of the interviewee's choosing (e.g. at the football club, at the office, on an outside terrace), except for one telephone interview (on request of the interviewee).

The football coaches (25–50 years old) constitute a diverse group in terms of their ethnic, socio-cultural and educational backgrounds. Their ethnic backgrounds vary; four of the coaches are of Surinamese origin, two of Moroccan origin, two of Turkish origin, and two of Moluccan/Indonesian origin (originating from the Molucca Islands which is an island group in eastern Indonesia). Most were born in the Netherlands or had lived in the Netherlands for the majority of their lives. The biographies of the interviewees show that the vast majority of the coaches had been active in professional Dutch football as players, mostly at the highest professional level in the Netherlands (the *Eredivisie*) or just one level below that. During their playing careers, the vast majority of the interviewees had played at central positions in the field – such as central midfielder, central defender, or goalkeeper. These positions are usually associated with qualities that are *also* seen as important for coaching/management such as leadership, tactical capacities and organizational qualities. In terms of coaching certificates, two interviewees had obtained the highest certificate possible (*UEFA Pro license*) while most had obtained their *UEFA A* degree at the time of the interview (one level below the UEFA Pro)[5]. Even though many respondents had obtained a coaching certificate that would allow them to be a head coach or assistant head coach at the highest professional level in football or a head coach one level below, in reality the interviewees did not occupy such a position at their clubs. Instead, they held positions as head coaches at the *amateur* level or as an assistant head coach in professional football. Only one of the ten interviewees had managed to become a head coach within the highest professional level, although not in the Netherlands.

Participants were recruited via diverse networks using the snowball method, and they were guaranteed anonymity. In general, the interviewee and interviewer did not know each other prior to the interview. A topic list was used for the interviews but the experiences and narratives of the interviewees were central in the interviews in order to make their stories heard (Bradbury et al., 2018). Interviews were audio recorded and transcribed literally. A thematic analysis using the steps of open coding, axial coding and selective coding (Boeije, 2010), in combination with a literature review and consultations with the other researchers in the project, enabled me to identify four main themes in the narratives of the coaches. These reflect the processes and practices which have limited or enabled the career pathways of the minority coaches who had been interviewed. In the next section I will present these themes more in depth.

Results

This results section is twofold. Firstly, it will provide the main results from the quantitative inventory (Peeters & Van Sterkenburg, 2017) followed by the results from the qualitative study that provide more context to the quantitative findings.

Underrepresentation of Dutch minority ethnic coaches

Our inventory of the racial/ethnic diversity in the Dutch football coaching corps shows how the vast majority of coaches within the three highest football divisions in the Netherlands are Whites of a majority ethnic background. More specifically, 95% of all head coaches and assistant head coaches who were active in the highest level of the Dutch professional football *Eredivisie* were males of a White majority ethnic background, while only 5% were of a minority ethnic background. These percentages are slightly more balanced for the two divisions below although the difference is rather minimal (7% minority ethnic coaches in the *Jupiler League* – and 10% in the *Second Division*). When we focus on the specific ethnic background of minority ethnic head coaches or assistant head coaches, it becomes clear that it is mainly men of Surinamese or Caribbean descent who occupy these roles (three head coaches and three assistant head coaches), while an ex-professional football player of Moluccan descent was the head coach of the Rotterdam-based club *Feyenoord*. The data also indicate that most minority ethnic coaches in our quantitative overview worked as an *assistant* head coach at the time of the project – with three of them of Surinamese descent, two of Moroccan descent, one of Moluccan/Indonesian descent and one of Turkish descent.

The skewed figures on race/ethnicity of coaches contrast sharply with the diversity in the *playing squads* of the *Eredivisie*. Both majority and minority football players participate in large numbers in *De Eredivisie*, with 60% of the players being of a majority ethnic background and 40% of a minority ethnic background, in the period under study. The latter group included many players of Surinamese and Moroccan descent.

Within a European perspective, the skewed percentages are not that surprising as the figures for the Dutch context are quite similar to those of other European elite football leagues as they were found some years ago. More specifically, Bradbury et al. (2014) showed that only 3.4% of all football coaches in the selected European club football competitions (England, Germany, Spain, Belgium, France, Italy and the Netherlands) were of a minority ethnic background.

In order to gain more insights into the reasons behind these numbers and percentages I now turn to the qualitative findings from the interviews with minority ethnic coaches. The following four themes emerged from the interviews with Dutch minority ethnic coaches: 'Implicit mechanisms of racial/ethnic exclusion and discrimination', 'Inclusivity/exclusivity of networks', 'Stereotypes, lack of role models and the role of the media', and 'Whiteness and playing down oppositional racial/ethnic identities'. The themes broadly overlap with the themes found on a European scale in the earlier overarching study by Bradbury et al. (2014) but with national distinctions for the Dutch case[6].

Implicit mechanisms of racial/ethnic exclusion and discrimination

When interviewees reflect on experiences of racial/ethnic inclusion, exclusion and discrimination, two strands of reasoning permeate the interviews. First of all, some coaches argue there is no racism in professional football and that *individual qualities* are key in achieving a coaching position. Even though these interviewees acknowledge that minority ethnic coaches may be underrepresented in football coaching positions, they argue this is unrelated to racial/ethnic discrimination within the football culture. Instead, they argue that minority ethnic coaches *themselves* are not ambitious enough, not disciplined enough to pass the educational KNVB (national football federation) courses, or have difficulty accessing the right networks because they have not mastered the Dutch language well enough (which hinders the process of networking). For some, this line of reasoning, with an emphasis on individual responsibility, individual agency and ambition, probably worked well in their own career; individual ambition and hard work were the ingredients necessary for them in their playing career or to reach the coaching position they currently occupy. In sum, they deal with a possible glass ceiling effect for minority ethnic coaches (Bradbury et al., 2014) by considering it quite irrelevant; if there is indeed a glass ceiling, their argument goes, it is just a matter of working harder to break through that glass ceiling.

> *If you close your eyes and work hard, you can exceed all. Suppose people or players feel disadvantaged, you have to work harder and neglect that.*
> (Surinamese-Dutch interviewee)

Another strand of reasoning among the coaches, *which was more dominant in the interviews*, was the experience of a range of overt and more institutional and cultural forms of racism that limited coaching career pathways. Various minority ethnic coaches speak of a racialized football culture which makes it relatively hard for them to reach the top as a coach. A recurring theme in many of the interviews is that minority ethnic football coaches feel they have to work harder than Whites to get the same opportunities.

> *Yes I believe you are being stigmatized easier. If a foreigner acts in a certain way, they will say; you see. They lump all individuals together like 'they are all...'. And for the majority Dutch this is different, I believe they get more chances...*
>
> (Surinamese-Dutch interviewee)

In line with this are remarks that minority ethnic coaches are watched more closely by relevant stakeholders in the football sector. For some interviewees, this has resulted in feelings of insecurity which hinders them in their career. Minority ethnic coaches feel they tend to be judged negatively because they are seen as culturally different in terms of their language, ways of talking and presenting themselves. Some experience real frustration for never being asked for vacant coaching positions even though their resume as a coach is good enough and they have the required certificates.

> [Interviewer: In the end your ambition is to become a head coach; Do you think you would have been in that position already if you had been White, do you think it would have been easier?]
>
> *Yes I think so, I do have that feeling. [...] That is frustrating yes. If I see what I have performed, others have performed less well. I do not know what are their qualities but if I look at their CV; I have a big name as a player, I have performed well as a coach, and I have not been engaged in messy stuff that may make clubs think 'we should not hire him as he gets into fights, he has been into trouble with the board' [...] Huistra has just been fired as the coach of FC Groningen, the coach at FC Bruges has been fired recently, I have a good name in Belgium. Then I am depressed for a week; why was my name not mentioned? I get really disappointed then; I feel really small.*
>
> [Interviewer: [...] and you cannot find out why your name is not being mentioned?]
>
> *No no. They have never said 'you are too black'.*
>
> [Interviewer: People probably never say such a thing explicitly. Is that something that could be the reason, in your opinion?]
>
> *Yes of course.*
>
> (Surinamese-Dutch interviewee)

In a similar vein, a few respondents who work as an assistant head coach in a professional football club report that club owners are reluctant to appoint them as the head coach of the first team because they are afraid of negative reactions on the part of fans and sponsors for whom a minority ethnic coach would not be acceptable.

> *Well look, our coach will leave this year. And the question is; who will be next year's coach? And the technical manager of the club wants to present me as the new head coach. I do not have the required certificate for that yet but it may be possible with his certificate. The only problem is that he says; 'How will the outside world react to that, how will sponsors react?'*
> [Interviewer: What do you mean?]
> *How will they react to a foreigner as a coach? He [the technical manager] supports me, he has brought me here. He knows my qualities but he asks himself 'how will the outside world react?' So, he is thinking about that, unconsciously.*
> (Moroccan-Dutch interviewee)

Inclusivity/exclusivity of networks

One of the aspects mentioned by interviewees as key in the coaching career pathway is being part of the right networks. The vast majority of respondents argue that individual networks are very important in making the transition from a player to a coach and in climbing the ladder as a coach. Some even state that being in the right network outweighs individual coaching qualities (also Bradbury et al., 2018): "*It is not about how much you know but about how many people you know*" (Moroccan-Dutch interviewee). And even though some do *not* agree with the key importance ascribed here to having the right contacts, most do mention the importance of certain key figures when reflecting on their transition from player to coach. These key figures – almost all White male head coaches or club owners – provided them with the opportunity to start to work as a coach after their career as a player. At the same time, most emphasize that these opportunities were not sufficient to make the transition; opportunities given by others should be combined with individual initiative. Coaches should, for instance, build a network themselves and get in touch with relevant people, preferably during their period as a player already; "*you really have to go after it yourself*" (Moroccan-Dutch interviewee). Not surprisingly, therefore, the interview data show that having been an active player at the highest levels of Dutch professional football is a huge advantage for making the transition from player to coach in the professional game. Those who have been active as professional players generally report to have a broader network of people within the football sector who may hire them as a coach or manager after their career compared to those who have passed the coaching education successfully but have *not* been active as a player at the highest level.

> *It is important in the football world that you establish contacts here and there, even if that means that you start a conversation with those who pay your salary after the match [...] I was always open to people, also with sponsors, they also want to... then you just talk to those people.*
> (Turkish-Dutch interviewee about his playing career)

Some interviewees explain the underrepresentation of minority ethnic coaches in elite football – *an underrepresentation which they all acknowledge* – by pointing to a lack of such individual initiative on the part of the minority coaches themselves. They describe minority ethnic players or coaches as being, amongst other things, more relaxed than Whites, as giving up relatively easy and as going for alternative career paths. Having said that, many interviewees also, regardless of having played at the elite level or not, consider the underrepresentation of minority ethnic coaches a serious problem. In their opinion, the quality of football coaching in general would improve when more minority ethnic coaches would be active at the highest levels, amongst other things because minority ethnic coaches are better able to motivate and work with (the many) minority ethnic players who are active in Dutch football. The following quotation from a youth coach at a professional football club illustrates this:

> *I have noticed that, if there is some issue with a minority ethnic player, they tend to approach me, or their parents approach me, instead of them going to [...]. Just the other day I received a phone call from a parent of a player of another team who is also of minority ethnic background. They were not satisfied about something. I advised them to talk to their own coach. So, they approach me, it has to do with the fact that I have the same ethnic background, it makes it easier for them.*
> (Moluccan-Dutch interviewee)

Some respondents argue that their minority background has helped them in their coaching career because those who hired them perceived their background as an advantage to cope with players that shared their (minority) ethnic background. This was an exception, however. In general, interviewees stated their minority ethnic background was *not* an enabling factor in their coaching career and was *not* seen as an advantage by clubs or the football association.

Some interviewees suggest a direct link between the underrepresentation of minority ethnic coaches and the underrepresentation of minority ethnic groups in powerful governance positions in the football world who decide on hiring new coaches. Most are careful to make such a direct connection between the whiteness of football governance and the whiteness of coaching positions, though. Some do mention, however, that White football managers and club owners hold racial/ethnic stereotypes that frame racial/ethnic minorities as good athletes but not as good managers or coaches. I will return to the role of racial/ethnic stereotypes in more detail in the next section.

Stereotypes, lack of role models and the role of the media

One aspect that interviewees experienced as further marginalizing their position as a coach is the widespread circulation of racial/ethnic stereotypes. Interviewees argue that specific stereotypes are commonly used in the football sector resulting in racial/ethnic minorities being seen as good football players but not fit for management or leadership.

> *It will never be expressed explicitly, but there is a certain feeling that minority ethnic people are less educated and that it [their underrepresentation in coaching] has to do with that; 'They can play football well but they are not fit for certain positions or for policy making', they just do not see that.*
>
> (Moluccan-Dutch interviewee)

Paradoxically, the interviewees also often use the same hegemonic stereotypes *themselves* to give meaning to players of various racial/ethnic backgrounds. In other words, even though the interviewees are critical of these stereotypes in the context of coaching and realize the stereotypes may have a detrimental effect on their careers, the coaches are also complicit with the maintenance and reproduction of these stereotypes when they describe players.

> *If you had to play against a Black player, you knew in advance he would probably be fast. But he often was. If you played against a Moroccan, they are technically gifted. What is very striking is that when you take a look at Africa, or Asia, Saudi Arabia is a good example, they have plenty of opportunities, financially etcetera, but their play is very poor in terms of tactics, reading the game.*
>
> (Surinamese-Dutch interviewee)

Sometimes, the coaches challenged the commonly held stereotypes that associate Black players with physical strength and poor tactical or management qualities:

> *There are all kinds of stigmas [...] but I do not think in that way. Brazil has become world champions five times, there are enough tactically-gifted Black players. I think it is too silly to talk about. I do know what you mean, but I believe it is too irrelevant to talk about.*
>
> (Surinamese-Dutch interviewee)

Related to the issue of stereotyping was a discussion about *role models*. Most interviewees argued that role models of football coaches are usually White and that role models of a (non-White) minority ethnic background are lacking. This is unfortunate, they stress, as role models may show minority ethnic youth/players that it *is* possible to achieve a career as a football coach. This may be important as many minority ethnic youth do not really seem to consider this as a realistic career path. However, even though the importance of role models is acknowledged by some of the interviewees, these interviewees *also* state they do not consider the lack of role models as a key reason for the current underrepresentation of minority ethnic coaches in football. Furthermore, a Turkish-Dutch coach states that Turkish-Dutch youth do not want to pursue a coaching career in the Netherlands anyhow; *if* they have the ambition to become a coach, then this will be in Turkey instead of the Netherlands. These kinds of statements were also applied when discussing minority ethnic *players*; some argue that talented minority ethnic players in Dutch clubs may not feel represented at the coaching level which is mainly White, and therefore do not feel completely at home at their clubs. This makes it easier for them to opt for a club abroad or (when having a double passport) to choose the national team of the country of familial origin instead of the Dutch national team. The assumption underlying this line of thought is that minority ethnic players may feel more included when they feel represented at the coaching or leadership level by people who share their racial/ethnic background.

Whiteness and playing down oppositional racial/ethnic identities

In general, and as has become clear from the preceding sections, the interviewees see the football coaching industry as a predominantly White context. Results show that minority ethnic coaches negotiate carefully their racial/ethnic identity vis-a-vis other actors in a White-situated football world. Some interviewees use a different strategy to deal with their minority ethnic status in the football context. They say not to care about racism in football as they do not look at football in that way and do not 'see' race or ethnicity themselves. Some, on the other hand, consciously downplay their minority ethnic identity as they feel that may disadvantage them. This may have negative repercussions, however, for their coaching career. One respondent argues that, due to his minority background, he is always careful in what he says and does, ensuring he does not make any missteps as those missteps may be linked to his race/ethnicity. At the same time, he argues this carefulness is also counterproductive as it does not facilitate making new contacts and creating new networks which are important to make the next step in his career.

> *We are not good in networking, we are not good in lobbying. [...] We are perhaps a bit too modest, as we always had to maneuver in a careful, modest role while it would be better to actually open our mouths.*
>
> (Surinamese-Dutch interviewee)

Another interviewee expresses similar concerns and also refers to other actors than the football industry per se, such as the media. In particular, he states that the media have the tendency to focus on his minority status, as an explanation for the choices he makes. This happened to him, for instance, when he hired players who share his (Moroccan-Dutch) ethnicity.

> *I have had a few questions about that earlier in my career, after I had hired five players of Moroccan descent. I have asked [the journalist] about the reason for his questions: 'I do not understand why you ask me this, can you explain that to me?' Well, then the standard reply was 'Well it is a legitimate question or not? You are of Moroccan origin, you have been engaged with the theme of ethnicity in football, and you now have five Moroccan-Dutch players in the squad'.*
>
> (Moroccan-Dutch interviewee)

It is interesting, of course, to consider whether similar questions would have been posed to a White majority ethnic coach if he would have hired five players who share his (White majority) ethnic background. This seems unlikely and shows how normative whiteness operates in football management and leadership. I will return to that in the Discussion section.

Discussion

This chapter has shown how the hegemonic and often naturalized narrative of professional football as an egalitarian and meritocratic space reflexive of multi-ethnic society deserves some critical reflection (Bradbury et al., 2018; Rankin-Wright et al., 2016). Using cultural studies and CRT insights, this chapter has revealed how implicit and often unacknowledged forms of racial/ethnic stereotyping and racial/ethnic inclusion and exclusion negatively influence the opportunities and ambitions of minority ethnic football coaches in the Netherlands. Based on the narratives of our interviewees, it seems that meanings about the football coaching profession that circulate within the (Dutch) football industry have racialized/ethnicized *sub-texts* in which those of a majority ethnic (White) background tend to be associated with 'normative' management and leadership skills and those of a (non-White) minority ethnic background with natural 'playing' and 'athletic' skills (also Bradbury et al., 2018). Much research has been done about how the sport *media* draw on and reproduce such stereotypes (e.g. Ortega & Feagin, 2017; Hylton, 2009), with White players being represented as capable in terms of tactical capabilities and organizational skills, and Black players as naturally athletic, fast and strong. However, scholars have paid only very little attention to how such racialized meanings may linger on in the domain of football coaching as well. The narratives presented in this chapter show how the racial/ethnic stereotypes and racialized myths also seem to permeate the discourses surrounding football coaching, with negative effects for the careers of minority ethnic coaches. This is combined with a lack of minority ethnic role models in football coaching (Peeters & Van Sterkenburg, 2017). Hylton (2018) argued in this respect that the racial/ethnic homogeneity within the football coaching corps can create an image of football organizations as *"effective at keeping marginalized groups away because those environments do not reflect them"* (Hylton 2018: 31).

Such experiences of racial/ethnic exclusion and marginalization in management and leadership have been found for other sports and contexts as well such as football in the English and French contexts, and cricket and rugby in England (Bradbury et al., 2014; Bradbury et al., 2018; Hylton 2018; Long & Hylton, 2002). It also illustrates how whiteness operates within the sport and football domains. Whiteness can be seen as a discourse which privileges White people, amongst other things by framing racial/ethnic minorities as different from the norm, and by associating White majority ethnic people with traits that are seen as normative and desirable for positions of leadership and management. Within such a discourse of whiteness, non-White people become associated with executive (playing) rather than managerial roles (e.g. being seen as a good athlete or a good 'natural' entertainer). Our results illustrate how minority ethnic coaches experience such operation of whiteness on a regular basis. This is evident when coaches report that club owners are reluctant to appoint them as the head coach of the first team because they are afraid of negative reactions on the part of fans and sponsors, or when minority ethnic coaches feel they are being judged in negative ways because they are seen as culturally 'different' in terms of their language, ways of talking and presenting themselves (see results section). There was a consensus amongst most interviewees in this study about the existence of subtle racisms of this kind in the Dutch football sector. At the same time, the minority coaches who were interviewed deal with this in different ways – some say they ignore it, some work harder to overcome the prejudice, some become frustrated. Regardless of the variation in coping strategies, though, a recurring theme in many of the interviews was that minority ethnic football coaches feel they have to work harder than their majority ethnic counterparts to get the same opportunities. Furthermore, most interviewees consider the whiteness of the (Dutch) football coaching corps problematic. Many coined the underrepresentation of minority ethnic coaches in Dutch professional football a serious issue.

Paradoxically, the coaches in our study not only criticized the racialized stereotypes and myths but they also reinforced them using the same racial stereotypes when talking about players of diverse origins. It reflects the pervasiveness of stereotypes and that whiteness is being *"produced by everyone"* (Hylton, 2018: 45). A discourse of whiteness was also evident when interviewees argued that they feel the need to conform to whiteness norms in their actual coaching practices, as a way to gain acceptance within a White-dominated football world. Interviewees argued, for instance, they had to maneuver "in a modest role", not make any missteps, and downplay their minority identities, amongst other things (see also results section). It reveals how minority coaches seem to internalize a White-situated perception of themselves as the racial/ethnic 'Other' and how minority coaches feel the need to conform or adjust to whiteness in their coaching practices and behavior. Such adoption of whiteness discourses and norms may facilitate their individual careers in the short term, but it also serves to reinforce racial/ethnic hierarchies, stereotypes and myths of blackness in football in the longer term (Hylton, 2018).

Conclusions and recommendations

By giving voice to the (anonymized) narratives of ten Dutch coaches of a minority ethnic background, this chapter hopefully contributes to increase the awareness of the role that whiteness and racial/ethnic stereotypes play in the underrepresentation of minority ethnic coaches in professional football. This is especially relevant since the obstacles to a more diverse and inclusive football coaching culture are persistent. This applies to the Dutch professional football (and sport) context as well, where an emphasis on individual/team performance and individual 'quality' seems to go hand in hand with a relatively limited focus on how race/ethnicity may operate in a more structural way in football coaching and leadership. I will, therefore, end this chapter with a few recommendations that can help break the glass ceiling as experienced by minority ethnic coaches in this study, in a more or less structural manner. Many of these recommendations originate from the coaches that have been interviewed. The recommendations can be sorted in four main areas which are (1) coach education support, (2) coach employment practices, (3) improved networking, and (4) media stereotypes.

Firstly, in relation to coach education support, interviewees argued that the (Dutch) football association can provide stronger support for minority ethnic coaches in their transition from player to coach. This can be achieved, for instance, by giving extra 'points' to those with a minority ethnic background who want to access the top-level UEFA Pro course so that they have a slight advantage in reaching the required threshold to get access. A certain number of points is required for a candidate to get access to the UEFA Pro course and the number of points a candidate gets is based on a variety of criteria such as educational capacities, learning abilities (openness to new ideas), performance in earlier coach education, experience as a coach and as a player, etcetera (information from Dutch ex-football coach Co Adriaanse in the earlier mentioned broadcast *Studio Voetbal* [Studio Football]). Some interviewees reject such affirmative action, but nevertheless state that the football association can encourage football clubs to hire minority ethnic coaches and monitor their progress within these clubs.

Secondly, regarding coach employment opportunities, some interviewees recommend the implementation of the Rooney Rule which means that clubs have to invite (at least) one minority ethnic candidate for a vacancy for a head coach. Respondents mention that this will increase the opportunities for minority ethnic coaches to be invited for a job interview. Moreover, they argue that being invited *in itself* is of added value (even when not getting the job) since this enhances network building. Moreover, I would add, such face-to-face interviews may challenge some deeply ingrained popular stereotypes on the part of (usually White) club owners about Black people and/or minority ethnic groups.

Thirdly, given the importance of networking and the obstacle this poses to minority coaches (see results) it was suggested that football associations and/or UEFA create a database that includes the names of all certified coaches of minority ethnic background who passed the UEFA Pro course. A database would enable football associations to widen their network and pro-actively contact capable minority ethnic coaches when relevant, for instance when there is a vacancy in the organization but also for smaller activities – like when a guest speaker is needed for an educational course, a conference, or otherwise. Such a database would also be useful to minority ethnic players wanting to become a coach. Again, this will broaden the network of minority ethnic coaches.

Fourthly and lastly, given the detrimental effect of racial/ethnic stereotyping on the popular perception toward minority ethnic groups, in particular toward Black (ex-)footballers as fit for playing but not for organizing sport, it is important to turn to the role of sport media. I concur with Ortega and Feagin (2017: 28) who argue that *"white media owners and associated media decision makers must end the constant barrage in reproducing [...] racialized narratives of racist framing by implementing creative and accurate programming of people of colour instead of lazily employing the old racist frames"*. An important part of such 'accurate programming', I would argue, are also debates and discussions in mainstream media programs that address the underrepresentation of minority ethnic coaches at the elite level, thus raising awareness of the topic amongst relevant stakeholders like football journalists or those working in football governance. In that regard, the football talk show *Studio Voetbal* that I discussed in the beginning of the chapter was unique and offers some hope. At the same time, however, the broadcast *also* showed the persistent use of a hegemonic narrative of football and football coaching as merely meritocratic and independent from any racialized discourse. It illustrates how any change in this regard will require long-term reflections and intervention projects (Ortega & Feagin, 2017) as well as ongoing research that keeps monitoring, exploring and discussing (unequal) treatment of and access to coaching positions for minority ethnic coaches.

Notes

1 I use the term 'minority ethnic' here since this reflects the Dutch everyday discourse where those who are perceived as belonging to a racial or ethnic minority group are usually referred to as 'minority ethnic groups' *['etnische minderheden']* (rather than minority *racial* groups). At the same time, race and ethnicity are often used in a conflated manner in everyday talk. I will return to the use of the terms 'ethnicity' and 'race' in Dutch everyday discourse later on in this chapter.
2 The term used in the official statistics to refer to this ethnic group is '(former) Dutch-Antilles and Aruba'. The term 'Antilles/Antillean' is more commonly used in everyday Dutch discourse, though, to refer to people who originate from the islands/countries that constitute the (former) Dutch-Antilles and Aruba, and I therefore also use that terminology here.
3 The category of 'Latin-American' was not mentioned explicitly in Bradbury et al. (2014) but is relevant in the Dutch football context given the presence of Latin-American football players.
4 In total 11 interviews have been conducted but one was with a White KNVB (Dutch football association) educator in order to gain more insight into the coach education. I want to thank the KNVB for their cooperation in this respect, and the assistant researcher Kelly Elskamp for the effort she has put into the interviewing and transcription.
5 One of our interviewees had only obtained his UEFA C certificate and had mainly been active in leadership instead of coaching roles in professional football.
6 It also means that some of the quotations by the coaches mentioned in this chapter overlap with those in Bradbury et al. (2014; 2018).

References

Abbink, M. (2019). Trends van de jaren tien [trends of the 2010s]. In Voetbal International (Ed.) *Voetbal International Seizoensgids 2019/2020* (pp. 6–10). Alkmaar: Voetbal International.
Boeije, H. (2010). *Analysis in qualitative research*. London: Sage.
Bradbury, S., Van Sterkenburg, J., & Mignon, P. (2014). *The glass ceiling in football in Europe. Levels of representation of 'visible' ethnic minorities and women in leadership positions, and the experiences of elite level 'visible' ethnic minority coaches*. London: FARE/UEFA.
Bradbury, S., Van Sterkenburg, J., & Mignon, P. (2018). The under-representation and experiences of elite level minority coaches in professional football in England, France and the Netherlands. *International Review for the Sociology of Sport*, 53, 313–334. https://doi.org/10.1177/1012690216656807.
Bruce, T. (2004). Marking the boundaries of the 'normal' in televised sports: The play-by-play of race. *Media, Culture & Society*, 26, 861–879.
Carrington, B. (2011). 'What I said was racist – but I'm not a racist': Anti-racism and the white sports/media complex. In J. Long, & K. Spracklen (Eds.) *Sport and challenges to racism* (pp. 83–99). Houndmills, Basingstoke, UK: Palgrave Macmillan.
Centraal Bureau voor de Statistiek [CBS] (2018). Bevolking Kerncijfers 2017 (gewijzigd op 30 oktober 2018) [Population Key Numbers 2017] (updated October 30, 2018). Retrieved from https://opendata.cbs.nl/statline/#/CBS/nl/dataset/37296ned/table?dl=107C4.

Essed, P., & Trienekens, S. (2008). 'Who wants to feel White?' Race, Dutch culture and contested identities. *Ethnic and Racial Studies*, 31, 52–72. https://doi.org/10.1080/01419870701538885

Frankenberg, R. (2004). On unsteady ground: Crafting and engaging in the critical study of whiteness. In M. Bulmer, & J. Solomos (Eds.) *Researching race and racism* (pp. 104–118). London/New York: Routledge.

Hylton, K. (2009). *'Race' and sport: Critical race theory*. London/New York: Routledge.

Hylton, K. (2018). *Contesting 'race' and sport. Shaming the colour line*. London/New York: Routledge.

Long, J., & Hylton, K. (2002). Shades of white: An examination of whiteness in sport. *Leisure Studies*, 21, 87–103. https://doi.org/10.1080/02614360210152575.

'Marokkanen in de Eredivisie: viercategorieën, vierzekerheidjes, veelpotentie' [Moroccans in Eredivisie; four categories, four certainties, much potential] (2017, November 14). Retrieved from www.voetbalprimeur.nl.

Ortega, F. J., & Feagin, J. R. (2017). Framing. The undying White racial frame. In C. Campbell (Ed.) *The Routledge companion to media and race* (pp. 19–30). London/New York: Routledge.

Peeters, R., & Van Sterkenburg, J. (2017). *Etnische en gender diversiteit in topbesturen en coaching posities in het Nederlandse profvoetbal* [ethnic and gender diversity in top government and coaching positions in Dutch elite football]. Rotterdam/Ede: Erasmus University Rotterdam/Knowledge Centre Sport (KCS).

Rankin-Wright, A. J., Hylton, K., & Norman, L. (2016). Framing race equality in sport coaching. *Sociology of Sport Journal*, 33, 357–368. http://dx.doi.org/10.1123/ssj.2015-0174.

Sykes, H. (1998). Turning the closets inside/out: Towards a queer-feminist theory in women's physical education. *Sociology of Sport Journal*, 15, 154–173.

Van Sterkenburg, J. (2011). *Race, ethnicity and the sport media*. Amsterdam: Amsterdam University Press/Pallas Publications.

Van Sterkenburg, J., Knoppers, A., & De Leeuw, S. (2012). Constructing racial/ethnic difference in and through Dutch televised soccer commentary. *Journal of Sport and Social Issues*, 36 (4), 422–442. https://doi.org/10.1177/0193723512448664.

Van Sterkenburg, J., Peeters, R., & Van Amsterdam, N. (2019). Everyday racism and construction of racial/ethnic difference in and through football talk. *European Journal of Cultural Studies*. https://doi.org/10.1177/1367549418823057.

Vlietstra, B. (2017, November 14). Eredivisie is kleine vijver voor Marokkaanse bondscoach Renard [Eredivisie small pool for Moroccan's national team coach Renard]. *De Volkskrant*.

Vlietsra, B. (2019, May 17). Oranje moet een warm bad zijn [Orange needs to be a warm welcome]. *De Volkskrant*.

Wekker, G. (2016). *White innocence. Paradoxes of colonialism and race*. Durham/London: Duke University Press.

Chapter 5

British Asian football coaches
Exploring the barriers and advocating action in English football

Daniel Kilvington

Introduction

Although people with South Asian heritage have a history in British football that stretches back over a century (Kilvington, 2016), there have been very few success stories observed within English professional football. British Asians[1] have historically been excluded from the 'beautiful game' as players, fans, administrators, managers, coaches and scouts. Although many studies have explored the exclusion of British Asian football players (Bains & Patel, 1996; Bains & Johal, 1998; Burdsey, 2004a, 2004b; 2007; Johal, 2001; Kilvington, 2012, 2013, 2016, 2017; McGuire et al., 2001; Randhawa, 2011), very few have investigated the exclusion of British Asians as coaches and managers.[2] This chapter intends to critically understand the barriers that British Asian football coaches encounter and promote recommendations for reform, at various levels of the game.

A racialised disparity exists between on- and off-field representation when considering black and South Asian heritage inclusion within football. While a quarter of the 3,700 professional players are black, with black British players accounting for 15 per cent of all professionals since the mid-1990s, British Asians, on the other hand, constitute around 0.25 per cent of professional players (Bradbury, 2001; Kilvington, 2018). This under-representation is worthy of critical examination as evidence suggests that football is a popular pastime among British Asian communities (Sport England, 2018). Furthermore, recent studies have shown that of 482 senior coaches in professional football, 20 are black (Bradbury, 2017a) while only two are British Asian (Kilvington, 2018). While black players are in fact over-represented on the playing field, British Asians are doubly marginalised as they are absent as players, coaches and managers. Considering that the British Asian population is double that of the black British population, it is perhaps noteworthy and intriguing as to why the former group is marginalised both on and off the field (Kilvington, 2016, 2017, 2018). This chapter aims to desegregate generalised BAME[3] (Black, Asian and minority ethnic) experiences and focus on the stories of British Asian football coaches.

This chapter begins by briefly conceptualising 'race' and racisms before contextualising British Asian experiences in English football. Second, a methodology, which utilises a Critical Race Theory (CRT) framework, will critically discuss the employed methods. Third, oral testimonies of British Asian coaches will be presented to help us comprehend the exclusion of British Asian coaches. Exclusionary barriers will be highlighted such as access and pathways, racisms, and a lack of role models. The final section concludes and offers several recommendations for reform, generated from the experiences of British Asian coaches.

'Race', racism and the experiences of British Asians in football

This chapter draws on CRT to help 'examine the racism in society that privileges whiteness as it disadvantages others because of their "blackness"' (Hylton, 2009: 22). CRT scholars postulate that 'race' is a central component in the structuring of contemporary societies. Conversely, football is often presented as an exception because fairness, egalitarianism and meritocracy *lay* at its core (Hylton, 2009; Kilvington, 2016; Lusted, 2017). Burdsey (2007), Kilvington (2016) and Ratna (2014) all illustrate how racisms have worked to exclude British Asian male and females within English football, at all levels. The power and perseverance of 'race' must not be understated as it acts as the precursor to racism – the effect of 'race' thinking.

Racism has adapted to survive and we now live in a world where multiple forms of racism exist. Overt racism, which is very visible and relatively easy to identify, was a major problem within English football during the 1960s and 1970s as more black players started to emerge. Back et al. (2001) and Burdsey (2007) both provide evidence of anti-Asian and anti-Muslim football chants, respectively, within English football.

Another form is inferential racism, otherwise called 'stealth racism' (Johnson, 2007: 27). This type of racism is strongly influenced by stereotypes, which Stangor (2009: 2) describes as *'the traits that come to mind quickly when we think about the groups'*. As Kilvington (2012) notes, inferential racism has marginalised British Asian players within the recruitment system as they are commonly perceived by some scouts to be physically weaker than their white or black counterparts.

Arguably, inferential racism influences social actions and structures and leads to another type of racism, known as institutional racism. Institutional racism, a form which is integral to this chapter, is often hidden and invisible. The very fact that scouting networks overlook predominantly British Asian football environments showcases an inequality of opportunity and thus, by definition, illustrates institutionalised racism (Kilvington, 2016). Yet, the foundations of contemporary racism are to be found disguised within institutions and organisations, meaning that it is very hard to identify and challenge. As Zarate (2009: 388) notes, it is possible for one to '*document the underrepresentation of minorities among elected and appointed officials*', but it may be '*virtually impossible to identify any specific instance of racism*'. This form of racism '*operates as a boundary keeping mechanism whose primary purpose is to maintain social distance between racial elite and racial non-elite*' (Coates, 2011: 121 cited in Farrington et al., 2015: 36). Within a sports context the 'racial elite' becomes a synonym for whiteness while the 'racial non-elite' refers to BAME communities. Scholars including Back et al. (2001), Kilvington (2016, 2018), Singer et al. (2010) and Regan & Feagin (2017) have documented how institutionally racist practices operate and manifest within sport.

Feagin (2006) argues that racism is structurally embedded within institutions, such as football. He notes that racism exists at a societal level as well as an individual level. In other words, if racism was magically eradicated from the consciousness of every individual, racism would still be embedded in the institutional structures that continue to oppress minority ethnic communities, such as housing, education, the legal system, healthcare, and so on. Racism is therefore manifest within society and is socially reproduced across generations. Bonilla-Silva (2003) suggests that the 'white habitus', for example, encourages solidarity and connectedness amongst whites and reinforces 'white' behaviour, practices and performances. Within football, whites thus remain in control and this maintains the exclusion of current and aspiring BAME coaches due to the institutionalised tendency of white decision makers promoting and hiring white candidates over people of colour (see Cunningham & Sagas, 2005; Kilvington, 2018; Sartore & Cunningham, 2006). For Feagin (2006), these decisions made by gatekeepers are influenced by the white racial frame – whites' collective memories and histories which are influenced by cultural representations and stereotypes.

A plethora of studies have highlighted the role 'race' and the various forms of racism have played in the continued exclusion of British Asians in English football (Burdsey, 2007; Kilvington, 2016, 2017; Ratna, 2014). Although Roy Smith, Ricky Heppolette and Jimmy Carter, all South Asian descent, blazed a football trail between the 1950s and early 1990s, very little has changed regarding British Asian participation at elite level. Because there have been few success stories at the professional level, racially motivated stereotypes remain, such as that parents prioritise education, religion outweighs sport, football is unpopular and physical sports are not suited to the 'Asian frame'. Although there may be a degree of truth to *some* of these common-sense rationales (particularly among first generation migrant experiences), they have continued to be embellished and popularly employed to explain the exclusion of British Asians from English professional football. In turn, British Asians are perceived as the determining agents in their own exclusion (Burdsey, 2007).

Several recent studies have investigated the BAME exclusion from coaching and management positions within football (Bradbury 2014, 2016). Bradbury

(2014) found that only 1 per cent of senior coaching positions at elite level professional clubs and national teams across Europe are held by minority personnel. The LMA (2015) similarly provide detailed quantitative statistics to illustrate the exclusion. In short, research indicates that BAME coaches and managers are largely excluded within English professional football. However, it could be argued that British Asians, the UK's largest minority ethnic group, perhaps encounter additional barriers when compared to other BAME football communities (Bradbury, 2017b; Kilvington, 2016, 2018).

Bradbury (2017b) suggests that minority coaches who have little connection to the professional game struggle to gain support from senior club staff to attend Higher Level Coach Education (HLCE) courses. While well-known black players are generally welcomed onto HLCE courses based on their prior status, British Asian coaches are arguably '*doubly marginalised by their lack of prior professional experience as players and by their embodied (and negatively assumed), ethnic, cultural and religious distinctiveness*' (Bradbury, 2017b: 19).

Bourdieu (1984) notes that participating in sport depends on the economic, cultural and physical capitals that we possess. For Tinning and Fitzclarence (1992), ideologies are shaped through one's relationships with popular culture, media and institutional sites. Valued bodies are thus understood, and contextualised, via a negotiation through '*today's image-heavy, postmodern and individualised world where self-worth and one's place in society are closely tied to the self-managed, but fluid, body*' (Hill & Azzarito, 2012: 265). Kilvington (2018: 6) postulates:

> *British Asians are not considered the traditional embodiment of a football coach... Because of this, due to their paucity in football, and a lack of role models, individuals are racially framed according to external markers such as 'race', ethnicity and religion... In turn, British Asian coaches continue to be perceived as a gamble.*

These stereotypes arguably help preserve the status quo as clubs continue to operate '*patterns of institutional closure*' by recruiting '*within the dominant (white) social and cultural networks of the professional football industry*' (Bradbury, 2017b: 12–13). Previous literature has identified the multiple barriers that BAME football coaches encounter but it could be suggested that greater attention and scrutiny should be awarded to British Asian experiences to, first, uncover whether there are additional obstacles and, second, highlight what these are, if any, and how they impact upon British Asian coaching experiences.

Methodology

This chapter employs CRT because it allows us to critically comprehend '*the all-encompassing web of race to further our understanding of inequality*' (Zamudio et al., 2011: 3). Hylton (2009; 2010), among others, notes that there are five main themes of CRT. First, 'race' is considered a central component when investigating inequality. Racial inequality is not on the margins of social life but, as Zamudio et al. (2011: 3) postulate, it *'permeates every aspect of social life from minute, intimate relationships ... to the neighbourhoods we live in, and the schools we go to ... all the way to the macro-economic system'*. Second, 'race' neutrality, which is arguably manifest in the football psyche, is challenged. The third tenet seeks social justice and transformation as CRT advocates suggest that *'gains made through the legal system, and state sponsored racial equality is unsatisfactory and slow'* (Hylton, 2010: 339). This chapter concludes with recommendations for reform to challenge racial inequality. Fourth, storytelling is employed to examine 'race' and racism within social institutions. Providing 'oral testimonies' helps us to *'uproot the dysconscious racism or uncritical and distorted ways of thinking about race that have led to tacit acceptance of the dominant White norms and privileges'* (Singer, 2005: 370 in Burdsey, 2007: 9). For CRT scholars, racism is not a 'thing of the past' as racial subordination is still a major problem of the present, and has contributed to the exclusion of British Asian football coaches and managers. The final tenet acknowledges that CRT is transdisciplinary as it draws on knowledge from other disciplines such as ethnic studies, women's studies, sociology, history and the law to further comprehend the experiences of BAME groups.

CRT therefore provides scholars with an important theoretical lens to help critically understand, underpin and contextualise findings. Methodologically, it challenges colour-blindness, promotes social justice, and attempts to empower marginalised voices. For these reasons alone, it suits any researcher that is attempting to highlight injustice and challenge it. As noted, several studies have explored British Asian player experiences within English football, but few have specifically focused on the high-level British Asian coach experiences. This work therefore centralises excluded voices – British Asian football coaches.

My investigation into British Asians and football, which first began in 2007, has seen over 50 hours of data being collected through interviews and focus groups, with the total number of transcribed words totalling over 140,000. Although my work has predominantly focused on British Asian male playing experiences, my recent work has begun to explore the experiences of British Asian coaches. Using already established contacts in the game, I approached four British Asian coaches who had achieved either a UEFA A or UEFA B Licence[4] to gain a deeper insight into the barriers that British Asian football coaches, working in the system, encounter. All the participants currently coach at academy level and/or semi-professional[5] level. Due to their experience and understanding of the coaching qualification system, the participants were perfectly placed to reflect on barriers British Asian coaches encounter and offer recommendations for reform. A purposive sampling strategy was thus enforced as it *'allows the researcher to home in on people or events which there are good grounds for believing will be critical for the research'* (Denscombe, 2003: 16).

Although four participants may appear a small number, qualitative methods such as semi-structured interviews are concerned with generating rich, detailed and quality data over the need for a large, representative sample. Due to the paucity of British Asians in football, especially when the targeted sample is either UEFA A or UEFA B Licence qualified coaches, the sample is necessarily small.

The interviews aimed to explore general ideas which had been constructed through literature consultation such as the paucity of networks; stereotypic assumptions; and the power of role models. Of course, like all semi-structured interviews, the researcher must approach each interview open-minded and let the interviewee guide the interview, to some extent. Therefore, this flexibility allowed new and unintended themes to arise and be explored in greater depth. The significance of names, for example, was noted by the first participant and the lack of standardisation allows the researcher to pursue this emerging theme within subsequent interviews. The interviews were largely biographical, allowing the participants freedom and space to tell their story. The interviews were analysed using the coding mechanism of constructivist grounded theory. Open, axial and selective coding was therefore used (Strauss & Corbin, 1990) to help further construct themes.

British Asian football coaches: exploring the barriers

Bringing together the data collected from these semi-structured interviews with data from previous literature and research, this section will critically discuss the barriers that British Asian coaches appear to face. Multiple overt and subtle racist practices and processes form barriers for British Asian football coaches. Overt racism, which is now commonly justified as 'banter' (see Burdsey, 2011; Kilvington, 2016), can make some feel uncomfortable and isolated. Farenet note that some BAME coaches encounter

> experiences of intentional and unintentional racism ... This has included explicit racist name calling and more subtle and nuanced forms of racial 'banter' and a lack of recognition of or willingness to address racisms of this kind by FA coach tutors.
>
> (Farenet, 2014: 15)

The following oral testimony emphasises the participants' powerlessness while attempting to gain his FA coaching badges:

> *Basically I was in a classroom environment and a lot of racist and derogatory remarks were said; not directly to me but as a figure of speech. I didn't challenge it at the time because I was going to be with these players for two or three weeks ... so it was important for me to remain calm but it did create a little bit*

of unease. I was surprised and the thing that annoyed me was that some of the facilitators within this session could have done better. So, what happened was that I saw the few weeks through because I had to. Obviously, if you're gonna get your badges you're gonna have to play the system.

(British Indian Sikh coach, cited in Kilvington, 2016: 74)

This oral testimony correlates with Fanon's (1986) conceptualisation of the 'white mask'. To succeed, one must downplay their difference(s) and, quite simply, 'play the system' (Kilvington, 2016). Ratna (2013) argues that many of the British Asian players, for example, who 'make it' in football not only do so on merit, but also because of their 'ability to tolerate racism and "get on with it"'. For the above participant, to challenge the 'racist and derogatory remarks' that were being casually made would have isolated him and marked him out as 'Other'. Put simply, he had to suppress his feelings as whiteness encapsulates this space. Problematically, however, downplaying or denying indecencies of racism exonerates those accused of engaging in such acts (Burdsey, 2011).

Numerous studies have explored the ingrained nature of institutional racism within sport and highlighted the significance of names, for example, within the hiring process (see Bertrand & Mullainathan, 2004; Pilkington, 2003). This is highlighted by the following oral testimonies:

Names are a barrier as people might look at somebody's name and think 'well he's not going to be able to coach' because his name isn't right.

(British Asian UEFA B Licence coach, 22 August 2016)

When you apply for jobs and they see certain names, they [football clubs] tend to be put off.

(British Asian UEFA B Licence coach, 24 August 2016)

Three participants commented that their 'foreign sounding' names have disadvantaged their progress. Another participant noted that his football enthused British Asian friend formerly used his real name on football-related application forms but failed to gain any interviews. After changing his name for job applications and adopting his racially ambiguous nickname instead, he was increasingly shortlisted for interviews. This individual is now a relatively high-profile and respected figure within the game. As Burdsey (2009) notes, racially ambiguous nicknames can be employed to resist institutionalised forms of racism. Wider research highlights the significance of names within the hiring process not only in sport but across many different work sectors (see Pilkington, 2003). For example, Bertrand & Mullainathan (2004) found that people with 'black sounding names' are 50 per cent less likely to be called back for a job interview. Likewise, Adesina & Marocico (2017) state that applicants with a perceived 'white' or 'English' sounding name are three times more likely to acquire a job interview than those with a 'Muslim' sounding name. In short, 'foreign' or 'non-traditional' English sounding names can exclude some individuals from gaining an interview, thus again highlighting institutional racism.

The following oral testimony highlights the racial exclusivity of football. Back et al. (2001: 37) add that *'networks of white knowledge'* play a significant role in the hiring of coaches:

> *I applied four times to the club I was previously at. I didn't know anybody. But when I did get the opportunity [for interview] I missed out because the individual who got the job was a former YTS [Youth Training Scheme player] at the club. I met all the essentials and desirables, I had done my level 2, but I was told that I didn't have enough experience. A couple of months down the line on the off chance I met the individual who got the job, and fair play to him, but he said he had just recently passed his level 2.*
> (British Asian UEFA B Licence coach, 24 August 2016)

This illustrates that coaching networks are mono-ethnic (white-to-white) which reproduces social alienation (Feagin, 2006). Because economic resources and power are generationally passed down by family and institutional means, a hierarchical power structure between whites and BAME communities has been established within major institutions. Sport is no exception as Hill (2004) notes that over the course of 22 years, NCAA Division IA[6] teams appointed just 19 black head coaches out of a total of 381 vacancies. In addition, other studies have highlighted how black coaching opportunities are limited as white decision makers regularly employ qualified and unqualified white coaches over qualified black coaches (Cunningham & Sagas, 2005; Sartore & Cunningham, 2006). McIntosh's (2014: 35) work on white privilege is fitting within this discussion as *'one's life is not what one makes it; many doors are open for certain people through no virtues of their own'*. Due to the overwhelming whiteness of the game at institutional level (Lusted, 2009; Sporting Equals, 2011), white networks continue to tap into pre-existing white networks thus institutionally reproducing the racial status quo (Burdsey, 2007; Feagin, 2006; Kilvington, 2016, 2018). This narrative is similarly encapsulated within the following interview:

> *I apply for jobs, semi-pro jobs, all the time... I've applied for about 200 to 300 jobs. I never get an interview... My CV reads: [UEFA] A Licence; managed a national team, I have a [supporting] letter from (current international manager). But, this is how it works. The job comes up. I email. They acknowledge the email. A couple of weeks later they email and say unfortunately you have not been selected. The only time I have ever been able to manage in England was because I knew the chairman personally.*
> (British Asian UEFA A Licence coach, 15 January 2018)

This participant, who achieved his UEFA A Licence at the age of 22, and has managed at international level, said that he struggles to even gain an interview at semi-professional level. He has even offered his coaching services for free and has still been unsuccessful in gaining interviews. It is significant that his only break within England came through utilising a personal network. It could be argued that networking between insider/outsider groups can help challenge and destabilise the traditional process of 'white-to-white' networks. However, some British Asian coaches may feel intimidated, apprehensive and uncomfortable at the prospect of venturing into the 'unknown'. Nonetheless, the following participants suggested:

> *In life in general, and especially in professional football, you've got to be in those social circles to advance. It's about developing good relations with people and having them respect the work you do.*
> (British Asian UEFA B Licence coach, 24 August 2016)

> *I've had to go out of my way and do the networking and meet people I don't know. I think of other people and they might not have had to have done that. They might not have had to go out of their comfort zone and they might have had it put on their plate a little bit more. That feeling of going out there in that environment and feeling like an outsider, it's an uncomfortable feeling and many people wouldn't do that.*
> (British Asian UEFA B Licence coach, 22 August 2016)

If one is to succeed within football then, it is paramount that networks are constructed. Rich (2013) highlights the importance of networks as *'over 80 percent of Americans … Get their jobs through acquaintance contracts. Racially homogenous friendship networks can segregate people out of important networks, and thus out of important opportunities'* (2013). To challenge barriers based around access and pathways, white male networks must be destabilised. The participants highlighted that due to the traditional paucity of British Asians playing professional football, it not only maintains negative stereotypes, but it also indicates that they are less connected in comparison to black players, for instance, who represent over a quarter of the professional game.

Cohen's (1996) discussion of racial 'no-go' areas whereby 'race' becomes a marker of territory is useful to consider. Said (1985: 54) argues that designating a *'familiar space' which 'is "ours" and an unfamiliar space beyond "ours" which is "theirs" is a way of making geographical distinctions'*. These 'geographic boundaries' are thus split along 'social, ethnic and cultural' lines (ibid). This notion could be applied to football as coaching and management roles have traditionally been racially exclusive. When coaches do attempt to cross the 'colour-line', and forge links, some are met with resistance. The complexity of 'race' and multi-faceted role of racism must not be underestimated.

It could be argued that physical and cultural stereotypes held by key power brokers question the competence of British Asian coaches. These key power brokers, often white, rely on centuries-old *'white-crafted racial stereotypes, interpretive concepts, images, emotions, ideologies, and inclinations'* which prevent *'whites from seeing and treating blacks as equals'* (Regan & Feagin, 2017: 18). This perpetuates societal racism and is encapsulated by the following oral testimony:

> *People may automatically assume because of your appearance or your background that you can't coach or that you don't know about the game... Those stereotypes manifest and cause barriers.*
> (British Asian UEFA B Licence coach, 22 August 2016)

This story is also shared by the following British Asian grassroots coach:

> *They [football's gatekeepers] don't see any Asian coaches out there... So they think, 'who is this guy'? They'd probably respect a black guy or a white guy more than they would an Asian guy because they know that white people are already there, they know that black people are already there but they don't see Asian people. They don't see them play or coach... They think: 'well who's he? He's a Mickey Mouse coach'.*
> (pers comms, 4 April 2011)

Back et al. (2001: 214) note that BAME players are racialised in terms of their *'attributes, sporting capacity and professional competence'*. As the above interviews suggest, British Asian football coaches as well as players are racialised and stereotyped. Because British Asians have traditionally been associated with stick sports such as cricket and hockey, football is falsely, but commonly, perceived to be an unimportant subculture among British Asian communities (Bains & Johal, 1998; Burdsey, 2007; Kilvington, 2016). In turn, the British Asian 'body' is perceived to be paradoxical to 'football bodies'.

Feagin's (2006) notion of the white racial frame, as well as Omi & Winant's (1986) Racial Formation Theory, helps us critically understand the above oral testimonies. Omi & Winant argue that ideological beliefs have certain structural consequences. These oral testimonies indicate that the BAME 'knowledge' of the game continues to be implicitly or explicitly questioned by football insiders. This questioning, which could be categorised as inferential racism, has been founded on the collective memories and histories of the white racial frame (Feagin, 2006). In turn, British Asian coaches are perceived to possess fewer desirable characteristics associated with the qualities of 'good' coaches when compared with whites (Tomkiewicz et al., 1998). These common-sense assumptions remain because there are so few role models in elite positions. Inferential racism (common-sense assumptions and stereotypes) leads to institutional racism (under-representation in coaching positions). As Omi & Winant (1986) argue then, these ideological beliefs reinforce structural consequences and therefore shape and reproduce the social order. The concept of 'social cloning' (Ahmed, 2012) is relevant as people in powerful positions tend to recruit and surround themselves with others who share similar worldviews and cultural norms. Lawrence (2017: 141) adds that social cloning is a '*strategically important enabler of white male supremacy in football*'. As this section has illustrated, various forms of racism work to maintain white supremacy within football. Institutionalised forms of racism based on 'foreign sounding names' and perceived racial bias has thus worked to ignore and exclude British Asian football coaches. One way to challenge perceptions is to create and celebrate role models.

Role models have the power to overturn stereotypes (Coyle, 2010; Kilvington, 2012; Saeed & Kilvington, 2011). Within football, Back et al. (2001: 34) suggest that stereotypical perceptions of black players' skills and attributes have been '*exploded by the variety of black players in the professional game*'. However, due to limited British Asian involvement in football, elite figures may adhere to timeworn notions of physical incapabilities (Fleming, 2001; Kilvington, 2012) or alleged sociocultural differences (Bains and Patel, 1996; Burdsey, 2007) that have been prevalent throughout media and society (Farrington et al., 2012). British Asian coaches, a rarity within the professional game, can act as positive symbols and mentors for emerging coaches. Fletcher et al. (2014: 31) suggest that British Asian role models help promote an '*inclusive ideology*' while Sporting Equals (2011) postulate that a lack of trailblazers is a key barrier as coaching is something which is not feasible for BAME communities. They continue, highlighting that the establishment is 'all white' and this lack of visibility affects their perceptions of 'fitting in' and feeling welcome. The power of role models is emphasised by the following participants:

> *If you want to succeed at the top, whether that means working with the under 11s, 16s or 21s or whatever, you need people there to show you that they've made the breakthrough... I do agree that if there were more faces out there it does give you that confidence.*
> (British Asian UEFA B Licence coach, 24 August 2016)

> *The lack of role models is a massive thing. Because there's so few role models, people might, at the back of their minds, stereotype and think, 'do these guys know what they're doing'?*
> (British Asian UEFA B Licence coach, 24 August 2016)

Role models therefore have the power and ability to change the perception of coaching from a 'cul-de-sac' career to a field where one can succeed.

Coyle (2010) argues that this notion equates with the idea of 'ignition' whereby if we visualise something as a realistic or viable career, it ignites us to further motivate ourselves and pushes us to work harder to improve our talents. But, without a revision of the football system, role models will remain few and far between. Confronting these barriers is essential if we are to observe greater diversity within coaching and management positions.

Discussion and recommendations for reform

This chapter sought to critically understand and address the barriers facing British Asian football coaches with the aid of oral testimonies. The empirical work undertaken for this study builds on the research by Bradbury (2017a), LMA (2015) and Sporting Equals (2011). However, while these studies focused on BAME groups more generally as well as employing quantitative methods, this research used qualitative methods to help us critically understand British Asian experiences. CRT enables this by centralising minority voices to help '*inform anti-racist agendas and action*' (Kilvington, 2016: 7). The oral testimonies illustrated that networks, multiple forms of racism, and a paucity of role models continue to marginalise British Asian football coaches. Participants were also asked what action should be enforced to help achieve inclusion and their suggestions are critically discussed below.

First, networks must be established, developed and solidified. Kick It Out's 'Raise Your Game' programme, Black and Asian Coaches Association (BACA), and Creating and Developing Coaches, to name but a few, facilitate networking events and profile BAME role models in the process. As illustrated in this chapter, British Asians are arguably less likely to have established networks in the game due to systemic forms of racism such as social alienation and reproduction. The FA traditionally employs a generalist approach to engagement in elite coach education programmes. Although these courses are perceived to be 'open to all', they rely on aspiring coaches to have the necessary economic capital, professional playing experience and foundational coaching qualifications. For a coach to secure a position at elite level, they must be '*identified, selected and supported by professional clubs or national associations as suitable candidates*' and have '*access to work with elite players to fulfil the practical "on the job" requirements requisite for the completion of these awards*', i.e. UEFA B, UEFA A, UEFA Pro-Licence (Farenet, 2014: 10). However, it has been argued that coaches tend to be hired on 'personal recommendation' (ibid. 16) and that 'outsider' coaches, such as British Asians, are frequently overlooked in favour of 'insiders' (Sporting Equals, 2011). The FA should consider franchising out a networking model, physically or digitally, to help counter the isolation that BAME coaches, and British Asians in particular, encounter. It is important that these inclusion events understand the nuances between BAME communities as well as the nuances and differences among British Asian groups.

Second, coach inclusion organisations should develop relationships and pool resources rather than competing against one another. As a result, organisations would avoid duplicating schemes. There are several groups challenging the British Asian exclusion such as Kick It Out, the FA, various professional football clubs, Sporting Equals, etc. Often, similar strategies are created and it could be argued that a 'British Asians in football activist group' should be established, perhaps facilitated by the FA. By bringing together experts within this field they could develop bespoke strategies to increase the number of British Asian football coaches, as well as players, scouts, fans, etc. This recommendation could help create a more holistic 'strategic plan' with regards to achieving coach inclusion, equality and diversity.

Third, although the participants appeared hesitant and sceptical of positive action strategies, such as the Rooney Rule, it could be argued that they offer benefits. The door of the interview room was closed but because of the Rooney Rule, for example, it is ajar for at least one BAME candidate to walk through. Positive action policies alone are not *the* solution to the problem as such policies must be complemented by other means. While the Rooney Rule is concerned with coach recruitment, other initiatives link well, such as the Coach Inclusion and Diversity Programme, which focuses on coach education. Implementing a combination of well-resourced combative measures within different spaces, such as recruitment and education, creates a more holistic approach.

Finally, I argue that equality and diversity (or unconscious bias) training for academy personnel, coach educators and selection committees is advisable to challenge narrow and unfair perceptions of minority groups that permeate the white racial frame. In turn, this may reduce the 'social cloning' that is manifest within the game (Ahmed, 2012).

This chapter has critically investigated the experiences of British Asian football coaches, and highlighted key exclusionary barriers. The proposed recommendations for reform have been born out of the counter narratives and existing literature. To achieve inclusion, racialised stereotypes must be challenged; racially exclusive networks must be constructed and developed; and role models must be championed.

Notes

1 British Asian is a commonly used term to refer to a person who is of South Asian descent, i.e. of Bangladeshi, Indian, Pakistani or Sri Lankan descent, and was born, raised or is living in Britain.
2 A football coach is employed to train (or coach) the players, to analyse their performances and develop them. They are also tasked with encouraging and motivating them to reach their full potential. A manager, on the other hand, has the main responsibility for the team. This article focuses on participants' experiences who have both coaching and managerial experience. A manager, also sometimes called

the 'head coach', has the ultimate responsibility for the team as they are tasked with choosing, buying and selling players, deciding on the teams' formation, tactics and overall style of play. The manager is responsible to the clubs' chairperson.
3 BAME, within the British context, refers to a person who belongs to a minority ethnic group. BAME, which first emerged within policy documentation, replaced black and minority ethnic (BME) as its precursor was accused of homogenising 'blackness'. It is recognised that such terms and acronyms are problematic, but within this chapter BAME has been chosen as the preferred term.
4 A UEFA B Licence is a football coaching qualification that takes between 9–12 months to complete and allows holders to become assistant coaches at professional level. The UEFA B Licence is the precursor to the UEFA A Licence which is one qualification below the highest coaching qualification in football, the UEFA Pro-Licence. The A Licence takes 12 months to complete and has a taught element which lasts for 18 days. Upon successful completion, holders can coach youth teams up to 18 years of age, reserve teams in the highest division, and men's second tier clubs. Awards such as the UEFA B, UEFA A, and UEFA Pro-Licence are sometimes referred to as Higher Level Coach Education (HLCE) courses.
5 Semi-professional football clubs refer to those who compete in leagues below the four professional leagues, i.e. The English Premier League, The Championship, League One, and League Two. In non-league football, the National League is the highest tier, following jointly by National League North and National League South. In non-league football, clubs are regarded as semi-professional meaning that some, or most, of the players will be paid for playing football. However, the majority of players do not receive a 'liveable wage' for playing at semi-professional level and therefore rely on other employment.
6 The NCAA Division 1A is the top level of college football in the United States.

References

Adesina, Z. & Marocico, O. (2017) 'Is it easier to get a job if you're Adam or Mohamed?' BBC Online. 6 February. Available at: http://www.bbc.co.uk/news/uk-england-london-38751307.

Ahmed, A. (2012) *On Being Included: Racism and Diversity in Institutional Life*, Durham and London: Duke University Press.

Back, L., Crabbe, T. & Solomos, J. (2001) *The Changing Face of Football: Racism, Identity and Multiculture in the English Game*, Oxford: Berg.

Bains, J. & Johal, S. (1998) *Corner Flags and Corner Shops: The Asian Football Experience*, London: Gollancz.

Bains, J. & Patel, R. (1996) *Asians Can't Play Football*, Birmingham: D-Zine.

Bertrand, M. and Mullainathan, S. (2004) 'Are Emily and Greg more employable than Lakisha and Jamal? A field experiment on labor market discrimination', *The American Economic Review*, 94, 4: 991–1013.

Bonilla-Silva, E. (2003) *Racism without Racists: Color-blind Racism and the Persistence of Racial Inequality in the United States*, Lanham, MD: Rowman & Littlefield.

Bourdieu, P. (1984) *Distinction: A Social Critique of the Judgement of Taste*, London: Routledge.

Bradbury, S. (2001) *The New Football Communities: A Survey of Professional Football Clubs on Issues of Community, Ethnicity and Social Inclusion*, SNCCFR, University of Leicester.

Bradbury, S. (2014) 'Ethnic minorities and coaching in elite level football in England: A call to action'. Sports People's Think Tank, FARE Network and Loughborough University. Available at: http://www.farenet.org/wp-content/uploads/2014/11/We-speak-with-one-voice.pdf.

Bradbury, S. (2016) 'Levels of BME coaches in professional football in England: 2nd annual follow report'. A report from the Sport People's Think Tank in association with the Fare network and the University of Loughborough. Available at: http://thesptt.com/wp-content/uploads/2016/11/SB-final-report-screen3-1.pdf.

Bradbury, S. (2017a) 'Ethnic minorities and coaching in elite football in England: 2017 update: A report from the Sport People's Think Tank in association with the Fare network and the University of Loughborough'. Available at: http://thesptt.com/wp-content/uploads/2017/11/2017-SPTT-report-print.pdf.

Bradbury, S. (2017b) 'The under-representation and racialized experiences of minority coaches in high level coach education in professional football in England', in D. Hassan and C. Acton (eds) *Sport and Contested Identities: Contemporary Issues and Debates*, London: Routledge, pp. 11–29.

Burdsey, D. (2004a) 'Obstacle race? "Race", racism and the recruitment of British Asian professional footballer', *Patterns of Prejudice*, 38, 3: 279–299.

Burdsey, D. (2004b) 'One of the lads? Dual ethnicity and assimilated ethnicities in the careers of British Asian professional footballer', *Ethnic and Racial Studies*, 27, 5: 757–779.

Burdsey, D. (2007) *British Asians and Football: Culture, Identity, Exclusion*, Oxon: Routledge.

Burdsey, D. (2009) 'Forgotten fields? Centralising the experiences of minority ethnic men's football clubs in England', *Soccer and Society*, 10, 6: 704–721.

Burdsey, D. (2011) 'That joke isn't funny anymore: Racial microaggressions, colorblind ideology and the mitigation of racism in English men's first-class cricket', *Sociology of Sport Journal*, 28: 261–283.

Cohen, P. (1996) 'Homing devices', in V. Amit-Talai & C. Knowles (eds) *Re-situating Identities: The Politics of Race, Ethnicity and Culture*, Hadleigh: Broadview.

Coyle, D. (2010) *The Talent Code: Greatness Isn't Born, It's Grown*, London: Arrow Books.

Cunningham, G. & Sagas, M. (2005) 'Access discrimination in intercollegiate athletics', *Journal of Sport and Social Issues*, 29: 148–163.

Denscombe, M. (2003) *The Good Research Guide: For Small-scale Social Research Projects*, Berkshire: Open University Press.

Fanon, F. (1986) *Black Skin, White Masks*, London: Pluto Press.

Farenet (2014) 'Ethnic minorities and coaching in elite level football in England: A call to action'. Available at: http://www.farenet.org/wpcontent/uploads/2014/11/We-speak-with-one-voice.pdf.

Farrington, N., Hall, L., Kilvington, D., Price, J. & Saeed, A. (2015) *Sport, Racism and Social Media*, London: Routledge.

Farrington, N., Kilvington, D., Price, J. & Saeed, A. (2012) *Race, Racism and Sports Journalism*, London: Routledge.

Feagin, J. (2006) *Systemic Racism: A Theory of Oppression*, New York: Routledge.

Fleming, S. (2001) 'Racial science and South Asian and Black physicality', in B. Carrington and I. McDonald (eds) *'Race', Sport and British Society*, London: Routledge.

Fletcher, T., Piggott, D., North, J., Hylton, K., Gilbert, S. & Norman, L. (2014) 'Exploring the barriers to South Asian cricket players' entry and progression in coaching', Research Institute for Sport, Physical Activity and Leisure, Leeds Metropolitan University.

Hill, F. (2004) 'Shattering the glass ceiling: Blacks in coaching', *Black Issues in Higher Education*, 21, 4: 36–37.

Hill, J. & Azzarito, L. (2012) 'Representing valued bodies in PE: A visual inquiry with British Asian girls', *Soccer & Society*, 17, 3: 263–276.

Hylton, K. (2009) *'Race' and Sport: Critical Race Theory*, London: Routledge.

Hylton, K. (2010) 'How a turn to critical race theory can contribute to our understanding of "race", racism and anti-racism in sport', *Sociology of Sport*, 45, 3: 335–354.

Johal, S. (2001) 'Playing their own game: A South Asian football experience', in B. Carrington and I. MacDonald (eds) *'Race', Sport and British Society*, London: Routledge.

Johnson, N. (2007) 'Building an integrated society', in M. Weatherell, M. Lafleche and R. Berkeley (eds) *Identity, Ethnic Diversity and Community Cohesion*, London: SAGE.

Kilvington, D. (2012) 'The "Asian Frame", football and the sport media', *Networking Knowledge*, 5, 1: 201–218.

Kilvington, D. (2013) 'British Asians, covert racism and exclusion in English professional football', *Culture Unbound*, 5, 34: 587–606.

Kilvington, D. (2016) *British Asians, Exclusion and the Football Industry*, London: Routledge.

Kilvington, D. (2017) 'Two decades and little change: British Asians and calls for action', *Soccer and Society*, http://www.tandfonline.com/doi/full/10.1080/14660970.2017.1366902.

Kilvington, D. (2018) 'Does English football warrant the Rooney Rule? Assessing the thoughts of British Asian coaches', *Sport in Society*, https://www.tandfonline.com/doi/full/10.1080/17430437.2018.1490269.

Lawrence, S. (2017) 'A Critical Race Theory analysis of the English Premier League: Confronting the declining significance of "race" and racism myth', in R. Elliott (ed) *The English Premier League: A Socio-cultural Analysis*, London: Routledge, pp. 133–149.

LMA (2015) 'Black, Asian and Minority Ethnic Managers 2015'. Available at: http://www.leaguemanagers.com/documents/24/LMA_BAME_Managers_Report_Feb_2015.pdf.

Lusted, J. (2009) 'Playing games with "race": Understanding resistance to 'race' equality initiatives in English local football governance', *Soccer & Society*, 10, 6: 722–739.

Lusted, J. (2017) 'Understanding the varied responses to calls for a "Rooney Rule" in English football', in D. Kilvington and J. Price (eds) *Sport and Discrimination*, London: Routledge, 44–58.

McGuire, B., Monks, K. & Halsall, R. (2001) 'Young Asian males: Social exclusion and social injustice in British professional football?' *Culture, Sport and Society*, 4, 3: 65–80.

McIntosh, P. (2014) 'White privilege: Unpacking the invisible knapsack', in G. B. Rodman (ed) *The Race and Media Reader*, New York: Routledge, pp. 33–36.

Omi, M. & Winant, H. (1986) *Racial Formation in the United States: From the 1960s to the 1990s*, London: Routledge.

Pilkington, A. (2003) *Racial Disadvantage and Ethnic Diversity in Britain*, Basingstoke: Palgrave Macmillan.

Randhawa, K. (2011) 'Marrying passion with professionalism: Examining the future of British Asian football', in D. Burdsey (ed) *Race, Ethnicity and Football: Persisting Debates and Emergent Issues*, New York: Routledge.

Ratna, A. (2013) 'Intersectional plays of identity: The experiences of British Asian female footballers', *Sociological Research Online*, 18, 1: 108–117.

Ratna, A. (2014) '"Who are ya?" The national identities and belongings of British Asian football fans', *Patterns of Prejudice*, 48, 3: 286–308.

Regan, M. & Feagin, J. (2017) 'College sport leadership: Systematic racial employment barriers', in D. Kilvington and J. Price (eds) *Sport and Discrimination*, London: Routledge, pp. 15–31.

Rich, W. (2013) *The Post-Racial Society Is Here: Recognition, Critics and the Nation-State*, New York: Routledge.

Saeed, A. & Kilvington, D. (2011) 'British-Asians and racism within contemporary English football', *Soccer and Society*, 12, 5: 602–612.

Said, E. W. (1985) *Orientalism*, Harmondsworth: Peregrine.

Sartore, M. & Cunningham, G. (2006) 'Stereotypes, race, and coaching', *Journal of African American Studies*, 10, 2: 69–83.

Singer, J., Harrison, C. & Bukstein, S. (2010) 'A critical race analysis of the hiring process for head coaches in NCAA college football', *Journal of Intercollegiate Sport*, 3: 270–296.

Sporting Equals (2011) *Insight: BME Coaching in Sport*, London.

Sport England (2018) 'Active Lives Survey 2018'. Available at https://activelives.sportengland.org/.

Stangor, C. (2009) 'The study of stereotyping, prejudice and discrimination within social psychology', in T. D. Nelson (ed) *Handbook of Prejudice, Stereotyping and Discrimination*, New York: Taylor and Francis.

Strauss, A. L. & Corbin, J. (1990) *Basics of Qualitative Research*, London: SAGE.

Tinning, R. & Fitzclarence, L. (1992) 'Postmodern youth culture and the crisis in Australian secondary school physical education', *Quest*, 44, 3: 287–303.

Tomkiewicz, J., Brenner, O. & Adey-Bello, T. (1998) 'The impact of perceptions and stereotypes on managerial mobility of African Americans', *Journal of Social Psychology*, 138, 1: 88–92.

Zamudio, M. M., Russell, C., Rios, F. A. & Bridgeman, J. L. (2011) *Critical Race Theory Matters: Education and Ideology*, New York: Routledge.

Zarate, M. A. (2009) 'Racism in the 21st century', in T. D. Nelson (ed) *Handbook of Prejudice, Stereotyping and Discrimination*, New York: Taylor and Francis.

Part II

Racialised identities, diversity and intersectionality in sports coaching

Chapter 6

Finding the 'natural'

Talent identification and racialisation in sports coaching and selection practices in Australia

Brent McDonald and Ramón Spaaij

Introduction

At the beginning of the 2010 Australian Football League (AFL) season, the then CEO, Andrew Demetriou, launched the league with a speech about his imagination for the future of the competition, especially in relation to the diversity of its players. He stated:

> It'll be faster and more spectacular than ever before. We'll follow the game using technology that we can only dream about. We'll have players from all corners of the world. Imagine, Majak Daw captaining North Melbourne. Imagine AFL players regularly drafted from South Africa or the Pacific Islands. Imagine Kevin Sheedy at age 72 unveiling his latest batch of Western Sydney's version of the Baby Bombers. In 2020 not only will the game look very different, Australia will be a different country. More Australians than ever before will have either been born overseas or have a parent who was born overseas. Our country – and our game – will have moved further away from its Anglo-Celtic roots and reflect Australia's ever evolving cultural diversity.
>
> (Demetriou, 2010)

Demetriou, also at the time on the board of the Australian Multicultural Commission, is an advocate for sport's (and especially the AFL's) role in contributing to multiculturalism and social inclusion, and has a vision that every Australian, regardless of their ethnicity, can find a place to belong in the AFL. However, what we would like to focus on here is his particular 'dream' of who is actually playing the game. In this case the imagination is narrowed. Majak Daw is a Sudanese Australian with a refugee background, and represents a small but growing migrant diaspora in Australia. The talent pool to be drafted from lies not within Australian borders but more specifically the Pacific Islands and (black) Africa. This imagination is not necessarily a speculative one, rather it is based on the reality that the AFL had already established various programmes, academies and pathways from these locations and their related communities in Australia. What is noticeable though is that the imagination doesn't include Australia's populous neighbours (and much larger migrant groups) such as Indonesia, China or India.

Simply put, this is a 'white' dream about 'blackness' and resonates with Ghassan Hage's (1998) critique of 21st century multiculturalism in Australia, which sees the non-white other deployed and consumed according to the suitability of the migrant's abilities and the tastes of the dominant cultural force. The suitability for sport draws on the concept of the 'natural' which is positioned in the logic of the nature/nurture debate essentially inferring that ability is the result of a genetic or *'inherited predisposition to a particular task without effort or training'* (Cobley et al., 2011: 3). When the concept of the 'natural' intersects with the concept of 'race' the effect is to conflate individual performativity in sport to a racialised group. For example if the performance of a Black athlete is connected to 'natural' talent, then the genetic information responsible for this talent is conferred, via the erroneous concept of biological race, to all potential Black athletes.

The concept of the 'natural' is particularly pervasive when applied to bodies of diversity in 21st century Australia, as it draws on both the discredited legacy of biological race, and its contemporary colour-blind meritocracy. The 'natural' satisfies both constructs, as the meritocracy justifies the over-representation of 'black' bodies as the result of equal opportunity whilst the lingering biological position explains this as evidence of racial genetic difference and suitability to physical tasks. Indeed Demetriou's dream includes legendary coach, and pioneer advocate for Indigenous players, Kevin Sheedy. Sheedy, an evangelical supporter of the game, encourages the spread of AFL 'for community-spirited reasons, and also from the football slant. Some people smile when I say these things, but some of those young, tall, loose-hipped Africans have playing in the ruck stamped all over them' (Sheedy in Legge, 2010).

This chapter is an interrogation of the logic of Sheedy's throwaway statement and Demetriou's dream. We are interested in how talent is identified and developed in Australian sport. Talent identification (ID) and coaching have become tightly interlinked in the 21st century. Indeed, many talent ID actors are also coaches embedded in sport labour market pathways, simultaneously coaching and identifying. Placing these practices in a broader cultural context, we investigate the role of sport science as the underpinning logic that shapes where and who is targeted as potential talent.

We combine data from a series of earlier and ongoing research projects that we have undertaken to empirically illustrate and validate the arguments made. The first project examined the experiences of Pacific Islanders living in Australia and the place of rugby in their social trajectory and life choices. This project was multi-sited focusing on coaching (McDonald, 2016), pathways (McDonald, 2014), intervention programmes (McDonald et al., 2019) and life histories (Rodriguez & McDonald, 2013; McDonald & Rodriguez,

2014). The second project is a critical examination of sport science (methods, research dissemination, textbooks and other knowledge production) and racialisation, which concerns *'the process by which racial and neo-racial meanings are constructed, appropriated, recalibrated, and given utilitarian social valence'* (Ochonu, 2019: 6). This project involved ethnographic fieldwork in a sports science laboratory, interviews with sport scientists and research assistants, analysis of textbooks and sport science publications, and focus groups with sport science students. Finally, we draw on data from 'Participation versus performance: Managing gender, cultural diversity and (dis)ability in junior sport' (Farquharson et al., 2018; Spaaij et al., 2018a, 2018b, 2019; Schaillée et al., in press). This study aimed to identify how diversity is understood, experienced and managed in local sports clubs (and particularly junior sports clubs). This project was funded by the Australian Research Council (ARC) and conducted by four universities in partnership with the Victorian Health Promotion Foundation, Australian Football League, and Centre for Multicultural Youth. The project worked closely with a range of local sports clubs throughout the research process, and produced rich data on the intersection between 'race', racialisation, talent identification and coaching.

In the remainder of the chapter we explain the application of Critical Race Theory to the scientific production of 'race' and some of its consequences. Following this, we discuss how the discourse of racialised science pervades the sport industries in Australia, especially talent identification programmes, before considering the effects of this discourse on practices of sport organisations, coaches and players. Finally, we conclude by recommending that sport organisations and coaches critically reflect on and challenge their own privilege and taken-for-granted knowledge in order to de-bunk the natural and the biological racialisation it draws upon.

Critical race theory and biological racism

This chapter utilises a Critical Race Theory (CRT) framework. CRT allows the critique of the *'complex personal, cultural, institutional and structural arrangements'* at work in the relationship between 'race', sport and society (Hylton, 2018: 7). In particular CRT offers insight into the ways 'race' and racism appear in the processes of racialisation, which enables a *'sharper focus on the past and present utilisation of racial categories, both implied and explicit'* (Hylton, 2009: 6). In the context of sport in 21st century Australia, CRT is powerful as it has the capacity to challenge the overwhelming dominant ideologies surrounding sport especially *'meritocracy, colour-blindness, race neutrality, objectivity, and ahistoricism'* (Hylton, 2018: 7). This is particularly true as both sport and sport science are overwhelming organised by and representative of the interests and agendas of white men (Hylton, 2018). Through highlighting the invisible whiteness related to leadership, management, coaching and research design, CRT is useful in placing 'race' as central to the structural arrangements and social experiences in sport. By focusing on 'race' in both talent ID practices and sport science research we are able to consider the huge cultural influence both institutions are able to effect in the Australian context without losing sight of the way race intersects with other social factors such as gender, class, educational background and physical or sporting ability.

Scientific and cultural discourses operate in a type of loop, continually feeding on each other (Hartigan, 2008). Hence popular concepts of 'race' (involving biological and cultural notions) inform scientific method and design, and the findings of this science are then fed back into a cultural context to validate the original popular position. In many cases 'race' is not explicitly referred to which is a process that Gillborn (2016: 366) describes as the absent presence of 'race', that it is *'hidden in the background'*. As such, sports practitioners such as talent identifiers, coaches, journalists, and indeed players, don't have to understand or utilise genomics in order for racialised science to directly and indirectly affect their actions and choices.

The discourse of biological racialisation is particularly apparent in a variety of media outputs, both those from within and outside Australia. Global sport media and the over-represented presence of black bodies in high-profile sporting events (Olympics, World Championships) and competitions (NBA, NFL, European football) provides audiences inferentially primed to ideas of biological race with the evidence to support such beliefs. The link between biological determinism and black athleticism is well documented in a variety of English language media sources including Australian (Hughey & Goss, 2015). Kowal & Frederic (2012) examined Australian newspapers for genetic discourse, racial prejudice and Indigenous Australians and Torres Strait Islanders. They found articles supporting both anti-deterministic and deterministic arguments with the three major topics being disease, sporting ability and addiction. Coram (2007: 406) goes further suggesting that the Australian media's coverage of Indigenous players creates a racial other through positively intended narratives of 'race' difference and dominance and more *'ambivalent constructs'* evoking the savage, the mimic, and the child.

Racialised science has informed various institutional practices and has therefore contributed to the phenomenon of the over-representation of racialised populations in these institutions. For example, racial profiling techniques used by law enforcement result in statistically racialised prison populations (see for example Henne & Shah, 2015; McDonald et al., 2019); epidemiologists employ racial categories in diagnosis and treatment of diseases that are seen to reside within certain racialised populations (Outram & Ellison, 2006; Hartigan, 2008); deterministic discourses (exemplified in texts such as *The Bell Curve*) influence the way that predominantly white teachers engage with diversity, producing different educational trajectories for differently racialised children (Picower, 2009; Azzarito & Harrison, 2008). For example, Maori researcher Brendan Hokowhitu (2004) has written at length about the funnelling of young Maori students into physical education and 'hands on' subjects and away from 'intellectual' classes such as maths and science. Gillborn (2016) warns of the potential re-inscription of biological race in education through the science of new geneism which he suggests threatens to bring back genetic determinism and provides the conditions for the revival of eugenics.

Based on the above it should not be a surprise that an institution such as sport would be similarly influenced by racialised science (St Louis, 2003; Carrington, 2010; Hoberman, 1997). Hawkins's (2010) work on black athletes in American college sports demonstrates with clarity the way that racial ideology had produced and continues to produce the idea that black success in sport is a result of 'natural' ability based in advantageous biology that essentialises black men (see also Hoberman, 1997; Carrington, 2010). At the level of structure entire sport industries rely on and create pathways for their labour and at the level of agency large numbers of young men choose to chase the sporting dream as part of their biological destiny. Deterministic thinking grounded in biology also produces the phenomenon of stacking or positional segregation of over-represented racial groups (see for Australian examples Hallinan et al., 1999; Hallinan & Judd, 2009), and a corresponding absence from leadership and post-playing career opportunities such as coaching, management and the media (Bradbury, 2013; Bradbury et al., 2014; Hallinan & Judd, 2009).

Kevin Hylton (2015) discusses the ways in which various forms of 'race' are activated and perpetuated in physical education discourses and the subsequent practices that emanate from these discourses. He demonstrates clearly how students studying to become PE teachers simultaneously draw on a range of explanations for racialised athletic performance that are colour-blind, valourising of the Black athlete, and relying on reductionist notions of biological difference. Racialised science is also evident in Australian physical education discourses. McDonald (2013) examined twenty years' worth of textbooks utilised as part of high school PE curriculum to find that just over two thirds discussed 'race' as a factor that influenced performance in sport. Most of this usage drew on the conception of 'race' as 'biologically real' and used racialised science to explain the differences in athletic performance between racialised populations, predominantly 'why blacks beat whites' (Malpeli et al., 2000 in McDonald, 2013: 189).

This is exemplified further at a national level of sport governance. Accordingly, maintaining Australian sport's continued prominence internationally will require 'innovative talent identification techniques' to keep up with overseas initiatives, which are able to 'recruit young athletes of different ethnic/racial background, who possess certain physical characteristics that give them a performance advantage in several sports over athletes of

Anglo-Celtic origin' (Bloomfield, 2002 in Sotiriadou, 2010: 18). As one of the most multicultural nations in the world it is difficult to make sense of Bloomfield's position, unless one understands that he is referring to a particular 'ethnic/racial background', namely from Africa. At the time of Bloomfield's quote many European countries were represented by athletes through post-colonial migration from Africa. Whilst Black African migration to Australia has a long history, it has only accelerated in recent decades, especially the increasing numbers of refugee and humanitarian settlers who have come to Australia from Africa (Hugo, 2009).

Talent identification and discourse

Talent identification happens at all levels of sport in Australia. This includes scouts from super rich clubs in Europe and America hoping to discover new sporting labour; governmental agencies such as the Australian Institute of Sport (AIS) and the various national and state sporting organisations; professional sport clubs and leagues and their recruiting personnel who develop relationships with community and grassroots sports clubs; private schools with scholarships on offer in order to bolster their first teams' performance; and indeed even at the interpersonal level when one invites a new acquaintance (who looks likely) to 'come down to training to have a run'.

The relationship between talent identification, coaching and sport science is undeniable, and the latter continues to develop novel ways of locating talent. Most recently we have seen the rise of sport genomics, which offers application at both ends of the sport labour market. At one end it offers the '*potential application of knowledge about the genetic characteristics of elite athletes*' providing an '*enhancement of talent identification programmes*' (Heffernan et al., 2015: 464). At the other end is the commercialisation of genomic testing whereby one can apply the technology to the self in order to ascertain one's predisposition for a particular sport (Collier, 2012).

Sport genomics in itself is not necessarily problematic. Elite sports clearly demand that their players are exceptional in relation to certain physiological characteristics such as endurance, explosive speed and power, or vertical leap, not to mention conceptual and tactical game sense, motivation and competitiveness, and ability to work under pressure. The problem that sports genomics and other sports sciences pose is their tendency to produce racialised science. This racialisation occurs at several levels of research design, method and knowledge dissemination. The beginning point is often found in the rationale for the research in the first place, namely to answer the apparently '*enduring and fascinating question in exercise science regarding the dominance of specific populations groups at the extreme ends of the competitive running spectrum*' (Tucker et al., 2013: 545) and to '*identify potential ethnic differences in the genetic predisposition to athletic performance*' (Pitsiladis et al., 2016: 186).

Subsequently 'race' or 'ethnicity' is used as a controlling variable in participant recruitment. For example, a systematic review of literature focusing on the ACTN3 gene, colloquially known as the 'speed gene', revealed that of the 35 articles examined, 34 controlled for ethnicity (Caucasian, African or Asian) (Eynon et al., 2013). The population categories used here have a striking resemblance to previously used continentally based racial groups. This is significant because, despite the fact that there is no genetic basis to 'race' and that it is a *'meaningless marker of anything'* (Editorial, 2005, 903), the effect is to reify 'race' as scientifically real.

Finally, in relation to knowledge production such research outputs revive and reify the scientifically discredited concept of 'race' as being based in biology and genetics rather than being socially constructed categories. In doing so they take highly complex physiological explanations of individual athletic performance and essentialise entire racialised populations. In other words the reductionist and popular notions of 'race' existing within Australian society are validated and as such entire socially constructed population groups become pre-disposed to exceptional performance in particular sports. Two points need to be made here. The first is that biological racialisation has the effect of reducing Indigenous Australians, Pacific Islanders and black Africans to the homogenous category of the black athlete, an athlete seemingly in exclusive possession of a genetic makeup designed to excel in sport. The second is that racialised thinking is not limited to sport but exists across a variety of fields including health, education and crime (McDonald et al., 2019). This is significant because it strengthens the 'natural athlete' narrative. Hence in a racialised society like Australia, the application of sports science and genomics to talent identification, coaching and selection processes in sport is not necessarily explicit. Racialised scientific knowledge underpins the conscious and subconscious decision making of sport coaches and talent scouts. In other words those responsible for targeting particular black communities do not perform genetic tests nor do they necessarily read or understand the racialised science, rather the discourse produced from this science recreates and validates the concept of biological race and it is the subsequent reductionist logic that sport organisations apply in their search for talented sports labour.

The effects of finding the 'natural'

The effects of the search for the 'natural' as informed by racialised athletic science is threefold. At an organisational level in relation to programmes and pathways, at an interpersonal level in relation to coaches and scouts sourcing talent, and at an embodied level in relation to individuals' explanations of their own performance and ability. Below we discuss each level in turn.

Organisational level

Sport organisations and clubs make strategic decisions about where to spend their resources to recruit potential talent. Informed by the discourse of biological race, sports simultaneously operate from the perspective of enlightened and inferential racism (Hallinan & Judd, 2009). That is, that the positioning of the black athlete in Australian sport is inherently positive and celebrated; sport provides the space for the expression of 'natural' ability. Yet this expression is limited to athletic labour and mostly does not include managerial, coaching or leadership roles.

The effects of the racialisation and deterministic thinking can be seen in the organisation of many sports talent identification practices in Australia, as reflected in this comment from basketball development director James Kerr: 'They (African youth) are going to be amazing athletes if they get the right support and exposure. They can change the face of the sport in Australia without a doubt' (Kerr in Topsfield, 2018). The AFL, for example, has fast tracked African Australian youth into their development academies due to their 'incredible athleticism' and their capacity to 'add a unique and exciting element' to the game (Cherny, 2016). This is mirrored by other sports such as soccer and athletics through the creation of African pathways programmes (Larkin, 2018). Rugby union and league have established links with Pasifika communities and talent programmes and pathways (McDonald, 2014). These pathways also stretch into the education system, either in the form of rugby programmes as education (McDonald et al., 2019), or in the form of sporting scholarships to elite schools around the country (Lutton, 2010).

Interpersonal level

These effects are not limited to elite sport; they also permeate interpersonal relations within sub-elite and grassroots sport systems. This is evidenced by the language used by coaches at the grassroots level, who regularly make explicit reference to black athleticism. For example, a coach (White male, 40s) in a grassroots cricket club explained:

> 'The amazing thing is these [black African] children are quite talented as well, and for say high performance people in cricket that see these tall strapping strong Sudanese boys, it's very attractive'.
>
> (White male, 40s)

In a similar vein, a basketball coach (White male, 40s) made explicit reference to genetics:

> With the South Sudanese kids in particular, 90% of them, and there's a big number, 90% of the boys are fantastic basketballers. Like, why is that? They are just awesome. So, you just look at these kids and they're so athletic and so

fast and it's obviously a genetic thing and they play a lot. [...] If we were to rank our teams one to 15, you literally could have in your first three teams of nine boys, 27 kids, you could literally put 25 Sudanese boys, if it was just purely on skill. So, then you face this issue of well OK, we really want to cap it at two. [...] You're like, well... some of the coaches love it. We'll win every game but then some of them have a few issues with reliability and communication, they won't turn up.

Similar to the aforementioned racial dynamics in elite sport, this coach limits his appreciation of black athleticism primarily to athletic labour. His reference to reliability issues – a common concern expressed by community sports coaches about culturally diverse participants and their families (Spaaij et al., 2018a) – suggests that this appreciation does not extend to managerial, coaching or leadership roles. This idea of black people as limited to athletic labour is likely to create barriers to black coaches being seen as legitimate.

Attesting to this prevailing sentiment of 'natural' ability, a volunteer (White female, 40s) at a grassroots AFL club observed with a sense of irony:

'Well a lot of people who you might consider to be more conventional and more narrow thinking in this club have really embraced it [cultural diversity] because they will say things like "got to get those Black kids [of African background] here because they're really fast" [laughs]'.

(White, Female, 40s)

These comments by coaches and volunteers reveal that the search for the 'natural' extends beyond the confines of sport science or elite sport, right down into the grassroots level. In such cases, it is often biologically determined racial stereotypes around black African Australians, Pasifika and Indigenous Australians and their 'natural' ability to excel in sport that lead grassroots clubs to reach out to these demographics (Spaaij et al., 2014). In contrast, these clubs are generally less likely to reach out to population groups that are considered less 'naturally gifted' or 'built' for high performance in sport, notably South Asian migrants such as Australia's Karen community (with the exception of South Asian Australians in cricket) (cf. Thangaraj, 2015).

Embodied level

Finally, the discourse of racialised athletic ability is apparent at an embodied level. Israel Folau, who is Australian of Tongan ancestry, is dual international for Australia in rugby league and rugby union who also played AFL for expansion team Greater Western Sydney. Both he, and Karmichael Hunt (also of Pasifika ancestry), were signed on enormous contracts to launch expansion teams in AFL and both were broadly deemed failures. For many, their failure was as a result of their inability to adapt to the physiological requirements of AFL which could be considered a much more aerobically demanding sport than rugby league or union. What is interesting is that both utilised genetics and science to justify their apparent inability in AFL and exceptional talent in rugby (Australian Associated Press, 2014). In an interview Folau contended:

> With my heritage and background, we're not built as athletes to be good runners. We're natural athletes with explosive power. I've got to work on my aerobic capacity, which is improving. I guess that's part of our genes that come from our heritage as Polynesian people. We're built for more explosive, powerful stuff rather than aerobic running. Some of my trainers within the NRL [National Rugby League] and now the AFL have been saying it and I see it as being true. A lot of Polynesian athletes, they struggle aerobically but when it comes to being quick and powerful they've certainly got that.
> (Conn, 2012)

Folau makes sense of his aerobic struggles through the support of the 'expert' voice, in this case trainers, who it would seem have provided some genetically based explanation regarding sporting suitability. Such an understanding is not limited to elite athletes. Indeed, as we have suggested, this type of racialised athletic science pervades sport at all levels and the black athletes present. The following two examples come from Pasifika men playing in grassroots rugby codes when explaining the enormous over-representation of Pasifika in the codes:

> *I think genetics wise, it's just more suited to an Islander sort of body shape, because we're all big boned, we're explosive off the mark, we can take impact and you know, got hard heads. So it's probably more suited, that's why I think they're natural talents, because their bodies are suited to the sport. Where you've got your normal European kid is a bit smaller, has to work harder, like has to go to gym hard and that sort of stuff to build the body mass to equal these (Pacific Islander) blokes.*
> (Samoan Australia, male, 30s)

> *It's definitely in the blood for Pacific Islanders, this sport is definitely in the blood of Pacific Islanders. I think that's why I struggle with footy (AFL), because we've got – and it's been proven in some studies that have been done that we have a larger makeup of fast twitch fibres, which allows us to sprint faster, be stronger, on short distances, versus running long distances, we just burn out too easily. So structurally this game suits us better.*
> (Cook Islander, male, 30s)

Yet again both respondents draw on scientific language and research to make sense of Pasifika over-representation. In doing so, the reductionist category of 'Pacific Islander' is meaningfully and biologically othered to 'European' and presumably other categories of ethnicity. The scattering of authoritative scientific language through these quotes indicates the discursive relationship between concepts of 'race', talent for sports, and the processes of racialisation. Considering the hegemonic nature of this scientific discourse, it is not surprising to see large numbers of boys and young men of Indigenous, Pasifika and African ethnicity concentrating on sport as a vehicle to some form of social mobility. Indeed sport is one of the few spaces in Australian society where successful role models from these communities are regularly seen, and there is no doubt that for most of these young people sport is an enjoyable pursuit. To become a professional athlete affords these individuals with symbolic and cultural capital and they become a source of pride for their communities (Rodriguez et al., 2015). However the 'natural' explanation to success renders invisible the fact that coaches and sport organisations actively target these populations, and similarly fails to recognise the levels of individual commitment, sacrifice, time and determination that the successful players all make. In the context of the sports labour market it is clear that the possibility of 'making it' trumps the probability. The Black athlete in Australia becomes what Brooks and McKail (2008: 370) describe as the *'preferred worker'*, that is niche labour that allows the maximisation of cost efficiency and profit. Coaches and talent spotters exist in the same market, and make strategic choices of where to best maximise their efforts and resources in finding talent. Backed by racialised ideas of athletic performance it is therefore not surprising that they target groups who are really 'ready to play'. In the next section, we reflect on the implications of the discourse of racialised athletic ability.

Conclusion

In this chapter, we have argued that the access and opportunities to succeed in sport are facilitated via a system of coaching and talent identification that bases its practice on ideas tied to biological 'race' and deterministic thinking. Underpinned by the logic of 'race' and the (perceived) inherent suitability of particular groups of people for particular sports, sport organisations and coaches actively target such populations in the hope of finding the 'natural'. In the Australian context, the 'natural' reflects a recolonisation of racialised bodies and the affects that inform the choices of the broader ethno-racialised communities. The 'natural athlete' narrative extends to coaching at all levels of sport, from elite to grassroots, and is strengthened by racialised sport science.

How can this dynamic be challenged and changed? Our analysis indicates that any effective challenge to the discourse of racialised athletic ability needs to be multi-pronged. We call for sport organisations and coaches to critically challenge their own privilege and taken-for-granted knowledge in order to de-bunk the natural and the biological racism it draws upon. With regard to coaching and talent identification, there is an urgent need to include elements of critical inquiry into 'race' in coach education and training programmes. As an absent presence, racialised practices around natural ability are accompanied by a deficit discourse in relation to psychological characteristics such as reliability, work ethic and decision making. Sport organisations not only need to provide education to coaches to address unconscious racial bias, they also need to create pathways for black athletes to occupy positions of power in sport post playing career, so that the level of representation in those playing the sport is mirrored in managerial, coaching and other roles. This would at least have the immediate effect of countering the current deficit position of such racialised practices.

Moreover, the discourse can be challenged at the micro level in everyday sports practices. For example, in one of our studies we observed a concerned parent querying the coach of his son's grassroots sports team why he had positionally segregated black and white children on the team during a match. The coach suggested, drawing on the 'natural athlete' narrative, that the black children were naturally better suited to attacking positions because they could run fast and had better technical skills, whereas the white children made more dependable and intelligent defenders. The parent challenged the coach's thinking, pointing out what he had learnt from our research (which had been presented to club members in a public forum). This led the coach to acknowledge his own racial bias and change the way he determined players' field positions to a rotation system.

Our analysis shows how, ultimately, racialised sport science fuels and reproduces the discourse of natural ability. The discourse produced from this science recreates and validates the concept of biological race and it is the subsequent reductionist logic that sport organisations apply in their search for talented sports labour. It also strengthens our fascination with the search for the 'natural' in elite performance. There is thus a need to systematically challenge racialised sport science on a variety of fronts including research design and knowledge production, in the classrooms where sport science is taught and new experts are created, in coach training and in talent identification practices. This would also necessitate listening to the voices, stories and experiences of black athletes and coaches so that sport organisations work *with* and not *on* these communities.

References

Australian Associated Press (2014). Karmichael Hunt says his 'genetics' couldn't cope with AFL. *The Guardian*, 28 August. Retrieved from: https://www.theguardian.com/sport/2014/aug/28/karmichael-hunt-leaves-afl-super-rugby.

Azzarito, L. & Harrison Jr, L. (2008). 'White men can't jump': Race, gender and natural athleticism. *International Review for the Sociology of Sport* 43 (4): 347–364.

Bradbury, S. (2013). Institutional racism, whiteness and the under-representation of minorities in leadership positions in football in Europe. *Sport in Society* 14 (3): 296–314.

Bradbury, S., van Sterkenburg, J., & Mignon, P. (2014). *Cracking the glass ceiling: Levels of representation of 'visible' minorities and women in leadership and coaching in* football in Europe and the experiences of elite level 'visible' minority coaches. Loughborough, UK: Loughborough University and the Football Against Racism in Europe (FARE) Network.

Brooks, S. & McKail, M. (2008). A theory of the preferred worker: A structural explanation from Black male dominance in basketball. *Critical Sociology* 34 (3): 369–387.

Carrington, B. (2010). *Race, sport and politics: The sporting black diaspora*. London: Sage.

Cherny, D. (2016). AFL adds African players to academy to fast-track development. *The Age*, 11 September. Retrieved from: https://www.theage.com.au/sport/afl/afl-adds-african-players-to-academy-to-fasttrack-development-20160911-grdqic.html.

Cobley, S., Schorer, J., & Baker, J. (2011). Identification and development of sport talent: A brief introduction to a growing field of research and practice. In J. Baker, S. Cobley & J. Schorer (eds.), *Talent identification and development in sport: International perspectives* (pp. 1–10). London: Routledge.

Collier, R. (2012). Genetic tests for athletic ability: Science or snake oil? *Canadian Medical Association Journal* 184 (1): 43–44.

Conn, M. (2012). Israel Folau believes he faces a genetic disadvantage in endurance sports. *The Daily Telegraph*, 15 June. Retrieved from: https://www.news.com.au/sport/afl/israel-folau-believes-he-faces-a-genetic-disadvantage-in-endurance-sports/news-story/94f0c2474bc0414e951fa1f006246962.

Coram, S. (2007). Race formations (evolutionary hegemony) and the 'aping' of the Australian Indigenous athlete. *International Review for the Sociology of Sport* 42 (4): 391–409.

Demetriou, A. (2010). AFL launches 2010 season. 19 March 2010. Retrieved from: http://www.goldcoastfc.com.au/news/2010-03-19/afl-launches-2010-season.

Editorial. (2005). Illuminating BiDil. *Nature Biotechnology* 23(8): 903.

Eynon, N., Hanson, E., Lucia, A., Houweling, P., Garton, F., North, K., & Bishop, D. (2013). Genes for elite power and sprint performance: ACTN3 leads the way. *Sports Medicine* 43: 803–817.

Farquharson, K., Spaaij, R., Gorman, S., Jeanes, R., Lusher, D., & Magee, J. (2018). Managing racism on the field in Australian junior sport. In P. Essed, K. Farquharson, K. Pillay & E. J. White (Eds.), *Relating worlds of racism: Dehumanisation, belonging, and the normativity of European whiteness* (pp. 165–189). Houndmills: Palgrave Macmillan.

Gillborn, D. (2016). Softly, softly: Genetics, intelligence and the hidden racism of the new geneism. *Journal of Education Policy* 31 (4): 365–388.

Hage, G. (1998). *White nation: Fantasies of white supremacy in a multicultural society*. New York: Routledge.

Hallinan, C., Bruce, T., & Coram, S. (1999). Up front and beyond the centre line. *International Review for the Sociology of Sport* 34 (4): 369–383.

Hallinan, C. & Judd, B. (2009). Race relations, Indigenous Australia and the social impact of professional Australian football. *Sport in Society* 12 (9): 1220–1235.

Hartigan Jr, J. (2008). Is race still socially constructed? The recent controversy over race and medical genetics. *Science as Culture* 17 (2): 163–193.

Hawkins, B. (2010). *The new plantation: Black athletes, college sports, and predominantly white NCAA institutions*. New York: Palgrave Macmillan.

Heffernan, S., Kilduff, L., Day, S., Pitsiladis, Y., & Williams, A. (2015). Genomics in rugby union: A review and future prospects. *European Journal of Sport Science* 15 (6): 460–468.
Henne, K. & Shah, R. (2015). Unveiling white logic in criminological research: An intertextual analysis. *Contemporary Justice Review* 18 (2): 105–120.
Hoberman, J. (1997). *Darwin's athletes: How sport has damaged black America and preserved the myth of race.* Boston MA: Houghton Mifflin.
Hokowhitu, B. (2004). Physical beings: Stereotypes, sport and 'physical education' of New Zealand Maori. In J. Mangan and A. Ritchie (Eds.), *Ethnicity, sport, identity: Struggles for status* (pp. 192–218). London: Routledge.
Hughey, M. & Goss, D. (2015). A level playing field? Media constructions of athletics, genetics and race. *The Annals of the American Academy* 661 (September): 182–211.
Hugo, G. (2009). Migration between Africa and Australia: A demographic perspective: Background paper for African Australians: A review of human rights and social inclusion issues. Sydney: Australian Human Rights Commission.
Hylton, K. (2018). *Contesting 'race' and sport: Shaming the colour line.* New York: Routledge.
Hylton, K. (2015). 'Race' talk! Tensions and contradictions in sport and PE. *Physical Education & Sport Pedagogy* 20 (5): 503–516.
Hylton, K. (2009). *Race and sport: Critical race theory.* New York: Routledge.
Kowal, E. and Frederic, G. (2012). Race, genetic determinism and the media: An exploratory study of media coverage of genetics and Indigenous Australians. *Genomics, Society and Policy* 8 (2): 1–14.
Larkin, S. (2018). New Socceroos the latest African Australians to blaze sporting pathway. *The West Australian*, 16 October. Retrieved from: https://thewest.com.au/sport/new-socceroos-the-latest-african-australians-to-blaze-sporting-pathway-ng-b88992469z.
Legge, K. (2010). How the west will be won. *The Australian*, 8 June. Retrieved from: https://www.theaustralian.com.au/life/weekend-australian-magazine/how-the-west-will-be-won/news-story/beda0c0f3b0e3f7c2e711d00bb675f5a.
Lutton, P. (2010). Rugby students commodities to be traded. *The Brisbane Times*, 14 April. Retrieved from: https://www.brisbanetimes.com.au/sport/rugby-union/rugby-students-commodities-to-be-traded-20100412-s3zc.html.
McDonald, B. (2016). Coaching whiteness: Stories of Pacifica Exotica in Australian high school rugby. *Sport, Education and Society* 21 (3): 465–482.
McDonald, B. (2014). Developing 'home-grown' talent: Pacific Island rugby labour and the Victorian rugby union. *International Journal for the History of Sport* 31 (11): 1332–1344.
McDonald, B. (2013). The reproduction of biological 'race' through physical education textbooks and curriculum. *European Physical Education Review* 19(2): 183–198.
McDonald, B. & Rodriguez, L. (2014). 'It's our meal ticket': Pacific bodies, labour and mobility in Australia. *Asia Pacific Journal of Sport and Social Science* 3 (3): 236–249.
McDonald, B., Rodriguez, L., & George, J.R. (2019). 'If it weren't for rugby I'd be in prison now': Pacific Islanders, rugby and the production of 'natural' spaces. *Journal of Ethnic and Migration Studies* 45 (11): 1919–1935. doi:10.1080/1369183X.2018.1492909.

Ochonu, M. E. (2019). Looking for race: Pigmented pasts and colonial mentality in 'non racial' Africa. In P. Essed, K. Farquharson, K. Pillay & E. J. White (Eds.), *Relating worlds of racism* (pp. 3–37). Houndmills: Palgrave Macmillan.

Outram, S. & Ellison, G. (2006). Improving the use of race and ethnicity in genetic research: A survey of instructions to authors in genetics journals. *Science Editor* 29 (3): 78–81.

Picower, B. (2009). The unexamined whiteness of teaching: How white teachers maintain and enact dominant racial ideologies. *Race, Ethnicity and Education* 12: 197–215.

Pitsiladis, Y., Tanaka, M., Eynon, N., Bouchard, C., North, K., Williams, A., Collins, M., Moran, C., Britton, S., Fuku, N., Ashley, E., Klissouras, V., Lucia, A., Ahmetov, I., de Geus, E., Alsavrafi, M., & AthlomeProject Consortium. (2016). Athlome Project Consortium: A concerted effort to discover genomic and other 'omic' markers of athletic performance. *Physiol Genomics* 48 (3): 183–190.

Rodriguez, L., George, J., & McDonald, B. (2015). Constructing legitimate and illegitimate Pasifika masculinities in the global diaspora. *Culture, Society and Masculinities* 7 (2): 102–121.

Rodriguez, L. & McDonald, B. (2013). After the whistle: Issues impacting the health and wellbeing of Polynesian players off the field. *Asia-Pacific Journal of Health, Sport and Physical Education* 4 (3): 201–215.

Schaillée, H., Spaaij, R., Jeanes, R., & Theeboom, M. (In press). Knowledge translation practices, enablers, and constraints: Bridging the research–practice divide in sport management. *Journal of Sport Management*. doi:10.1123/jsm.2018-0175.

Sotiriadou, P. (2010). The Australian sport system and its stakeholders: Development of cooperative relationships. In K. Toohey and T. Taylor (Eds.), *Australian sport: Antipodean waves of change* (pp. 6–24). London: Routledge.

Spaaij, R., Farquharson, K., Gorman, S., Jeanes, R., Lusher, D., Guerra, C., White, S., & Ablett, E. (2018a). *Participation versus performance: Managing (dis)ability, gender and cultural diversity in junior sport*. Melbourne: Centre for Multicultural Youth.

Spaaij, R., Magee, J., Farquharson, K., Gorman, S., Jeanes, R., Lusher, D., & Storr, R. (2018b). Diversity work in community sport organizations: Commitment, resistance and institutional change. *International Review for the Sociology of Sport* 53 (3): 278–295.

Spaaij, R., Farquharson, K., Magee, J., Jeanes, R., Lusher, D., & Gorman, S. (2014). A fair game for all? How community sports clubs in Australia deal with diversity. *Journal of Sport and Social Issues* 38 (4): 346–365.

Spaaij, R., Lusher, D., Jeanes, R., Farquharson, K., Gorman, S., & Magee, J. (2019). Participation-performance tension and gender affect recreational sports clubs' engagement with children and young people with diverse backgrounds and abilities. *PLoS ONE* 14 (4): e0214537.

St Louis, B. (2003). Sport, genetics and the 'natural athlete': The resurgence of racial science. *Body and Society* 9 (2): 75–95.

Thangaraj, S. (2015). *Desi hoop dreams: Pickup basketball and the making of Asian American masculinity*. New York: New York University Press.

Topsfield, J. (2018). Red Roos disappointed after Sudanese basketball tournament cancelled. *The Age*, 21 July. Retrieved from: https://www.theage.com.au/politics/victoria/red-roos-disappointed-after-sudanese-basketball-tournament-cancelled-20180720-p4zsmb.html+.

Tucker, R., Santos-Concejero, J., & Collins, M. (2013). The genetic basis for elite running performance. *British Journal of Sports Medicine* 47: 545–549.

Chapter 7

From freedom to oppression?
A Freirean perspective on coaching and indigenous players' journeys to the NRL and AFL

Richard Light and John Evans

Introduction

This chapter draws on a three-year ARC (Australian Research Council) funded study that inquired into the journeys of Indigenous Australians from growing up in local communities to playing at the most elite levels in their sports of rugby league and Australian football, also referred to as Australian rules football (Evans & Light, 2016). The term Indigenous is used to collectively refer to those who identify as Aboriginal and Torres Strait Islanders in Australia. The term Aboriginal refers to people who are indigenous to mainland Australia and Tasmania. In our study the participants referred to themselves as Indigenous and Aboriginal people but described their culture and way of playing sport most commonly as being Aboriginal. The study identified two distinct phases in the participants' development into elite athletes which were (1) the development of expertise and a distinctive Aboriginal style of play up until around the age of 13 (see Light & Evans, 2017) and, (2) a process of cultural transitioning into the global culture of professional sport (Light et al., 2017). The first phase of the participants' development involved learning through playing informal, competitive games from very young ages and playing a range of different sports (Light & Evans, 2018a). From around the age of 13 their movement towards, and then into, professional sport presented significant challenges for them when compared to how they had developed the foundations of expertise in small communities where Aboriginal culture formed a prominent influence (Light & Evans, 2018b). The cultural transitioning (see Ryba et al., 2016) also involved adapting to radical changes in the coaching pedagogy that shaped their learning. It involved moving from often having no formal coaching and learning through informal play to the highly structured coaching of professional sport and moving from play to work.

We begin with a brief outline of Paulo Freire's work (see 1996) to compare what Freire describes as the objectivist, anti-dialogic 'banking' education that operates as a form of oppression with the dialogic, 'problem-posing' approach that he proposes in which learning is subjective and liberating. We then identify how learning through open and equal interaction with peers and relatives in communities influenced by Aboriginal culture that supported this approach in our study was dialogic and how it contrasted with the anti-dialogic, structured approaches to coaching they experienced as they moved into professional environments. Following this we examine how the ways in which adjusting to this anti-dialogic approach to coaching presented a significant challenge for the participants due to its radical contrast with the implicit pedagogy of learning as children, shaped by Aboriginal culture. While this may often characterise a shift from youth sport to professional sport in non-Indigenous settings it was far more marked in this study due to the nature of sport as an Aboriginal cultural practice and its role in the participants' lives.

Contrasting coaching pedagogy

Drawing on Freire's (1996) *Pedagogy of the Oppressed* we use his notion of dialogic and anti-dialogic pedagogy to identify the radical differences for the 16 participants between learning as children and the anti-dialogic pedagogy of professional sport. Freire's work and the critical pedagogy developed from it focus on the use of dialogic pedagogy in schools to liberate students from the limitations, constraints on thinking and oppression of formal schooling created by the 'banking' approach that dominates formal education. Somewhat in reverse, this chapter examines how the participants had been empowered through learning to play 'footy' (rugby league and Australian football) from an early age through dialogic learning and how they had to adapt to the challenge of the inherently anti-dialogic pedagogy of professional sport. The term 'footy' is commonly used in Australia in reference to Australian rules football, rugby league and rugby union and to the football used in these sports.

In this chapter our use of the term coaching pedagogy is not limited to what a coach does to achieve articulated learning outcomes, or even to being the theory and practice of teaching and its influence on learning. It also goes beyond notions of pedagogy in the critical pedagogy literature such as that of Giroux (1992: 3) who sees it as being: '*a configuration of textual, verbal, and visual practices that seek to engage the processes through which people understand themselves and the ways in which they engage others and their environment*'. Our use of pedagogy in this chapter refers to a broader conception of it as anything that shapes or influences learning and which includes the implicit pedagogy of participation in the practices of a cultural field or subfield (Bourdieu, 1986), or of a community of practice (Lave & Wenger, 1991) in sport (see Light, 2006).

We suggest that the implicit pedagogy through which the participants learned to play 'footy' as children was dialogic in nature with verbal and non-verbal dialogue lying at the centre of learning 'footy' and culture as a humanising and liberating experience. We then contrast this with the structured and prescriptive pedagogy of non-Indigenous, professional sport with its objective perception of knowledge and its emphasis on measurement as being anti-dialogic, dehumanising and, ultimately, oppressive. In doing so we highlight what can be seen as implicit cultural discrimination through sport coaching that does not consider Indigenous values and ways of learning.

Dialogic learning

Dialogic learning is learning that takes place through dialogue and can be linked to the Socratic dialogues in Western thought and to the development of Buddhism in Eastern traditions. In comparatively contemporary thinking such as that of Freire (1996), learning arises from egalitarian dialogue and arguments with the notion of dialogic pedagogy used in reference to student learning generated through teacher and student dialogue. The central role of dialogue in learning is also a feature of what is commonly referred to as athlete-centred coaching when applied to team sports (see Pill, 2018) and more recently to coaching individual sports such as swimming and athletics through *Positive Pedagogy for sport coaching* (Light, 2017). These approaches emphasise empowering athletes to be active learners by developing relationships between coach and athletes through which the coach guides and facilitates learning instead of trying to determine or direct it. What Freire (1996) refers to as egalitarian dialogue is central to these innovative approaches to coaching. Within the sport coaching field these are innovations but their influence on practice has been limited by the dominance of direct instruction and the view of coaching as being the transmission of objective knowledge from the coach to passive learners, as anti-dialogic pedagogy (see Light, 2013).

Within schools and other educational institutions dialogic learning typically involves learners interrogating the focus of their study, listening to different points of view and creating equitable relationships in the classroom. Both the idea of dialogic learning in the classroom, and Freire's (1996) dialogic pedagogy refer to an explicit pedagogy with clearly articulated learning outcomes. However, in this chapter we are using it to consider the implicit pedagogy of participation in the practice of 'footy' that is difficult to identify and take account of within very different cultural fields and sub-fields and communities of practice (see Bourdieu, 1986).

Banking versus problem-posing education (coaching)

Freire (1996) argues that the dominant, traditional approach to education controls learners through prioritising conformity and by limiting thinking, imagination and creativity. This *banking approach* to education sees the learner as an empty vessel to be filled with knowledge by the teacher and with knowledge seen to be an object that is transmitted from teacher to student.

For Freire this involves the objectification of knowledge, learning and the learner in ways that limit thinking and action and inhibit creative power. This focus on learning as an objective process, on knowledge as an object, and on the learner as an object obfuscates the subjective nature of our being and, in doing so, is dehumanising:

> To deny the importance of subjectivity in transforming the world and history is naive and simplistic. It is to admit the impossible: a world without people... World and humans do not exist apart from each other, they exist in constant interaction.
>
> (Friere, 1996: 32)

Willis (cited in Beabout, 2008: 22) argues that this banking approach produces students who are mere *'fodder for the factories and prisons of a capitalist society'*. Beabout suggests that this dehumanising approach to education is evident in the ways that oppressive forces such as racism, sexism and classism attempt to isolate and force humans to live silently in the world rather than interact with it. As Collins (1998) suggests in regard to injustice from the interlocking of sexism and racism for Afro-American women, the dominant group uses controlling influences to justify racism, sexism, poverty and other forms of oppression as a natural part of day-to-day life. This approach is also central to the role that educational institutions play in maintaining social control (see, Light & Light, 2016).

Challenging the dominance of the banking approach to education and the ways in which it dehumanises and objectifies learning, Freire argues for the adoption of a problem-posing approach that promotes active learning rather than the passive reception of knowledge and a conception of learning as being adding on new knowledge. It typically involves students working in groups or as a whole class to solve a problem through inquiry, collaborating, cooperating and egalitarian dialogue between students and between teacher and students. Dewey's (see 1933) thinking on inquiry learning advocates a similar approach as do later variations such as problem-based learning (PBL – see Schmidt, 1998). These ideas also inform contemporary athlete-centred developments in sport coaching such as in Game Sense (Light, 2013), and Positive Pedagogy for sport coaching (Light, 2017).

In the problem-posing approach knowledge is not seen to be an object passed down to students by the teacher but, instead, something developed or constructed through dialogue between students and between student and teacher. Underpinned by constructivist epistemology it sees learning as arising from listening, egalitarian dialogue and action to create a dialogic bond between people (Freire, 1996; Wallerstein, 1987). The problem-posing approach aims to promote learning and knowing through interaction between people and between people and their world by enabling them to 'read the word and read the world' (Freire, cited in Beabout, 2008).

Problem-posing pedagogy is evident in contemporary coaching approaches such as Game Sense, game-based approaches, athlete-centred coaching and Positive Pedagogy for sport coaching as opposed to 'traditional' coach-centred and directive coaching that align more with Freire's banking pedagogy. It recognises and accounts for the individual's agency in the world and encourages showing 'respect for the intelligence of the students' (Beabout, 2008; Giroux, 1992) and by implication, athletes. Freire (1996) argues that challenging the dominance of a banking approach to education by replacing it with a problem-posing approach can liberate the oppressed classes such as those from racial minorities. However, Freire argues that this should not be through leaders showing the way as an attempt to 'save' them but, instead, through the use of dialogic learning to engage and empower learners in shaping '*their own* preferred future' (original emphasis) that is evident in TGfU, Game Sense and other athlete-centred coaching approaches.

Methodology

Methods

The study drawn on in this article combined narrative inquiry and constructivist, grounded theory methodology to provide a subjective perspective and a holistic understanding of experience and learning in particular sociocultural settings (Lal et al., 2012). It used a life history type interview as used to capture the participants' own perceptions of their lives (see Goodson & Sikes, 2001) and complemented the importance of telling stories in Aboriginal culture (Bamblett, 2013), which was enhanced by aligning it with the Indigenous concept of *dadirri* that requires empathy, sensitivity and openness on the part of the researcher. Grounded theory suited this purpose due to its rigorous, open ended and inductive approach. Over the study we strove to be non-judgemental and generate understanding through non-intrusive observation, deep, active listening, sensitivity and awareness, contemplation and reflection (Atkinson, 2000: 16), which helped us address any possible power differences between researcher and participants.

Participants

Sixteen male Indigenous players participated in the study with eight having played in the Australian Football League (AFL) and eight in the National Rugby League (NRL). Both cohorts were selected using a purposive and snowballing approach to recruit participants with the criteria being that they had to be Indigenous and were playing in, or had played in, the AFL or NRL within the past 15 years. One had retired 15 years before the study but the others had retired no more than ten years before the study with two of them having retired no more than three years before the study. In the AFL cohort two participants came from the Northern Territory, one from remote Western Australia, two from the suburbs of Melbourne and Adelaide and one from Sydney. In the NRL cohort two came from Sydney, four from northern rural NSW and two from rural Queensland. More details on the participants and their backgrounds are available in Light & Evans (2017, 2018a, 2018b).

Data generation and analysis

Data were generated using an initial life history type interview of approximately one hour in which the participants were asked to tell their story from their first exposure to their sport to making the AFL or NRL with the duration of the interviews varying from 50 to 70 minutes. We used initial coding of this narrative data and then focused coding (Charmaz, 2006) and shifted to grounded theory at this stage. This involved the use of two more rounds of shorter and more focused semi-structured interviews, totalling three interviews with most participants. Through the constructivist grounded theory process we developed emergent, and then substantive, theories grounded in the data that we connected with the formal theory of Bourdieu and of athlete transitioning in the latter stages where we integrated substantive theories to move to conceptual theory. The University of Sydney granted ethical approval for this study with pseudonyms used for all names and places or institutions where possible to maintain anonymity.

In the main body of the chapter we first trace the participants' experiences of learning to play footy up to the age of around 13, shaped by Aboriginal culture and implicit, dialogic pedagogy. We then outline and contrast this with their learning experiences on the way towards, and into, the AFL and NRL, which were marked by being increasingly confronted with the structure of professional approaches to coaching and conditioning driven by anti-dialogic pedagogy. This is followed by a discussion of the implications this had for the participants and for Indigenous Australians more broadly

Laying the foundations of expertise through dialogic pedagogy

The participants' exposure to footy began from early childhood as a prominent cultural practice & growing up in small, Indigenous communities in the Northern Territory, West Australia, rural New South Wales and Queensland (see Evans and Light, 2016). Two grew up in suburban settings in Melbourne, Adelaide (2) and Sydney (1) that were characterised by cultural diversity but in which Aboriginal culture shaped learning (Light & Evans, 2017). Two factors most shaped their learning as children in these settings, which were, in order of importance: (1) through informal play like games that were self-regulated, (2) playing a range of different games when younger.

Learning through informal games

The role of informal games had the most significant influence on learning for all the participants in the study. Competitive games were important community activities for children and were always social activities with much discussion and dialogue. This learning began at a very early age at social gatherings such as at community barbeques at which the participants' memories were of continually playing modified games of team sport such as cricket, rugby league, Australian football and basketball.

The participants recognised the pivotal importance of playing games every day and whenever possible in their development of expertise (Light & Evans, 2017; Evans & Light, 2016). They were not exposed to formal or semi-formal coaching until the later years in primary school with Alistair (AFL) noting how the skills and knowledge he learned through games often 'don't get noticed'. Playing against older siblings, cousins and extended family provided opportunities to problem solve in environments that encouraged experimentation, creativity and innovation. The development of a practical sense of the game (Bourdieu, 1986), or game sense, creativity and flair emerged from designing and managing informal games that were often adapted to environmental conditions and modified to account for a lack of resources. For example, they played modified Australian football on squash and basketball courts such as playing the game 'court footy':

> It (learning) just becomes natural, it just all happens and you don't think about it because you're playing with your mates, playing with your cousins, you're just enjoying it and is not really structured. It's just; have fun, enjoy yourself and whether that was in my court whether it was in my mate's court against his brothers.
>
> (Jack [AFL], Interview 1)

The participants were convinced of the central role these games played in their development:

> We were always doing stuff down at the place called the low level and we'd all have barbies (barbeques) and that, and that was it. That's where you learned all your skills, you know, you'd chase your older cousins around and that sort of stuff so I think that was massive in the obviously the early development.
>
> (Max [AFL], interview 1)

They were exposed to a range of sport and games growing up when younger as part of life in their communities, which included boxing, cricket, athletics, basketball, rugby union, Australian football, football (soccer) and rugby league. Mark grew up in the Northern Territory and received a scholarship to play rugby union and study at an elite independent school in Sydney where he also played Australian football in the club system and, after completing his schooling, played AFL. Many excelled in more than one sport and some had to make a difficult choice in their early teens to choose which sport they would specialise in. Their memories of community gatherings when younger were of playing a range of different sports that involved social interaction during and around the games they played.

> The earliest memory of growing up was pretty much going to parties, going to barbeques, cousins, uncles, and it would be always sport, whether it was the game we used to play, fly, or we'd play other games, ball games, soccer, cricket was a big thing. We'd always have two teams and cricket would go all day, just in the backyard.
>
> (Austin [NRL], Interview 1)

Jarrod (AFL) moved to Darwin at age 10 and took up rugby league: 'I always played rugby when I got to Darwin, I was a sort of rugby man', but continued playing Australian football and cricket at school. Austin (NRL) captures the central role sport played in the lives of the participants in this study as they grew up and the range of sports they played:

> In high school I wasn't physically as strong as everybody else, but I knew I had the skills, you know, the skills to play the game, so the things I was doing without even knowing were helping me become football player. Doing it just out of the love of playing touch football at lunchtime or you know, playing soccer on the footy field, just yeah, it put me in the position that I am today.
>
> (Austin [NRL], Interview 1)

Up to the age of around 13 the participants learned to play Australian football and rugby league through interaction, dialogue and the freedom to experiment, reflect and modify what games and the skills and abilities they were learning, comparatively free of adult interference and instruction. Learning was a subjective experience that was largely self-regulated and acutely influenced by the emphasis of Aboriginal culture, on gathering, social interaction and competition that Gordon articulates here:

> It's part of our culture to do things as a group, to enjoy each other's company and all that sort of stuff… Indigenous people play football the way they do and why they enjoy training the way they do.
>
> (Gordon [NRL], Interview 1)

This can be seen to be learning that is generated by implicit, dialogic pedagogy and which contrasts with the anti-dialogic pedagogy we identify as dominating coaching and the development of expertise in the NRL and AFL.

The anti-dialogic pedagogy of professional sport

The participants grew up with 'footy' as a meaningful practice in their communities and culture (Light & Evans, 2017) but their movement towards and into the AFL and NRL involved increasing exposure and adjustment to the practice of footy with different practices and meanings to what they had learned in primarily Indigenous communities. From an objective point of view the rules, aims and movements of footy may look the same but from a subjective perspective the meaning made of them and experience of learning in small communities and in quasi-professional/ professional sport were very different. We found stark contrasts between the collective and supportive nature of the mostly Indigenous communities the participants grew up in and the highly individualised and objectified non-Indigenous world of professional sport and the socio-cultural environments around them. For example, Danny's NRL club placed him in a nearby private school in Sydney where he felt lonely, isolated and unsupported:

> *I went to Madison College (pseudonym) and just could not get over, you know, the fact that people stuck to themselves a lot and there were not many people to interact with and so I used to spent a lot of time in the library by myself.*
>
> (Interview 1)

After having learned to play 'footy' through playing a range of sports and informal games free of interference from adults or coaches, the increasing structure of training and its objectification formed part of a transition from 'footy' as play to footy as work from around 13 years of age. This began with exposure to non-Indigenous 'footy' well before their entry into the professional leagues as Carl explains:

> *I was training three nights a week, Monday, Wednesday, Friday, a 15 year old coming into a system that I had no idea what was going on, you know, the weights start coming out and I'm like, this is not football, this is weight training and so that was a big surprise to me but the most thing that I sort of took out of it, is I looked around and kids around me that were developed, I mean developed in their arms were developed, their legs were developed, their body was developed, they'd been doing weights for two or three years before me.*
>
> (Interview 1)

They did not talk in detail about the nature of the coaching they received in the NRL or AFL in terms of it being coach or player-centred but did offer detail on adapting to regimes of training for fitness and strength. For example, Danny (NRL) talked about the problems he had adapting to an emphasis on individual responsibility and accountability when compared to the collective nature of learning and playing shaped by Indigenous culture that he enjoyed so much:

> It's part of our culture to do things as a group, to enjoy each other's company and all that sort of stuff and I think that's what comes into why Indigenous people play football the way they do and why they enjoy training the way they do.
>
> (Interview 1)

The highly individualised approach to training the participants all experienced as they approached and entered the AFL and NRL was characterised by constant measuring and monitoring of performance and fitness, individual accountability with expectations of individual discipline as reflections of an objectivist view of learning and athletes as learners. This involved having to adapt to a challenging shift from Aboriginal culture to the non-Indigenous, global culture of the sporting industry with radically different sets of beliefs and assumptions. Bernie (NRL) found being 'up' and 'on' every day in a highly competitive environment without a sense of community and adequate interaction a challenge for him and one that is often faced by Indigenous players (Schinke et al., 2006). The contexts in which the participants learned their skills, their abilities and the way they played were shaped by Aboriginal culture, which might also be seen as being racialised. The culture of professional sport they had to transition into was dramatically different and not so much because it was shaped by non-Indigenous, European or white values and beliefs but more so how it was shaped by the global culture of the sport industry.

Carl (AFL) struggled to deal with the highly structured approach to training in higher-level teams in his mid-teens, always being told what to do and repeating drills and patterns instead of playing free flowing games. This led him to quit a representative schoolboy team and return to his local club at the age of 15. Two years later he was drafted into an AFL club in Melbourne where he again struggled to deal with structure and being told what to do, how to do it and when. He found the emphasis placed on fitness, strength training and demands for meeting measurable standards de-motivating. Carl enjoyed anything where he had ball in hand and that he could see as being relevant to the game:

> The speed I was okay at, the weights? I wasn't lifting the heaviest weights but as soon as the footballs came out there was a sense of – how would you say? I was comfortable.
>
> (Interview 1)

This suggests the importance of the meaning 'footy' held for Carl and the lack of relevance of fitness training for him and should not be misinterpreted as reinforcing the hegemonic image of Aboriginals as 'natural born athletes' who do not work hard enough in their sport because this study identified how what seems natural is actually learned through lifetimes of effort and training. What is more central to understanding differences between Indigenous and non-Indigenous athletes in this study is the meaning the sport held for them. It should also be noted that the qualities Indigenous athletes are renowned for in Australia are not limited to them and are valued in some non-Indigenous athletes. For example, former Wallaby David Campesie was renowned for his creativity, flair and unpredictability, which are characteristics he sees and lauds in current All Black, Damien McKenzie. He sees McKenzie as a player who has the willingness to *'take a risk, the lack of conformity, the spark of magic'* he values (Cully, 2019: 26). For Campese, McKenzie is successful *'because he is not a structured player'* and has the flair that *'is impossible to coach'* (Cully, 2019: 26).

On their journey to the AFL and NRL from their early teens the participants shifted from playing footy for enjoyment and cultural expression to footy being work. This involved a disjunction between the way of learning that they had grown up with and the formal coaching and management they were subjected to in professional sport (see Schinke et al., 2006). Even in the communities a few grew up in that were not Indigenous, learning was influenced by an Aboriginal approach to playing footy that has been identified in research on Indigenous sport (see Butcher & Judd, 2016). Carl (AFL – Melbourne) and Toby (AFL – Sydney) did not grow up in Indigenous communities but had a strong sense of identity as Indigenous Australians and played with other Indigenous Australians as they developed. The links between early informal play and later creativity, flair and game sense has been suggested in Australia by former Wallabies (Australian national rugby team) coaches (Light & Evans, 2010) and more broadly, linked with the development of expertise in later life regardless of culture (see Côté et al., 2007). However, in this study it was far more dominant than any of the literature suggests anywhere else and is distinctive due to the role of sport as an important cultural practice.

There are several hundred Indigenous peoples in Australia that existed before colonisation who have their own country within Australia and Toby's mentor in Adelaide helped him find his country. This, he said, helped him deal with the challenges of adapting to a new culture and the loneliness he so often suffered from in his first few years in the AFL by strengthening his Aboriginal identity. Indeed, all participants drew on their sense of identity as Indigenous Australians to deal with the challenges they faced in adapting to professional sport and its anti-dialogic coaching pedagogy.

Discussion

For the participants in our study learning to play footy as children involved verbal and non-verbal interaction in developing embodied and cognitive understandings of their sport through dialogue and egalitarian relationships rather than being compelled to act as prescribed by someone in a position of power such as a coach. In fact, most of them had no coach or adult acting as a coach until senior primary school age. Even at primary school age the coaching they received was relatively informal and not too far removed from the informal games they grew up with. They learned most effectively through their own informal games played before school, at lunchtime and after school with these informal self-managed games played whenever the opportunity arose and typically dominated each day of their lives.

There is similarity between Freire's dialogic approach and Australian Indigenous views on education that reject the premise that the learner is an empty vessel and that learning is episodic in nature. Indigenous scholars such as Nakata (2007), Rigney (2001), Sarra, (2011) and Yunkaporta & Kirby (2011) make the point that learning takes place in unique socio-cultural contexts where the individual is exposed to a range of pedagogical mediums that include discussion, listening and practice and where their identity and culture are embraced (Burgess & Evans, 2016). The value of direct instruction in this perspective on learning is not rejected but is considered as part of a wider philosophical view of learning as being complex and shaped by engagement and which includes non-verbal and implicit learning.

Most of our participants grew up and learned their sport in predominantly Indigenous communities where sport formed a central cultural practice, in rural, remote and urban settings. Even for the boys who grew up in more culturally diverse communities where Aboriginal culture was not dominant, such as in the outer suburbs of Melbourne, sport was an important community practice. Despite the diversity of communities they grew up in these few participants had extended families and networks within which they experienced cultural learning. As young boys most grew up watching fathers, uncles and older brothers playing 'footy' and described these learning experiences to us as not only providing powerful learning in their sport but also as being central to cultural learning, developing a sense of personal and cultural identity. For all of them sport and the informal games they learned through were the most meaningful activity in their lives as children.

The participants' memories of childhood were of community gatherings, lively interaction and games. Engagement in these games involved constant dialogue between peers and relatives that promoted what Freire calls dialogical bonds and promoted interaction with each other and their world. Playing games and the social interaction involved formed a cultural practice through which they embodied the values and assumptions of Aboriginal culture. Looking at their communities as communities of practice helps understand how continually playing games as children constituted learning through social relationships and interaction as active learners (Lave & Wenger, 1991). Communities of practice is one of three core concepts used by Lave & Wenger along with 'situated learning' and 'legitimate peripheral participation' to understand how we learn implicitly through participation in the practices of communities, which always involves learning the culture of the community. Through participation in these games they not only developed skill and understanding of their sports but also learned the Aboriginal culture with the increasingly structured nature of training that they found constraining as they moved towards professional sport. This anti-dialogical and prescriptive approach imposes the view of the coach or coaches on the players with Freire (1996: 29) arguing that, *'Every prescription represents the imposition of one individual's choice upon another, of the milieu within which they also created a shared identity'*.

The participants' experiences of playing games over their childhood contrasted sharply transforming the consciousness of the person prescribed into one that conforms with the prescriber's consciousness. In this way the antidialogical pedagogy of professional sport acted to oppress the participants and in a way that can be seen as being culturally inappropriate. It acted to dehumanise and objectify the learner and learning as a process of passing on knowledge to passive learners through unequal power relationships. Learning as children involved very subjective experience but the pedagogy of the AFL and NRL objectified it.

Learning to play sport primarily through informal games with friends from the local area and relatives is not limited to Indigenous Australians or to Indigenous people more generally. Indeed, this 'deliberate play' as children has been identified as making a significant contribution to the development of sporting expertise in later life across a range of cultures and societies (see Côté et al., 2007). In a study on rugby coaching a former coach of a national team suggested the importance of 'knock up games' in the backyard or local park for the development of creativity, flair and being able to play 'what is in front of you' (Light & Evans, 2010). This rugby coach also made reference to his experiences of growing up short of resources and having to be creative to get a game going that extended to tying a spare jersey up to use as a ball when they did not have one.

The challenge of adapting from learning through informal games in local communities to the structures and demands of professional sport are likely not limited to Indigenous Australians. Non-Indigenous players from remote or rural areas of Australia may possibly have similar experiences but none would have experienced the stark contrast that the participants dealt with in this study, which was largely due to how their learning as children was inseparable from Aboriginal culture.

Conclusion

The participants in this study met the immense challenges involved in moving from local and familiar communities to the NRL and AFL. These involved the significant challenges of cultural transitioning into the global culture of sport as business with its vastly different meanings and practices when compared to where they learned to play their sport. Within this culture of the global sport industry the dominant pedagogy (implicit and explicit) is anti-dialogical, which contrasted with the implicit dialogical pedagogy through which they learned their sport and embodied Aboriginal culture.

The ways in which the participants succeeded in meeting the significant challenges they faced was tied into their strong cultural identity and speaks volumes about the capacity of Indigenous Australians to succeed in such competitive and even ruthless environments (Light & Evans, 2018b). A critical consideration of the implications of their exposure to the anti-dialogic pedagogy of professional sport and how it contradicted and contrasted with their learning of sport and culture as children also has some significant implications beyond their sport. From a critical pedagogy perspective the increasingly anti-dialogic pedagogy they were exposed to on their journeys from local communities to the NRL and AFL could also be seen as preparing them as 'fodder' for the NRL and AFL and the global sport industry in which sport and athletes have been reduced to commercial commodities (Nauright, 2004). It is also guilty of not accounting for their culture and the significance of 'footy' as an important cultural practice.

The dialogic pedagogy through which the participants laid the foundations of expertise sits upon a conception of developing sporting expertise and player improvement as a process of learning that, like any learning, is inseparable from culture (see Bruner, 1990). When we consider how the participants learned to play with the skill, flair, creativity and sublime game sense reflective of the Aboriginal ethic (Butcher & Judd, 2016) we are compelled to ask what mainstream coaching could learn from the inductive, athlete-centred Aboriginal approach. The constraints the participants experienced with the professional, anti-dialogic, approach to player development also seems to parallel some of the problems Indigenous people have to wrestle with in formal, mainstream education. Drawing on Freire's work and ideas on education in this paper also lends support to criticism of contemporary schools and the banking education they continue to employ. Many AFL and NRL clubs have made considerable progress with understanding Aboriginal culture and developing supportive structures in their clubs that this study justifies. It should, however, encourage further thinking about cultural sensitivity and consideration of the central role that Aboriginal cultures play in the development of elite level Indigenous athletes and in them meeting the significant challenges required when crossing the cultural borders to enter the world of non-Indigenous, professional sport.

References

Atkinson, J. (2000) *Trauma trails, recreating song lines. The transgenerational effects of trauma in Indigenous Australia*, Melbourne: Spinifex Press.
Bamblett, L. (2013) *Our stories are our survival*, Canberra: Aboriginal Studies Press.

Beabout, B. (2008) 'More fully human: Principals as Frieran liberators', *Journal of Thought*, Spring/Summer/Spring/Summer, 21–39.

Bourdieu, P. (1986) *Distinction*, London: Routledge and Kegan Paul.

Bruner, J. (1990) *Acts of meaning*, Cambridge, MA: Harvard University Press.

Burgess, C. M. & Evans, J. R. (2016). 'Culturally responsive relationships focused pedagogies as the key to quality teaching and quality learning environments'. In *Handbook of Research on Promoting Cross-Cultural Competence and Social Justice in Teacher Education*.

Butcher, T. & Judd, B. (2016) 'The Aboriginal football ethic', *Griffith Review: Our Sporting Life*, 52, 167–184.

Charmaz, K. (2006) *Constructing grounded theory: A practical guide through qualitative analysis*, London: Sage.

Collins, P. H. (1998) *Fighting words: Black women and the search for justice*, Minnesota, MN: University of Minnesota Press.

Côté, J., Baker, J. & Abernathy, B. (2007) 'Practice and play in the development of sport expertise', in G. Tenenbaum and S. R. C. Ecklund (eds.), *Handbook of sport psychology* (3rd ed, pp. 184–202). Hoboken, NJ: Wiley.

Cully, P. (2019, 3 Feb) 'McKenzie has Aussie great Campese excited again', *Sunday Star Times* (p. 26).

Dewey, J. (1933) *How we think: A restatement of the relation of reflective thinking to the educative process*, Boston: D.C. Heath.

Evans, J. R. & Light, R. L. (2016) 'The roots of exceptional performance: Indigenous players' early development in Australian football', in M. Drummond and S. Pill (eds.), *Advances in Australian football: A sociological and applied science exploration of the game* (pp. 128–135), Hindmarsh, South Australia: ACHPER.

Freire, P. (1996) *Pedagogy of the oppressed* (2nd ed), London: Penguin.

Giroux, H. A. (1992) *Border crossings: Cultural workers and the politics of education*, New York: Routledge.

Goodson, I. & Sikes, P. (2001) *Life history research in educational settings: Learning from lives*, Buckingham: Open University Press.

Lal, S., Suto, M., & Ungar, M. (2012) 'Examining the potential of combining the methods of grounded theory and narrative inquiry: A comparative analysis', *The Qualitative Report*, 17 (41), 1–22.

Lave, J. & Wenger, E. (1991) *Situated learning: Legitimate peripheral participation*, Cambridge: University Press. doi:10.1017/CBO9780511815355..

Light, R. (2006). 'Situated learning in an Australian surf club', *Sport, Education & Society*, 11 (2), 155–172.

Light, R. L. (2013) *Game sense: Pedagogy for performance, participation and enjoyment*, London and New York: Routledge.

Light, R. L. (2017) *Positive pedagogy for sport coaching: Athlete centred coaching for individual sports*, London and New York: Routledge.

Light, R. L. & Evans, J. R. (2010) 'The impact of Game Sense pedagogy on elite level Australian rugby coaches' practice: A question of pedagogy', *Physical Education and Sport Pedagogy*, 15 (2), 103–115.

Light, R. L. & Evans, J. R. (2017) 'Socialisation, culture and the foundations of expertise in elite level Indigenous Australian sportsmen', *Sport, Education and Society*, 22 (7), 852–863. http://dx.doi.org/10.1080/13573322.2015.1105208.

Light, R. L. & Evans, J. R. (2018a) 'Learning as transformation in the development of expertise by elite Indigenous Australian athletes', *Sport Mont Journal*, 1–4.

Light, R. L., & Evans, J. R. (2018b) *Indigenous stories of success in Australian sport: Journeys to the AFL and NRL*, London: Palgrave MacMillan. 10.1007/978-973-319-66450-7.

Light, R. L., Evans, J. R. & Lavallee, D. (2017) 'The transition of Indigenous Australian athletes into professional sport', *Sport, Education and Society*. Published ahead of print, 19 October, http://dx.doi.org/10.1080/13573322.2017.1391085.

Light, R. L. & Light, A. L. (2016) Making the games lesson the 'laboratory of the possible' through Game Sense, in J. Bruce and C. North (eds.) *Proceedings for the 2015 Game Sense for Teaching and Coaching* (pp. 74–85). Christchurch, New Zealand: University of Canterbury.

Nakata, M. (2007) 'The cultural interface'. *Australian Journal of Indigenous Education*, 36 (Supplementary), 7–14.

Nauright, J. (2004) 'Global games: Culture, political economy and sport in the globalised world of the 21st century', *Third World Quarterly*, 25 (7), 1325–1336. doi:10.1080/014365904200281302..

Pill, S. (ed.) (2018) *Perspectives on athlete centred coaching*, London and New York: Routledge.

Rigney, L.-I. (2001) 'A first perspective of Indigenous Australian participation in science: Framing Indigenous research towards Indigenous Australian intellectual sovereignty', *Kaurna Higher Education Journal*, 7, 1–13.

Ryba, T. V., Stanbulova, N. B., & Ronkainen, N. J. (2016) 'The work of cultural transition: An emerging model', *Frontiers in Psychology*, 7, 427. doi:10.3389/fpsyg.2016.00427.

Sarra, C. (2011) *Strong and smart: Towards a pedagogy for emancipation: education for first peoples*: Routledge.

Schinke, R. J., Michel, G., Gauthier, A. P., Pickard, P., Danielson, R., Peltier, D., … Peltier, M. (2006) 'The adaptation to the mainstream in elite sport: A Canadian Aboriginal perspective', *The Sport Psychologist*, 20, 435–448.

Wallerstein, N. (1987) 'Problem posing education: Freire's method for transformation', in I. Shor (ed.), *Friere for the classroom*, Portsmouth, NH: Boynton/Cook.

Willis, P. (1977) *Learning to labor: How working class kids get working class jobs*, New York: Columbia University Press.

Yunkaporta, T. & Kirby, M. (2011) 'Yarning up Indigenous pedagogies: A dialogue about eight Aboriginal ways of learning', in N. Purdie, G. Milgate, and H. R. Bell (eds.), *Two way teaching and learning: Toward culturally reflective and relevant education*. Camberwell, Vic: ACER Press.

Chapter 8

Black women, intersectionality and sport coaching

Alexandra J. Rankin-Wright and Kevin Hylton

Introduction

In the United Kingdom (UK), as is the case globally, current statistics and research suggests that racial and gender diversity within sport coaching and sports leadership remains low. Sport research, equity policies and practice have been criticised for failing to adequately address 'race', gender and their intersections. This chapter provides an examination of intersecting 'race' and gender issues in sport coaching in the UK. In particular, it highlights the dynamic nexus of 'race' and gender, drawing on primary research from the experiences of Black women coaches in the UK and supplemented by narrative from the autobiography of ex-England football manager, Hope Powell (Powell, 2016). Our arguments are underpinned by Critical Race Theory (CRT) and draw from the work of Black feminism and intersectionality scholarship. While acknowledging critiques of the term 'Black', and recognising the multiplicity of experiences within and across different groups of people, we adopt the term Black as an inclusive, theoretical and political term to refer to a diverse group of racialised women, both in our review of literature and when talking about Black women coaches as a group[1]. Rearticulating the scholarship of Black feminists, including Hill Collins, and hooks, Crenshaw (1989) coined the term intersectionality to emphasise the salience and intersections of 'race', gender and social class with other related identities and forms of oppressions, masked and exacerbated by structural and institutional power. Such phenomena contribute to why Hylton (2018: 1) has reasserted that "*'race' continues to be one of the most significant problems of the twenty-first century*" and one that continues to structure sport coaching and leadership domains in the UK.

Notwithstanding legislative drives for equality in British sport across all levels of participation and governance, a stark racial and gender imbalance remains at the highest and most powerful levels of sport coaching (Hylton, 2018; Rankin-Wright et al., 2017; Sporting Equals, 2011). When Black coaches have come to prominence they have been presented with a set of circumstances that their White counterparts rarely contend with. They often have to be more successful than their previous incumbents, are given less time to prove their worth, while regularly being relieved of their posts with a better record than those that have come before them (Hylton, 2018). Hope Powell is a Black woman football coach from a working-class Jamaican family in London who has been inducted into the British National Football Museum. She has achieved a number of 'firsts' over the course of her career which include being the first female England women's national team manager. Appointed by the governing body of association football in England in 1998–2013 (The Football Association: The FA) Powell brought to a close a successful playing career when she moved into coaching. Though an inspired appointment, The FA has been criticised about its approach to diversity by Dame Heather Rabbatts, the chair of its own inclusion advisory board (Press Association, 2017) as well as being described as institutionally sexist (Conn, 2016). As a successful club and England player with few others emulating her achievements since she ended her playing career, in an interview for *The Coaches' Voice* (nd) she stated,

> I was always battling. Every day I went into The FA, it felt like I was in a fight. And I was fighting. I was fighting for women's football. It was tough. I was female and black. The decision-makers? White. Male. And middle-class.

For Powell, in this moment we can see that she recognises that being in a male dominated, patriarchal and white dominated institution was always going to present multifarious challenges to her presence and progression within sport coaching. As Hylton (2018: 26) argues elsewhere, "*stereotyping, institutional racism, prototypes of effective managers and narrow conceptions of effective leadership reproduce the ideologies of those who can and cannot lead at the highest levels*".

The chapter is structured as follows. First, we review and address the absence of Black women's voices, perspectives and insights in the sociology of sport and sport coaching literature. Following this review, we then discuss an intersectional approach drawing on the work of critical race theorists, Black feminists and intersectionality scholarship. We highlight that this approach both supplements and challenges previous established epistemologies, methodologies and theoretical perspectives in sport coaching (Rankin-Wright & Norman, 2018). We go on to discuss Black women's experiences in sport coaching, including Hope Powell's, that provide a counter-narrative to the dominant ideologies espoused in sport coaching. We then facilitate an understanding of a group of coaches whose contributions and voices have long been systematically marginalised or ignored. We conclude by reaffirming the imminent need for critical research that theorises 'race', ethnicity and gender and their intersections from the perspectives of Black women coaches themselves.

'Silenced' voices in sport sociology and sport coaching

In her seminal works in 1989 and 1990, Susan Birrell urged sport scholars to broaden their theoretical frameworks and understanding of race relations to provide more sophisticated analyses of 'difference' in the field of gender and sport. In particular, Birrell (1990: 185) revealed the general absence of women of colour in sport scholarship and the stark neglect of 'race' and racial power relations. Following Lorde (1984: 117), they both assert that *"ignoring the differences of race between women and the implications of those differences presents the most serious threat to the mobilization of women's joint power"*. A decade after Birrell's call, Scraton (2001) similarly expressed grave concerns with the lack of theorisation of 'difference' and the omission of consistent critiques of sport as a racialised arena by feminists. This was despite, Scraton (2001) noted, the abundance of work outside of sport initiated by Black feminists (Anthias & Yuval-Davis, 1993; Brah, 1996; Hill Collins, 1990; hooks, 1984, 1989; Mirza, 1997; Bhavnani & Phoenix, 1994).

Birrell's call to broaden theoretical frameworks within the field of gender and sport to create space and a platform to counter the systematic silencing of 'invisible voices' retains its significance. Ratna & Samie's (2018) insightful collection, *'Race, Gender and Sport: The Politics of Ethnic 'Other' Girls and Women'*, reasserted how mainstream pursuits for knowledge in the sociology of sport have traditionally been framed by a white, Western, male Eurocentric hegemony. As such, the dominant voices and epistemologies in sport have been framed by a white masculine standpoint limiting discourses of 'race' and gender (Bruening, 2005). These approaches to the sociology of sport have been regularly criticised for failing to adequately theorise and critically problematise the place of 'race', gender and their intersections in our understanding of sport and society (Birrell, 1989; Birrell, 1990; Scraton, 2001; Ratna & Samie, 2018; Ratna, 2017).

In the dominant work on sport, gender and women's experiences, scholarship is critiqued for failing to *"speak to, with, and for the diverse group of women"* through a failure to understand and fully connect the interrelatedness of multiple oppressions that shape Black women's experiences, struggles and achievements (hooks, 1984: 14; Hargreaves, 2000; see Ratna & Farooq's 2018 chapter: *'Mapping the field: ethnic 'Other' females'*, for a comprehensive critical review of scholarship on sport, race relations and gender in sport sociology). The omission of subjugated knowledges of racialised power relations and reproduction of dominant discourses has silenced the voices and constructions of knowledge from Black women, erasing how they may construct and understand 'truths' about their own realities, and accounting for multiple interconnecting forms of oppression (Ratna, 2017). This is particularly evident in sport coaching research and scholarship, which has largely overlooked discussions pertaining to 'race', racialised power relations and whiteness, and has often failed to include the voices of

Black women coaches as knowledge formers. Scholarly attention to date that has theorised 'race' and gender has tended to focus on women's experiences as participants or athletes/players of sport. Thus, the alternative lived realities of Black women that take into account the diverse and varied ways Black women participate or engage in sport as coaches, for example, have been marginal (Toffoletti & Palmer, 2017). As Carter-Francique & Olushola (2016: 81) reaffirm:

> Women of color occupy a distinctive space in which race and gender cannot be disentangled. Racism and sexism create an "Othered" experience for women of color in sport, including those pursuing coaching careers. Thus, the experiences of women coaches of color must be understood from the standpoint of synergistic effects of multiple forms of oppression that intersect to further marginalize women of color beyond what women and men of color endure.

Critical sociological scholarship that has foregrounded the intersecting racialised and gendered structural and relational experiences of Black women coaches has demonstrated that Black women confront persistent, multiple and complex oppressions. Serious critique of Black women's intersecting identities that constitute Hill Collins' matrix of domination underpins much of this work. Bruening (2005) is part of a vanguard of critical scholars intent on illuminating the experiences of Black women in sport. Her commitment to delineating the bounded discourses of 'race' and gender in sport reveals a sector and cognate disciplines that habitually see "all women as White and all men as Black". Though we join these scholars to emphasise that Black women coaches' experiences are not homogenous we do however stipulate that there are assumptions, processes and practices at play recognisable by them in sport. These include: feeling 'tokenistic' and hypervisible in their organisations and within their coaching roles, prejudice assumptions regarding their capabilities as a coach and leader, and everyday experiences of racism and sexism, often intertwined, that isolate, intimidate, and can leave them feeling under-valued (Borland & Bruening, 2010; Carter-Francique & Olushola, 2016; Norman et al., 2014; King, 2007; Rankin-Wright & Norman, 2018; Rankin-Wright et al., 2017). To include a gendered dimension to Fanon's analogy of the 'white mask', King (2007) argued that Black women coaches in the UK adopt a 'gendered white mask' to negotiate the multiple and layered oppressions they face in the coaching and leadership spaces of football.

Analogous to this, there is a stark under-representation of women in all leadership positions across British sport and continued calls for the need to hear and include more women coaches' voices and perspectives to inform sport research, policy and practice (Women in Sport, 2015). More specifically, there is an acute lack of visibility of women from Black, Asian and minoritised ethnic groups in policy contexts and sport scholarship (Ratna &

Samie, 2018; Rankin-Wright & Norman, 2018; Armstrong, 2007). On the whole, the majority of research on women's experiences of sport coaching has by default been concerned with white middle-class women in Western countries, who represent a racial majority (Caudwell, 2011). In these works, 'race' has been arguably lost almost entirely. Whiteness operates as the dominant norm and there is limited debate of political and historical contexts. Too little is known about the personal, political and historical experiences, insights and standpoints of Black British women sport coaches from diverse backgrounds (Scraton, 2001; King, 2007; Ratna, 2011). Borland & Bruening (2010) support this further by adding to Bruening's (2005) thesis above that where diversity has been the focus of scholarship it has tended to have a discrete focus on gender or race. Black women in sport, and specifically Black women sport coaches, have thus fallen through the legislative and academic discourse cracks when 'race' and gender have been addressed as mutually exclusive categories of analysis and experience in both organisational monitoring and research (Rankin-Wright et al., forthcoming).

Power, privilege and resistance

In his book *Contesting 'Race' and Sport: Shaming the Colour Line*, Hylton (2018) makes reference to Du Bois' notion of 'living within the veil', 'double consciousness' and the idea of 'twoness'. A recognition that racialised people understand the politics of living in a world dominated by the privileges and supremacy of whiteness that forces them to skilfully comprehend and navigate it. The sovereignty of whiteness and the oft unspoken significance of 'race', forces performances of whiteness in social spaces by the sensitised Black 'other' where cultural norms associated with whiteness are highly valued. The whiteness of boards, leadership groups, fandom, presenters and commentators, referees and officials are not part of common sporting discourses outside of the frequent spikes in racism. Though things have improved in regard to increased women's sport coverage on television and in the newspapers, when gender becomes part of the mainstream conversation in sport it is often because of a reaction to extraordinary, rather than everyday, events. These issues may arise from, in the example of Hope Powell, being sacked from her position as manager of the England women's team after 15 years, the disruption of somatic and/or gender norms valued or privileged in key societal or organisational spaces, or in the case of Eniola Aluko, a player of the England women's football team, a sensational display of institutionalised racial and gendered harassment in the upper echelons of football by the England women's team manager (BBC Sport, 2017). Aluko's precarious position as a Black England women's player was exacerbated in the asymmetrical gendered and racialised team culture led by its manager Mark Sampson. Sampson's ill-considered racist joking and the English FA's inappropriate attempts to keep the issue quiet was heavily criticised by independent barristers and a committee made up of members of parliament. It later transpired that a number of people connected to the team and The FA were implicated in the investigation from The FA Chairman Greg Clarke down to the goalkeeping coach Lee Kendall. The FA later apologised for its 'systemic, historic failings'. For Black women, it is in these moments of raced/gendered disruption where critical identity work takes place that can simultaneously engender dynamics of accommodation, assimilation and resistance by women who have to work hard to fit in. It is in the liminal spaces that Black women coaches occupy where they must tend to the additional and stressful work of establishing their professional status, competence and compatibility with the role in hand (Harlow, 2003; Hylton, 2018). Yet it is a critical undertaking to understand how 'race' and gender intersect to enhance our understandings of the experiences and context of Black women coaches.

Black Feminism has many similarities with feminism in its resistance to omnipresent patriarchy and gendered oppression. However, it is in relation to 'race' where the Black Feminist thinkers differ from more traditional feminist thought in their approach to understanding and challenging oppression. Like Critical Race Theory, which is fundamentally connected to its founders' core ideas about the centrality of 'race' in society and the permanence of everyday racism (Gillborn, 2008; Hawkins et al., 2017; Hylton, 2010, 2018), Black feminists acknowledge that it is at this juncture where past and present racialised gendered experiences facilitate the need for a fundamental shift in standpoints. As Harris (2007: 57) argues, "*the salience of one's racial identity whether internally or externally imposed, forces one to live a 'double life'*". Ladson-Billings (1998), Bell (1992) and Gillborn (2008) argue that the salience of 'race' in society cannot be under-played. The centrality of 'race' is the starting point of any critique while its position at the nexus of other intersecting identities is crucial to its applicability as an inclusive critical lens. CRT aims to centre and transform the racialised experiences of those often on the margins of sport epistemologies, methodologies and theory (Hylton, 2018; Burdsey, 2011; Hawkins et al., 2017). These experiences, often described as the 'voice' of the marginalised, are privileged in a broader contextualisation of racial dynamics within society. Intersectionality is a legacy of Black feminism, though regardless of its intellectual beginnings it is not fixed to any particular intersections, and closely interconnected as a key element of Critical Race Theory (Carbado, 2013). Lee (2012: 468) describes the intersectional dialectic and power associated with social dynamics when she considers how,

> *Intersection enables and disables, allows and hinders, does and undoes: it is a hinge, a point of convergence. 'Seemingly' formal and neutral in its silent workings, intersection also 'presses' on, forward and inward.*

We all have intersecting identities yet the configuration of some enhance our ability to move through institutions and societies better than others. And though there are consistencies among subordinated and dominant groups they are contingent on context, geography and time. Black feminism puts the experiences of Black women coaches at the centre to ensure that they are a visible and substantive part of research, professional and social agendas. It is at this point where CRT and Black feminism coalesce. CRT and Black feminism speak truth to the power of influential actors in sport coaching through analogous standpoints that challenge the pseudo-meritocracy and colour-blindness in common approaches to sport policy and practice (Hawkins et al., 2017; Bruno Massao & Fasting, 2014; Ratna & Samie, 2018; Burdsey, 2011). Further, microaggressions, interest convergence, whiteness critiques and intersectionality make essential contributions to examining racialised relations in sport and society (Coram & Hallinan, 2017; Hylton, 2010; Fletcher & Hylton, 2018; Hylton, 2017; Hylton & Morpeth, 2014; Rankin-Wright et al., 2017; Rankin-Wright et al., 2016). Crucially, CRT and Black feminism challenge preoccupations with 'objectivity' for standpoints that recognise social justice, and the bias of cultural, epistemic and social discourses that privilege particular approaches to knowledge formation over others. They therefore advocate that debates in sport such as the experiences of Black women coaches that have traditionally operated at the margins are centred in the context of sport coaching.

'Talking back': the research

This section presents passages from Hope Powell's biography juxtaposed with findings from Black women coaches interviewed in Rankin-Wright's doctoral study. Before presenting this, it is worth reflecting upon how the inconsistencies of organisations contribute to the inclusion/exclusion of Black women coaches. In the equalities literature, it has often been argued that reactive or gestural institutions will often take a minimalist approach to diversity, equity and inclusion (Hylton & Totten, 2013; Lusted, 2017; Lusted, 2009). This can be manifest in basic provision, terms and conditions in place to comply with legal requirements. In some cases, the symbolism of charters, campaigns and action plans have been viewed by organisations as evidence in themselves of action rather than the *actual* implementation and recording of progress. Such activities have been described as types of 'performance' or 'symbolic gestures' that act as devices to distract and obfuscate weak or superficial approaches to equalities work (Ahmed, 2007; Ahmed, 2009). Race and gender equality in sport coaching has been described by us (Rankin-Wright et al., 2017) as 'blind spots' for many national governing bodies. For example, The FA's 2018–21 Equality, Diversity and Inclusion action plan (The FA, 2018) states that (1) equality, diversity and inclusion means valuing and celebrating our differences, (2) differences can be something tangible like gender, race and ethnicity, and (3) they believe embracing equality, diversity and inclusion makes us stronger, and better equipped to meet the challenges of the modern game.

There are few that would actively argue against policy commitments toward equality, diversity and inclusion especially where complex identities in historically disparate organisations are concerned. Yet, as an informed insider, Hope Powell's assessment of her appointment at The FA was initially quite sceptical and perhaps more reflective of her lived reality of working in football. When asked why she thought she was appointed she remarked in The Coaches' Voice interview,

> Why me? I felt it was a bit of a token gesture. Black. Female. Ticked a box.
> (Coaches' Voice, nd)

It should be noted that The FA Inclusion Advisory Board had its first meeting in January 2014, a year after Powell left the England coaching job. The notion of box ticking for Hope Powell may have seemed more pronounced in a period where there may have been less of a focus on 'race', gender and broader equalities concerns. Carter-Francique & Olushola (2016: 81) further discuss the *"synergistic effects of multiple forms of oppression"* that intersect and further marginalise Black women coaches in a sport coaching field that privileges whiteness and maleness. These multiple oppressions were poignantly articulated by the coaches who shared their experiences for Rankin-Wright & Norman's (2018) chapter, 'The inclusion of Black women in sport coaching in the United Kingdom'. Eight coaches, from different sports with a range of coaching experience, qualifications and from different ethnic backgrounds, shared their journeys and experiences of entering and progressing in coaching. This fear of evidencing an organisational commitment to diversity and the continual physical and emotional toll of 'standing out' within an occupation traditionally dominated by whiteness and masculinity was reinforced by the coaches interviewed for Rankin-Wright's doctoral research:

> *That's what I kind of worry about sometimes, I don't want people thinking "oh we'll tick, she's Black and she's female".*
> (Amelia, cited in Rankin-Wright & Norman, 2017)

> *When I got the job with [NGB] I think there's a tick box that everybody has to tick isn't it? [...] so I think that was just a tick box, "Oh we got a Black girl, Black female".*
> (Carol, cited in Rankin-Wright & Norman, 2017)

One can never underestimate the additional pressures of everyday racism and the microaggressions related to being a Black woman in UK coaching structures, particularly at the high-performance level. The processes of racialisation and gendered relations not only marked the coaches' bodies as different but also challenged their presence within the spaces of sport coaching (Rankin-Wright & Norman, 2017). Consequently, the coaches often felt the need to legitimise their existence, to justify their visibility as the only female and only Black coach even if motives are continually questioned and actions continually challenged (Rankin-Wright & Norman, 2017).

Research has shown that a number of similarities can be drawn across women's experiences in and of sport coaching. However, women as individuals, within and across groups, also face layered privileges and oppressions heightened by multiple and interconnecting identities and positionalities. LaVoi (2016) advocates centring intersectionality and power relations to address the multi-level and complex challenges facing women coaches and leaders. For the Black women coaches who shared their experiences in Rankin-Wright's doctoral research, a 'gendered racism' (Essed, 1991) was similarly in operation where 'race' and gender were inextricably linked in day-to-day interactions as coaches in their respective sports and organisations (Rankin-Wright & Norman, 2018; Rankin-Wright et al., 2017). Seema, an Asian British Pakistani woman who had previously coached at grassroots level, explained:

> BME [sic] women are fighting a different battle than White Caucasian [sic] women.
>
> (Seema, cited Rankin-Wright & Norman, 2018: 213)

Carol, a Black Caribbean coach for an individual sport who was actively coaching at high-performance level at the time of the interview, discussed the interconnecting oppressions she frequently negotiated in relation to feeling stereotyped:

> I think some of it's to do with race but I think some of it's to do with being a woman ... they tarnish every Black person with the same brush. I say to people just because that person is like that, don't tarnish me! So, I'm not sure if it's racism, sexism... do you know what I mean? I think it's all of it.
>
> (Carol, quote from Rankin-Wright et al., 2017: 11)

These coaches had, and would continue to have, a more challenging journey to navigate compared to their White female counterparts due to compounding intersecting racialised relations within White dominated organisations (Rankin-Wright et al., 2017). In this case, Carol recognises the multiple inflected way her sport can impact her experience materially, discursively and affectively as a Black woman coach. Powell recognised that she would always have an added barrier of having to manage a gendered culture, assumptions about ability and fitness for purpose as a woman football coach. She emphasised this point when stating that,

> Just because you're a man, it's assumed you have more knowledge. As a woman, you always have to prove yours. […] It has to change […] It's another fight.
>
> (Coaches' Voice, nd)

All coaches have to cajole and persuade stakeholders to release resources to achieve their visions for success. *Another fight*, for Hope Powell, is an additional one that men coaches in The FA have the privilege to avoid thus saving their energies for other generic challenges for the job in hand. However, in this case she does not stop short at her observation of the primacy of masculinity. Hope Powell recognises the added dimension of racial dynamics at play within the English Football Association that required her to critically manage the double-burden of gender and 'race'. In her autobiography, she also acknowledges that as a gay woman she had to take the unfortunate step of having to reveal her sexuality to her prospective employers because of the fear that they (The FA) may not want to take her on.

> I told The FA from the off that I lived with my partner Michelle, just in case the press wanted to make any kind of issue about it. […] Overall, the press gave me a very enthusiastic welcome, albeit in the limited amount of column inches that women's football gained in those days.
>
> (Powell, 2016: 69)

In this example Hope Powell's White women coach counterparts have the privilege of not having to manage the racialised assumptions that coalesce with gender that draw on stereotypes of fitness for play over leadership, physicality over intellect. Sexuality and everyday homophobia in the press adds a further layer of complexity and pressure to this Black woman's professional being. Being a body out of place in football coaching for Hope Powell is more than gender, more than 'race'. It is 'both', further, it is 'both' 'and' (Hill Collins and Bilge, 2016: 3). Powell's openness about her sexuality as a gay Black woman exemplifies the multiple interlocking oppressions that adds to considerations of the intersections of 'race' and gender that we have unpacked in this chapter. Everyday sexism and racism for Black women coaches encompasses a myriad of interconnecting oppressions that are more or less pertinent at different times and in different contexts (Rankin-Wright & Norman, 2018). Specific intersecting processes are experienced and negotiated by Black women coaches in multifaceted, complex and dynamic ways. Yet there are similarities that can be drawn from these counter-narratives that enfeeble the dominant perspectives espoused from the coaching system. To understand the experiences of Hope Powell and the Black women coaches interviewed in Rankin-Wright's study, it is clear that the intersection of gender, 'race' and their intersections with other identities and oppressions, with coaching, require a critical unpacking. Although these stories were individualised and multidimensional, and therefore cannot be essentialised nor generalised, the counter-narratives together highlight the racialised and gendered structures, power processes, and practices that reinforce the dominance of both whiteness and masculinity within sport coaching organisations (Rankin-Wright & Norman, 2018).

Conclusion

The trends towards the silencing of Black women's experiences within sport coaching research and practice highlights the imminent need for critical research that theorises 'race', ethnicity, gender and their intersections from the perspectives of Black women coaches themselves. We write this chapter in the context of a research environment where the marginality of such issues in sport coaching and the sociology of sport are being exacerbated by anti-intellectual research assessment exercises that encourage writing in more established domains. Thus, reinforcing dominant epistemologies. We must offer a word of caution that these pressures must not be acceded to. We also remind readers that great writing and seminal texts can still emerge from challenging educational environments. For instance, Patricia Hill Collins (2015: 2349) remarked about her book *Black Feminist Thought* that,

> I had no idea who would read the book, and I certainly did not evaluate its worth by contemporary metrics of categorizing, ranking and evaluating everything.

The Black women coaches whose voices we reflect upon here are tacit reminders of how little knowledge we have of their entry and experiences of progression in sport coaching and of how important it is for us to continue to find out. Regardless of levels of celebrity there are strong similarities and patterns that emerge from them in regards to (i) how they view their sports as racialised entities and (ii) how the double-burden of 'race' and gender offers a 'both'-'and' dynamic that requires a more detailed comprehension that moves beyond mainstream additive approaches to 'race' and 'gender'. These narratives further illustrate the interrelatedness of multiple oppressions that shape Black women coaches' experiences within sport coaching that are unique from those of Black men and White women, and are unique to each individual coach within their ethnic group (Bruening, 2005). In many cases 'race' OR gender debates lend themselves to overly simplistic conclusions.

Critical Race Theory and Black feminism's engagement with transforming racialised and gendered power in sport and society reflects a definite centring of important contemporary issues and hints at alternative ways to view the location and experience of Black women coaches in sport coaching. They disavow sport coaching of notions of colour-blindness, meritocracy and 'race' neutrality and underscore approaches that fundamentally challenge traditional laissez faire policy and practice. Sport coaching research must explore the interconnections between and among systems of oppressions and how such interconnecting oppressions are organised regarding structural domains of power relations (Hill Collins, 2000: 12). Hence, questions about equalities, identities, leadership and role models in sport coaching become underpinned by a tacit understanding of intersectionality and how it might affect considerations for the coaching workforce and the success of the sport. Further, questions of social justice and transformation naturally lead to reflections about 'who we are', 'how we know?' and 'what are we going to do about it?'. Such questions disrupt the status quo and engender a more productive debate concerning Black women and their contribution to the success of sport coaching.

Note

1 The debates around terminology are complex. Whilst acknowledging critiques of the term 'Black', and recognising the multiplicity of experiences within and across different groups of people we use this term in the political and theoretical sense, as solidarity in the commonalities of shared oppressions and empowerment for communities. However, we shift terminology when citing particular writers and coaches to reflect their use of terminology as relevant to their own context and politics.

References

Ahmed, S. 2007. 'You end up doing the document rather than doing the doing': Diversity, race equality and the politics of documentation. *Race, Ethnicity & Education*, 30, 590–609.

Ahmed, S. 2009. Embodying diversity: Problems and paradoxes for Black feminists. *Race, Ethnicity & Education, Special Issue Black Feminisms and Postcolonial Paradigms: Researching Educational Inequalities*, 12, 41–52.

Anthias, F. & Yuval-Davis, N. 1993. *Racialized boundaries: Race, nation, gender, colour and class and the anti-racist struggle*, London, Routledge.

Armstrong, K. L. 2007. The nature of Black women's leadership in community recreation sport: An illustration of Black feminist thought. *Women in Sport & Physical Activity Journal*, 16, 3–13.

BBC Sport. 2017. Mark Sampson: FA sorry over race remarks to Eniola Aluko & Drew Spence [Online]. Available: https://www.bbc.co.uk/sport/football/41617223 [Accessed 4 May 2018].

Bell, D. 1992. *Faces at the bottom of the well: The permanence of racism*, New York, Basic Books.

Bhavnani, K. & Phoenix, A. 1994. Shifting identities shifting racisms. *Feminism & Psychology*, 4, 5–18.
Birrell, S. 1989. Racial relations theories and sport: Suggestions for a more critical analysis. *Sociology of Sport Journal*, 6, 212–227.
Birrell, S. 1990. Women of color: Critical autobiography and sport. In: MESSNER, M. & SABO, D. (eds.) *Sport, men, and the gender order: Critical feminist perspectives.* Champaign, IL: Human Kinetics.
Borland, J. F. & Bruening, J. E. 2010. Navigating barriers: A qualitative examination of the under-representation of Black females as head coaches in collegiate basketball. *Sport Management Review*, 13, 407–420.
Brah, A. 1996. *Cartographies of diaspora: Contesting identites*, London, Routledge.
Bruening, J. E. 2005. Gender and racial analysis in sport: Are all the women White and all the Blacks men? *Quest*, 57.
Bruno Massao, P. & Fasting, K. 2014. Mapping race, class and gender: Experiences from Black Norwegian athletes. *European Journal for Sport and Society*, 11, 331–352.
Burdsey, D. 2011. Applying a CRT lens to sport in the UK: The case of professional football. In: HYLTON, K., PILKINGTON, A., WARMINGTON, P. & HOUSEE, S. (eds.) *Atlantic crossings: International dialogues on Critical Race Theory.* Birmingham: The Higher Education Academy Network.
Carbado, D. 2013. Colourblind intersectionality. *Journal of Women in Culture and Society*, 4.
Carter-Francique, A. R. & Olushola, J. 2016. Women coaches of color: Examining the effects of intersectionality. In: LAVOI, N. (ed.) *Women in sports coaching.* Oxon: Routledge.
Caudwell, J. 2011. Gender, feminism and football studies. *Soccer and Society*, 12, 330–344.
COACHES' VOICE. nd. The journey: Being first [Online]. Available: https://www.coachesvoice.com/being-first/ [Accessed 25 January 2019].
Hill Collins, P. 1990. *Black feminist thought: Knowledge, consciousness, and the politics of empowerment*, London, Routledge.
Hill Collins, P. & BILGE, S. 2016. *Intersectionality*, Cambridge, Policy Press.
CONN, D. 2016. Women in Football survey exposes 'ingrained, sexist culture'. *Guardian*, [Accessed 8 March 2019].
Coram, S. & Hallinan, C. 2017. Critical race theory and the orthodoxy of race neutrality: Examining the denigration of Adam Goodes. *Australian Aboriginal Studies*, 1, 99–111.
Crenshaw, K. 1989. Demarginalizing the intersection of race and sex: A Black feminist critique of antidiscrimination doctrine, feminist theory and antiracist politics. *University of Chicago Legal Forum*, 139–167.
Essed, P. 1991. *Understanding everyday racism: An interdisciplinary theory* (Vol. 2). London: Sage.
Fletcher, T. & Hylton, K. 2018. Whiteness in event organisation. *Journal for Policy Research in Tourism, Leisure and Events.*
Gillborn, D. 2008. *Race and racism: Coincidence or conspiracy?*, London, Routledge.
Hargreaves, J. 2000. *Heroines of sport: The politics of difference and identity*, London, Routledge.
Harlow, R. 2003. "Race doesn't matter, but…": The effect of race on professors' experiences and emotion management in the undergraduate college classroom.

Social Psychology Quarterly, Special Issue: Race, Racism, and Discrimination, 66, 348–363.

Harris, T. 2007. Black feminist thought and cultural contracts: Understanding the intersection and negotiation of racial, gendered, and professional identities in the academy. *New Directions for Teaching and Learning*, 100, 55–64.

Hawkins, B., CARTER-FRANCIQUE, A. & COOPER, J. N. (eds.) 2017. *Critical Race Theory: Black athletic sporting experiences in the United States*, New York: Palgrave Macmillan.

Hill Collins, P. 2000. Gender, Black feminism, and Black political economy. *The ANNALS of the American Academy of Political and Social Science*, 568(1), 41–53.

Hill Collins, P. 2015. No guarantees: Symposium on Black Feminist Thought. *Ethnic and Racial Studies*, 38, 2349–2354.

hooks, B. 1984. *Feminist theory: From margin to center*, Boston, MA, South End Press.

hooks, B. 1989. *Talking back: Thinking feminist, thinking black*, Boston, MA, South End Press.

Hylton, K. 2010. How a turn to critical race theory can contribute to our understanding of 'race', racism and anti-racism in sport. *International Review for the Sociology of Sport*, 45, 335–354.

Hylton, K. 2017. I'm not joking! The strategic use of humour in stories of racism. *Ethnicities*, 18, 327–343.

Hylton, K. 2018. *Contesting 'race' and sport: Shaming the colour line*, London, Routledge.

Hylton, K. & Morpeth, N. D. 2014. 'Race' matters, and the East End. In: Bloyce, D. & Smith, A. (eds.) *The 'Olympic and Paralympic' effect on public policy*. London: Routledge.

Hylton, K. & Totten, M. 2013. Developing 'Sport for All'. In: Hylton, K. (ed.) *Sport development: Policy, process and practice*. London: Routledge.

King, C. 2007. Football in England and the gendered white mask. In: Magee, J., Caudwell, J., Liston, K. & Scraton, S. (eds.) *Women, football and Europe: Histories, equity and experiences*. Oxford: Meyer & Meyer Sport (UK) Ltd.

Ladson-Billings, G. 1998. Just what is Critical Race Theory, and what's it doing in a nice field like education? *Qualitative Studies in Education*, 11, 7–24.

Lavoi, N. 2016. A framework to understand experiences of women coaches around the globe: The Ecological-Intersectional Model. In: Lavoi, N. (ed.) *Women in sports coaching*. Oxon: Routledge.

Lee, K. 2012. Rethinking with Patricia Hill Collins: A note toward intersectionality as interlocutory interstitiality. *Journal of Speculative Philosophy*, 26.

Lorde, A. 1984. Age, race, class, and sex: Women redefining difference. *Sister outsider: Essays and speeches*. Berkley, CA: Crossing Press.

Lusted, J. 2009. Playing games with 'race': Understanding resistance to 'race' equality initiatives in English local football governance. *Soccer and Society*, 10, 722–739.

Lusted, J. 2017. Understanding the varied responses to calls for a 'Rooney rule' in English football. In: Kilvington, D. & Price, J. (eds.) *Sport and discrimination*. London: Routledge.

Mirza, H. S. (ed.) 1997. *Black British feminism: A reader*, London, Routledge.

Norman, L., North, J., Hylton, K., Flintoff, A. & Rankin, A. J. 2014. *Sporting experiences and coaching aspirations among Black and Minority Ethnic (BME) groups*, Leeds, Sports Coach UK.

Powell, H. 2016. *Hope: My life in football*, London, Bloomsbury.

Press Association. 2017. Heather Rabbatts to stand down as a nonexecutive director of the FA. *theguardian.com*, Available: https://www.theguardian.com/football/2017/jun/14/heather-rabbatts-stand-down-fa-director-paul-elliott?CMP=Share_iOSApp_Other [Accessed 14 June 2018].

Rankin-Wright, A. J., Hylton, K. & Norman, L. 2016. Off-colour landscape: Framing race equality in sport coaching. *Sociology of Sport*, 33, 357–368.

Rankin-Wright, A. J., Hylton, K. & Norman, L. J. 2017. Negotiating the coaching landscape: Experiences of Black men and women coaches in the United Kingdom. *International Review for the Sociology of Sport*, 1–9.

Rankin-Wright, A. J. & Norman, L. 2018. Sport coaching and the inclusion of Black women in the United Kingdom. In: Ratna, A. & Farooq, S. (eds.) *Race, gender and sport: The politics of ethnic 'Other' girls and women*. Leeds: Routledge.

Ratna, A. 2011. 'Who wants to make aloo gobi when you can bend it like Beckham?' British Asian females and their racialised experiences of gender and identity in women's football. *Soccer & Society*, 12, 382–401.

Ratna, A. 2017. Black women, Black voices: The contribution of a Spivakian and Black feminist analysis to studies of sport and leisure. In: Long, J., Fletcher, T. & Watson, B. (eds.) *Sport, leisure and social justice*. Routledge.

Ratna, A. & Farooq, S. 2018. Mapping the field: Ethnic 'Other' females. In: Ratna, A. & Farooq, S. (eds.) *Race, gender and sport: The politics of ethnic 'Other' women*. Leeds: Routledge.

Ratna, A. & Samie, S. (eds.) 2018. *Race, gender and sport: The politics of ethnic 'Other' girls and women*, Oxon, Routledge.

Scraton, S. 2001. Reconceptualising race, gender and sport: The contribution of black feminism. In: Carrington, B. & McDonald, I. (eds.) *'Race', sport and British society*. London: Routledge.

Sporting Equals. 2011. *Insight: BME coaching in sport*. Birmingham.

The Football Association. 2018. *In pursuit of progress: The FA's equality, diversity and inclusion plan 2018–2021*, London, The Football Association.

Toffoletti, K. & Palmer, C. 2017. New approaches for studies of Muslim women and sport. *International Review for the Sociology of Sport*, 52, 146–163.

Women in Sport. 2015. *Trophy women? No more board games*.

Chapter 9

Beyond the Xs and Os
The representation of black college coaches

Joyce Olushola-Ogunrinde and Akilah R. Carter-Francique

Introduction

Sport is a microcosm of society, and therefore, it is not immune to the varying ways that racism and racial discrimination can reify social problems (Singer, 2005). While race and its intersections with other social identities (i.e., ethnicity, gender, social class, religion, sexual orientation) create an "Othered" experience for Black people specifically, and people of color generally, in the cultural context of sport discriminatory challenges shape the access and treatment for those pursuing careers in college coaching (Carter-Francique & Olushola, 2016; Sagas & Cunningham, 2005). College sports in the United States (U.S.) are organized by various organizations at a varsity and club level. For the purpose of this paper, we are focusing on those varsity sports governed by the National Collegiate Athletic Association (NCAA). The NCAA was formed in 1906 in the United States of America to increase the safety and well-being outcome of student-athletes. Currently, the NCAA oversees 420,000 college athletes for 1000 member institutions (e.g., colleges, universities). Participation in college sports is key to training and development of professional athletes, coaches, and administrators as it serves as the direct feeding platform to professional and Olympic sports. College athletes are recruited as early as adolescence to play at this level and these athletes serve as the largest pool of potential college coaches. Therefore, the forces shaping sport participation, namely racial and gender ideologies, also shape the opportunities and experiences of Black coaches.

Parallel to the larger U.S. society, the manifestation of racism on the experiences of racially and ethnically "Othered" coaches is attributed to the devaluation of the contributions to their team, the higher performance standards, decreased job satisfaction, and high job turnover rates (Sagas & Cunningham, 2005). Yet, in spite of these experiences, the stories of Black coaches like Charlie Strong and C. Vivian Stringer demonstrate that Black college coaches have found success intrinsically and extrinsically. These individuals represent a larger group of underrepresented coaches whose experiences can provide insight into unpacking and dismantling the isomorphic forces that continue to privilege Whiteness over non-White people in college coaching.

With a growing recognition of diversity in sport in the U.S., more scholarly attention has been given to exploring the coaching experiences for Black people and increasing the quality of these experiences and quantity of their representation (Carter-Francique, 2018; Singer et al., 2010). Extant literature and contemporary realities promote the need for a sociohistorical perspective of the enablers and barriers influencing Black coaches' experiences (Lapchick et al., 2015). Capturing these experiences is necessary to redress the *"sporting myths of meritocracy and inclusion"* (Rankin-Wright et al., 2017: 616) that pathologize coaching disparities faced by Black coaches as innate to their race as opposed to socially constructed through racialized and gendered sport structures.

Statistical data demonstrate Black coaches are continuously underrepresented at the college level in comparison to their levels of participation as players across a range of college sports (Lapchick, 2018; NCAA, 2019). For instance, in football, the percentage of Black college athletes is 39%, while only 11% of the head coaches, 10% of offense coordinators, 20% of defensive coordinators and 29% of assistant coaches are Black. Similarly, in men's basketball, which has the highest percentage of Black student-athletes at 45%, Black head coaches were 17% and assistant coaches 33%.

More directly, Lapchick (2018) from The Institute for Diversity and Ethics in Sport (TIDES) found college sport reflected a C+ (78.3%) grade for diverse racial representation and C+ (75.1%) grade for gender (male, female) representation (see Lapchick [2018] for more details on the grading rubric). Despite being overly represented in the sports of football, basketball, and track and field as athletes, Black college coaches are grossly underrepresented in their profession. Scholars have examined this reality throughout the years, and while the challenges of Black women were examined (Abney, 1989, 2007; Abney & Richey, 1991; Borland & Bruening, 2010; Carter-Francique & Olushola, 2016), an overwhelming number of research examinations focus on Black men (Agyemang & DeLorme, 2010; Cunningham, 2010; Cunningham et al., 2001; Day & McDonald, 2010; Latimer & Mathes, 1985; Mixon & Treviño, 2004; Sagas & Cunningham, 2004; Singer et al., 2010). To address this oversight, this chapter employs an intersectional perspective to explore the factors shaping the coaching landscape for Black coaches and provides strategies for increasing the quantity and quality of their experience.

Therefore, the purpose of this chapter is to (a) identify and analyze the structural, representational, and political challenges experienced by Black men and women coaches and (b) provide recommendations for transformative policies and practices to enable greater equity in the recruitment and retention of Black men and women coaches in college sport. To be consistent with the NCAA's terminology used to describe and collect data on coaches of African descent, "Black" will be used in addressing coaches in this article.

Theoretical framework: intersectionality theory

To better understand and identify the enablers and barriers for Black collegiate coaches, there is a need to provide a framework that explicates how the historic construction of the U.S. works to perpetuate myths and stereotypes and inhibits efforts of marginalized groups while justifying the actions and philosophical beliefs of dominant groups. Hence, we found that a critical perspective is best to support these experiences, particularly through the perspective of Critical Race Theory (CRT). Critical Race Theory was born out of Critical Legal Studies (CLS) in the 1980s in the U.S. and sought to take CLS into action by centering race and providing a space for social transformation. Therefore, CRT emerged as a framework that could continue the efforts of the Civil Rights movement and speak about "Othered" people and groups that are often rendered silent in society and cultural institutions like sport.

Critical race theory has five fundamental tenets that work to guide our understanding of marginalization, yet illuminate actionable efforts to redress social inequalities that include: (a) the centrality of race and racism and their intersectionality with other forms of subordination, (b) the challenge to dominant ideology, (c) the commitment to social justice, (d) the centrality of experiential knowledge, and (e) the transdisciplinary perspective (Solorzano, 1997, 1998; Solorzano & Bernal, 2001; Solorzano & Yosso, 2000). For the purpose of this chapter, and as alluded, we employ the centrality of race and racism and their intersectionality with other forms of subordination. Employing this tenet to examine the experiential realities of Black college coaches can prove beneficial as it centers race and racism and acknowledges the intersecting identities such as sex, social class, religion, sexual orientation, age, disability, and geographic location that can differentially impact the quality of life for people and groups. Thus, we will utilize intersectionality theory to identify, analyze, and transform the quality of Black college coaches' experiences and the quantity of their representation.

To address the purpose of this chapter it is necessary to identify and understand the experiences, patterns, and pathways, utilizing a critical theory. Critical theories can unpack the similarities and differences between Black men and women, yet link their experiences to a broader conversation of diversity and inclusion. Therefore, Kimberle Crenshaw's (1991) intersectionality theoretical framework will be used to contextualize the current state of Black college coaches by exploring (a) the ways in which race and ideologies are manifested through the evaluation of the quantity and quality of Black coaches; (b) the legislation and political landscape shaping opportunities for Black coaches; and (c) experiential excerpts from current and former Black collegiate coaches to triangulate the data uncovered in the literature and to describe the lived effects of the concepts explored. Intersectionality posits that marginalized individuals' lived experiences are shaped by various social factors (i.e., race, social class, religion, gender) simultaneously. Hence, social factors work in concert on a macro level to push groups to the margins of society and/or hinder their growth and development within institutional contexts and organizations on a meso level. The effects result in a multiplicative layering of oppression felt on a personal micro level.

Intersectional challenges of Black college coaches

Intersectionality theory offers the opportunity to act through informing and creating transformative policies and best practices on three levels within society and sport: structural, representational, and political (Crenshaw, 1991). Therefore, we employ structural intersectionality to focus on how Black coaches' lived experiences are qualitatively different from White coaches' experiences (i.e., daily treatment). Representational intersectionality is utilized to provide insight on how media and popular cultures' portrayal of Black women and men coaches suppresses the realities of their lived experiences. And, political intersectionality is used to demonstrate how legislation and institutional policies have systematically decreased access and opportunities for Black coaches.

Structural challenges

College coaching is overwhelming White. Approximately 9% of college head coaches and 15% of assistant coaches are Black, numbers that have remained stagnant for the last 20 years (NCAA, 2019; Lapchick, 2018). While many factors are considered in choosing a coach, many scholars have called for a deeper look into these numbers to further understand how racial ideologies shape the opportunities afforded for Blacks (and people of color generally) to enter the coaching ranks (Cunningham & Sagas, 2005; Lapchick, 2018; McDowell, 2008). Even from the practitioner's standpoint, Johnson (2017) affirms scholarly examinations of college sport on the "systemic barriers to entry" into college coaching discern how the "pipeline," or pathway, to achieve a coaching position reflects distinct differences based on race. Therefore, we begin our investigation of Black college coaching with the structural factors shaping this phenomenon.

Structural intersectionality interrogates the policies and regulations, rooted in social categorizations, which create differential treatment and experiences for marginalized groups and shape the political and physical position of Black college coaches. Sport environments are entrenched with racialized beliefs about a person's abilities which are institutionalized through policies (or the lack thereof) and practices that leave objective hiring criteria to subjective interpretation (Cunningham & Sagas, 2005). For example, Black people's athletic participation fuels such notions of physical superiority and intellectual inferiority (Sailes, 1993) through their service in the roles of "physical positions," rather than the roles of "thinking" positions in some sports (e.g., quarterback in American Football) which is evidenced not only on the playing field (i.e., stacking) but also in the positions of Black coaches. Of the 138 Football Bowl Subdivision (FBS) schools, considered the highest level of college sports, only 12 schools have Black head football coaches; these numbers are similar in men and women's basketball. With college athletes serving as the potential pool of college athletes, the low and stagnant number of Black coaches becomes more alarming (Everhart & Chelladurai, 1998). Though the increasing number of Black coaches would suggest progress, the percentage and position rank of these coaches remains the same (Lapchick, 2018; NCAA, 2019). The stagnation in these numbers can be attributed to institutionalized practices of access discrimination and treatment discrimination based on race and gender that often go unchecked because they are seen as normal and the ideologies guiding them seen as true.

Access discrimination refers to the prejudice Black coaches face in gaining access to positions, resources, and influence vital to acquiring and sustaining positions within their field. In 2005, Cunningham and Sagas found Black men represented 33% of assistant basketball coaches though they consisted of 48% of the former athletes. While Black athletes are highly sought after as participants, or labor, that same desire is not reflected in coaching positions, or as administrative leaders. White coaches and athletic administrators are hiring White coaches to the exclusion of Black coaches creating an isomorphic view of who has the capacity to coach. Cunningham and Sagas (2005) found Black coaches were more likely to obtain the position when under Black head coaches than White head coaches with one in six White head coaches having no Black coaches on their staff. Furthermore, Black coaches' ability to be hired is compounded by the lack of Black head coaches and, more specifically, the smaller number of Black sport administrators (e.g., Athletic Director, Associate Director, Assistant Director).

For Black men, beliefs about their cognitive ability denied them access to head coaching positions as they were presumed incompetent to be head coaches and that their "talent" is in recruiting. The overrepresentation of Black coaches in recruiting and special assistant positions suggests they are not considered able to handle a "thinking" position (Anderson, 1993). The roles and responsibilities of special assistants and recruiters are informed by and dependent on the often highly subjective needs of head coaches and college sports organizations and are not officially recognized by the NCAA. Therefore, experience in these roles is difficult to quantify and leverage for promotion in the coaching ranks. For Black women, beliefs about their attitude and leadership abilities (Carter-Francique, In Press; McDowell, 2008; McDowell et al., 2009) foreground their entrance into college sport administration and participation and the experiences during their tenure. Carter-

Francique (In Press) reviewed the archetypes that often frame Black women in society, namely as mammies, jezebels, and sapphires and discerned that the racialized representations of Black women create biases and a culture of microaggressions within college sport. Under these lenses, Black women are characterized as having undesirable coaching traits ranging from angry to aggressive to sexually permissive to nurturing. Consequently, these same traits are also used to justify the clustering of Black women in positions that focus on nurturing college athletes and their families (i.e., academic advising, special assistants).

The statistics also indicate Black college coaches have one opportunity to succeed in their position as few of them are rehired after being fired or relieved of duty (Johnson, 2017). Therefore, the limited access and coaching opportunities for Black men and women also limits their potential ability to serve in administrative capacities as the pool for these positions is often filled from persons in the coaching ranks (Carter-Francique, 2018). While Seebruck & Savage (2014) indicated Black coaches benefit from being on the staff of White head coaches, without Black people gaining social capital to influence hiring and promotion decisions in college athletics, the institutionalized practices of homogenous reproduction will continue (cf., Powell, 2008).

Treatment discrimination references the behaviors, attitudes, and limited opportunities to access resources (e.g., education, leadership development) for advancement. In college athletics, treatment discrimination is rooted in racial and gender stereotypes which create unrealistic beliefs and expectations about Black coaches that are often utilized to evaluate their performance (Harrison, 1998). Sagas & Cunningham (2004) explained that leaders in sport organizations are more likely to associate and appreciate those with similar demographics (i.e., race, gender, age) as themselves (e.g., homogenous reproduction). Moreover, leaders are more likely to attribute preferred characteristics of employees based on race. Over time, these preferences become the structural habitus of sport organizations, normalizing these social beliefs through hiring and promotion criteria, behavior policies, and differential, often discriminatory, treatment. Unfortunately, discrimination becomes harder to prove as it does not manifest in overt acts and often is explained away by personal preference, the will of stakeholders, and/or lack of professional experience.

Treatment discrimination also occurs in the form of resource distribution. The concentration of resources – physical, financial, and social – in college sport lies within those in power, namely White males, who are more likely to provide those resources to other White males (Cooper et al., 2017; Cunningham & Sagas, 2004; McDowell, 2008). This preference creates a deep divide between the resources available to White and Black coaches, which is exacerbated for Black women, in obtaining, maintaining, and excelling in the coaching profession. For example, sharing and providing opportunities to obtain professional development training (e.g., NCAA Leadership Institute, National Football League (NFL) Coaches Academy). Another example reveals that White coaches are more likely to hire other White coaches creating challenges for Black coaches to gain the experience needed to qualify for promotions. A powerful example of this phenomenon occurred in 2014: She was a four year letterman (an award given to student-athletes who meet the school's standard of athletic excellence) at the University of Southern California (USC) Trojans basketball team, sixth in NCAA history for career points and third in rebounding, a three time Naismith College Player of the Year, and a Wade Trophy recipient. She later became the first USC basketball player to have her jersey retired; and, participate in the Olympic Games, Pan American Games, and Goodwill Games, and played professionally for the Women's National Basketball Association (WNBA). But, even with all of these accolades and social and athletic capital, she had difficulties attaining an intercollegiate head coaching position. You may ask yourself, "How can a person fail to obtain a coaching position with this resume?"

Cheryl Miller, inducted into the Basketball Hall of Fame in 1995, pondered this very notion during her job search before being hired as the head women's basketball coach at Langston University in 2014. Despite her aforementioned resume, Miller said, "*It was very humbling .... Sometimes we get in the mindset where it should be easy, and it wasn't. There were a lot of doors that were slammed*" (Steckley, 2014, personal communication). Miller's story highlights how objective criteria of success (e.g., coaching experience, winning championships, personal statistics) can still be viewed subjectively through the color of their skin.

Representational challenges

Acknowledging the present-day implications of U.S. structural and political history, the limitations placed on Black coaches can be further exacerbated and ultimately repackaged by mediated (re)presentation. The mediated image of Black men and women as coaches has the ability to maintain and/or alter how they are perceived in society and sport. Crenshaw (1991) contends the most influential method to devalue Black people is through their cultural representation. Specifically, she states representational intersectionality "*would include both the ways in which these images are produced through a confluence of prevalent narratives of race and gender, as well as a recognition of how contemporary critiques of racist and sexist representation marginalize*" Black people (Crenshaw, 1991: 1283).

Furthermore, the mediated image of Black men and women as coaches affects how they are perceived as qualified leaders within college sport. This (re)presentation manifests through stereotypes and myths and the stories and personal narratives within the college sport environment and beyond. There is a historical practice of utilizing myths and negative stereotypes to describe Black people as a race and characterize their behavior, work ethic, and intellectual capabilities in society and sport (Harrison, 1998; Vertinsky & Captain, 1998). Social myths are legitimized through the *"attitudes, values, beliefs, stereotypes, and ideologies that provide moral and intellectual justification for the social practices that distribute social value within the social systems"* (Sidanius & Pratto, 1999: 45). In sport the utilization of stereotypes and perpetuation of myths are commonly utilized through announcers' and media journalists' characterizations and framing of Black athletes at the college and professional levels (Billings, 2004; Bruce, 2004; Denham et al., 2002; Eastman & Billings, 2001; McCarthy & Jones, 1997; Mercurio & Filak, 2010).

For example, Mercurio and Filak (2010) examined how Black college football quarterbacks were framed by a major print media entity finding that writers used racial stereotypes to describe the physical attributes of a Black quarterback as being:

> a big guy with a rifle arm, good mobility, good feet, shows good overall toughness and a good feel for the game.

SI [Sports Illustrated], though, ended its description of this player with the following statement:

> His biggest adjustment will be in the mental area, as he will face sophisticated NFL defenses, and his ability to learn a new system quickly and make the right decisions will be critical to his early NFL success.
> (Mercurio & Filak, 2010: 66–67)

These descriptions of Black male college athletes' abilities reflect notions of athletic superiority and intellectual inferiority which are noted to influence how athletic directors and institutional administrators perceive Black men and women as coaching candidates.

Stereotypes are defined as *"an exaggerated belief associated with a category. Its function is to justify (rationalize) our conduct in relation to that category"* (Allport, 1979: 191). Sport scholars examined how the use of stereotypes rationalized, or biased, Black coaches' perceived abilities due to their subjugated racial categorization (Sagas & Cunningham, 2004; Sartore & Cunningham, 2006). In 2006, Sartore & Cunningham examined the influence of stereotypes on potential leaders (White men and women) and their management practices (i.e., hiring, promotion) in relation to college coaches of color and found the perceived potential of Black coaches is undermined by racial stereotypes that can be *"activated by simply presenting the face of the applicant"*(Sartore & Cunningham 2006: 79).

Hence, (re)presentation and perceptions can play an influential role in the actual hiring and retention of Black college coaches. The importance of illuminating such a truth is to then identify who is telling these stories, conveying these messages, and (re)presenting the Black athlete and in some cases Black coaches as we watch the football, basketball, track and field, and other college athletic competitions. As discussed in the structural perspective, management practices which favor White men are significant as they speak to issues of homogenous reproduction, tokenism, and the need for diversity education and management training. Nevertheless, the fact remains that Black head coaches and assistant coaches are underrepresented and identifying ways to redress these challenges is required.

Political challenges

Employing structural and representational intersectionality revealed a number of overlapping marginalizations and in this section of political intersectionality, we illuminate the ways policies and legislation can limit Black coaches' experiences. Political intersectionality acknowledges that living at the intersections of racial and gender subordination creates *"conflicting political agendas"* (Crenshaw, 1991: 1251). For Black male and female coaches, the political challenges are similar yet different. While Black male coaches face discrimination based on race, policies around family leave (e.g., maternity) and the loss of human capital due to childbirth contribute to the "motherhood wage penalty" for Black women (cf., Budig & Hodges, 2010). In addition, hiring practices and work standards create differential treatment of Black women. For example, preferences for sport administrators who are overwhelming white males, to hire other white males (e.g., homogenous reproduction), also contribute to hiring practices and work environments that are hostile. In addition, due to the "white male norm" Black women are susceptible to evaluation based on higher standards of performance "success." Structural and representational ideologies undergird societal legislation and NCAA policies which create divergent pathways for Black men and women, and work to limit their access to positions and eligibility for promotions based on their sex. Thus, Black men and women are often viewed from a single-axis race-based perspective, rather than as multidimensional beings (i.e., based on race, gender, and experiential status) which can hinder their opportunities for support (i.e., developmental training, career support organizations, interpretation of diversity policies and best practices) and eventual promotion into positions of leadership (Mathewson, 1995).

To redress these instances of disparate treatment, activists' efforts shifted the political atmosphere to pass Title VII of the Civil Rights Act of 1964 which provides legal protections against discrimination based on race, gender, and religion. Unfortunately, this legislation fails Black people when its implementation does not address the structural inequalities that still limit their coaching opportunities and their experiences when hired. Moreover,

Black coaches represent various communities in concert with their race; and unfortunately, structural remedies neglect the experiences of those who represent more than one subordinate group. This is most evident in the treatment of Black women.

Title IX of the Education Amendments of 1972 (Title IX) was enacted to provide legal protection based on gender; however, it also failed to adequately address the structural inequalities Black women face given the intersection of their race, gender, *and* social class. Therefore, while Title IX opened the door for more sport opportunities for women, a closer look at the sport participation data uncovers these opportunities are concentrated in sports that were geographically and/or economically inaccessible to Black women (i.e., lacrosse, swimming, soccer, softball; Carter-Francique, 2016; Rhoden, 2007). Without access and exposure to these sports as athletes, Black people are systematically denied opportunities to coach these sports and take advantage of the legal privileges afforded them. Moreover, the historical marginalization of these groups has created a culture around who coaches these sports that serves to preemptively exclude them from being considered for these positions.

To draw attention to this reality would be to question the gendered and racialized division of labor in college sports. Therefore, when Black coaches fail, the narrative used to explain their failure reflects a fulfilled prophetic stereotype, yet when they succeed Black coaches are deemed the exception and their success is attributed to skill and/or luck. Issues of gender relations are also subsumed under the category of race to the detriment of both Black men and women. As Dr. Harry Edwards (Moody College of Communication, 2015) stated:

> [The focus on interracial conflict between black and white men] overall it outright precludes and is dismissive of gender-based conflicts and contradictions and issues. And today, this limitation, this ... major blind spot in our overall social and political analysis and strategies, in our paradigm for understanding the world that we are attempting to impact, promises to be as costly as it is intolerable. So while I am elated that athletes are beginning to stand up and speak out, I am equally concerned that their actions do not reflect a much-needed, even imperative change in our paradigmatic perceptions of the issues. America today has a major human rights problem and it particularly afflicts Black America. And that human rights crisis is the circumstances, the outcomes, the status of women and girls.

Intersectional remedies for Black college coaches

Our analysis of the current landscape of Black coaches illustrates the intersectional factors shaping hiring and promotion practices in sport coaching:

access and treatment discrimination and stereotypes limiting individual agency. These factors sustain the institutional racialized and gender-based processes within college sport administration by normalizing and privileging White people in sport coaching (Rankin-Wright et al., 2017). The disparity between the number of Black coaches and Black college athletes in football and basketball, and blinding absence of Black coaches and athletes in emerging sports, speaks to the matrix of oppression Black people must navigate to obtain, maintain, and thrive in college coaching positions. This oppression creates a dearth of Black coaches that limits the organizational effectiveness of sport teams and the job satisfaction of its employees (Cunningham, 2010). As Singer (2005) warns, if the sport management field, researchers and practitioners alike, continue to consciously or unconsciously ignore the ways in which race shapes sport, particularly to the detriment of Black coaches, athletes, and administrators, we will continue to operate within and reinforce racial ideologies that blind us to recognizing racism and cripple us from redressing its effects.

Black coaches face subordination in many forms and therefore require a multilevel approach to meaningful interventions on their behalf. Intersectional subordination created by race, gender, and ultimately class *"need not to be intentionally produced; in fact, it is frequently the consequence of the imposition of one burden that interacts with pre-existing vulnerabilities to create yet another dimension of disempowerment"* (Crenshaw, 1991: 1249). Therefore, sport administrators dedicated to increasing the number of Black coaches and the quality of their experiences must create policies to address the intersecting factors outlined above. Specifically, sport administrators need clear and transparent equity policies at a broader level and in relation to coaching appointments; and, sport administrators need stakeholder involvement in the process with ongoing evaluation to measure the effectiveness of these policies and hiring practices.

Through clear evaluation criteria and stakeholder accountability, structural remedies can reduce the influence of racial bias and create more transparent hiring and promotion practices. Including community stakeholders in every aspect of the process and allowing them to provide input in the candidate pool and interview process can redress institutional habitus to conflate Whiteness with quality coaching and the groupthink mentality that occurs in homogenous groups.

Another layer of accountability should occur through the governing body in the form of annual evaluations of programs' diversity efforts, cultural competency training (e.g., NCAA Inclusion Forum), and recognition for programs and administrators who employ effective inclusionary practice. Annual reviews of each department's progress are needed to promote accountability and identify schools in need of assistance by creating and maintaining inclusive environments for Black coaches. Data from sport scholars can inform campus athletic policies and governing bodies to support the efforts to fund training for campuses and implement best practices based on these policies. Incentives (e.g., more scholarships, recruitment dollars, recognition) for organizations that implement these policies and practices can be given to promote diversity as vital to the athletic department's success (e.g., financially, athletically, socially).

At the representational level, successful mentoring relationships are linked to internal and external job success (Carter-Francique, 2018). From a structural standpoint, mentoring needs to have a formal professional development role for head coaches and administrators. Mentoring should include opportunities for "deep talk" that allow the concerns of Black coaches to be heard by the administration and redress the "presumed incompetence" Black coaches face in academic settings due to the stereotypes about their race and/or gender (Borland & Bruening, 2010; cf., Gutiérrez y Muhs et al., 2012).

Moreover, mentors should serve as advocates for these coaches and promote their well-being as synergetic with the welfare of the sport organization. Mentors in head coaching and administrative positions can promote clear hiring and promotion guidelines that value the contributions of Black coaches through more competitive pay and promotion to positions more central to their team's success and the longevity of one's coaching career. The relationship between mentors and mentees should also provide access to resources traditionally inaccessible to Black coaches without making these coaches feel inferior for doing so. Beyond financial compensation, Black coaches need an infrastructure within college sports that values their existence and promotes their success. Key to enabling sport infrastructures to support the growth and development of Black coaches is focusing their intent and implementation on redressing discrimination as opposed to "fixing" their Blackness.

Conclusion

The focus of this chapter was to critically examine how race is used to frame the experiences of Black coaches. Building upon previous literature from critical sport scholars who critiqued current narratives around Black coaches and sought to robustly understand their sociopolitical position, we employed intersectionality as a theoretical framework. Intersectionality allows us to frame race and racial inequalities as structural, representational, and political processes and practices of Whiteness; and therefore, better articulate the dearth of Black coaches and quality of their coaching experiences. Therefore, this chapter not only progresses our understanding of the current status of Black college coaches, but it also reaffirms the importance of applying a socioecological (e.g., multilevel) approach to understanding how sport policies are created and implemented. By using intersectionality, we demonstrate the strengths of CRT to identify, explore, and challenge the dominant ideologies that work to make sport appear color blind. Specifically, the use of intersectionality allowed us to overcome the blind spots (Mirza, 2009) left in our examination of Black coaches when we view them from a single identity as opposed to multidimensional beings who are socially viewed through various lenses, namely race and gender.

Oppression is understood as a matrix in which race and gender intersect in different ways to create similar but divergent experiences for Black female and male coaches. This is most evident in the treatment of Black females as underscored by Bruening's (2005) question, "Are all the women White and all Blacks men"? Bruening's review of sport scholarship demonstrated that in research and practice, efforts to address racism and sexism do not benefit all women equally because current research, and consequently, policy and legislation, only addresses the nature of their oppression in silos (race or gender). In the face of these hegemonic forces, CRT and intersectionality provide a systematic justice approach and representational voice for marginalized groups. These theoretical frameworks and their methodological implications proffer an essential critical lens for relevant critiques of dominant epistemologies and create inclusive practices in sport coaching. In advocating for the equitable treatment of Black college coaches, the need for Black sport administrators is glaring. Increasing the number of Black sport administrators is vital to having the experience of Black people centered in the decision-making processes affecting coaches' (and student-athletes') success and their well-being on and off the playing field. By centralizing race and the experiences of Black coaches, we desire to ensure the presence of Black coaches is made visible in sport coaching research and practice.

Centering Black coaches in the exploration, critique, and revision of sport administration, our desire is to better equip college sport organizations to identify and challenge color blind policies. We seek to disrupt the normalization of White maleness, the criminalization of Blackness, and the insignificant nature of femaleness in college coaching that limits the number of Black coaches in the profession and the college administrators' effectiveness to address the needs of an increasingly diverse student-athlete, employee, and consumer population. The difficulty for college sport personnel to acknowledge race and gender, and how they intersect, can be attributed to the overwhelmingly homogenous makeup of coaches (White male) and, moreover, the isomorphic forces (e.g., media) of commercialized sport. Yet, through the acknowledgment of race and gender as non-neutral factors that shape *everyone's* experience in sport, privileging some (Whites) at the expense of the "Other", we continue the work of critical race scholars to promote political and legal changes that lead us closer to racial and gender equality and equity. As many sport scholars including Akilah Carter-Francique and Jacqueline McDowell posit, race and gender need to be at the center of research, policy, and practice if sport is to adequately meet the needs of its student-athletes, employees, sponsors, and consumers (Carter-Francique, 2018; McDowell et al., 2009).

For college sport organizations to fulfill their mission of increasing the safety and well-being of student-athletes and provide the best quality coaches for fulling this mission, it is imperative that college sport administrators and governing bodies understand the nature, realities, and influence of the intersectional matrix of oppression on institutional processes and individual preferences.

References

Abney, R. (1989). *The effects of role models and mentors on career patterns of Black women coaches and athletic administrators in historically Black and historically White institutions of higher education.*

Abney, R. (2007). African American women in intercollegiate coaching and athletic administration: Unequal access. *Diversity and social justice in college sport: Sport management and the student athlete*, 51–75.

Abney, R., & Richey, D. (1991). Barriers encountered by Black female athletic administrators and coaches. *Journal of Physical Education, Recreation & Dance*, 62(6), 19–21.

Agyemang, K., & DeLorme, J. (2010). Examining the dearth of black head coaches at the NCAA football bowl subdivision level: A critical race theory and social dominance theory analysis. *Journal of Issues in Intercollegiate Athletics*, 3, 35–52.

Allport, G. W. (1979). *The nature of prejudice.* Cambridge, MA: Addison-Wesley.

Anderson, D. (1993). Cultural diversity on campus: A look at intercollegiate football coaches. *Journal of Sport and Social Issues*, 17(1), 61–66.

Billings, A. C. (2004). Depicting the quarterback in black and white: A content analysis of college and professional football broadcast commentary. *Howard Journal of Communications*, 15(4), 201–210.

Borland, J. F. & Bruening, J. E. (2010) Navigating barriers: A qualitative examination of the under-representation of Black females as head coaches in collegiate basketball. *Sport Management Review*, 13, 407–420.

Bruce, T. (2004). Marking the boundaries of the 'normal' in televised sports: The play-by-play of race. *Media, Culture & Society*, 26(6), 861–879.

Bruening, J. E. 2005. Gender and racial analysis in sport: Are all the women White and all the Blacks men? *Quest*, 57.

Budig, M. J., & Hodges, M. J. (2010). Differences in disadvantage: Variation in the motherhood penalty across White women's earnings distribution. *American Sociological Review*, 75(5), 705–728.

Carter-Francique, A. R. (In Press). Intersectionality and the influence of stereotypes for Black sportswomen in college sport. In V. Farmer (ed.), *Critical Theory in the Academy*. Charlotte, NC: Information Age Publishing.

Carter-Francique, A. R. (2016). Sports and health and their impact on African American girls. In P. Larke, G. Webb-Hasan, & J. Young (Eds.), *Cultivating achievement, respect, and empowerment (CARE) for African American girls in PreK-12 settings: Implications for access, equity, and achievement* (pp. 303–336). Charlotte, NC: Information Age Publishing.

Carter-Francique, A. R. (2018). Is excellence inclusive: Examining Black female college athletes' sense of belonging. *Journal of Higher Education and Athletic Innovations*, 1(3), 48–73.

Carter-Francique, A. R., & Olushola, J. (2016). Women coaches of color: Examining the effects of intersectionality. In *Women in sports coaching* (pp. 95–108). Routledge.

Carter-Francique, A. R. & Richardson, F. M. (2016). Controlling media, controlling access: The role of sport media on Black women's sport participation. *Race, Gender & Class*, 23(1/2), 7–33.

Cooper, J. N., Nwadike, A., & Macaulay, C. (2017). A Critical Race Theory analysis of big-time college sports: Implications for culturally responsive and race-conscious sport leadership. *Journal of Issues in Intercollegiate Athletics*, 10, 204–233.

Crenshaw, K. (1991). Mapping the margins: Intersectionality, identity politics and violence against women of color. *Stanford Law Review*, 43(6), 1241–1299.

Cunningham, G. B. (2010). Understanding the under-representation of African American coaches: A multilevel perspective. *Sport Management Review*, 13(4), 395–406.

Cunningham, G. B., Sagas, M., & Ashley, F. B. (2001). Occupational commitment and intent to leave the coaching profession: Differences according to race. *International Review for the Sociology of Sport*, 36(2), 131–148.

Cunningham, G. B., & Sagas, M. (2005). Access discrimination in intercollegiate athletics. *Journal of Sport and Social Issues*, 29(2), 148–163.

Davis, L. R., & Harris, O. (2002). Race and ethnicity in US sports media. In *Media Sport* (pp. 168–170). Routledge.

Day, J. C., & McDonald, S. (2010). Not so fast, my friend: Social capital and the race disparity in promotions among college football coaches. *Sociological Spectrum*, 30 (2), 138–158.

Denham, B. E., Billings, A. C., & Halone, K. K. (2002). Differential accounts of race in broadcast commentary of the 2000 NCAA Men's and Women's Final Four basketball tournaments. *Sociology of Sport Journal*, 19(3), 315–332.

Eastman, S. T., & Billings, A. C. (2001). Biased voices of sports: Racial and gender stereotyping in college basketball announcing. *Howard Journal of Communication*, 12 (4), 183–201.

Everhart, B. C., & Chelladurai, P. (1998). Gender differences in preferences for coaching as an occupation: The role of self-efficacy, valence, and perceived barriers. *Research Quarterly for Exercise and Sport*, 68, 188–200.

Finch, B., McDowell, J., & Sagas, M. (2010). An examination of racial diversity in collegiate football. *Journal for the Study of Sports and Athletes in Education*, 4(1), 47–58.

Gutiérrez y Muhs, G., Niemann, Y. F., González, C. G., & Harris, A. P. (2012). *Presumed incompetent: The intersections of race and class for women in academia*. University Press of Colorado.

Harrison, C. K. (1998). Themes that thread through society: Racism and athletic manifestation in the African-American community. *Race Ethnicity and Education*, 1 (1), 63–74.

Hylton, K. (2012). Talk the talk, walk the walk: Defining critical race theory in research. *Race Ethnicity and Education*, 15(1), 23–41.

Johnson, R. (2017). College football's lack of black head coaches is the result of a flawed pipeline. Retrieved January 5, 2019 from https://www.sbnation.com/college-football/2017/8/9/15959410/black-coaches-rooney-rule-assistants-quarterbacks.

Lapchick, R., Baker, D., Bounds, J., Bullock Jr, T., Malveaux, C., May, J., & Tymeson, A. (2015). *Regression throughout collegiate athletic leadership: Assessing diversity among* campus and conference leaders for football bowl subdivision (FBS) in the 2015–16 Academic Year. The Institute for Diversity and Ethics in Sport, University of Central Florida. Retrieved from http://nebula.wsimg.com/981af17829f7a5a304eaa2160bfeb884

Lapchick, R. (2018) *The 2018 Racial and Gender Report Card*. Institute of Diversity and Ethics. University of Central Florida.

Latimer, S. R., & Mathes, S. A. (1985). Black college football coaches' social, educational, athletic and career pattern characteristics. *Journal of Sport Behavior*, 8(3), 149.

Mathewson, A. D. (1995). Black women, gender equity and the function at the junction. *Marq. Sports Law Journal*, 6, 239.

McCarthy, D., & Jones, R. L. (1997). Speed, aggression, strength, and tactical naivete: The portrayal of the Black soccer player on television. *Journal of Sport and Social Issues*, 21(4), 348–362.

McCarthy, D., Jones, R. L., & Potrac, P. (2003). Constructing images and interpreting realities: The case of the Black soccer player on television. *International Review for the Sociology of Sport*, 38(2), 217–238.

McDowell, J. (2008) Head Black women in charge: An investigation of Black female athletic directors negotiation of their gender race and class identities. *Dissertations Abstract International* (69(7), m3210 (UMI No.3321745).

McDowell, J., Cunningham, G. B., & Singer, J. N. (2009). The supply and demand side of occupational segregation: The case of an intercollegiate athletic department. *Journal of African American Studies*, 13(4), 431–454.

Mercurio, E., & Filak, V. F. (2010). Roughing the passer: The framing of black and white quarterbacks prior to the NFL draft. *The Howard Journal of Communications*, 21(1), 56–71.

Mirza, H. S. (2009). *Race, gender and educational desire: Why Black women succeed and fail*. Oxon: Routledge.

Mixon, F. G., & Treviño, L. J. (2004). How race affects dismissals of college football coaches. *Journal of Labor Research*, 25(4), 645–656.

Moody College of Communication (2015, January 22). Harry Edwards presents the keynote at the 2015 Black Student-Athlete Conference at UT Austin [Video File]. Retrieved from https://www.youtube.com/watch?v=Z93a1NVWWnY.

National Collegiate Athletic Association (NCAA) (2019). Demographics database: Executive Summary 2018-19. http://www.ncaa.org/about/resources/research/ncaa-demographics-database

Powell, S. (2008). *Souled out? How blacks are winning and losing in sports*. Human Kinetics.

Rankin-Wright, A., Hylton, K., & Norman, L. (2017). Negotiating the coaching landscape: Experiences of Black men and women coaches in the United Kingdom. *International Review for the Sociology of Sport*. https://doi.org/10.1177/1012690217724879.

Rhoden, W. C. (2007). *Forty million dollar slaves: The rise, fall, and redemption of the Black athlete*. Broadway Books.

Sabo, D., Jansen, S. C., Tate, D., Duncan, M. C., & Leggett, S. (1996). Televising international sport: Race, ethnicity, and nationalistic bias. *Journal of Sport and Social Issues*, 20(1), 7–21.

Sagas, M., & Cunningham, G. B. (2004). Treatment discrimination in college coaching: Its prevalence and impact on the career success of assistant basketball coaches. *International Sports Journal*, 8(1), 76.

Sagas, M., & Cunningham, G. B. (2005). Racial differences in the career success of assistant football coaches: The role of discrimination, human capital, and social capital. *Journal of Applied Social Psychology*, 35(4), 773–797.

Sailes, G. A. (1993). An investigation of campus stereotypes: the myth of black athletic superiority and the dumb jock stereotype. *Sociology of Sport Journal*, 10(1), 88–97.

Sartore, M. L., & Cunningham, G. B. (2006). Stereotypes, race, and coaching. *Journal of African American Studies*, 10(2), 69–83.

Seebruck, R., & Savage, S. V. (2014) The differential effects of racially homophilous sponsorship ties on job opportunities in an elite labor market: The case of NCAA basketball coaching. *Sociological Inquiry*, 85(1), 75–101.

Sidanius, J. & Pratto, F. (1999). *Social dominance: An intergroup theory of social hierarchy and oppression*. 2nd Edition. Cambridge: Cambridge University Press.

Singer, J. N. (2005). Addressing epistemological racism in sport management research. *Journal of Sport Management*, 19(4), 464–479.

Singer, J. N., Harrison, C. K., & Bukstein, S. J. (2010). A critical race analysis of the hiring process for head coaches in NCAA college football. *Journal of Intercollegiate Sport*, 3(2), 270–296.

Solorzano, D. (1997). Images and words that wound: Critical race theory, racial stereotyping and teacher education. *Teacher Education Quarterly*. Summer 1997 1997.

Solorzano, D. (1998). Critical race theory, race and gender microaggressions and the experiences of Chicana and Chicano scholars. *Qualitative Studies in Education*, 11 (1), 121–136.

Solorzano, D., & Bernal, D. (2001). Examining transformational resistance through a critical race and LatCrit theory framework: Chicana and Chicano students in an urban context. *Urban Education*, 36(3), 308–342.

Solorzano, D., & Yosso, T. J. (2000). Maintaining social justice hopes within academic realities: A Freirean approach to critical race/LatCrit pedagogy. *78 Denv. U. L. Rev.*, 595.

Steckley, K. (2014). Miller is new Langston coach. Retrieved on July 4, 2019 from https://www.pressreader.com/usa/tulsa-world/20140501/282256663503647.

Vertinsky, P., & Captain, G. (1998). More myth than history: American culture and representations of the black female's athletic ability. *Journal of Sport History*, 25(3), 532–561.

Chapter 10

Transnational coaches
A critical exploration of intersections of race/ethnicity and gender

Annelies Knoppers and Donna de Haan

Introduction

> At its home Winter Olympics in Sochi in 2014, Russia came a confident first in the medal table, with 13 gold, 11 silver and nine bronze medals. … it is beyond doubt that a large part in the victory was played by the numerous foreign specialists hired to assist them [the athletes].
>
> (Shestakova, 2016)[1]

In an attempt to achieve elite sporting success, athletes are offered access to a plethora of performance related experts including, nutritionists, psychologists, physiotherapists, exercise scientists and world-class coaches. The quote at the start of this chapter reflects a popular mediated understanding of the role 'foreign coaches' play in elite sport. Their purpose is to improve athlete performance so that a country can win more medals. Across most sports the athlete and coach experiences typically occur in contexts that are male dominated and which favor men (Norman, 2016).

The role of the coach, however, goes beyond influencing performance on the pitch, field or court. Coaches also play a vital and visible role in maintaining and challenging dominant sporting discourses (Denison et al., 2015). Norman (2016) suggests that coaches are important agents of social change who could implement visions and values of equity, equality and inclusion. Within this context we assume that coaching is a complex social and cultural practice that is embedded within a specific country's sport structure and culture (Hassanin & Light, 2014). The scholarly literature on migration and international sport refers to such coaches as transnationals since they cross national borders to work/live and are therefore part of social processes that occur between nation-states (Leonard, 2010). Basch et al. (1994: 7) refer to transnationalism as *"a social process whereby people forge and sustain multi-stranded social relations that transverse geographic, political, and cultural borders"*.

In this chapter we present the argument that transnational coaches contribute to intersectional social processes that go beyond improving athletic performance and that these processes tend to be ignored by those appointing these coaches and by scholars who study coaching. Since this chapter is part of a book with a central focus on race/ethnicity, we primarily focus on the intersection of race/ethnicity and gender. Therefore, the aim of this chapter is to add to understandings of how transnational coaches disrupt, challenge or reinforce dominant ideologies of race/ethnicity and gender. Various scholars have shown that many coaches in Western countries are white heterosexual men (e.g. Bradbury, 2013; Bradbury et al., 2018; Calhoun et al., 2011; Kamphoff & Gill, 2013). Therefore, we also aim to reflect on the position of coaches in terms of gender, heteronormativity and whiteness and the invisibility of this positioning in the scholarly literature. Specifically, we use a post-structural lens to draw on scholarly work on migration, critical management, gender, intersectionality and sport to explore how transnational coaching may contribute to and challenge complex figurations of race/ethnicity and gender.

We begin with a theoretical section in which we briefly explain a post-structural approach and introduce the key concepts relevant to this chapter, including whiteness, discourses of masculinity and heteronormativity. This is followed by two sections that review available literature relating to transnational coaches with a specific focus on race/ethnicity, the gendered complexity of coaching and becoming an elite coach. In the final section of this chapter we discuss the limitations of existing research and suggest the use of potential 'new/alternative' concepts that may advance the field.

Theoretical framework

A post-structural lens assumes that socially constructed boundaries are used to create categories that are subsequently hierarchically arranged (Anthias, 2012). For example, the structure of most sport organizations at the local, national and/or international level is based on two categories using constructed definitions of gender that have been used to create a hierarchy in which more financial, support and media resources flow to men than they do to women. Post-structuralism assumes reality is not only socially constructed but also constituted by discourse. Such an approach attempts to reveal how certain practices are accepted knowledge or common sense and become regimes of truth while other practices and knowledges become invisible (Foucault, 1972). If the presence and practices of transnational coaches, for example, are only seen through the dominant discursive lens of their involvement in the performance of elite athletes, then the ways this presence contributes to social power relations such as race and gender will be obscured to those hiring/working with them, to coaches themselves and to scholars.

We consider whiteness, heteronormativity and masculinity to be discursive practices that advantage those defined as white, heterosexual and male (McDonald & Shelby, 2018). Long & Hylton (2002: 3) have argued that the intersection of whiteness and masculinity produces "*everyday invisible and hegemonic processes that privilege (and normalize) the position of White [male] identities*". This intersection positions white male coaches as being essentially or 'naturally' better or superior coaches than those marked as nonwhite and/ or female. These practices of whiteness and heteronormative masculinity have become the norm in sport/coaching (Hylton, 2009; Lenskyj, 2013; Spracklen, 2013). Whiteness or being labeled as white can serve as a resource for transnational coaches and may intersect with a contextual masculinity to construct a skilled transnational coach. Their apparent skill as well as their position in society gives transnational coaches specific privileges. Their knowledge, perceived authority and expertise and the ways they constitute athletes and sport while negotiating cultural forces in their host country (as well as from their country of 'citizenship') may be used to strengthen and shift meanings in local and national constructions of gender, race, ethnicity and nationality (see also Christian, 2018). The privileges of whiteness and desired masculinity may not always be automatic, however, since their meanings depend on time and place (see also Leonard, 2010). We return to this point further on.

The ways in which discursive practices of and about white male transnational coaches reinforce and challenge dominant notions about whiteness and masculinity in sport may receive little attention because they are 'common sense' and often invisible (Hughey, 2010). Leonard (2010) contends that privilege in the 'skilled' transnational labor market is often based on categorical constructions of 'race', gender and citizenship. Analyses of how elite transnationals such as coaches practice gender, race and other relations of power could therefore add to understandings of the gendering and racialization of sport in a specific context. In the following section we summarize the research based on empirical data about the experiences of transnational coaches. Much of the available empirical scholarship around transnational coaching and sport has focused on gender and race as separate categories and ethnicity as being conflated with race and/or nationality. We attempt to show how the focus of such scholarship generally ignores the role of these coaches in the gendering and racialization of sport in the host country.

Review: empirical research on the experience of transnational coaches

> Coaches in rugby from New Zealand, gymnastics from Russia, and wrestling from Cuba are among the dozens of outsiders brought in to share their expertise in sports not traditionally associated with Brazil.
>
> (Ramil & Downie, 2015)

In this section we present a general review of empirical research that focuses on the experiences of transnational coaches at the micro and meso levels and highlight the relatively little attention that has been paid to intersections of race/ethnicity and gender. Much of this empirical research on transnational coaches has been conducted at the micro or individual level and is situated within cross-cultural psychology. The focus of these *micro*-level studies is on the adjustments transnational coaches have made while coaching elite athletes in the hosting country. For example, in the quotation used at the start of this section, the coaches are referred to as 'outsiders', so what is the lived experience of an outsider like? The results from *micro*-level studies reveal that these coaches primarily attributed the necessity and scope of their adjustments to perceived differences between the culture of host and birth country and to the goal of optimal performance for their athletes. For example, Cummings (2014) describes in detail the adaptation strategies used by immigrant coaches from China, Belarus, Ukraine, Romania, Soviet Union, Jamaica, Mexico, New Zealand, the United Kingdom and Germany who coached high performance athletes in boxing, judo, rowing, synchronized swimming and badminton in Canada. The strategies of these coaches included acquiring necessary communication skills, developing a "sense of belonging" and understanding the nature of (non)hierarchical relationships including those between athlete and coach and contextual constructions of respect. Sasaba et al. (2017) used a similar approach and found that coaches of national gymnastic teams from Japan, Mexico and the USA, working in the USA, attributed differences between themselves and the athletes they coached, to culture. Relatively little attention was paid in these studies, however, to how coaches influence and are influenced by broader social forces related to race and gender (see also De Jong, 2016; Primecz et al., 2016).

Not all scholars who have looked at transnational coaches have used a cross-cultural framework, however. Others have examined the context in which the practice of coaching takes place and the power of knowledge/discourses. For example, Kerr & Moore (2015) used a Foucauldian framework to study the experiences of coaches from the Soviet Union who coached gymnastics in New Zealand. The researchers found that these coaches drew on discourses about childhood, parenting and social ideologies to make sense of their experiences. The use of this theoretical framework enabled the researchers to show how the actions and ways of thinking of transnational coaches not only reflected individual preferences but were also informed by broader social forces.

Others have used a more *meso*-level analysis to explore why coaches migrate. Wicker and colleagues (Wicker et al., 2018; Orlowski et al., 2016, 2018) for example, concluded that push factors such as having a degree in sport science and pull factors such as larger salaries and a permanent contract, played a role in the decisions of German coaches to coach in another country. Borges et al. (2015) found that transnational Spanish coaches in professional football and handball had been recruited informally and had relied on their networks to attain such positions. Kerr & Obel (2018) also tried to take broader structures and societal forces into account by using actor-network theory to show how multiple human and nonhuman factors together facilitated the migration of ten Russian gymnastic coaches to New Zealand. The material factors included illness, leotards, work visas, finances and education systems while the human factors pertained to individual choices, the support offered by spouses and the wellbeing of their children.

None of the above cited studies explored how the presence of these coaches informed or disrupted the discourses that shaped the structure of sport in the host country. Do transnational coaches, for example, practice colonization in their attempt to transform the system and the athletes they encounter in the host country to mirror the one they have developed elsewhere? A tentative answer to this question is presented by Bairner & Barbour (2005) in their exploratory study of seven elite coaches from South Africa, New Zealand and Australia who migrated to Ireland to develop rugby programs/clubs. The findings suggest the influence of these rugby coaches may have extended beyond the teams they currently coach. The coaches believed they were able to influence the playing style in a significant manner. Specifically, the Irish style of playing was replaced with a style that the coaches had 'successfully' used elsewhere. Bairner & Barbour concluded that the practices of transnational coaches may increase the homogenization of playing style in a sport. The presence of a transnational coach could, therefore, shape a sport, athletes and local coaches in ways that go beyond the current winning of games and improving player performances (see also Carter, 2011). We contend that this influence includes ways transnational coaches and their presence may challenge, reconfigure and reproduce gender and racial hierarchies and power inequalities that may be part of the context in which a transnational coach practices coaching. We return to this point of colonization further on.

The *meso-* or institutional-level impact of the movement of coaches, across national borders, may displace national coaches. Although the media presents announcements about the hiring of 'foreign' coaches as a positive development for the hosting country, local coaches and athletes may see such appointments in other ways. A few accounts in the media point to resistance from national coaches to the advent of transnational coaches. For example, Akhil Kumar, a championship boxer from India argues that:

> We should be encouraging young coaches in India. They are the ones who know the system and realities of sport inside out... We shouldn't allow foreign experts to dictate us... If the foreign coaches are so good, then why are they not employed at the sub-junior level? If they are so good, let them shape youngsters. Why are finished products handed to

them? If I come into the national camp after winning the national title, am I not an almost finished product given to them?

(Rediff.com, 2018)

Similarly, Ryan Giggs, the former Manchester United winger and assistant manager, argued that there are too many foreign coaches in the Premier League leaving little opportunity for local talent:

> There's a lot of top quality foreign coaches in the Premier League, but there's also a lot of quality British coaches and managers out there but they don't get the chance to prove what you can do and see what you can do with a talented team. I just think on the balance, there's too many foreigners at the moment and British coaches probably just don't get the chances.
>
> (Eurosport, 2017)

While it could be argued that transnational opportunities are equally available for British coaches, they are not filling positions in other national leagues at the same rate as transnational coaches are filling up the Premier League (Spencer, 2018).

This preference for the appointment of transnational coaches instead of national coaching talent is not confined to professional sport but also occurs in amateur/Olympic sports. Kerr & Cervin (2016) investigated the lack of appointment of women coaches of elite gymnasts in New Zealand and Australia. They found that boards looked to other countries and recruited men instead of first looking at those available in New Zealand and Australia. These available coaches were often women. None of the studies cited above looked specifically at how and why these specific coaches were recruited and hired.

Although most of the transnational coaches described in the above-mentioned studies seemingly adapted to normative practices in their host country, at the same time, possibly contributing to the cultural homogenization of a sport, relatively little scholarly attention has been paid to how their presence may disrupt sport systems and gender and racial hierarchies. In the following we expand on ways the presence of transnational coaches may contribute or challenge the racialization and gendering of sport and comment on the lack of research in this area. This emphasis on what is lacking and needed should contribute to a research agenda on this topic.

Transnational coaches: race and ethnicity

> Billy, listen to me. White men can't jump.

The above quotation is a line taken from the 1992 film 'White Men Can't Jump' about two basketball hustlers, one black, one white. In the movie this line is spoken by Sidney to Billy Hoyle, a former college basketball player who makes his living by hustling 'streetballers' who assume he cannot play well because he is white. Billy uses his opponents' racial stereotypes to his advantage as he hustles them in pickup games by encouraging his opponents, most of whom are black, to falsely believe they have a natural advantage over him due to his race and clothing style. While this example plays out between two fictional players, research has shown how coaches use racial or gender discourses to describe the skills and work habits of (male) athletes (e.g. Cunningham et al., 2006; De Haan & Knoppers, 2019; Rankin-Wright, Hylton, & Norman, 2016). Khomutova (2016) is one of the few researchers who looked at constructions of both race and ethnicity in international sport. She explored how professional basketball coaches of multicultural basketball teams in Central Europe constructed race and ethnicity. These teams consisted of athletes whom coaches identified as differing in ethnicity, nationality and race. Khomutova found that these coaches engaged in productive strategies to negotiate what they constructed as different playing styles. The coaches attributed these differences in styles to ethnicity and saw them as emerging from various subcultures based on ethnicity/country of origin. The coaches said they respected these ethnic and national differences and that they worked hard to try to accommodate them. This was different for perceived racial differences in behaviors and playing styles of black athletes, all of whom were African-American. Specifically, these coaches constructed black players and their playing styles as a source of problems. Few, if any, coaches had developed constructive strategies to overcome these 'racial differences'. 'Race' was seen as fixed and as black.

The migration of skilled sport labor such as occurred in these multicultural basketball teams seems, therefore, to have included a transnational migration of discourses about black and white bodies. Specifically, dominant negative discourses about African-American athletes were accepted uncritically. Khomutova did not attribute the actions of these coaches to practices of whiteness and/or masculinity nor did she examine why coaches attempted to accommodate (white heterogenous) ethnicity that they saw as fluid while constructing race as fixed, homogenous, synonymous with being black and conflating it with nationality (American). The intersections between ethnicity, race and nationality in transnational sport and coaching, and the role masculinity plays in that, has been largely ignored (see also Ryan & Martin, 2013). Yet, as we argue in the following these are social relations of power that shape both transnational coaches and the contexts in which they work (and travel).

Hylton (2009) and Fenton (2003) have argued that race and ethnicity are often conflated. They contended that relations of power converge in race and ethnicity since both are often used to construct categories that are used to create social hierarchies. These hierarchies are used to distinguish minority populations from numerical majorities and to label these minorities as

Other. Hylton emphasizes the constructedness of these definitions by pointing out that *"there is a 'naturalness' attributed to socially constructed, sometimes shared categories that sets up arbitrary boundaries"* (Hylton, 2009: 15). Race and ethnicity may be confounded even more when transnational coaches move to a specific country other than their own. They may be privileged due to skin color or ethnic markers in one setting while their status in another setting may limit those privileges. For example, nationality is also often conflated with ethnicity, and both may be seen as being synonymous with culture. The example of Ruud Gullit, a Dutch football player and manager of Surinamese descent, illustrates this. He was a famous Dutch football player who later became a football manager and worked as coach in England beginning in 1995. He named himself an "overseas coach" rather than naming himself a black [male] coach (King, 2004). This example suggests identities are fluid and that race/nation/ethnicity and gender intersect in different ways depending on the situation and who is doing the defining.

These categories of ethnicity and nationality that are assumed to produce identities are not homogenous, nor is behavior an automatic reflection of (ethnic) identity. Coaches may reproduce and participate in certain traditions or customs and they themselves or researchers may assign them a certain ethnicity based on that behavior. This behavior may, however, be instrumental instead of being an expression of self-perceived identity or subjectivity. For example, various transnational coaches and their athletes in their 'host' country in the studies cited above, suggested that the transition to being a coach in Canada and the United States meant they could not engage in what is seen as authoritarian behavior. They seemed to associate this behavior with ethnicity/nationality (Cummings, 2014; Sasaba et al., 2017; Schinke et al., 2013). Various studies on physical and emotional abuse and authoritarian behavior in sport coaching have shown, however, that such behavior is not specific to one area of the world or to a stable ethnic descriptor (see, for example, Kerr & Stirling, 2012; Jacobs et al., 2017; Pinheiro et al., 2014). Rather, these scholars argued that such behavior is often a result of dominant discursive practices about developing mental toughness in young athletes.

Nationality is not only often associated with ethnicity but may also be constructed as an actual community that exists in a specific place. However, as Anderson (2006) argues, this community is more a social imaginary than it is actual since all those living within the borders of a country do not know each other. Anthias (2002) contends that such an imagined community needs an Other from which it can imagine itself as being different or separate. Also, those living within the borders of a nation state or community are not all assigned the same ethnic status. Someone with a Dutch passport may be ethnically rooted in China and be seen as Chinese, as an Other, although born and raised in the Netherlands. When she becomes a transnational coach, the ways in which she is 'seen' in her host country may depend more on how Chinese race/ethnicity is constructed in that time and place than meanings assigned to Dutch-ness and will intersect with constructions of gender by transnational coaches.

Gender: transnational coaches

> *The male coaches thought that they had a harem. We [female athletes] were the harems of women that followed them around and did everything the men said, and they got a bit carried away with that. I'm talking about two specific foreign coaches...*
> (de Haan & Norman, 2019: 6)

As the foregoing quote suggests, transnational coaches come to a country with internalized conceptions of masculinity and femininity that shape their behavior. Gender and nationality of athletes are explicitly institutionalized and policed in international sport through the use of fixed categories defined by the International Olympic Committee while race and ethnicity as categories of analysis are often more contextual as the other chapters in this book show. In contrast to athletes, a coach does not need to undergo gender verification nor does s/he need to be a national of the country s/he is representing. Transnational coaches that are recruited to work in countries other than where they live, can work freely across national boundaries assuming they can obtain a visa. There are no formal institutional requirements for coaches that restrict their participation in international competition and their transnational mobilities. Informally, race/ethnicity/nationality and gender and heteronormativity will, however, play a role in selection procedures and, consequently, in the mobility of transnational coaches (Tudor, 2018). The host country bears a great deal of responsibility for their choice of coach, recruitment and selection but also the ways such appointments may shape a sport and sport culture and contribute to its racialization and gendering.

In the migration literature gender is often associated with women (Hearn et al., 2006). Gender tends to be constructed as an individualized expression of skilled transnationals and may ignore the culturally specific contexts of such constructions. Consequently, transnational coaches may vary in the ways in which they construct women's and men's sports and difference. Conversely, gender is institutionalized in sport within a specific nation so that time and place may shape these localized constructions as well (Knoppers & Anthonissen, 2003). Comparative research is needed that looks at how transnational coaches negotiate, challenge and strengthen these discourses.

Although the underrepresentation of women in coaching has received a great deal of scholarly attention (see Burton, 2015 for a summary), gender is often neglected in scholarly research on skilled labor migration of professionals including that in coaching. A recent exception is our own work (De

Haan & Knoppers, 2019; De Haan & Norman, 2019). We looked at the gendered practices used by transnational coaches to constitute elite athletes. We found that these coaches, regardless of country of origin, created an essentialist gendered hierarchy in which male athletes were the norm and the actions and ideas of elite female athletes were discounted. We did not examine how these gendered practices were connected to constructions of ethnicity and nationality, however.

Although research has explored the experiences of lesbian coaches (Krane & Barber, 2005; Norman, 2012), little research is available that has focused on transnational coaches and explored *"existing heterogeneous expressions of queerness across the globe"* (Mizzi, 2015, no page number). We assume this lack of research includes transnational coaches as well. Mizzi, who compared the work experiences of gay male educators teaching overseas, found that gay male educators who had moved from the global south to Canada felt that in order to 'fit' or assimilate they had to take on an identity based on sexual orientation that to them was a problematic Western concept.

Ward & Schneider (2009: 438) argue, however, that such a focus on identities in a transnational context is too narrow in scope. They contend that:

> *heteronormativity shapes the production of identities, relationships, cultural expressions, and institutional practices, revealing it to be a force with consequences well beyond the discrimination against lesbians and gay men... heteronormativity gives form to a broad range of cultural forms and societal institutions that are all too often analyzed without attention to the specter of queerness but also to the ways that racism, socioeconomic inequalities, and the colonial gaze are dependent upon ideas about normal bodies, identifications, and sex practices.*

Much of the work on migration and sport does not specifically address gender, however, let alone heteronormativity. Similar to work done in migration studies when gender is addressed, the focus is on men (and their wives); gendered practices and institutions rarely receive critical attention (see also Kunz, 2016; Pessar & Mahler, 2003). An exception is the work of Kerr & Obel (2018). They paid attention to women partners of male transnational coaches. Some of these women accompanied their husbands while others stayed in the country of origin. This focus is a welcome addition to the transnational sport literature since it illustrates how transnational coaching practices have consequences for more than the elite athletes whom they coach. A focus on transnational coaches and their partners could explore how such practices strengthen sport as a site for the practice of heteronormativity.

Research is therefore needed on gender as a construction in transnational coaching to explore how it *"permeates a variety of practices, identities, and institutions implicated in immigration"* (Hondagneu-Sotelo, 2003: 9 see also Yuval-Davis, 1997). As we have argued in previous sections this heteronormativity intersects with race/ethnicity and nationality. This complexity has however rarely been captured in research on transnational coaches.

Possible approaches: researching transnational coaches and their intersectional practices

In this section we present various ways such research could be conducted. The possibilities presented here are not meant to be exhaustive but are briefly described to encourage readers to conduct research in this area.

Post-colonial approach

Current constructions of race and gender in sport at both local and transnational levels can be viewed through the lens of post colonialism (Chen & Mason, 2018; Leonard, 2010; Lugones, 2007). A post-colonial lens questions normalized assumptions of the cultural binary representations of the Self/Other. Fechter & Walsh (2010: 1203) contend that *"the post-colonial self becomes figured as competent, capable and 'developing the Other'"*. The quote at the beginning of this chapter illustrates this well. Transnational coaches are recruited because they are assumed to be skilled and able to develop athletes. The transnational coach is the colonizer and the athletes in the host country are the colonized. Much of the expansion of sport across the globe is based on Western sport so that in essence the practices of transnational coaches can be seen as a colonial endeavor (Chen & Mason, 2018). A post-colonial approach, however, assumes that the distinction between the athletes as the Other and the coach as the Self is a false distinction since culture is assumed to be hybrid and fluid. A post-colonial approach explores continuities and disruptions over time in ways of thinking, relationships and attitudes about the Self and Other. Specifically, the use of such an approach means scholars need to pay attention to the multilayered and intersectional contexts in which transnational coaches are situated and how they create expertise and regimes of truth (Fechter & Walsh, 2010).

Intersectionality and translocational positionality

A queer perspective is an approach that could inform intersectional analyses of whiteness and masculinity of transnational coaches. It is an approach that assumes heteronormativity is an organizing principle of *"the matrix of domination"* (Ward & Schneider, 2009: 434). The use of a queer lens makes visible and problematizes practices that strengthen or reproduce heteronormativity (see also Calhoun et al., 2011; Tudor, 2018; Ward & Schneider, 2009). This could include an examination of how heteronormative discursive practices of transnational coaches are racialized and how those practices circulate in a specific sport to become regimes of truth, that is, how they become discourses that coaches and those around them accept and make function as true (see also Foucault, 1972). Such a queer analytical focus could be used to explore how ethnicized/racialized and gendered bodies are embedded in (post-colonial) constructions of transnational coaches and their practices, what sustains these practices and the norms that emerge from them. This intersectional focus can add to understandings of the dynamic relationships between white normativity and heteronormativity and how "'*normative sexual hierarchies' structure global processes such as migration*" (Ward & Schneider, 2009: 435).

Power relations are fluid, however, and simultaneously operate in contradictory and different forms. Any research project on transnational mobility must not only explore intersectionality but also *differentiate* between various relations of power such as race/nationality/ethnicity/ gender. Tudor (2018: 14) suggests that differentiations among these power relations "*are necessary to be able to define and deconstruct specific oppressions, ascriptions, exclusions and abjectifications*". A focus on differentiation could give researchers insight into "*the specificities of these various relations of power and to formulate the precise and ever shifting forms of resistance*" and how those might be specific to not only time and place but also to a sport (Tudor, 2008: 14). Tudor also argues that this exploration of specific power relations should be part of a larger research agenda in which scholars are: "*able to think of them [various power relations] as assemblages… by analyzing ambivalences, contradictions and blurry cross-fadings…*" (Tudor 2008: 14).

A focus on a specific location of a transnational coach may be a way to explore this differentiation. A transnational coach, for example, may be in a position of dominance in her or his function as coach but the meanings assigned to this function or position may intersect with other subordinate ascribed categories of race, gender and ethnicity not only within the sport system but also in her/his life outside of sport. Transnational coaches may move from one country to another after an Olympic or World Cup cycle. The ways in which these coaches strengthen or disrupt local or national dominant practices of heteronormativity, masculinity and their intersection with whiteness may vary by location. Anthias (2002) suggests using the term 'translocational' and 'translocational positionality' to describe conflation and intersection of social relations of power such as race, ethnicity, nationality, gender and sexuality in a specific location. This concept can be used to:

> *denote the ways in which social locations are products of particular constellations of social relations, and in terms of relationality and experience at determinate points in time; it considers them within a spatial and temporal context. It points to the existence of contradictory and shifting social locations where one*

might be in a position of dominance and subordination simultaneously on the one hand or at different times or spaces on the other.

(Anthias, 2002: 501–502)

The concept of translocational positionality to study differentiation in transnational practices in coaching does not necessarily mean those meanings and their associated practices are fixed. Nor does a focus on constructions of race/ethnicity and gender mean they should be seen as separate narratives in which a study of gender or race assumes but does not mention specific practices of masculinity and/or whiteness (Hylton, 2009).

The gendered and racialized meanings assigned to practices of transnational coaches may also be very unstable and perhaps not reflective of a socially constructed category of race or gender at all. They may also replicate dominant ways of coaching that have become part of a sport over time. A coach from Russia may be constructed as authoritarian due to perceived notions of ethnicity/race/gender generally assigned to such nationals. This construction may overlook the presence of many coaches in the host country who also use such styles as we indicated earlier. Transnational coaches will engage in/perform and emphasize certain practices of masculinity and femininity that intersect in some ways with whiteness, but they may differ relatively little from those in which national coaches engage in the same sport. The ways in which translocational positionality informs practices of transnational coaches could therefore give further insight into the fluidity of the conflation of race/ethnicity/nationality and gender.

Conclusion

To conclude, we suggest research is needed that explores how discursive practices of transnational and national coaches reconfigure and challenge dominant ideologies of race/ethnicity and gender, their intersections as well as power inequalities and how these meanings and configurations are negotiated in a specific time and place. Does the increase in transnational coaches strengthen dominant gender and race/ethnic ideologies and norms in sport and/or does it also challenge or question them? (see also Pessar & Mahler, 2003). Such research not only could provide insight into the ways social relations of power are challenged and reproduced through national and transnational coaching practices but could also enrich scholarship in other areas such as critical studies of (sport) migration, gender, race/ethnicity and of diversity management (De Jong, 2016).

Note

1 This does not exclude the possibility that other factors such as doping and home advantage played a role in 'the victory' as well.

References

Anderson, B. (2006). *Imagined communities: Reflections on the origin and spread of nationalism (revised edition)*. London: Verso Books.

Anthias, F. (2002). 'Where do I belong?' Narrating collective identity and translocational positionality. *Ethnicities*, 2 (4) 491–514.

Anthias, F. (2012). Transnational mobilities, migration research and intersectionality: Towards a translocational frame. *Nordic Journal of Migration Research*, 2, 102–110.

Bairner, A., & Barbour, D. (2005). Where the grass is greener: Irish rugby union, migrant coaches and the globalisation debate. *Football Studies*, 8 (1), 27–41.

Basch, L., Glick Schiller, N., & Szanton Blanc, C. (1994). *Nations unbound: Transnational projects, postcolonial predicaments and deterritorialized nation-states*. Amsterdam: Gordon & Breach.

Borges, M., Rosado, A., de Oliveira, R., & Freitas, F. (2015). Coaches' migration: A qualitative analysis of recruitment, motivations and experiences. *Leisure Studies*, 34 (5), 588–602.

Bradbury, S. (2013). Institutional racism, whiteness and the under-representation of minorities in leadership positions in football in Europe. *Soccer & Society*, 14(3), 296–314.

Bradbury, S., Van Sterkenburg, J., & Mignon, P. (2018). The under-representation and experiences of elite level minority coaches in professional football in England, France and the Netherlands. *International Review for the Sociology of Sport*, 53 (3), 313–334.

Burton, L. J. (2015). Underrepresentation of women in sport leadership: A review of research. *Sport Management Review*, 18 (2), 155–165.

Calhoun, A. S., LaVoi, N. M., & Johnson, A. (2011). Framing with family: Examining online coaches' biographies for heteronormative and heterosexist narratives. *International Journal of Sport Communication*, 4 (3), 300–316.

Carter, T. (2011). Re-placing sport migrants: Moving beyond the institutional structures informing international sport migration. *International Review for the Sociology of Sport*, 48 (1), 66–82.

Chen, C., & Mason, D. S. (2018). A postcolonial reading of representations of non-western leadership in sport management studies. *Journal of Sport Management*, 32 (2), 150–169.

Christian, M. (2018). A global critical race and racism framework: Racial entanglements and deep and malleable Whiteness. *Sociology of Race and Ethnicity*, 1–17 (preprint).

Cummings, J. (2014). *The adaptation challenges and strategies of immigrant high performance coaches working within the Canadian sport system* (Doctoral dissertation, Laurentian University of Sudbury, Ontario, Canada).

Cunningham, G. B., Bruening, J. E., & Straub, T. (2006). The underrepresentation of African Americans in NCAA Division IA head coaching positions. *Journal of Sport Management*, 20 (3), 387–413.

De Haan, D., & Knoppers, A. (2019). Examining gendered discourses in coaching high performance sport: A Foucauldian perspective. *International Review of the Sociology of Sport*. doi:1012690219829692.

De Haan, D., & Norman, L. (2019). Mind the gap: The presence of capital and power in the female athlete–male -coach relationship within elite rowing. *Sports Coaching Review*, doi:10.1080/21640629.2019.1567160.

De Jong, S. (2016). Converging logics? Managing migration and managing diversity. *Journal of Ethnic and Migration Studies*, 42 (3), 341–358.

Denison, J., Pringle, R., Cassidy, T., & Hessian, P. (2015). Informing coaches' practices: Toward an application of Foucault's ethics. *International Sport Coaching Journal*, 2(1), 72–76.

Eurosport. (2017). Ryan Giggs: Too many foreign managers in Premier League. https://www.eurosport.com/football/premier-league/2016-2017/ryan-giggs-too-many-foreign-managers-in-premier-league_sto6068456/story.shtml.

Fechter, A. M., & Walsh, K. (2010). Examining 'expatriate' continuities: Postcolonial approaches to mobile professionals. *Journal of Ethnic and Migration Studies*, 36 (8), 1197–1210.

Fenton, S. (2003). *Ethnicity*. Cambridge: Polity Press.

Foucault, M. (1972). *The archaeology of knowledge*. London: Tavistock Publications.

Hassanin, R., & Light, R. (2014). The influence of cultural context on rugby coaches' beliefs about coaching. *Sports Coaching Review*, 3 (2), 132–144.

Hearn, J., Metcalfe, B., & Piekkari, R. (2006). Gender and international human resource management. In Günter, K., Stahl, G., & Björkman, I. (eds) *Handbook of research in international human resource management* (pp. 502–522). Cheltenham, UK: Edward Elgar.

Hondagneu-Sotelo, P. (Ed.) (2003). *Gender and US immigration: Contemporary trends*. Los Angeles, CA: University of California Press.

Hughey, M. (2010). The (dis)similarities of white racial identities: The conceptual framework of 'hegemonic whiteness'. *Ethnic and Racial Studies*, 33 (8), 1289–1309.

Hylton, K. (2009). *'Race' and sport: Critical race theory*. London: Routledge.

Jacobs, F., Smits, F., & Knoppers, A. (2017). 'You don't realize what you see!' The institutional context of emotional abuse in elite youth sport. *Sport in Society*, 20 (1), 126–143.

Kamphoff, C., & Gill, D. (2013). Issues of exclusion and discrimination in the coaching profession. In Potrac, P., Gilbert, W. & Denison, J. (Eds) *Routledge handbook of sports coaching* (pp. 52–66). London: Routledge.

Kerr, G. A., & Stirling, A. E. (2012). Parents' reflections on their child's experiences of emotionally abusive coaching practices. *Journal of Applied Sport Psychology*, 24, 191–206.

Kerr, R., & Cervin, G. (2016). An ironic imbalance: Coaching opportunities and gender in women's artistic gymnastics in Australia and New Zealand. *The International Journal of the History of Sport*, 33, 2139–2152.

Kerr, R., & Moore, K. (2015). Hard work or child's play? Migrant coaches' reflections on coaching gymnastics in New Zealand. *World Leisure Journal*, 57 (3), 185–195.

Kerr, R., & Obel, C. (2018). The migration of gymnastics coaches from the former Soviet Union to New Zealand: An actor–network theory perspective. *Leisure Studies*, doi:10.1080/02614367.2018.1482367.

Khomutova, A. (2016). Basketball coaches' experience in working with multicultural teams: Central and Northern European perspectives. *Sport in Society*, 19 (7), 861–876.

King, C. (2004). Race and cultural identity: Playing the race game inside football. *Leisure Studies*, 23 (1), 19–30.

Knoppers, A., & Anthonissen, A. (2003). Women's soccer in the United States and the Netherlands: Differences and similarities in regimes of inequalities. *Sociology of Sport Journal*, 20, 351–370.

Krane, V., & Barber, H. (2005). Identity tensions in lesbian intercollegiate coaches. *Research Quarterly for Exercise and Sport*, 76(1), 67–81.

Kunz, S. (2016). Privileged mobilities: Locating the expatriate in migration scholarship. *Geography Compass*, 10 (3), 89–101.

Lenskyj, H. J. (2013). Reflections on communication and sport: On heteronormativity and gender identities. *Communication & Sport*, 1(1–2), 138–150.

Leonard, P. (2010). *Expatriate identities in postcolonial organizations: Working whiteness*. Burlington, VT: Ashgate.

Long, J., & Hylton, K. (2002). Shades of white: An examination of whiteness in sport. *Leisure Studies*, 2 187–103.

Lugones, M. (2007). Heterosexualism and the colonial/modern gender system. *Hypatia* 22 (1), 186–209.

McDonald, M., & Shelby, R. (2018). Feminism, intersectionality and the problem of Whiteness in leisure and sport practices and scholarship. In Mansfield, L., Caudwell, J., Wheaton, B., & Watson, B. (eds) *The Palgrave handbook of feminism and sport, leisure and physical education* (pp. 497–514). London: Palgrave Macmillan.

Mizzi, R. (2015). Sexualities on the move: A comparison of the work experiences of gay male educators teaching overseas. *Canadian Journal of Educational Administration and Policy*, issue 173.

Norman, L. (2012). Gendered homophobia in sport and coaching: Understanding the everyday experiences of lesbian coaches. *International Review for the Sociology of Sport*, 47(6), 705–723.

Norman, L. (2016). The impact of an "equal opportunities" ideological framework on coaches' knowledge and practice. *International Review for the Sociology of Sport*, 15 (8), 975–1004.

Orlowski, J., Wicker, P., & Breuer, C. (2016). Determinants of labor migration of elite sport coaches. *European Journal of Sport Science*, 16 (6), 711–718.

Orlowski, J., Wicker, P., & Breuer, C. (2018). Labor migration among elite sport coaches: An exploratory study. *International Review for the Sociology of Sport*, 53 (3), 335–349.

Pessar, P., & Mahler, S. (2003). Transnational migration: Bringing gender in. *International Migration Review*, 37, 812–846.

Pinheiro, M. C., Pimenta, N., Resende, R., & Malcolm, D. (2014). Gymnastics and child abuse: An analysis of former international Portuguese female artistic gymnasts. *Sport, Education and Society*, 19 (4), 435–450.

Primecz, H., Mahadevan, J., & Romani, L. (2016). Why is cross-cultural management scholarship blind to power relations? Investigating ethnicity, language, gender and religion in power-laden contexts. *International Journal of Cross Cultural Management*, 16 (2), 127–136.

Ramil, T., & Downie, A. (2015). Top-10 finish the aim for Brazil with one year to go. https://www.reuters.com/article/us-olympics-rio-sports/top-10-finish-the-aim-for-brazil-with-one-year-to-go-idUSKCN0Q926J20150805. The one that is mentioned now seems not to work.

Rankin-Wright, A. J., Hylton, K., & Norman, L. (2016). Off-colour landscape: Framing race equality in sport coaching. *Sociology of Sport Journal*, 33 (4), 357–368.

Rediff.com. (2018). Why the obsession with foreign coaches? http://www.rediff.com/sp orts/report/why-the-obsession-with-foreign-coaches-cwg-akhil-kumar/20180327.htm.

Ryan, I., & Martin, S. (2013). The practice of intersectionality: The amateur elite sport development game. *Equality, Diversity and Inclusion: An International Journal*, 32 (7), 688–700.

Sasaba, I., Fitzpatrick, S. J., Pope-Rhodius, A., & Sakuma, H. (2017). Elite gymnastics coaches' perceptions of coaching athletes from different cultures. *International Journal of Coaching Science*, 11 (2), 15–30.

Schinke, R. J., McGannon, K. R., Battochio, R. C., & Wells, G. D. (2013). Acculturation in elite sport: A thematic analysis of immigrant athletes and coaches. *Journal of Sports Sciences*, 31 (15), 1676–1686.

Shestakova, I. (2016). Russia's foreign Olympic sports coaches head home as money runs out. https://www.rbth.com/news/2016/11/08/russias-foreign-olympic-sports-coa ches-head-home-as-money-runs-out_645907.

Spencer, J. (2018). The 13 foreign coaches leading countries other than their own at the World Cup. https://www.90min.com/posts/6067448-the-13-foreign-coaches-lea ding-countries-other-than-their-own-at-the-world-cup.

Spracklen, K. (2013). *Whiteness and leisure*. London: Palgrave Macmillan.

Tudor, A. (2018). Cross-fadings of racialisation and migratisation: The postcolonial turn in Western European gender and migration studies. *Gender, Place & Culture*, 1–16. doi:10.1080/0966369X.2018.1441141.

Ward, J., & Schneider, B. (2009). The reaches of heteronormativity: An introduction. *Gender & Society*, 23 (4), 433–439.

Wicker, P., Orlowski, J., & Breuer, C. (2018). Coach migration in German high-performance sport. *European Sport Management Quarterly*, 18 (1), 93–111.

Yuval-Davis, N. (1997). Women, citizenship and difference. *Feminist Review*, 57 (1), 4–27.

Part III

Formalised racial equality interventions in sports coaching

Chapter 11

When the law won't work
The US National Football League's extra-judicial approach to addressing employment discrimination in coaching

N. Jeremi Duru

Introduction

In 2003, the most prominent American football league in the United States, the National Football League (NFL), implemented a modest interviewing protocol in an attempt to fend off accusations of racial inequity with respect to promotions among the league's coaches. Historically, the league's head coaching ranks had been virtually all white, with only a rare black coach, or an even rarer Latino coach, among them. Although all 32 club owners ultimately agreed to the interviewing protocol – mandating that a club searching for a head coach interview a person of color before making a hire – the initiative was, initially, an afterthought. Two of the first three clubs to hire a head coach after the policy's implementation ignored it and pundits maligned it as another half-hearted and hollow NFL attempt to project progressiveness (Hack, 2003; Duru, 2018), pp. 530–531). Fifteen years later, however, the protocol, known as the Rooney Rule, has not only altered the complexion of the NFL, it is an established employment best practice, relied upon in the United States and abroad, and in government as well as the private sector. Notably, the NFL did not hatch the Rooney Rule idea. Two civil rights lawyers, Johnnie Cochran and Cyrus Mehri, who were known for aggressive litigation and charismatic media presence, and who happened to love football, proposed the concept and pressured the NFL to adopt it. While understanding the Rooney Rule's operation and impact are important, the reason these seasoned and committed litigators chose this mechanism rather than litigation is just as important, and this chapter will explore both fronts.

The chapter will examine the racial inequity facing coaches of color in the NFL near the turn of the twenty-first century, the legal system's inadequacy in remedying that inequity, the effectuation of an alternative, extra-legal, solution to the problem, and the impact that solution – the Rooney Rule – has had across a range of sports and non-sports organizations. Ultimately, the chapter illustrates the law's limitations with respect to ensuring racial equity in employment and the consequent need for creative non-legal approaches to workplace fairness within sport and otherwise.[1]

The problem: racial inequity among coaches in the NFL

In 2002, Cyrus Mehri and Johnnie Cochran were two of the United States' most successful lawyers. Cochran was known principally for his successful, and certainly controversial, murder trial defense of former American football star O.J. Simpson, but he was most proud of the civil rights victories he had won for clients over the years. Mehri was less renown but similarly effective for his clients, securing hundred million dollar settlements from corporate titans such as Coca-Cola and Texaco on behalf of employees alleging racial discrimination. Together, they were in the midst of a civil rights lawsuit against pharmaceutical giant Johnson & Johnson when the NFL's Minnesota Vikings and Tampa Bay Buccaneers in quick succession fired their head coaches, both of whom were black. The terminations were startling for two reasons: (1) both coaches – Dennis Green and Tony Dungy – had performed well in their jobs; and (2) with Green and Dungy out, only one of the 32 NFL head coaches was of color, notwithstanding a roughly 70% player population of color. In the league's 80-year history, there had only been eight head coaches of color. Green, Dungy and the one remaining head coach of color in the league, Herm Edwards, had together constituted a high water mark of three head coaches of color in the league at one time, and the backslide to one discouraged those who believed things were trending in the other direction.

Mehri and Cochran were among those discouraged and they shared the view that coaches of color were systematically disadvantaged in pursuing head coaching positions. To test their hypothesis, they commissioned Dr. Janice Madden, a labor economist at the University of Pennsylvania, to analyze the win-loss records of all NFL head coaches over the previous 15 years and to then compare them by race. Dr. Madden's analysis confirmed their suspicion. Because there had been so few head coaches in the league who were neither white nor black, she focused her analysis on those two groups. However the data was sliced, it revealed that black head coaches outperformed white head coaches (Cochran & Mehri, 2002). Black head coaches averaged 9.1 wins over the course of a 16-game season, while white head coaches averaged 8 wins. Importantly, that ninth win generally meant the difference between a successful season and an unsuccessful one, as 60 percent of teams with 9 wins during that 15-year span made the playoffs and fewer than 10 percent of those with 8 wins made the playoffs. In black head coaches' last year before being fired, the disparity was even greater: they won, on average, 1.3 more games than white head coaches (Cochran & Mehri, 2002). In conclusion, Dr. Madden wrote, *"No matter how we look at success, black coaches are performing better. These data are consistent with black having to be better coaches than the whites in order to get a job as head coach in the NFL"* (Cochran & Mehri, 2002: 6).

With Dr. Madden's study, which was both statistically significant and peer reviewed, as the foundation, Mehri and Cochran drafted a report – titled *Black Coaches in the NFL: Superior Performance, Inferior Opportunities* – and released it at a press conference during which they threatened litigation if the NFL did not address the issue of inequity in coaching opportunities. The threat inspired dramatic headlines in newspapers across the country and applied public pressure to the NFL, but it was extremely unlikely to evolve into a successful lawsuit, and both Mehri and Cochran knew it. The report and the threat were first steps in a strategy designed, instead, to change the NFL from within.

The absence of a viable legal remedy

While a layperson may have seen litigation as a potentially fruitful means of creating change, seasoned civil rights lawyers knew a litigation approach would not have been promising. Though not impossible, for multiple reasons successfully suing the NFL for employment discrimination would have been extremely difficult. First, the NFL does not control any individual club's personnel decisions, and a court would therefore likely deem it an inappropriate defendant. While the NFL is an umbrella organization that helps coordinate the activities of its member clubs, it has no authority to instruct a club to hire or terminate a coach or any other employee (except, under rare circumstances, as a disciplinary matter). The NFL, therefore, could not reasonably be held liable for the Vikings firing Green or the Buccaneers firing Dungy or for any other club's head coach termination.

A potential exception might lie in the doctrine of juridical links. A juridical link describes a legal relationship wherein multiple defendants are connected in a way that would suggest a single resolution would be preferable to numerous separate suits (*Leer v. Washington Educ. Asn*, 172 F.R.D. 439, 450 (1997)). Because the juridical links exception has carried the day in employment discrimination cases involving employers connected by a collective bargaining agreement (CBA), it could at first blush appear to come into play in the NFL context, in which a CBA binds the league and its teams together. In those cases, however, the CBA relationship giving rise to the juridical links argument bound those employers with the prospective plaintiffs (*Marchwinski v. Oliver Tyrone Corp.*, 81 F.R.D. 487, 489 (1979)). The NFL CBA binds the employers – the clubs – to the players, but it does not bind coaches, the parties who would be plaintiffs in the prospective lawsuit. Moreover, some case law suggests the juridical links doctrine is only applicable in cases where there exists an allegedly discriminatory uniformly applied rule or policy (Henderson, 2000). With no actual league-wide policy to target, a suit against the league as a whole, even by way of juridical links, would not likely be successful. In the absence of a path through the juridical links doctrine to sue the NFL, any employment discrimination argument would have to target a particular club, and would almost certainly revolve around a claim born of the Civil Rights Act of 1964 (the "1964 Act" or "Act").

Title VII

The Act is the United States of America's most significant civil rights legislation. Congress passed the Act in the midst of, and in response to, deep racial discord and discrimination that enveloped the United States. Although the Thirteenth Amendment to the US Constitution outlawed chattel slavery in 1865, Jim Crow segregationist policies and other governmental and private discriminatory mechanisms followed in slavery's wake, oppressing blacks throughout the nation (Edwards and Thompson, 2010). The Act, unquestionably *"the most far-reaching bill on civil rights in modern American history,"* was designed to quash that oppression (Iheukwumere & Aka, 2001: 14). The Act's 11 titles outlaw discrimination in a wide swath of American life, from voter registration to public accommodations access. Title VII outlaws discrimination in employment. Although the entire Act has been generally impactful, *"Title VII has emerged as having the most significant impact in helping to shape the legal and policy discourse on the meaning of equality"* (Belton, 2005: 432–433). The Act applies to both public and private employers and reads, in relevant part, as follows: "[i]t shall be an unlawful employment practice for an employer ... to fail or refuse to hire or to discharge any individual, or otherwise to discriminate against any individual with respect to his compensation, terms, conditions, or privileges of employment, because of such individual's race, color, religion, sex, or national origin" (42 U.S.C.A. § 2000e-2).

An employment discrimination claim for a head coach of a professional sports club presents a unique circumstance. As noted above, because the club, not the league, employs the coach, the league would likely not be an appropriate defendant. The coach would, instead, have to bring his or her Title VII action against the employing club. Title VII allows for liability under two basic theories: disparate treatment and disparate impact. Disparate treatment liability applies when a defendant is found to have intentionally discriminated, while disparate impact liability applies when a defendant's selection process, though seemingly neutral on its face, produces a racially disproportionate outcome. As will be argued below, however, because of the specificities of the coach selection process, neither theory is likely to be fruitful for an aggrieved coach.

Disparate treatment

As impactful as Title VII has been in United States history, it is difficult today to prove intentional racial discrimination in a particular instance

(Green, 2003). While unabashed racists exist today, just as they have throughout US history, racial discrimination in the post-civil rights era is often expressed covertly, and perhaps subconsciously (Patterson, 2011; Williams, 2005). This is the case in sport as it is in society generally. Bringing a successful intentional racial discrimination claim, as an aggrieved coaching candidate might want to do, therefore, would be difficult.

In order to be successful with a disparate treatment Title VII lawsuit, a coach would have to overcome an inevitable motion for summary judgment, a legal mechanism that permits a defendant to defeat a plaintiff's claim before it gets to trial on the grounds that "there [exists] no genuine issue as to any material fact" in the case (*Celotex Corp. v. Catrett*, 477 U.S. 317, 322 (1986); Fed. R. Civ. P. 56). In order to do so, the coach would have to first establish a *prima facie* case of discrimination. While direct evidence, such as an admission or a document indicating the coach was denied the position due to race, would on its own establish a *prima facie* case, such overtly expressed discrimination is rare in today's society, as noted above. Without access to direct evidence, establishing a *prima facie* case would require that the coach make several showings, each by a preponderance of the evidence. Under this framework, established by the United States Supreme Court in the seminal case of *McDonnell Douglas Corp. v. Green*, the plaintiff would have to prove that he or she: (1) is a member of a protected class; (2) is qualified for the position; (3) was rejected; and (4) that someone else was selected (Lawrence, 1987).

As a person of color, the coach would unquestionably be in a protected class, satisfying the first element, and elements three and four would obviously be satisfied as well. The rub would be in the second element, where subjectivity with respect to how the term "qualified" is defined would come into play. Courts tend to erect a low bar for what constitutes "qualified": generally, a plaintiff need not prove he or she was as qualified as or better qualified than the person selected, but rather that he or she merely met the position's minimum criteria. The courts, however, are rather deferential to a defendant's view as to what criteria are required for success in a particular position, creating an opening for defendants to design job searches to advantage a select individual or group of selected individuals.

If a plaintiff is able to prove he or she is qualified under the *McDonnell Douglass* framework and meets the other three prongs as well, he or she does not win the case, but instead creates as rebuttable presumption of Title VII discrimination. The defendant then has the opportunity to shield itself from liability by articulating a legitimate, non-discriminatory reason for the hiring decision. The defendant's threshold here is exceedingly low. Indeed, courts have routinely found that articulating virtually any lawful reason discharges a defendant's burden on this score. As one court has put it, an "employer may fire an employee for a good reason, a bad reason, a reason based on erroneous facts, or for no reason at all, as long as the action is not for a discriminatory reason" (*Nix v. WLCY Radio/Rahall Commc'ns*, [1999] 738 F.2d 1181, 1187 (1984)).

Because the showing necessary to return the burden to the plaintiff is so low, defendants generally do so without difficulty. To prevail, the plaintiff must then prove the defendant's articulated reason was pretext and that racial discrimination played into the decision. This is not easily done. As noted above, courts in employment discrimination cases are generally quite deferential to defendants' decisions as to what constitutes the best candidate for a job. This is particularly the case with respect to sport; courts simply do not want to substitute their judgment for that of the sports club executive making the decision. So, if a club's principal decision maker articulates that he or she hired a coach other than the plaintiff because the other coach possessed a particular trait, the court will, in the absence of suspicious circumstances, find no disparate treatment occurred.

Disparate impact

Failure under disparate treatment theory does not doom a plaintiff's Title VII claim, however, because disparate impact theory provides the possibility of Title VII liability even with no showing of intentional discrimination. Under this approach, a coach would have to show that a seemingly non-discriminatory requirement of the job has a disproportionate impact on his or her protected class. This theory allows for the possibility that employment discrimination may exist even when an employer has not set out to discriminate and, indeed, may not know that he or she is discriminating. As such, it would seem an attractive litigative option for an aggrieved head coach.

Professional sports clubs, however, often do not apply identifiable hiring criteria when searching for coaches, making a disparate impact challenge somewhat contextually incongruous (Moye, 1998; Walker, 2006; Duru, 2018). Moreover, to surmount a summary judgment motion in this context, a plaintiff must show, generally through statistics, that the selection criteria the employer uses "causes the selection of applicants … in a racial pattern that significantly differs from that of the pool of applicants" and that the "disparity [is] so great it cannot reasonably be attributed to chance" (*NAACP v. Town of E. Haven*, 70 F.3d 219, 225 (1995)). Such a showing, though, generally demands analysis using a sample size large enough that the results constitute statistically reliable evidence. In the absence of statistical significance, which is difficult to establish in the context of a challenge to head coach hiring, a disparate impact claim will fail. An aggrieved head coach candidate of color's Title VII claim, therefore, whether brought under a disparate treatment theory or a disparate impact theory, is unlikely to succeed.

The seminal case of *Jackson v. University of New Haven* is illustrative. In that case, decided in 2002, James C. Jackson sued the University of New Hampshire (UNH), "alleging racial discrimination in hiring" when he was denied an opportunity to be head coach of the UNH football team (*Jackson v. Univ. of New Haven*, 228 F. Supp. 2d 156, 157 (2002)). In February of 1999, UNH posted the position and listed in the posting the following requirements:

> A bachelors degree is required, master's degree preferred. Successful collegiate coaching experience required. Experience in recruiting, game coaching and knowledge of NCAA rules and regulations is essential.
>
> (*Jackson* at 157)

Jackson, who was black, applied for the position along with 36 other applicants. UNH selected six finalists to interview, all of whom had two things in common: they were white and they had previously coached collegiate football. Jackson did not have collegiate football coaching experience, but he had been an outstanding minor league football coach, winning coach of the year awards on several occasions and being inducted into the minor league football hall of fame. Jackson's suit centered on Title VII and was two-fold, including both a disparate treatment and a disparate impact claim. Both claims, however, fell to a motion for summary judgment, with neither progressing beyond the *prima facie* stage. With respect to the disparate treatment claim, the parties agreed that Jackson was a member of a protected class, that he was declined the position, and that someone else received the position, but disagreed – as employment discrimination plaintiffs and defendants usually do – as to whether he was qualified.

Jackson acknowledged that UNH listed collegiate coaching experience as a required qualification for the job, but argued that such experience was not, in fact, necessary to be a successful collegiate head coach. The court, however, explained that "Jackson's subjective determination that he is qualified for the position is not enough to carry his burden of making out a *prima facie* case" (*Jackson* at 161). The court went on to emphasize that "broad deference should be afforded to employers in selecting hiring criteria … . Absent a showing by the plaintiff that the employer's demands were made in bad faith … an employer … is not compelled to submit the reasonableness of its employment criteria to the assessment of either judge or jury" (*Thornley v. Penton Pub., Inc.*, 104 F.3d 26, 29 (1997) (cited in *Jackson* at 157)). As noted above, this deference is the norm: rarely will a court look beyond a defendant's criteria for a position. If a plaintiff is able to show that a defendant's criteria apply differently to different applicants, a disparate treatment claim is in order, but when the criteria are applied uniformly, courts defer to the employer and a disparate treatment claim is likely to fail, as it did in *Jackson*.

Disparate impact analysis, as the *Jackson* case illustrates, would be similarly unavailing. Because the candidate pool for a head coaching position is typically small, statistical significance is difficult to attain. In *Jackson*, the plaintiff noted that 50 percent of the applicants for the head coaching position who identified themselves as black lacked college coaching experience, while only 10 percent of the candidates who identified themselves as white lacked college coaching experience. Because college coaching experience was required for the position, plaintiff argued that the disproportionate impact of the requirement potentially triggered disparate impact liability. The court, however, dug deeper into the numbers, noting that there were only 14 applicants for the position who identified their race, ten of whom were white and four of whom were black. So, the 10 percent figure represented 1 out of 10 and the 50 percent figure represented 2 out of 4. The court explained that these numbers were simply too small to yield a statistically significant result. The court went on to acknowledge that in the employment discrimination realm there is no definite sample size threshold above which a result is statistically significant and below which it is not, noting instead that the "substantiality of a disparity is judged on a case-by-case basis" (*Smith v. Xerox Corp.*, 196 F.3d 358, 366 (1999) (cited in *Jackson* at 157)). The number of applicants in the *Jackson* case, however, was clearly too small.

If courts are unwilling to find statistical significance in cases such as *Jackson*, it is not realistic that they would find statistical significance in an NFL coach's disparate impact challenge, as NFL club's head coach searches involve well fewer than 14 candidates. Indeed, a candidate pool of three or four is typical. NFL coaches passed over time and again for head coach positions, therefore, could not reasonably turn to Title VII analysis for relief. Even if there existed a viable path through the law, it is not clear that any aggrieved coach would be willing to take it. The professional sports world is small and club owners have long memories. Even if successful in a lawsuit, a plaintiff would stand the very real possibility of being ostracized and therefore unable to secure a meaningful job in sport going forward. Notwithstanding the University of Pennsylvania study and the Dungy and Green anecdotes, therefore, Mehri and Cochran knew that they could not reasonably turn to Title VII for relief. The law would not support them, and if it did, it is likely no prospective head coach would retain them. If they wanted to spark change, the courts were not a promising option.

The solution: the diverse candidate slate concept

Previous litigation successes, however, had led Mehri to what he believed could level the playing field for aspiring NFL coaches in the absence of a viable legal claim. In 1994, he had filed a class action racial discrimination lawsuit on behalf of employees against the oil titan Texaco, and in 1999 he had filed a similar suit against the Coca-Cola Company. In both cases, he possessed damning evidence that damaged the companies' arguments and brought them to the settlement table.

Texaco had initially been litigating fiercely, but its defense dissolved when Mehri's legal team discovered recordings of company executives spewing racial epithets suited for a "Ku Klux Klan rally" while destroying documents that were responsive to the plaintiffs' requests and would be damaging if revealed in court (Roberts & White, 1998: 255). The evidence in the Coca-Cola case was not as dramatic, but just as damaging from a legal perspective: hundreds of pages of employee compensation data revealing *"massive racially driven disparities"* (Hays, 2004: 214) After negotiations, Mehri settled both cases on behalf of his clients. The Texaco suit settled for $176 million and the Coca-Cola suit settled for $192.5 million. The economic terms were, by any measure, extraordinary, but the programmatic relief was also deeply impactful. For instance, as a part of both settlements, independent task forces were created to monitor the organizations going forward, and they were imbued with sweeping powers to reform human resources practices if the organizations went awry. The Coca-Cola settlement, however, included one provision the Texaco settlement did not: a diverse candidate slate requirement.

Mehri felt he had not addressed the glass ceiling impeding the ascent of non-white aspiring executives as well as he could have during the Texaco settlement negotiation, and he wanted to target it when settling the Coca-Cola case. To do so, he had to develop an approach that would open the possibility of diversifying the company's upper ranks in a way that would not startle those in power away from the negotiating table. He settled on the idea of working consideration of race into the interviewing process rather than at the decision node, as is traditionally done in affirmative action hiring processes. Such an approach would not guarantee any person of color a position and, further, would invite decision-makers to disregard race entirely when deciding to whom the position would be offered. The only requirement would be that the interview pool be diverse.

Mehri believed the principal challenge facing people of color who aspired to executive positions at Coca-Cola was getting in the door to be seen, heard, and deemed a viable candidate (Working Ideal). Requiring a diverse interviewing slate would open that door, and once in the room – once the decision maker and the candidate of color were able to discuss the job and what was required to do it well – Mehri believed previously overlooked talent would shine and candidates of color would begin ascending to executive positions (Working Ideal). Mehri was able to convince Coca-Cola to adopt diverse candidate interviewing and in the years that followed the settlement, diversity at Coca-Cola increased substantially (Herman et al, 2006). By 2006, "minority representation among Coca-Cola executives at the assistant vice-president level and above increased from 8.4% to 21%. Below the executive rank, minority managers increased from 16% to 25.5%" (Park, 2008: 3). And since then, minority representation has continued to climb (The Coca-Cola Company, 2017).

Mehri was not the first person to think about this type of reform. In the late 1990s, both Sara Lee Corporation and Allstate Insurance instituted diverse candidate slate interviewing for open positions (Bryan, 1998). And Catalyst Corporate Board Placement marketed its services in tailoring diverse slates for companies seeking more diverse interviewing pools (Pollak, 2000). Mehri, however, was the first person to weave diverse candidate slate interviewing into a class action lawsuit settlement agreement.

Because it had proved successful in the Coca-Cola context, when Mehri and Cochran got the NFL to the negotiation table with an opportunity to propose reform, Mehri pressed for diverse candidate slate interviewing with respect to head coach positions. Like Coca-Cola, the NFL was widely regarded as a conservative organization, and like Coca-Cola, the power positions in the NFL – including head coach – were overwhelmingly white. Intervention was necessary if head coaching aspirants of color were to have a chance, and a system in which candidates of color received a preference at the hiring stage would have been roundly rejected. Mehri believed diverse candidate slates were well suited to the NFL context and anticipated they could assist in diversifying the NFL's head coaching ranks just as they had diversified Coca-Cola's executive ranks.

After three months of sometimes tense negotiation and discussion, the league's owners agreed that they would interview at least one person of color for head coach openings. While the only viable head coaching candidates of color at the time were black, the approach recognized that as the game of American football continued to develop other non-white aspiring head coaches may face headwinds as well. Each owner's particular motivation was untold. Some certainly valued the prospect of increased diversity, either because they valued diversity for diversity's sake or because they felt it would strengthen their bottom line. Others may simply have grown tired of the negative press the league's virtually homogenous head coaching corps had attracted and sought the appearance of attention to diversity. Whatever the case, they moved forward with reform. The Rooney Rule – named after Dan Rooney, the Pittsburgh Steelers owner who championed the idea in internal league discussions – was born.

The NFL's diversity gains

The year after the Rooney Rule went into effect, the number of head coaches of color in the NFL returned to the high water mark of three. In 2004, the following year, it increased to five. In 2005, it increased to six. And in 2007, it increased to seven. The NFL – at one point derided in the press as homogenous with respect to coaching but now labeled a torchbearer for diversity and inclusion – was so pleased with the Rule's impact in the head coaching ranks that it expanded the rule to apply to clubs' general manager searches as well. In short order, the number of NFL general managers of color would also rise.

The racial complexion of the NFL is unquestionably different than it was before the Rooney Rule. Entering the 2017 season, a record 16 NFL Clubs were led by a head coach or general manager of color, and in all, since the Rooney Rule took effect, clubs have hired 14 head coaches of color and 12 general managers of color. Given the opportunity, head coaches and general managers of color have thrived. Indeed, since 2007, 10 NFL clubs have reached the Super Bowl led by a head coach or general manager of color. The rise of Mike Tomlin, head coach of the Pittsburgh Steelers, most clearly illustrates the Rooney Rule's impact. Tomlin was a young unheralded defensive coach who had only served as a defensive coordinator in the NFL for one year when the Steelers interviewed him for the club's vacant head coaching position in 2007. His competition for the job was fierce, with older more experienced coaches – who were white and who were already on the Steelers' coaching staff – leading the field. With the chance to interview and make his case for the job, however, Tomlin convinced the Steelers that he was the best candidate for the job. Within two years, he had led the Steelers to a Super Bowl championship and won Coach of the Year honors. Tomlin remains among the most highly respected head coaches in the league and his hire, and subsequent success, sparked a trend in the NFL of searching for fresh, young dynamic coaches rather than grizzled coaching veterans. Tomlin's image, and his success, have come to symbolize the Rooney Rule (Duru, 2011).

The Rooney Rule's spread

A fairly substantial body of scholarship emerged in the years following the Rooney Rule's enactment. Some scholars have questioned whether the Rule was, in fact, the force driving the NFL's diversity gains, arguing that other factors played a more substantial part. For instance, Chris Rider of Georgetown University's McDonough School of Business, together with several colleagues, argues that demographic trends in NFL coaching that existed before the Rule's implementation suggest the league would have experienced its head coaching diversity gains even in the Rule's absence (Rider et al., 2016). Other scholars have explicitly credited the Rule with those gains (Smith, 2008; Thornton, 2009; Madden & Ruther, 2010).

If mimicry is validation, the Rooney Rule is, indeed, validated. Like the NFL, the National Collegiate Athletic Association, which governs the great bulk of collegiate athletics in the United States, had long been pilloried for the homogeneity of the collegiate football head coach ranks. In 2008, after the NFL had begun to experience diversity gains, the Division I-A Athletic Directors' Association, which represents the athletic directors at the highest level of NCAA football, issued guidelines encouraging its members to use diverse candidate slates when searching for head football coaches. The

NCAA, itself, stood in the background, fearing that it did not have the authority to institute a collegiate version of the Rooney Rule, but it quietly supported the Athletic Directors' initiative.

That same year, the American state of Oregon took the Athletic Directors' efforts a step further, passing legislation that required all seven of its public universities to utilize diverse candidate slates when interviewing candidates for head coaching positions in all sports as well as for athletic directors. Other American states have considered following suit, and some American municipalities have done so. Pittsburgh, Pennsylvania for instance, has done so. Portland, Oregon has as well, but has taken the concept a step further still, expanding it beyond race. Pursuant to city council resolution, any interview process for a bureau directorship in the city government (e.g., Chief of Police or Chief of the Fire Department) must include an interview of at least one candidate of color, one woman candidate, and one candidate with a disability.

Not to be outdone by state or local efforts on this front, the United States federal government has pursued Rooney Rule-like initiatives as well. Former Commissioner of the US Securities and Exchange Commission Luis Aguilar spoke publicly while in office about the need for diverse candidate slates when considering membership on Corporate boards, and current Senate minority leader Chuck Schumer has pushed for and eventually secured agreement among all Senate Democrats to interview diverse applicants for all staff vacancies when at all possible.

Various leading corporations, including Xerox, Intel, Microsoft, Facebook, and Pinterest, have adopted forms of the Rule as well. A conglomeration of law firms has taken a similar step. Thirty large US-based firms, most of which have international offices, have adopted the Mansfield Rule – named after the first woman ever licensed to practice law in the US – under which they commit to using diverse candidate slates with respect to "hiring for leadership and governance roles, promotions to equity partner, and hiring lateral attorneys" (Rubino, 2017, para. 4).

In addition, the Rooney Rule concept has taken hold outside of the United States. As explored in other chapters of this book, the top levels of soccer in England have long featured a starkly racially disproportionate corps of managers (the role equivalent to head coach in American football). Indeed, as of 2011, only two of the 92 clubs in the English Premier League (the top level) and the English Football League (the three tiers below the top level) employed managers of color (Bell, 2011). For several years prior to that, activists and soccer officials in England had consulted with Mehri about the Rooney Rule concept's potential application in England, but in 2011 the movement to enact a Rooney Rule analogue started to gain traction. That year Mehri gave a formal presentation to representatives of the English soccer community's key stakeholders: the Football Association (England's national governing body for soccer), the English Premier League, the English Football League, the League Managers Association, and the Professional

Footballers' Association (the players' union). Those stakeholders debated the matter for years going forward with little movement, but in December of 2017, all 72 clubs in the English Football League agreed in principle to interview at least one suitably qualified person of color for first team managerial positions, effective January 1, 2018 (Rudd, 2017). Within weeks, the Football Association adopted a similar rule, requiring that at least one suitably qualified person of color be interviewed for all national team managerial positions from the youth levels up to the senior level for both the men's and women's programs. These measures remain in their infancy, so their ultimate impact remains to be seen. The English Premier League has exhibited little interest in the Rooney Rule, and there is currently nothing to indicate that will change. Depending on the success of these initiatives in effectuating equal opportunity in the English Football League and Football Association, however, it is conceivable the English Premier League could re-examine the diverse candidate slate concept.

The Rooney Rule 2.0?

Notwithstanding the increase in diversity in the NFL following the Rooney Rule's enactment and the Rule's subsequent proliferation into other employment contexts, recent research suggests it is not as effective as it could be. In 2016, the Harvard Business Review reported that the Rooney Rule, while powerful in concept, is only as powerful in fact if *two* traditionally underrepresented candidates are on the diverse candidate slate. The article detailed a study conducted by University of Colorado scholars, in which they set out to determine if increasing the number of women or people of color on an interviewing slate to two would increase the likelihood of hiring a woman or person of color beyond what the laws of probability would suggest. They found that it did. Their research concluded that putting two women on the slate made the odds of hiring a woman 79.14 times greater, and putting two people of color on the slate made the odds of hiring a person of color 193.72 times greater. Notably, the results held no matter how many people overall were interviewed for the position (Johnson et al., 2016).

Two years later, another Harvard Business Review article explored the "two in the pool" concept specifically in the NFL context and found that, indeed, when two or more candidates of color were on the interview slate, the chances of a hire of color increased substantially (Johnson 2018). Had the NFL stakeholders who advocated for and instituted the Rooney Rule understood the benefits of diverse candidate slates with two or more people of color over those with only one person of color, perhaps they would have mandated that two people of color be interviewed for each head coach opening. And as other sports organizations concerned about diversity among coaches contemplate adopting the Rooney Rule concept, they would be wise to consider the Harvard Business Review's conclusions.

Conclusion

When inequality of opportunity for the NFL's head coaching aspirants of color reached a crisis point in 2002, anti-discrimination law promised no relief. The nature of the NFL coaching employment context rendered Title VII, the United States' bell-weather employment discrimination statute, essentially inapplicable. Moreover, the stigma of bringing suit would, in any event, likely have disincentivized prospective plaintiffs from attempting to press a legal claim. From the legal void, however, bloomed the Rooney Rule, an equal opportunity initiative that has gained traction in both the public and private sectors in the United States as well as in the United Kingdom's soccer community.

The Rooney Rule story teaches the importance of the opportunity to get into the proverbial room to make one's case, but it also teaches the importance of creative approaches to encouraging equal opportunity. While a lawsuit can be a powerful tool in this realm, various circumstances may thwart its use. The lack of a legal remedy, however, must not be equated with the lack of a remedy. When legal approaches to ensuring equal opportunity are unavailable or fail, other approaches can prove just as, or more, effective. The Rooney Rule is a testament.

Note

1 American Football has historically been played almost exclusively by Americans who are either black (of at least partial African heritage) or white. As such, the term "black" is frequently used in this article. In a presumed bid for inclusivity, however, the NFL's Rooney Rule applies to all people of color (all non-white persons) rather than just black people. When describing the Rule and its consequences, therefore, this article uses the term "people of color."

References

42 U.S.C.A. §2000e-2 (West).

Bell, J., 'British Soccer Officials Intrigued by N.F.L.'s Rooney Rule', *Goal - The New York Times Soccer Blog* (web blog), September 29, 2011, https://goal.blogs.nytimes.com/2011/09/29/in-britain-n-f-l-s-rooney-rule-is-seen-as-model-for-hiring-minority-coaches/, July 22, 2018.

Belton, R., 'Title VII at Forty: A Brief Look at the Birth, Death, and Resurrection of the Disparate Impact Theory of Discrimination', *Hofstra Labor & Employment Law Journal*, 22 (2), 2005, pp. 431–472.

Bryan, J.H., 'Diversity: A Strategic Business Imperative', *Vital Speeches of the Day*, 65 (2), 1998, pp. 44–47.

Celotex Corp. v. Catrett, 477 U.S. 317 (1986).

The Coca-Cola Company, 'Global Diversity Mission', https://www.coca-colacompany.com/our-company/diversity/global-diversity-mission, 2017, accessed June 25, 2018.

Cochran Jr., J. & Mehri, C., 'Black Coaches in the National Football League: Superior Performance, Inferior Opportunities', Washington, D.C., Mehri & Skalet, PLLC, 2002, http://media.wix.com/ugd/520423_24cb6412ed2758c7204b7864022ebb5d.pdf, accessed April 16, 2019.

Duru, N.J., *Advancing the Ball: Race, Reformation, and the Quest for Equal Coaching Opportunity in the NFL*, New York, Oxford University Press, 2011.

Duru, N.J., 'The Rooney Rule's Reach', in McCann, M. (ed.), *The Oxford Handbook of American Sports Law*, New York, Oxford University Press, 2018, pp. 525–540.

Edwards, F. & Thompson, G., 'The Legal Creation of Raced Space: The Subtle and Ongoing Discrimination Created through Jim Crow Laws', *Berkley Journal of African-American Law & Policy*, 12 (1), 2010, pp. 145–167, https://scholarship.law.berkeley.edu/cgi/viewcontent.cgi?article=1101&context=bjalp, accessed March 25, 2019.

Federal Rule of Civil Procedure 56.

Green, T.K., 'Discrimination in Workplace Dynamics: Toward a Structural Account of Disparate Treatment Theory', *Harvard Civil Rights-Civil Liberties Law Review*, 38 (1), 2003, pp. 91–158.

Hack, D., 'Pro Football; The N.F.L. Spells Out New Hiring Guidelines', *The New York Times*, December 9, 2003, https://www.nytimes.com/2003/12/09/sports/pro-football-the-nfl-spells-out-new-hiring-guidelines.html, accessed March 27, 2019.

Hays, C.L., *The Real Thing: Truth and Power at Coca-Cola Company*, New York, Random House, 2004.

Henderson, W.D., 'Reconciling the Juridical Links Doctrine with the Federal Rules of Civil Procedure and Article III', *University of Chicago Law Review*, 67 (4), 2000, pp. 1347–1378.

Herman, A.M. et al., 'Ingram, et al., v. The Coca-Cola Company Fifth Annual Report of the Task Force', 2006, p. 6, https://www.cocacolacompany.com/content/dam/journey/us/en/private/fileassets/pdf/unknown/unknown/task_force_report_2006.pdf, accessed March 27, 2019.

Iheukwumere, E.O. & Aka, P.C., 'Title VII, Affirmative Action, and the March Toward Color-blind Jurisprudence', *Temple Political & Civil Rights Law Review*, 11 (1), 2001, pp. 1–62.

Jackson v. Univ. of New Haven, 228 F. Supp. 2d 156, 157 (D. Conn. 2002).

Johnson v. Transportation Agency [1987], 480 U.S. 616.

Johnson, S.K., Hekman, D.R., & Chan, E.T., 'If There's Only One Woman in Your Candidate Pool, There's Statistically No Chance She'll Be Hired', *Harvard Business Review*, April 26, 2016, https://hbr.org/2016/04/if-theres-only-one-woman-in-your-candidate-pool-theres-statistically-no-chance-shell-be-hired, accessed May 15, 2018.

Johnson, S.K., 'What Amazon's Board Was Getting Wrong About Diversity and Hiring', *Harvard Business Review*, May 14, 2018, https://hbr.org/2018/05/what-amazons-board-is-getting-wrong-about-diversity-and-hiring, accessed April 15, 2019.

Lawrence III, C.R., 'The Id, the Ego, and Equal Protection: Reckoning with Unconscious Racism', *Stanford Law Review*, 39 (2), 1987, pp. 317–388.

Leer v. Washington Educ. Ass'n, 172 F.R.D. 439 (W.D. Wash. 1997).

Madden, J. & Ruther, M., 'Has the NFL's Rooney Rule Efforts "Leveled the Field" for African American Head Coach Candidates?', *Journal of Sports Economics*, 12 (2), 2010, pp. 127–142.

Marchwinski v. Oliver Tyrone Corp., 81 F.R.D. 487 (W.D. Pa. 1979).

Moye, J., 'Punt or Go for the Touchdown? A Title VII Analysis of the National Football League's Hiring Practices for Head Coaches', *UCLA Entertainment Law Review*, 6 (1), 1998, pp. 105–136, https://escholarship.org/content/qt43z5k34q/qt43z5k34q.pdf, accessed March 25, 2019.

NAACP v. Town of E. Haven, 70 F.3d 219 (2d Cir. 1995).

Nix v. WLCY Radio/Rahall Commc'ns, 738 F.2d 1181 (11th Cir. 1984).

Park, A., 'Making Diversity a Business Advantage', *Harvard Management Update*, 13 (4), 2008, pp. 1–4.

Patterson, E., 'Litigating Implicit Bias', *Poverty and Race Journal*, 20 (5), 2011, pp. 1–24, https://prrac.org/newsletters/sepoct2011.pdf, accessed March 25, 2019.

Pollak, M., 'Catalyst corporate board placement: new seats at the table', in Burke, R. J. and Mattis, M.C. (eds.), *Women on Corporate Boards of Directors, Issues in Business Ethics*, vol. 14, Dordrecht, Springer, 2000, pp. 263–269.

Purkett v. Elem [1995] 514 U.S. 765.

Rider, C.I., et al., 'Racial Disparity in Leadership: Performance-Reward Bias in Promotions of National Football League Coaches', *Georgetown McDonough School of Business Research Paper No. 2710398*, January 7, 2016, https://papers.ssrn.com/sol3/papers.cfm?abstract_id=2710398, accessed June 19, 2018.

Roberts, B. & White, J.E., *Roberts v. Texaco: A True Story of Race and Corporate America*, New York, HarperCollins, 1998.

Rubino, K., 'Get Ready for the Biglaw "Rooney Rule" as Firms Try to Actually Do Something about Diversity', *Above the Law*, June 8, 2017, https://abovethelaw.com/2017/06/get-ready-for-the-biglaw-rooney-rule-as-firms-try-to-actually-do-something-about-diversity/?rf=1, accessed July 22, 2018.

Rudd, A., '"Rooney Rule" Adopted by All 72 EFL Clubs', *The Sunday Times*, December 8, 2017, https://www.thetimes.co.uk/article/rooney-rule-adopted-by-all-72-efl-clubs-88n82tl3h, accessed July 22, 2018.

Smith v. Xerox Corp., 196 F.3d 358 (2d Cir. 1999).

Story, R., 'Abdallah, et al. v. The Coca-Cola Company, Settlement Agreement', 2000, pp. 18–19, https://digitalcommons.ilr.cornell.edu/cgi/viewcontent.cgi?referer=https://www.google.com/&httpsredir=1&article=1024&context=condec, accessed March 27, 2019.

Thornley v. Penton Pub., Inc. 104 F.3d 26 (2d Cir. 1997)

United Steelworkers of America v. Weber [1979], 443 U.S. 193.

Thornton, P.K., 'The Increased Opportunity for Minorities in the National Football League Coaching Ranks: The Initial Success of the NFL's Rooney Rule', *Williamette Sports Law Journal*, 6 (1), 2009, pp. 45–56.

Smith, E.R., 'The Rooney Rule: Affirmative Action Policy and Institutional Discrimination in the National Football League', PhD Dissertation, University of Miami, *Open Access Dissertations*, 354, 2008, accessed June 18, 2018.

Wah, L. (1999) 'Diversity at Allstate: A Competitive Weapon', *Management Review*, 88 (7), pp. 24–30.

Walker, A., 'Title VII & MLB Minority Hiring: Alternatives to Litigation', *University of Pennsylvania Journal of Business and Employment Law*, 10 (1), 2006, pp. 245–271, https://pdfs.semanticscholar.org/2922/bfb4d7b5e2dbe068f2ea74ab3da64d7043b6.pdf, accessed March 25, 2019.

Williams, A., 'Modern-Day Racism in the Workplace: Symbolic Diversity or Real Change?', *From Science to Practice: Organizational Psychology Bulletin*, 1 (2), 2015, pp. 6–10, https://www.vanguard.edu/uploaded/Academics/Graduate/Organizational_Psychology/Modern-Day-racism-in-the-workplace-Symbolic-diversity-or-real-change.pdf, accessed March 25, 2019.

Working Ideal. 'Results: Case Studies', *Working Ideal*, n.d., Increasing Diversity in Leadership: The Rooney Rule in the Workplace and on the Field, http://www.workingideal.com/results/#toggle-id-1, accessed March 27, 2019.

Chapter 12

The EFL voluntary code of recruitment

Using reflexive regulation to increase the racial diversity of professional football coaching in England

Sophie Cowell

Introduction

Despite advances in on-the-field racial diversity within English professional football, the underrepresentation of Black, Asian and Minority Ethnic (BAME) managers and coaches remains a significant issue. An established body of research into the experiences of BAME managers and coaches has recently emerged, which explores reasons behind this underrepresentation (see Sports People's Think Tank (SPTT) 2015; Cashmore & Cleland 2011; Bradbury et al., 2018). However, research into specific measures aimed at tackling underrepresentation, particularly recent policies introduced by football authorities, is still developing (see Bradbury 2016; and Conricode & Bradbury, Chapter 13 of this collection). Further, the broader issue of racism in football is "*still largely unexplored*" from an anti-discrimination law perspective (Veuthey 2013, 76). This chapter aims to fill this gap by considering the extent to which permissive, rather than mandatory, legislation may have encouraged the English Football League (EFL)[1] to introduce their Voluntary Code of Recruitment. Established in 2016, the Code is similar to the 'Rooney Rule' from the National Football League (NFL) in the United States. This chapter will provide background context to the Code, then outline the legal framework, before considering the extent to which the introduction of the Code demonstrates the legislative approach of 'reflexive regulation' or "enforced self-regulation" (McCrudden 2007) working effectively. It will conclude by using reflexive regulation theory to recommend ways to increase the success of the Code.

The chapter considers the Voluntary Code to be a form of positive action. Positive action is a contested term, with no clear legal definition. Barmes (2009: 623) defines positive action as an "*activity designed to improve the position, in terms of the distribution of benefits or dis-benefits, of a given social group or sub-group... on the basis that its members suffer systematic disadvantage in that regard*". This definition broadly informs the way in which the term is used in the chapter.

Additionally, the term 'Black, Asian and Minority Ethnic' or 'BAME' will be used throughout. It is acknowledged that homogeneous terms conceal *"substantial diversity"* (Aspinall 2011: 33). However, it is considered *"any official category will conceal some heterogeneity"* (Aspinall, 2009: 1425) and *"there is little in the lexicon of terms that is not contested"* (Aspinall, 2002: 804). Although ideally imposed categorisation should be avoided in ethnicity research, a theoretical analysis requires a consistent approach towards terminology, thus it is considered necessary to use the terms adopted by others who are researching, practising and developing policy in this area. The EFL's Voluntary Code utilises the term 'Black, Asian and Minority Ethnic' (The Football League 2015[2]); this is also used by key organisations in this area, such as the League Managers Association (LMA) and Kick It Out, English football's leading equality and inclusion organisation. BAME is also the salient term adopted throughout the UK beyond the football context, used within government reports, official healthcare, education and criminal justice settings, and beyond. This chapter will refer to 'minority' coaches/candidates when discussing the USA context, as this is the term generally adopted by those researching the Rooney Rule (see Collins, 2007; Corapi, 2012) and is thus the salient term in the given context. Further, this chapter will refer to both 'managers' and 'coaches'. In this context, a 'manager' is only the first-team head coach, who almost always will have wider responsibilities and duties beyond simply coaching, whereas 'coaches' includes all first-team coaches, and the development and youth squad coaches.

BAME managers and coaches – the current position

Since Viv Anderson became the first BAME footballer to play for the England first team in 1978, professional football in the English leagues has made significant advances in on-the-field racial diversity. Whilst high-profile incidents, such as West Ham United FC's Head of Recruitment, Tony Henry, stating African players "cause mayhem" (BBC, 2018a), and incidents of racist abuse aimed at BAME players including Raheem Sterling (BBC, 2018b) suggest an ongoing difficulty in embedding equality and inclusion, the level of diversity amongst players has significantly increased. Currently, up to 30% of all professional footballers are BAME, significantly higher than the general UK population of 14% (SPTT, 2017). Despite the advances in on-the-field racial diversity, the situation at managerial and coaching levels is different. In October 2018, 7 of 92 (7.6%) first-team managers were BAME. Whilst this was an improvement on previous years (on 1 September 2017, 3 of 92 (3.3%) first-team managers were BAME) it demonstrates a significant underrepresentation compared to both BAME players and the general population. This lack of representation is also seen in the wider coaching community: on 1 September 2017, 22 of 482 (4.6%) senior coaching positions[3] were held by BAME coaches, with only 18.5% of clubs employing BAME coaches in senior positions (SPTT, 2017).

Research by the SPTT identified key barriers to BAME coach career progression: over-reliance on networks-based recruitment; conscious and unconscious racial bias and stereotypes; and a consequent lack of BAME role models at all managerial and coaching levels (SPTT 2015: 4). A follow-up report in 2017 argued the statistics outlined above demonstrate these barriers are *"institutionally embedded"* and thus *"remain firmly in place"* (SPTT 2017: 9). Some studies have pointed to an actual and/or perceived lack of *qualified* BAME coaches (see Cashmore & Cleland's 2011 study on the views of 1,000 football fans). Consequently, commentators have called for action to redress actual and perceived disadvantage in this area. Peters (2014) argues to increase representation of BAME managers and coaches, the focus should be grassroots level, using positive action to encourage "under-represented groups to undergo training courses and gain relevant qualifications". Until recently, football authorities have focused positive action programmes on increasing numbers of qualified BAME coaches; for example, the COACH Bursary Programme funds coaching qualifications for BAME applicants (The Football Association 2015). Increasing access to coach education is much needed, and research by Bradbury (2016: 144) found the bursary helps coaches *"break into… some historically closed professional club coaching networks"*. However, this alone is insufficient to address the systematic barriers identified by the SPTT, and Bradbury (2018: 25) argues a *"holistic package of more strident positive action measures"* is needed.

Statistical evidence suggests a lack of suitably qualified managers and coaches is not the only issue. The proportion of high-level qualified BAME coaches is 8.3% (SPTT, 2015). Whilst this is significantly lower than the general population (14%) and, particularly, the number of BAME players (30%), it is almost double the number of coaches who are employed, outlined above as 4.6% (SPTT, 2015). This suggests that whilst the number of high-level qualified coaches is not representative of the number of BAME players, and work is required to address this, a fundamental problem for qualified BAME coaches appears to be accessing employment opportunities. Therefore, there have been calls for greater focus on assisting qualified coaches to gain employment, rather than continuing to roll out developmental opportunities like coaching courses. Although (in the UK at least) there have been various forms of Equality Standards for football clubs since 2004, the evidence suggests these have also been limited in the extent to which they have increased the representation of BAME managers and coaches (Bradbury, 2011). For several years there have been widespread calls for a version of the Rooney Rule, used within the NFL (National Football League) in the USA, to be introduced into English football. Calls for an 'English Rooney Rule' were made by notable BAME players and managers, including Paul Ince (Ornstein, 2014), Jason Roberts (BBC, 2014a) and Sol Campbell (Brown, 2015). Key organisations campaigned for its introduction for several years: the Professional Footballers' Association (PFA) began discussions with

Cyrus Mehri (instrumental in developing the NFL's Rule) in 2011 (Kick It Out, 2011) and Kick It Out have long been supporters of such a Rule (BBC, 2014b).

The Rooney Rule, named after Pittsburgh Steelers owner Dan Rooney, was introduced in 2003 following recommendations by the Workplace Diversity Committee. The Rule requires NFL teams to interview at least one minority candidate for all head coaching and senior football operations jobs (Duru, 2008). Collins (2007) argues the Rooney Rule works by countering the unconscious bias associated with minority coaches and reducing reliance on such networks, thus helping to resolve the catch-22 situation, whereby such networks were relied upon for recruitment, but minority coaches were not given opportunities to break into them. There is little room in this chapter to add to or evaluate the existing critique of the Rooney Rule (see Duru, Chapter 11 of this collection); however, it is important to note the impact it has had. Prior to its introduction, 70% of NFL players but only 3 of 32 head coaches were minority ethnic (Cashmore & Cleland, 2011). By 2015, 17 of 87 vacancies (20%) had been filled by minority ethnic candidates (Fox, 2015), with minority ethnic candidates now 19–21% more likely to fill an NFL head coach vacancy than prior to the Rule's introduction (DuBois, 2015). The Rule has strict sanctions and there has only been one identified breach, occurring in 2003 shortly after its inception. In response to this breach, the Detroit Lions' General Manager was personally fined $200,000; the then Commissioner promised the next breach would result in a $500,000 fine, showing the Rule had "teeth" (Duru, 2008). Given the Rooney Rule's relative success in combating barriers similar to those "institutionally embedded" in English football (SPTT, 2017), it is clear to see why there have been widespread calls for the Rule, or an equivalent, to be introduced.

Whilst there had been calls for the introduction of the Rule into English football for some time, this dialogue gained steam in 2014, when the EFL came under mounting pressure to act. The then EFL Chairman Greg Clarke was heavily criticised for failing to raise the issue at the 2013 Annual General Meeting, despite assurances he would do so – although he claims this was due to changes to the EFL Board (Ornstein, 2014). This led to claims by PFA Chief Executive Gordon Taylor that the EFL had failed to fulfil its promise (Conway, 2014), and Garth Crooks, a long-term campaigner for the introduction of the Rule, called on Clarke to resign (Ornstein, 2014). Considering that until this point the EFL had failed to act, arguably this wider pressure on both the EFL, and Clarke personally, led to the issue being raised at the 2015 AGM, where clubs agreed formal action should be taken (The Football League, 2015).

The EFL's initial proposals (summarised below) consisted of a Mandatory Recruitment Code for academy football, which was immediately rolled out to all 72 clubs, and Voluntary Recruitment Code for first-team football, to be trialled by ten teams (EFL, 2016). This chapter focuses on the Voluntary Recruitment Code; for a consideration of the Mandatory Recruitment Code, see Conricode and Bradbury's Chapter 13 in this collection.

In summary, the Voluntary Recruitment Code for *first-team football* involved the following:

- "During the season, clubs will be expected to interview one or more BAME candidate for any First Team managerial/coaching role (where an application has been received) in instances where they run a full recruitment process".
- "During the close season, clubs will be expected to run a full recruitment process for any First Team managerial/coaching role during which they must interview one or more BAME candidates (where an application has been received)". (EFL, 2016)

At the 2016 AGM, clubs gave their formal support to these proposals, which were introduced for the 2016–17 season (EFL, 2016).

There was a lack of detail provided on how this pilot scheme would be monitored and whether there would be sanctions for non-compliance. During the pilot, the Code came under criticism, particularly when club Wolverhampton Wanderers FC "completely failed to follow the process in appointing Walter Zenga" (SPTT, 2016). In total, the Code was not followed five out of a possible eight times (Slater, 2017). This raised questions around the lack of monitoring and evaluation of the Code, and the lack of sanctions for non-compliance (SPTT, 2016), particularly when compared to the Rooney Rule in the NFL where the one failure to follow the Rule resulted in significant penalties. Birmingham City, who did not interview a BAME candidate on two occasions, said they "abided by the agreement", as the Code is only required when clubs run a full recruitment process, thus still allowing clubs to select a specific manager (Slater, 2017). This further highlights the differences between the EFL's Voluntary Code and the Rooney Rule, with the latter required to be followed in all circumstances.

Chair of Kick It Out, Lord Ouseley, stated the pilot showed clubs had "got away with doing nothing to achieve fair outcomes" (Slater 2017). Despite this criticism, the EFL found the pilot "useful in terms of understanding the practicalities" of the Code (EFL, 2017a), eventually stating that they believe "this approach has the potential to deliver the right outcomes if operated by all clubs over a period of time" (EFL, 2017b). Therefore, it was announced that all 72 clubs had agreed to follow the Voluntary Code from 1 January 2018 to the end of the 2018–19 season (EFL, 2017b).

Positive action and the law

The EFL's measures can be considered a form of positive action, in line with Barmes' (2009) definition provided earlier; indeed, the EFL themselves have referred to the measures using this term (EFL, 2017a). Some argue the Rooney Rule as it operates in the NFL more readily fits into the realms of positive discrimination in the UK framework (Banton, 2014). Positive discrimination involves "recruiting or promoting a person solely because they have a relevant protected characteristic" irrespective of merit (Jarett, 2011) and is unlawful. Because of this, it is argued here the EFL's Code, which states clubs must appoint the successful candidate on merit alone (The Football League, 2015) is more closely aligned with positive action than positive discrimination.

Positive action in the UK is permitted by Sections 158 and 159 of the UK Equality Act 2010, which broadened the circumstances in which organisations could take positive action. S.158 applies to employment and beyond, where an employer (in this instance) *reasonably thinks*:

a "persons who share a protected characteristic[4] suffer a disadvantage connected to the characteristic",
b "persons who share a protected characteristic have needs that are different from the needs of persons who do not share it", or
c "participation in an activity by persons who share a protected characteristic is disproportionately low". (S.158(1) Equality Act 2010)

In such circumstances, employers are permitted to take special measures where it is a proportionate means of achieving the aim of: meeting needs, addressing underrepresentation, or enabling or encouraging persons who share the protected characteristic to overcome or minimise disadvantage (Equality Act 2010).

S.159 applies to recruitment and promotion and permits organisations to utilise preferential treatment in the form of 'tie-break' provisions. A candidate from a protected group can be favoured over another candidate where the candidates are *as qualified as* each other, and the employer "reasonably thinks" the protected group is at a disadvantage, has a particular need, or is underrepresented. This can only be exercised where the aim of the measure is to encourage or enable protected groups to overcome disadvantage, it is a proportionate means of achieving the aim, and there is not a policy of automatically treating protected groups more favourably (S.159(4) Equality Act 2010).

Sections 158 and 159 are mutually exclusive; where one applies, the other will not. To firstly consider the EFL's Voluntary Code in light of S.159, Corapi (2012, 381) argues an interview rule is most likely covered under this, because a guaranteed interview is "exactly what section 159 is intended to permit". He states that because S.159 permits organisations to factor in race when determining which candidates to recruit, a rule that requires clubs to interview at least one suitably qualified BAME candidate (where one applies) would be permitted under S.159, providing that if the club feels no such candidate has applied, the rule does not apply. However, it may be that the EFL's measures are not easily accommodated under S.159. As stated, S.159

relates to recruitment or promotion. S.159(5) outlines that, for this purpose, recruitment "means a process for deciding whether to... offer employment to a person...". It is not fully clear (and has not yet been tested in law) whether this only applies to the final decision regarding whom to appoint or promote, or whether it would cover the full recruitment process, including interview. As such, it may be that the EFL's measures are more aligned to the special measures anticipated under the more general S.158, which enables employers to take proportionate action where there is a need, underrepresentation or disadvantage.

Regardless of whether the EFL's measures are more closely aligned to S.158 or S.159, the key issue is that, to fall within the scope of the Act and therefore be lawful, the measures must be 'proportionate'. The positive action provisions of the Equality Act 2010 were introduced to bring positive action law in the UK in line with European Union (EU) law; therefore, we must look to EU law to determine what can be considered 'proportionate'. Connolly (2011) argues that for positive action to fall within the ambit permitted by EU law, there must be underrepresentation; the protected candidate must be equally qualified, and there must be a 'savings clause', requiring an objective assessment of all criteria specific to the individual candidates. Whilst it is clear that there is an underrepresentation of BAME managers and coaches, further research is needed to consider whether the EFL's measures would be proportionate considering the 'savings clause' requirement and the apparent lack of monitoring and review.

The EFL's Voluntary Code as reflexive regulation?

Positive action under the Equality Act 2010 is permissive rather than mandatory, so it is interesting to consider the extent that the law may have played a role in encouraging the EFL to act, given legislation did not require them to do so. The EFL's engagement with positive action could be considered a result of a 'new' legislative approach working effectively. 'Reflexive regulation' can be thought of as *"enforced self-regulation"* (McCrudden, 2007: 265. This focuses on the idea that, instead of introducing mandatory laws, it is more successful to introduce permissive legislation, whereby social systems can act but are not forced to do so. This recognises *"the inner logic of individual social systems"* (McCrudden, 2007: 265) and allows them to develop solutions as they see fit. McCrudden (2007) argues this legislative approach is evident within the positive action sections of the Equality Act 2010. As such, the EFL's introduction of a positive action measure may mean the permissive positive action provisions of the Act have had some success in encouraging action. Reflexive regulation theory can thus be used to consider whether the law may have triggered the EFL's action, and whether this might impact on its ultimate success.

Considering previous legislative approaches, Fredman (2012; 265) argues "*despite increasingly sophisticated antidiscrimination laws, discrimination and inequality have proved remarkably resilient*", therefore questions should be asked around the law's ability to achieve social change. She argues inequality is embedded within society so previous legislation, centred around a retrospective complaints-based approach, providing individuals with the ability to act if they have suffered discrimination, is limited in its ability to address "structural inequalities" (Fredman, 2012: 266). This is supported by Hepple (2011: 316), who argues under the complaints-based approach, individual cases can have a positive effect, but this is "*generally short lived, and can lead to defensive and negative attitudes to change*".

The limitations of the previous complaints-based legislative approach can be seen within football. Whilst there exist anti-discrimination laws that apply to football – as with any other area of society – which provide a complaints process if a BAME coach is discriminated against, BAME managers and coaches are still underrepresented. When considering the barriers identified above – particularly reliance on networks-based methods of recruitment and conscious and unconscious racial bias and stereotypes (SPTT, 2015) – it is clear to see how a complaints-based approach, reacting to instances of discrimination, would not work to combat more covert causes of inequality. In fact, using legislation to bring a claim in this regard may perpetuate inequalities, due to the "*defensive and negative attitudes to change*" (Hepple, 2011: 316) that often result from discrimination claims. The idea that challenging discrimination may lead to negative or defensive attitudes is seen within football, where those that challenge discrimination may be branded 'trouble-makers' (Kilvington 2016). Scott (2015: 1909) argues in European football, when BAME players complain about racialised behaviour, this has often been "*held against them… 'as a character issue'*", which is then hard to shake, thus BAME players often remain silent about racism due to their "*need to survive within white dominated institutions*". Given the networks-based methods of recruitment outlined above, being seen as a 'trouble-maker' will further increase difficulties for aspiring BAME coaches.

Because of the limited long-term impact of complaints-based approaches, Fredman (2012: 265) argues the way forward is to "*fashion new legal tools*". Teubner's solution is to utilise a reflexive regulation approach "*which does not seek to impose substantive rules on sub-systems but instead works with the internal dynamics of those systems*" (Hepple, 2011: 320). The core concept of reflexive regulation is "*enforced self-regulation*" (McCrudden, 2007: 265). Instead of solutions being imposed on a subsystem, it is "*required to come up with its own set of solutions*" (Fredman, 2012: 419), with law acting as "*a stimulus to self-regulation*" (McLaughlin, 2014: 5). It is argued here that enabling subsystems to devise their own solutions is particularly beneficial to professional football, given sport has such a level of 'specificity', a term used to refer to "*the inherent characteristics of sport which set it apart from other economic and social activities"* (European Commission, 2016). Sporting rules are distinct to societal norms and, particularly, general principles of equality law (Beloff, 2012: 97) This means laws based on a 'command and control' approach, where solutions aimed at society generally are imposed on subsystems, are unlikely to be successful in addressing inequalities that exist within sport. This may explain why the EFL used the positive action provisions of the Equality Act 2010, which enabled them to devise their own solutions and implement them in a way most suited to them.

Commentators have identified conditions required for measures devised through reflexive regulation to be successful. Considering the EFL's measures in light of these, we can consider the extent to which the law played a part in encouraging the EFL to act. Hepple (2011: 321) states reflexive regulation involves three interlocking mechanisms:

> *internal scrutiny by the organisation itself... The involvement of interest groups... who must be informed, consulted and engaged in the process of change ... [and] an enforcement agency... which should provide the back-up role of assistance, building capabilities and ultimately sanctions.*

Considering Hepple's first mechanism regarding internal scrutiny, prior to the introduction of the Voluntary Code, the EFL undertook some form of consultation, stating the measures were finalised by "a working party of clubs" (EFL, 2016). Internal scrutiny within each subsystem is an essential characteristic of reflexive regulation, building on the *"problem-solving expertise of those who are in the best position to bring about change"* (Fredman, 2012: 272). Given a working party of clubs appear to have devised the measures based on their own assessment of the problem, and their appreciation of the specificity of football, reflexive regulation theory suggests clubs will feel greater ownership over the solutions, which are therefore more likely to be followed.

Hepple's (2011) second mechanism concerns the involvement of different stakeholders, and the EFL do appear to have consulted stakeholders. When announcing the measures, the EFL stated several organisations provided them with advice, including the NFL, The FA, Premier League, LMA, PFA and Kick It Out (EFL 2016). However, there is little information on the way this was conducted, and little detail on the extent BAME managers and coaches were consulted. Fredman (2012: 272) argues *"deliberative democracy"* – involving the underrepresented group itself – is a key reason why reflexive regulation can be successful in addressing structural inequality. She argues that *"groups subject to discrimination inevitably have unequal bargaining power and are unlikely to achieve gains"* through previous approaches; therefore, the reflexive approach, which *"does not aim to resolve the issue according to the balance of political... power"* but through deliberation, will result in fairer outcomes. Considering Fredman's arguments, the failure to consult with BAME managers and coaches may mean the EFL's Code is far less likely to be successful in addressing structural inequalities BAME managers and coaches face. Even if BAME managers and coaches were consulted, the lack of transparency surrounding this process is a key limitation of the EFL's measures as a form of positive action.

The key principle of reflexive regulation is that subsystems are encouraged to act voluntarily. However, Braithwaite (2008) argues an important feature of successful reflexive regulation is ultimately it is supported by a gradual escalation of sanctions until compliance is reached. This supports Hepple's third mechanism, involving *"an enforcement agency... which should provide the back-up role of assistance, building capabilities and ultimately sanctions"* (Hepple, 2011: 321). The EFL's Code does not appear to align with reflexive regulation in this respect. There does not appear to be any external agency tasked with monitoring or evaluating the implementation and success of the measures, and the EFL do not appear to be imposing sanctions for non-compliance. The lack of sanctions has been one of the key criticisms of the EFL's Code, with several commentators stating sanctions are needed for there to be any real impact: Duru argues "for the Rooney Rule concept to be effective in English football, it must have teeth" (Kick It Out, 2017) and Lord Ouseley argued the Code needs to be "backed up by sanctions for non-compliance" due to the limited adherence during the pilot (Slater, 2017). Considering the EFL's measures in light of reflexive regulation theory demonstrates why the lack of sanctions is a concern for commentators. As both Braithwaite and Hepple argue, whilst reflexive regulation involves organisations devising their own solutions which, it is hoped, will mean they are more likely to be successful, it is important to have a gradual escalation of sanctions to ensure compliance. As the EFL did not support the Code with sanctions, the extent to which the law played a part in encouraging the EFL to act can be questioned. Further, as outlined, the Rooney Rule imposes strict sanctions for non-compliance, thus the lack of sanctions for the EFL's Voluntary Code can be said to make it a much watered-down version of the Rooney Rule.

Conclusion

The EFL's Voluntary Code could be considered an example of the legislative approach of reflexive regulation working effectively, given that the EFL introduced a positive action measure when they were not required to do so by law. However, a consideration of the EFL's Code shows that key features of measures introduced in response to reflexive regulation are missing, particularly concerning the lack of information regarding consultation with BAME stakeholders, in addition to the apparent lack of monitoring and enforcement. The positive action provisions of the Equality Act 2010 apply to all industries, yet *"there are relatively few employers who are prepared to embrace positive action initiatives"* (Davies & Robison, 2016: 11) This suggests something other than legislation acted as a trigger for the development of the measures. Given that the EFL's Voluntary Code was introduced following high-profile campaigning for the introduction of the Rooney Rule into English football, and the surface-level similarities between the Code and the Rule, it may have been the apparent success of the Rooney Rule – coupled with the pressure the EFL faced at the time – that caused them to act. Whilst this sporting precedent is likely to have played a greater role than legislative theory in encouraging action, arguably the Voluntary Code is a watered-down version of the Rooney Rule, as it does not apply on every occasion and is not supported by sanctions.

Further, it is argued here that whilst the key features of reflexive regulation (consultation, monitoring and escalation to reach compliance) may be present in the Rooney Rule, they are lacking from the EFL's Code. As above, the Rooney Rule must be followed on every occasion and failure to do so results in severe penalties. Perhaps it is for this reason that there has only been one breach. In contrast, the EFL's Voluntary Code was not followed five out of eight times in the pilot alone, with no repercussions for non-compliance (Slater, 2017). Arguably, as the EFL's Voluntary Code does not have all the characteristics of successful reflexive regulation, it is less likely to be successful.

It is acknowledged that the EFL's Code is voluntary, and reflexive regulation involves subsystems devising their own solutions, thus we should be cautious in arguing there are 'must have' characteristics. It may be that the EFL believe this version is likely to be most successful. However, for the Code to be more successful, the EFL should look to follow the characteristics of successful measures devised in response to reflexive regulation (consultation, monitoring and escalation to reach compliance) that are also present in the Rooney Rule in the NFL. Future research will consider the proportionality of the Voluntary Code in its current form in greater detail, as well as the impact that introducing sanctions, as with the Rooney Rule, may have on the legal status of a positive action measure in UK law, as affirmative action law in the USA is more permissive. It will consider whether this would take the measure outside of the scope permitted by Sections 158 and 159 of the Equality Act 2010, and the likely impact of sanctions on the success of the Code. However, it is argued here that, at a minimum, open and transparent consultation and monitoring processes should be introduced for the EFL's Voluntary Code. As well as increasing the likelihood of success of the Voluntary Code, this will also help to demonstrate proportionality under the positive action legal framework.

Notes

1 The EFL consists of the three professional leagues below the Premier League in the English football pyramid known as The Championship, League 1 and League 2.
2 The Football League was re-named the 'English Football League' (EFL) in November 2015 (EFL 2015).

3 Senior coaching positions include first-team manager, first-team assistant manager, first-team coach, development squad head coach, youth squad head coach, academy director (SPTT, 2015).
4 Protected characteristics are "the grounds upon which discrimination is unlawful" (Equality and Human Rights Commission, 2016). The Equality Act 2010 lists nine protected characteristics, these are: age, disability, gender reassignment, marriage and civil partnership, pregnancy and maternity, race, religion or belief, sex, and sexual orientation (Equality Act 2010).

References

Aspinall, P.J. 2002. "Collective Terminology to Describe the Minority Ethnic Population: The Persistence of Confusion and Ambiguity in Usage". *Sociology*, 36 (4), 803–816. doi: https://doi.org/10.1177%2F0038038502036000401.

Aspinall, P.J. 2009. "The Future of Ethnicity Classifications". *Journal of Ethnic and Migration Studies*, 35 (9), 1417–1435. doi: https://doi.org/10.1080/13691830903125901.

Aspinall, P.J. 2011. "Who is 'Black African' in Britain? Challenges to Official Categorisation of the Sub-Saharan African Origin Population". *African Identities*, 9 (1), 33–48.

Banton, E. 2014. "Fighting Discrimination in Sport: Positive Action v Rooney Rule". *LawInSport*. https://www.lawinsport.com/topics/sports/item/fighting-discrimination-in-sport-positive-action-v-rooney-rule.

Barmes, L. 2009. "Equality Law and Experimentation: The Positive Action Challenge". *Cambridge Law Journal*, 68 (3), 623–654. doi: https://doi.org/10.1017/S0008197309990171.

BBC. 2014a. "Jason Roberts: Harder than Ever for Black Managers to Get Jobs". *BBC Sport*, 23 September. http://www.bbc.co.uk/sport/football/29337157.

BBC. 2014b. "Kick It Out: Managers Not Hired on Merit, Says Anti-Racism Charity". *BBC Sport*, 3 October. http://www.bbc.co.uk/sport/football/29484593..

BBC. 2018a. "Tony Henry: West Ham Sack Head of Recruitment over African Player Comments". *BBC Sport*, February 2018. https://www.bbc.co.uk/sport/football/42925532.

BBC. 2018b. "Raheem Sterling Negative Press Coverage 'Emboldens Racist Rhetoric' – PFA". *BBC Sport*, 10 December. https://www.bbc.co.uk/sport/football/46504491.

Beloff QC, M.J. 2012. "The Specificity of Sport – Rhetoric or Reality?" *International Sports Law Review*, 4, 97–107.

Bradbury, S. 2011. "It's Not as Simple as Black and White: Challenging Racism in Professional Football through Locally Grounded Multi-agency Collaboration". In *Sport and Challenges to Racism. Global Culture and Sport*, edited by J. Long and K. Spracklen, 119–223. London: Palgrave Macmillan.

Bradbury, S. 2016. "The progression of Black and Minority Ethnic footballers into coaching in professional football: a case study analysis of the COACH bursary programme". In *Advances in Coach Education and Development: From Research to Practice*, edited by W. Allison, A. Abraham and A. Cale, 137–148. London and New York: Routledge.

Bradbury, S. 2018. "The Under-representation and Racialised Experiences of Minority Coaches in High Level Coach Education in Professional Football in England". In

Sport and Contested Identities, edited by D. Hassan and C. Acton, 11–29. London: Routledge.

Bradbury, S., van Sterkenburg, J. & Mignon, P. 2018. "The Under-representation and Experiences of Elite Level Minority Coaches in Professional Football in England, France and the Netherlands". *International Review for the Sociology of Sport*, 53 (3), 313–334. https://dspace.lboro.ac.uk/2134/21942.

Braithwaite, J. 2008. *Regulatory Capitalism: How it Works, Ideas for Making it Better*. Cheltenham: Edward Elgar.

Brown, M. 2015. "Sol Campbell Calls for 'Rooney Rule' to Increase Numbers of Ethnic Minority Football Managers". *ChronicleLive*, 18 January. http://www.chroniclelive.co.uk/news/north-east-news/sol-campbell-calls-rooney-rule-8465628.

Cashmore, E., & Cleland, J. 2011. "Why Aren't There More Black Football Managers?" *Ethnic and Racial Studies*, 34 (9), 1594–1607. doi: https://doi.org/10.1080/01419870.2011.595556.

Collins, B.W. 2007. "Tackling Unconscious Bias in Hiring Practices: The Plight of the Rooney Rule". *New York University Law Review*, 82 (3), 870–912.

Connolly, M. 2011. *Discrimination Law*. London: Sweet & Maxwell.

Conway, R. 2014. "Gordon Taylor: 'Hidden Resistance' to Hiring Black Managers". *BBC Sport*, 23 September. http://www.bbc.co.uk/sport/football/29333826.

Corapi, J. 2012. "Red Card: Using the National Football League's 'Rooney Rule' to Eject Race Discrimination from English Professional Soccer's Managerial and Executive Hiring Practices". *Fordham Intellectual Property, Media & Entertainment Law Journal*, 23, 341–395. https://ir.lawnet.fordham.edu/iplj/vol23/iss1/6.

Cunningham, T. 2015. "Monitoring Equality – Reflexive Regulation, Planning Systems, and the Role of Discrimination Law: Lessons from Northern Ireland". *The Equal Rights Review*, 14, 119–147.

Davies, C.M. & Robison, M. 2016. "Bridging the Gap: An Exploration of the Use and Impact of Positive Action in the United Kingdom". *International Journal of Discrimination and the Law*, 16 (2–3), 83–101. doi: https://doi.org/10.1177%2F1358229116655647.

DuBois, C. 2015. "The Impact of 'Soft' Affirmative Action Policies on Minority Hiring in Executive Leadership: The Case of the NFL's Rooney Rule". *American Law and Economics Review*, 18 (2), 208–233. doi: https://doi.org/10.1093/aler/ahv019.

Duru, N.J. 2008. "The Fritz Pollard Alliance, the Rooney Rules, and the Quest to 'Level the Playing Field' in the National Football League". *Virginia Sports and Entertainment Law Journal*, 7 (2), 179–197.

English Football League (EFL). 2015. "Football League Re-brand Explained". 12 November. https://www.efl.com/news/2015/november/football-league-re-brand-explained/.

English Football League (EFL). 2016. "EFL clubs Approve BAME Managers and Coaches Proposals". 16 June. http://www.efl.com/news/article/2016/efl-clubs-approve-bame-managers-and-coaches-proposals-3140386.aspx..

English Football League (EFL). 2017a. "EFL Clubs Support Extension of BAME Managers and Coaches Pilot". 17 July. https://www.efl.com/news/2017/july/efl-clubs-support-extension-of-bame-managers-and-coaches-pilot/.

English Football League (EFL). 2017b. "EFL Extends Voluntary Recruitment Code to All 72 Clubs". 7 December. https://www.efl.com/news/2017/december/efl-extends-voluntary-recruitment-code-to-all-72-clubs/.

Equality Act. 2010, c.1. Available at: https://www.legislation.gov.uk/ukpga/2010/15/part/2/chapter/1 [Accessed 6 June 2019].

Equality and Human Rights Commission. 2016. "Glossary of Terms". https://www.equalityhumanrights.com/en/secondary-education-resources/useful-information/glossary-terms [Accessed 6 June 2019].

European Commission. 2016. *Mapping and Analysis of the Specificity of Sport*. Luxembourg: Publications Office of the European Union.

Fox, A. 2015. "How the Rooney Rule Succeeds ... and Where it Falls Short". ESPN 14 May 2015. https://abc7ny.com/730588/

Fredman, S. 2012. "Breaking the Mold: Equality as a Proactive Duty". *The American Journal of Comparative Law*, 60, 265–288. https://www.jstor.org/stable/23251956.

Hepple, B. 2011. "Enforcing Equality Law: Two Steps Forward and Two Steps Backwards for Reflexive Regulation". *Industrial Law Journal*, 40 (4), 315–335.

Independent. 2018. "Crystal Palace's Wilfred Zaha Reveals Racist Abuse Suffered in Draw against Arsenal". 30 October. https://www.independent.co.uk/sport/football/premier-league/wilfried-zaha-racist-abuse-suffered-crystal-palace-arsenal-a8609611.html.

Jarett, T. 2011. *The Equality Act 2010 and Positive Action*. House of Commons Library Standard Note SN6093.

Kick It Out. 2011. "PFA Spearheads Moves to Address Imbalance in Coaching Positions". http://www.kickitout.org/news/pfa-spearheads-moves-to-address-imbalance-in-coaching-positions/#.WAPIuUtH2lI [Accessed 27 September 2018].

Kick It Out. 2012. "PFA Calls for English Version of the 'Rooney Rule'". http://www.kickitout.org/news/pfa-calls-for-english-version-of-rooney-rule/#.WAPAo0tH2lI [Accessed 25 September 2018].

Kick It Out. 2017. "Sports People's Think Tank Publish Latest BAME Coaching Statistics". http://www.kickitout.org/news/sports-peoples-think-tank-publish-latest-bame-coaching-statistics/#.W60x9mhKjIU [Accessed 27 September 2018].

Kilvington, D. 2016. *British Asians, Exclusion and the Football Industry*. Oxon: Routledge.

McCrudden, C. 2007. "Equality Legislation and Reflexive Regulation: A Response to the Discrimination Law Review's Consultative Paper". *Industrial Law Journal*, 36 (3), 255–266. doi: https://doi.org/10.1093/indlaw/dwm015.

McLaughlin, C. 2014. "Equal Pay, Litigation and Reflexive Regulation: The Case of the UK Local Authority". *Industrial Law Journal*, 43 (1), 1–28. doi: https://doi.org/10.1093/indlaw/dwu003.

Ornstein, D. 2014. "Greg Clarke 'Disingenuous' on Black Managers – Tony Kleanthous". *BBC Sport*, September 2014. http://www.bbc.co.uk/sport/football/29410247.

Peters, A. 2014. "How Can We Best Promote Racial Diversity in U.K. Football Management?" *LawInSport*. https://www.lawinsport.com/blog/squire-patton-boggs/item/how-can-we-best-promote-racial-diversity-in-u-k-football-management.

Ragowski, R. 2015. "The Emergence of Reflexive Global Labour Law". *Industrielle Beziehungen-The German Journal of Industrial Relations*, 22 (1), 72–90.

Scott, C-G. 2015. *African Footballers in Sweden*. New York: Palgrave.

Slater, M. 2012. "EFL to Extend 'Rooney Rule' Trial to All Clubs Despite Mixed Results Last Season". *Independent*, 11 July. https://www.independent.co.uk/sport/football/football-league/efl-rooney-rule-bame-birmingham-chesterfield-coventry-wolves-a7835256.html.

Slater, M. 2017. "EFL to extend 'Rooney Rule' trial to all clubs despite mixed results last season". *The Independent*. 11 July. www.independent.co.uk/sport/football/football-lea gue/efl-rooney-rule-bame-birmingham-chesterfield-coventry-wolves-a7835256.html

Teubner, G. 1987. "Juridification: Concepts, Aspects, Limits, Solutions". In *Juridification of Social Spheres: A Comparative Analysis in the Areas of Labour, Corporate, Antitrust and Social Welfare Law*, edited by G. Teubner, 3–48. Berlin: de Gruyter.

The Football Association. 2015. "Dr Wayne Allison Has Been Appointed as The FA's Black, Asian and Minority Ethnic Project Manager, in the Technical Directorate". 25 October. http://www.thefa.com/news/st-georges-park/2015/oct/wayne-allison-appointed-bame-project-manager.

The Football League. 2015. "Football League Clubs Back BAME Managers". 15 June. http://www.football-league.co.uk/news/article/2015/football-league-clubs-back-bame-managers-and-coaches-2483040.aspx.

The Sport's People Think (SPTT). 2015. "Levels of BME Coaches in Professional Football: 1st Annual Follow Up Report (October 2015)". http://thesptt.com/wp-content/uploads/2015/10/BME-coach-representation-update-report.pdf.

The Sports People's Think Tank (SPTT) and the Fare Network. 2016. "Ethnic Minorities and Coaching in Elite Level Football in England: 2016 Update". http://thesptt.com/wp-content/uploads/2016/11/SB-final-report-screen3-1.pdf.

The Sports People's Think Tank (SPTT) in association with the Fare Network and University of Loughborough. 2017. "Ethnic Minorities and Coaching in Elite Football in England: 2017 Update". http://thesptt.com/wp-content/uploads/2017/11/2017-SPTT-report-print.pdf.

Veuthey, A. 2013. "Racism in English Premier League: Is Football Operating in a Cocoon?" *International Sports Law Review*, 3, 76–96.

Chapter 13

Game changer or empty promise?
The EFL mandatory code of coach recruitment in men's professional football youth academies in England

Dominic Conricode and Steven Bradbury

Introduction: 'race', ethnicity and football coaching in England

Over the last 50 years, the higher echelons of men's professional football in England (and in other countries in Western Europe) have become characterised by the increasing racial, ethnic and cultural diversity of its playing workforce. However, during this period, there has been a minimal throughput of Black, Asian and Minority Ethnic (BAME)[1] players into senior coaching positions at elite club level (Bradbury et al., 2011, 2014; Cashmore & Clelland, 2011; Kilvington, 2017). For example, since 1992 just 32 BAME coaches have held 'head coach' positions at all 92 professional clubs competing annually in each of the four elite divisions of English football (LMA, 2017). Further, between 2014 and 2017 the levels of BAME representation in senior coaching positions at professional clubs have remained stagnant at around 4% at first team and youth academy level (SPTT, 2017). More promisingly, recent research undertaken by the authors has indicated that 17% of all professional club youth academy coaches are from BAME backgrounds, although around three-quarters (73%) of these coaches hold lower status part-time positions with limited occupational permanence or structured opportunities for career advancement (Bradbury & Conricode, 2020). Overall, the representation of BAME coaches in English professional football compares unfavourably with that of BAME youth academy players (40%), BAME professional players (30%), and the BAME population of England more broadly (15%) (SPTT, 2017).

Recent research has drawn on the informed experiential testimonies of elite level BAME coaches to examine the factors underpinning their under-representation in professional football in England and in other countries in Western Europe (Bradbury et al., 2014, 2018; Bradbury 2018). Broadly speaking, this research has identified three inter-connected barriers which have impacted negatively in constraining the extent and scope of BAME progression across the 'transition pipeline' from playing to coach education and coach employment in the professional game. Firstly, limited opportunities for organisational resource support to access high level coach education courses and negative experiences of racisms at courses of this kind. Secondly, the over-reliance on networks- (rather than qualifications-) based methods of coach recruitment at professional clubs premised on personal recommendation, patronage and sponsored mobility. And, thirdly, the existence of unconscious racial bias and stereotyping in the coaching workplace and the consequent problematisation of BAME coaches as lacking the relevant attitudinal and intellectual skills to become successful coaches. Taken together, this is argued to have positioned BAME coaches at a competitive disadvantage in the coach education and employment marketplace in comparison to White coaches drawn from within the dominant social and cultural insider networks of the professional football industry, and to constitute a form of institutional discrimination which has limited the potential for and realisation of equality of opportunities and outcomes in the coaching tiers of the sport (see also Bradbury in Chapter 2 in this collection). As a result, it has been argued that any targeted measures designed to address these racialised inequities should seek to challenge, disrupt and dismantle the normative arrangements of coach recruitment embedded within and maintained by the routinised practices of dominant individuals and institutions within professional football (Bradbury et al., 2018).

Promisingly, in recent years, a number of key stakeholders in professional football in England have responded to growing external pressures from national equality campaigns and media sources and have developed new programmes and initiatives designed to address racialised inequities in football coaching. These interventions differ markedly in their scope, focus and intended outputs, but have tended to prioritise the provision of resource support to empower BAME coaches to achieve high level coach education qualifications and to enhance their visibility and employability in the coaching marketplace. They include the targeted work of the Professional Footballers Association and League Managers Association to deliver professional development masterclasses, coaching clinics and interview preparation support to BAME coaches (LMA, 2018). They also include the work of the FA to deliver the expansive Coach Inclusion and Diversity programme, which since its inception as a smaller scale pilot project in 2012 has gone on to support around 100 BAME coaches per annum to achieve FA UEFA B, FA UEFA A, and FA UEFA Advanced Youth Awards (Bradbury, 2016, 2019). These elite level coaching qualifications are designed to equip coaches with the relevant technical and experiential skills considered requisite for employment within the increasingly formalised youth and adult tiered coaching infrastructures of professional clubs in England.

Other programmes have sought to move beyond notions of 'educative empowerment' to focus more specifically on addressing institutional barriers embedded in normative processes and practices of coach recruitment.

Programmes of this kind have been informed by the 'Rooney Rule' which was first implemented as a regulated approach to coach recruitment in the US NFL in 2002 and which has been hailed as a key mechanism through which the representation of racial minority head coaches has increased significantly in the sport over time (see Duru 2011 and Duru in Chapter 11 of this collection). Whilst in 2018 the FA announced that it would adopt a version of the 'Rooney Rule' in relation to the recruitment of all senior coaches at national team level (Football Association, 2018), arguably the most substantive efforts on this score have been undertaken by the English Football League (EFL) which in June 2016 launched the 'voluntary' and 'mandatory' codes of coach recruitment. These codes represent a tandem set of interventionist policy measures through which all 72 member clubs in the second, third and fourth tiers of the English professional game have been encouraged to adopt standardised and equitable practices of coach recruitment. The voluntary code is targeted specifically at adult first team operations and was first implemented at ten pilot clubs during the 2016–17 season and has since been extended to include all 72 member clubs (see Cowell in Chapter 12 in this collection). In contrast, the mandatory code is targeted specifically at professional club youth academies and was first implemented during the 2016–17 season at all 72 member clubs. EFL club youth academies are concerned with the technical, tactical, psychological and social development of elite level young players (9–21 years old) and each club academy operates a broadly comparable coaching infrastructure in which coaches are employed across a range of senior level operations, middle level development phase lead, and lower level age-specific coaching positions.

The mandatory code stipulates that all EFL club youth academies must run a full recruitment process for any coaching position that requires an individual to hold as a minimum an FA UEFA B licence, and that such positions should be advertised publicly on the EFL and club website for at least seven days. Further, clubs must interview at least one suitably qualified BAME candidate for any coaching position where an application has been received but will be permitted to opt-out of this full recruitment process when promoting a suitably qualified internal candidate regardless of ethnicity. To this end, the mandatory code can be understood as a distinctly positive action measure as outlined in sections 158 and 159 of the 2010 UK Equality Act which allows for employers to implement targeted practices of promoting and interviewing for vacancies in order to redress historical disadvantages and experiences of under-representation on the basis of ethnicity and other 'protected characteristics' such as gender, sexual orientation and disability (Government Equalities Office, 2010).

This chapter will provide an original empirical and theoretically grounded contribution to the study of 'race', racisms and the racial equality measures in sports coaching. More specifically, the chapter will examine the shape, scope and effectiveness of the EFL mandatory code of coach recruitment in the first year of its operation in professional football club youth academies in England. Firstly, the chapter will begin by examining the *operational implementation* of the mandatory code of coach recruitment. In doing so, it will focus on four inter-related and processual components of the code: *advertising, applications, interviews* and *appointments*. In particular, it will examine the extent and ways in which these components have been operationalised at club academies and the measurable impact they have had in ensuring greater racial equitability in all aspects of the coach recruitment process. Secondly, the chapter will proceed by examining the *attitudinal implementation* of the mandatory code of coach recruitment. In doing so, it will focus on two identifiably different *'race-conscious'* and *'race-neutral'* approaches to equality and diversity management exhibited by senior decision-making personnel at club academies. In particular, it will examine the ways in which these divergent attitudinal approaches have enabled or constrained the operational implementation and effectiveness of the mandatory code of coach recruitment in academy settings.

Theoretical framework

The presentation and analysis of findings featured in this chapter are informed by and draw on key tenets of Critical Race Theory (CRT). Firstly, in centralising 'race' as the key organising principle in social and public life and in considering racisms to constitute an endemic – rather than aberrational – feature of the everyday experiences of BAME populations in Western democracies such as the UK. From this perspective, racisms and racialised discrimination are understood to be enacted through the operation of often unconscious everyday routinised processes and practices which have become normalised within societal and sporting institutions to the point of invisibility (Delgado & Stefancic, 2001; Solórzano et al., 2001; Hylton, 2009). Secondly, CRT critiques dominant liberal ideologies around objectivity and meritocracy which individualise the concept of 'success' as resulting from talent, ability and hard work and consequently strip it from the deeply racialised societal and sporting contexts in which it occurs. From this perspective, such narratives are underpinned by an uncritical adherence to a set of 'colour-blind' ideologies which fail to recognise racisms unless in their most egregious forms and which actively seek to minimise the scope and naturalise the consequences of racialised inequalities as resulting from individual and cultural deficit rather than as being created and sustained by the practices of dominant individuals and institutions (Bonilla-Silva, 2010). For CRT scholars, these hierarchical systems of racial domination are underpinned by the power of Whiteness as a powerful structural and cultural practice to frame the unearned advantages of White privilege as the norm and to defend the contemporary racial order in societal and sporting contexts by protecting and endorsing existing institutional arrangements

(Long & Hylton, 2002; McDonald, 2005; McIntosh, 1990). And, thirdly, CRT argues that liberalism alone is not enough to address deeply embedded forms of institutional racism in societal and sporting contexts and that the operation of seemingly neutral approaches to recruitment tend to sustain rather than redress patterns and experiences of racial inequality and disadvantage in these settings. From this perspective, a strongly interventionist, redistributive and transformational approach to social justice is required at the policy level which recognises the unequal social locations and distinctive histories of different racial groups and the potential of radical positive action measures to challenge institutionalised racialised inequities and ensure equality of outcomes for BAME groups (Bradbury et al., 2018; Hylton, 2010; Rankin-Wright et al., 2017).

Study and methods

The findings presented in this chapter are drawn from a three-year study (2015–2018) examining the shape, scope and effectiveness of positive action measures in addressing racialised inequities in coach recruitment in men's professional football in England. The study was undertaken by the authors and funded by the Leverhulme Trust. The quantitative findings presented in this chapter are drawn from a comprehensive online survey of academy managers at professional club youth academies (n=23). In total, 20 club academy managers were White, and three were from BAME backgrounds. The survey was undertaken in June 2017 and sought to gather information as to the levels of representation of BAME coaches at club academies and the extent and ways in which the *operational implementation* of the mandatory code of coach recruitment had become embedded in academy settings. The qualitative findings presented in this chapter are drawn from extensive semi-structured interviews with academy managers (n=10), BAME academy coaches (n=16), and key organisational stakeholders, including national football federation, players union, and equality campaign group representatives (n=9). In total, ten interviewees were White (including eight academy managers) and 25 were from BAME backgrounds. The interviews were undertaken between July 2017 and May 2018 and sought to gather information as to the existence and types of racialised barriers in coaching in academy football and the *attitudinal implementation* and effectiveness of the mandatory code of coach recruitment in addressing racialised inequities of this kind.

Central to the mixed method approach to data collection and analysis featured within this chapter is the strong emphasis placed on prioritising the professionally and culturally informed experiential knowledge of the research participants. This is felt to be especially important in relation to efforts to 'give voice' to and 'make heard' the historically subjugated testimonies of BAME participants whose experiences and perspectives have traditionally been excluded from – but remain subject to – dominant narratives on the realities and impacts of 'race' and racism in sport (Hylton, 2005). In doing so, we remain cognisant of the inherent power imbalances between ourselves as White researchers and BAME participants and recognise that the normativity and invisibility of Whiteness embedded within the sporting contexts under review cannot be fully separated from those which exist in the research process, and that as a result we may at times unconsciously draw on White hegemonic discourses around 'race' and racisms in our discussion and analysis (Essed et al., 2008; Frankenberg, 2004; Sin, 2007). However, we contend that such influence is rarely definitive in its application or passive in its negotiation, and that our theoretically informed and lived engagement in the process of critical (and cultural) reflexivity provides us with a useful epistemological tool through which to better consider the self and the self in relation to others (Fletcher, 2014). It also enables us to extend the diversity of discourses we draw on to make sense of and contextualise the overlapping and contrasting narratives produced by research participants drawn from dominant and marginalised ethnicities in this chapter (see Bradbury et al., 2018 and Bradbury (Chapter 2) in this collection for additional reflections on (White) researcher positionality and conducting inter-racial research in sports related settings).

Findings

This section will begin by drawing on survey and interview data to present findings which examine the operational implementation of the mandatory code in relation to four key processual components: *advertising, applications, interviews* and *appointments*. The section will then draw on interview data to present findings which examine the attitudinal implementation of the mandatory code and in doing so will identify two distinct 'race-conscious' and 'race-neutral' approaches in this respect.

(i) Operational implementation of the mandatory code

Advertisements

Overall, survey and interview findings indicated that during the 2016–17 season the mandatory code of coach recruitment had engendered a broadly positive impact in increasing the incidence and length of publicly advertising coaching positions at club academies. For example, the overwhelming majority of academies reported publicly advertising all vacant coaching positions on 'every occasion' (86%) or on 'some occasions' (14%) during this period. Whilst almost all academies advertised these positions on their own club website (91%), around three-fifths also utilised other online mediums such as the EFL website (64%) and FA Licensed Coaches Club website (59%). Whilst these formalised approaches to advertising were often enacted alongside – rather than instead of – informal methods of vacancy promotion, they were nonetheless felt by interviewees to have become a standardised feature of the coach recruitment process during the period under review. One White academy manager reflects on these changing practices below:

> *Actually, because of that [mandatory code] intervention, the jobs now go on the EFL website, which I'd say is a massive step forward in the fact that probably around 18 months ago, before this came in, that never happened.*
> (Interviewee, White academy manager)

The majority of academies also reported they had gone beyond the stipulated seven-day period for publicly advertising coaching positions and had extended the 'reasonable time frame' to between 8–14 days (62%), 15–21 days (24%) or 22–28 days (14%). This was felt by some interviewees to have increased the awareness of vacancies at academies amongst all aspiring coaches and to provide an extended period in which to prepare and submit applications for positions of this kind. For some interviewees, this was considered to have had a particular resonance for BAME coaches whose marginality to dominant (White) social and cultural insider football coaching networks meant they were more likely than their better-connected White peers to be solely reliant on these formalised processes of vacancy promotion. Findings here chime with research undertaken in US college sports which suggest that normatively shorter time frames in which to conduct coach recruitment tend to generate '*unfair outcomes, as quick hiring decisions limit and inhibit the ability of racial minorities to gain genuine opportunities to engage in the interview process*' (Singer et al., 2010: 286). One BAME academy coach comments below on the benefits of extending the advertisement period within club academy settings:

> *Sometimes you see a job and you want to go away and think about how you're going to apply for that particular job and how you're going to edit your CV and your covering letter. And that might take some [BAME] individuals a little longer. So, I think it's definitely fair and important to have that time period.*
> (Interviewee, BAME academy coach)

Applications

Despite the increased incidence and length of advertising referred to above, survey and interview findings indicated that during the 2016–17 season this had not yet engendered a significant increase in applications for coaching positions at club academies from BAME coaches. For example, academies reported that just 9% of all applications for coaching positions during this period were from suitably qualified BAME coaches:

inclusive of applications for full-time (6%) and part-time positions (21%). For some interviewees, these figures were deemed to be reflective of the lower numbers of BAME coaches with requisite coaching qualifications and experience to be considered for employment at academies. Findings here are borne out to some partial extent by research which has alluded to the existence of racialised blockages in the coach education pipeline and a lack of a critical mass of highly qualified BAME coaches in some less ethnically diverse locales in which many lower division EFL clubs are based (Bradbury, 2016, 2018). This is arguably exacerbated further by the relatively low status and salaries associated with academy coaching positions and the consequent limited potential for such positions to engender significant geographical mobility or willingness to commute extensively on the part of aspiring coaches. For some interviewees, this was felt to have led to a lack of fit between BAME applicants' qualifications and the organisational expectations and requirements of club academies in some less ethnically diverse locales. One White academy manager comments further in this respect:

In terms of the key criteria for [BAME] people who would be eligible and be realistic to do the roles, a lot of it comes down to they just haven't got the experience of the qualifications to meet the mandatory criteria.

(Interviewee, White academy manager)

In other cases, interviewees felt that beyond the senior organisational tiers of the EFL and academy hierarchies there was little broader knowledge or awareness of the emphasis or implementation of the mandatory code of coach recruitment. This was felt to be the case amongst BAME coaches within and outside of academy coaching infrastructures for whom opportunities embodied in the code to ensure an interview for suitably qualified BAME candidates remained 'unknown' and 'out of sight'. As a result, a number of interviewees felt that the narrow public promotion of the mandatory code had thus far limited its potential to increase the numbers of applications from BAME coaches in the short term, and would continue to do so up until such a time as the code might become more widely publicised by the EFL and other key football bodies and through a more diverse range of traditional and community web-based mediums. One BAME academy coach comments further in this respect:

I think it will [increase applications] but I don't think you will see that until the next two or three years. And the only reason I say that is because it goes back to the whole, 'have they got the word out, do black and ethnic minority coaches know about this rule?'

(Interviewee, BAME academy coach)

Interviews

Survey and interview findings indicated that during the 2016–17 season there was a strong correlation between the number of applications made by and interviews awarded to suitably qualified BAME coaches. More specifically, academies reported that 97% of all BAME applicants were awarded an interview for coaching positions in academy settings during this period. Further, overall, academies reported that 27% of all coaches interviewed for coaching positions during this period were from BAME backgrounds: inclusive of interviews for full-time (19%) and part-time (35%) positions. Findings here indicate a strong operational adherence to this specific element of the mandatory code at most academies and an identifiable uplift in the numbers of BAME coaches progressing to the interview stage of the coach recruitment process. This was felt by some interviewees to have helped neutralise elements of unconscious racial bias and related preferences for 'homologous reproduction' (Cunningham, 2010; Sartore & Cunningham, 2006) inherent within the interview selection criteria at some academies and which was reported to have impacted negatively in limiting opportunities for some BAME coaches to access interviews in the past. One BAME academy coach articulates these themes further:

> I think something as little as a name that's foreign can be pushed aside. Whereas I think if they are progressing to an interview and you're giving that individual an opportunity to sit down and get to know the coach, and see them coach and see how good they are, you know, trying to overcome the obstacle of the name barrier, I think it's a good thing.
> (Interviewee, BAME academy coach)

A number of interviewees felt that the 'interview guarantee' embodied in the mandatory code had also enabled opportunities for suitably qualified BAME coaches to access an important 'interactional space' within which to showcase their technical and experiential skill sets directly to key decision makers at academies. These face-to-face opportunities to 'sit at the table' and 'make the case' as to their vocational suitability for emergent coaching positions were considered to be an essential factor in increasing the potential to secure employment as coaches thereafter. Findings here chime strongly with research examining the effectiveness of positive action measures in sports coaching more broadly and which highlight the importance of consideration forcing mechanisms in enhancing the professional visibility and favourability of BAME coaches within the consciousness of key decision makers with powers of appointment at professional sports clubs (Bradbury et al., 2014; Duru, 2011; Singer et al., 2010). One recently interviewed and appointed BAME academy coach offers some personal reflections on this score:

> *You could argue due to this rule at [club academy], I had the opportunity to sit down in front of the powers that be and from there I was able to make my case to say, 'this is why you need to hire me'. So, you could argue that if the rule wasn't there and they didn't have to interview someone from a BAME background, would I be the new foundation phase lead at the [club academy]? Probably not.*
>
> (Interviewee, BAME academy coach)

Appointments

Overall, survey and interview findings indicated that during the 2016–17 season the mandatory code of coach recruitment had engendered a strongly positive impact in enabling an increased number of appointments of BAME coaches at club academies. For example, academies reported that during the 12-month period under review, BAME coaches accounted for almost one-half (49%) of all new coaching appointments: inclusive of appointments for full-time (37%) and part-time (57%) positions. These annual snapshot figures show a marked upturn when set against figures drawn from the same survey which indicated that during the 2016–17 season in total BAME coaches accounted for 17% of the overall academy coaching workforce: inclusive of full-time (11%) and part-time (21%) positions. For some interviewees, these short-term representational gains were underpinned by a strong operational adherence to the mandatory code with respect to improved advertising procedures and processes of interview selection at some academies. Where these more equitable practices of coach recruitment were observed this was felt to have broadened the network radius of academies to incorporate a more ethnically diverse talent pool and to have enabled increased numbers of BAME coaches to progress through the previously blocked coach recruitment pipeline. One BAME organisational stakeholder comments below on these changing practices and their positive impacts:

> *The clubs will be seeing candidates that they might not have seen before. They'll maybe have seen 3 or 4 on their radar because they're within their networks, and those networks won't necessarily include people of other ethnicities. So, because of that [mandatory code], they'll see other talent.*
>
> (Interviewee, BAME organisational stakeholder)

However, in contrast to these more positive assertions, some interviewees questioned the extent to which the mandatory code was being enacted in a meaningful and transparent way at *all* club academies. These more critical accounts were mainly posited by BAME coaches who felt that despite being selected for and performing well in interview situations, they had still not been appointed to coaching positions which had instead been awarded to 'preferred' White candidates with strong social and cultural connections to senior staff at academies. The continued operation of such practices indicates that at some academies efforts to establish more equitable processes of coach recruitment have remained limited and perfunctory and have been undertaken performatively to satisfy the regulatory requirements of the mandatory code whilst ignoring the central principles of inclusivity to which it aspires. Findings here are broadly replicative of previous research which has drawn attention to the gestural and symbolic rather than meaningful and impactful implementation of racial equality policies in sports organisations in the UK and the related tendency to focus efforts on amending organisational processes whilst leaving the organisational cultures which underpin and operationalise them relatively untouched (Ahmed, 2006; Long et al., 2011; Lusted, 2014; Spracklen et al., 2006). As a result, the extent and effectiveness of the implementation of the code and its impact on increasing the representation of BAME coaches was felt by some interviewees to be underscored less by its core operational elements and more by the attitudinal approaches and consequent levels of organisational buy-in amongst key decision-making personnel at academies. In some cases, this was also felt to play a pivotal role in shaping the wider perceptions of and levels of engagement with the code amongst BAME coaches within and outside of the professional game. One BAME academy coach comments further in this respect:

> *You're going to get a certain few that are going take it on and embrace it, and you're going to have others of that mindset that it's an even bigger waste of time because until you make changes to the people and influence the mindsets of people making decisions, all these types of things will have no importance.*
> (Interviewee, BAME Academy Coach)

This chapter now turns to an evaluation of the attitudinal approaches of senior staff at academies, and the impact of this on the implementation and effectiveness of the mandatory code.

(ii) Attitudinal implementation of the mandatory code of coach recruitment

'Race-conscious' approaches to coach recruitment

Interview findings indicated that senior staff at a relatively small cluster of club academies exhibited a strong level of 'problem awareness' as to the existence, types and impacts of racialised barriers experienced by BAME groups seeking employment as coaches at the academy level. This seemed to be especially (but not exclusively) the case amongst senior staff at academies situated in ethnically diverse locales which featured significant numbers of young players and coaches from BAME backgrounds. Within these more multi-cultural occupational environments, these senior staff were also broadly supportive of wider calls for the development and implementation of new interventionist approaches designed to 'open-up' the coach recruitment process and to increase the numbers of BAME coaches in academy settings. One White academy manager summarises these perspectives below:

> *With coaches from a BAME background, I just think it does need a bespoke option or bespoke solution because if we keep doing what we're currently doing then the numbers aren't going to improve because we've been trying to do that already.*
>
> (Interviewee, White academy manager)

Senior staff at these academies were also likely to recognise the importance and value of cultural diversity in the coaching workplace and to view it as an important asset through which to enhance operational effectiveness and meet organisational goals. From this perspective, BAME coaches were conceptualised both in terms of their technical and experiential abilities and as possessing an important added value component as a positive pedagogical and intercultural resource through which to extend and diversify the 'cultural options' and developmental capacities of academies. This *'race-conscious'* approach to workplace diversity management was also felt by some interviewees to have enabled some academies to better 'connect with' and support the social, psychological and technical development of young BAME players especially and chimes strongly with prior research in the field which has drawn attention to the importance of cultural role models in youth football settings (Jowett & Frost, 2007). In this respect, within some contextually situated academy environments there appeared to be a strong recognition of the *'genuine relevance of identity for professional practice, beyond the limited scope of occupational qualifications'* (Johns et al., 2014: 109). One White academy manager comments further on the perceived importance of these racialised considerations to the player-coach relationship:

> *We do believe in role models for the boys and particularly in our club. Some of our [young] Black players have a different relationship with some of our Black coaches than with our other coaches, not on every single case, but I think there's definitely a pattern.*
>
> (Interviewee, White academy manager)

The establishment of a culturally diverse coaching workforce in which the varied professional, social and cultural experiences and skill sets of coaching staff were recognised and valued was also felt by some interviewees to have enabled impactful cultural learning opportunities for some White coaches in these academy settings. In particular, in engendering an increased (and increasingly nuanced) level of cultural awareness and understanding of equality and diversity. In some cases, this was felt to have led to improved social relationships with young BAME players and to the delivery of more culturally reflexive coaching practice. Findings here chime strongly with prior research in which White coaches have reflected positively on the valuable pedagogical experiences and benefits engendered through interracial coaching collaboration in youth academy settings (Bradbury, 2016). One White academy manager reflects below on some of the processes and impacts of these cultural learning opportunities:

> It's fantastic if we can get a real mix. Because for example a black coach from inner-city [club location] may have had some different experiences that he can share with us as staff, that can help us get better and better understand the kind of black inner-city areas of [club location]. It broadens our horizons and allows us to have more options and more capabilities.
> (Interviewee, White academy manager)

Overall, interview findings indicated that it was at these academies where cultural diversity was positively valued and where senior staff operated a distinctly *'race-conscious'* approach to coach and player operations, where there was a much stronger level of organisational buy-in to the principles of inclusivity embodied within the mandatory code. Here, the code was framed by senior staff as a useful policy tool which has enabled a tangible processual shift away from networks-based approaches to coach recruitment, to more formalised, equitable, and transparent systems in which an attitudinal commitment to cultural open-ness rather than cultural obstruction guided this operational process. One White academy manager reflects positively on these changing practices below:

> We've had problems in the past where we haven't gone through that process. People have been in the job and have done the recruitment where they'd brought in a friend, an ex-colleague, so there's never been a transparent recruitment process. Generally, it's (mandatory code) helped everything just move to transparency in what we do. Everything has to be really clear and concise and overall transparent to everybody. There's got to be a fairness to what you do.
> (Interviewee, White academy manager)

'Race-neutral' approaches to coach recruitment

In contrast to the more progressive assertions identified above, interview findings also indicated that senior staff at the majority of other club academies were much less likely to recognise or admit to the existence of racialised inequities in coach recruitment at the academy level. This seemed to be most marked (but not exclusively so) amongst senior staff at academies situated in ethnically narrow, or, at least, more ethnically polarised, locales, with lower numbers of BAME young players and where the make-up of coaching staff was predominantly White. At these academies, senior staff were keen to position the academy coaching landscape as a distinctly post-racial and egalitarian space which was separate from and more inclusive than other social fields in professional football in which overt forms of racisms were felt to be relatively commonplace. In doing so, these senior staff conceptualised the under-representation of BAME coaches as resulting from wider 'imported' societal exclusions or from the negatively assumed properties of BAME coaches, rather than as being shaped and maintained by the normative routinised practices of dominant individuals and institutions within the academy game (Bradbury et al., 2018; Burdsey, 2007; King, 2004). One White academy manager summarises these perspectives below:

> *I don't see there being major barriers to be honest as I think with the amount of jobs there are available now, if people are proactive and they want to get involved then I think it's quite easy.*
> (Interviewee, White academy manager)

Relatedly, senior staff at these academies were likely to downplay the positive pedagogical and intercultural value and associated beneficial organisational impacts which might be incurred through establishing a more culturally diverse coaching workforce. These perspectives seemed strongly underscored by a relatively rigid adherence to dominant liberal notions of objectivity, meritocracy and race-neutrality which remain a commonplace and normative feature of the societal and sporting landscape in late-modern Britain and in other Western countries (Bonilla-Silva, 2010; Delgado & Stefancic, 2001; Hylton, 2018). Further, in some cases, they were explicitly aligned with the related perception that efforts to ensure racial equality were antithetical to the 'competitive' process of coach recruitment and constitute an unnecessary and unwarranted distraction to the everyday operational concerns of academies. One White academy manager articulates further in this respect:

> *So no for me it's not about you have to have diversity, I don't think we do, I don't think that's important in my opinion, I think what is important is we have the right people in the right places who can do the jobs.*
> (Interviewee, White academy manager)

From this perspective, senior staff at these academies argued that pre-existing normative processes of coach recruitment were already inherently fair and unbiased and offered the reward of employment to the most talented and deserving candidates regardless of their ethnicity. In some cases, senior staff drew on their own racially unencumbered (and racially unacknowledged) experiences of occupational mobility in the professional football industry as evidence of the perceived meritocratic principles and practices embedded within it. Such narratives tended to downplay the privileges afforded by their own (White) racial identity and to preserve the illusion of a neutral social order which is perceived to be experienced in identical ways by all social groups (Bonilla-Silva, 2010; López, 2003). Further, the assumed (if not realised) operational and cultural impartiality of these approaches was deemed to be reflective of the (self-validated) personal integrity and professional even-handedness of senior decision-making staff at club academies. One White academy manager offers some personal reflections on this score below:

> *I would hate to think that I would need to follow BAME guidelines to recruit someone in order to recruit the best person for the job. I'd hate to think that I couldn't run a fair and appropriate recruitment process without people or without the game assuming that I'm gonna have a bias towards non-BAME candidates.*
>
> (Interviewee, White academy manager)

Overall, interview findings indicated that it was at these academies in which the value of cultural diversity was downplayed and where senior staff operated a distinctly *'race-neutral'* approach to coach recruitment, where there was a more limited level of organisational buy-in to the principles of inclusivity embodied within the mandatory code. In some cases, this was underscored by an explicit ideological and attitudinal resistance to the code on the part of senior staff who positioned it as an 'unfair' and 'anti-competitive' measure which favoured the 'underserving' and inhibited rather than enabled the recruitment of the 'best candidate for the job'. Further, whilst senior staff at these academies indicated that the mandatory code of coach recruitment had been implemented at an operational level, this had largely been done so as an additive and optional rather than central operating principle. As a result, its application in practice seemed gestural and performative and to have left the culturally unreflexive attitudinal approaches of senior decision-making personnel relatively untouched. One White academy manager summarises the minimal impact of the code in this respect:

> *It's not really impacted on anything because like I said earlier, I'll always be looking for the most positive kind of candidates that we've got... it's not really affected us within the coaching department much.*
>
> (Interviewee, White academy manager)

Discussion

This chapter firstly sought to examine the extent and effectiveness of the *operational implementation* of the mandatory code of coach recruitment and the measurable impact it has had on increasing the levels of representation of BAME coaches in club academies in the first year of its operation. In this respect, survey and interview findings indicated that there has been a generally strong operational adherence to the implementation of the code at most academies, with particular respect to efforts to formalise and broaden advertising procedures and to ensure that at least one suitably qualified BAME candidate is awarded an interview. Whilst these more equitable processes of coach recruitment have not yet engendered a marked upsurge in applications for coaching positions amongst BAME coaches, there is strong statistical evidence to suggest they have had a positive impact in enabling increased opportunities to progress through the applications to appointments pipeline and have led to some significant representational gains in increasing the employment of BAME coaches in academy settings. In doing so, it is the contention here that the mandatory code has thus far provided a useful policy-based platform on which to successfully begin the process of dismantling some of the foremost institutional barriers which have hitherto constrained the career progression of many BAME coaches (Bradbury et al., 2014, 2018). Not least of all, in engendering a positive shift from network-based to qualifications-based methods of coach recruitment at academies and in enabling opportunities for BAME coaches to showcase their evidential technical and experiential abilities and to challenge unconscious racial bias and stereotyping in interview situations. However, as prior research examining the implementation of racial equality measures in sports in the UK has indicated, the extent to which interventions of this kind can engender meaningful and sustainable representational impacts for BAME groups is to some extent underscored by the ideological value positions of key personnel and the levels of organisational commitment to enact such policies at the operational level (Ahmed, 2006; Long et al., 2011; Lusted, 2014; Rankin-Wright et al., 2016; Spracklen et al., 2006). In this respect, whilst the focus of the mandatory code in 'opening up' some previously closed organisational processes of coach recruitment has led to some positive numerical outcomes for BAME coaches, it has also arguably done less to address the ideologically narrow organisational cultures which underpin and operationalise them. As a result we concur with the cautionary words of Shaw (2007: 426) who argues that *'increasing the numbers of people who represent diverse groups does nothing to ensure that equality is a central part of organisational processes. All that it achieves is increased numbers of marginalised groups within organisations that are culturally and structurally unchanged'*.

Relatedly, the chapter secondly sought to examine the extent and ways in which the operational implementation and effectiveness of the mandatory code has been enabled or constrained by the *attitudinal approaches* of key decision-making personnel at club academies. In this respect, interview findings identified divergent perceptions amongst senior staff at academies as to the relevance and applicability of the code and differing levels of organisational buy-in to the principles of inclusivity embodied within it and its application in practice. Drawing on key tenets of CRT it is the contention here that these contrasting perceptions and approaches have been underscored by a broadly (but, not exclusively) oppositional ideological adherence to *'race-conscious'* or *'race-neutral'* philosophies and associated preferences for managing equality and diversity in societal and sporting contexts, including in coach recruitment. For example, amongst a smaller cluster of *'race-conscious'* senior staff there appeared to be a stronger acknowledgement of the salience of 'race' as an important operating principle in the lives of BAME groups (Delgado & Stefancic, 2001; Hylton, 2009) and a recognition of the existence and impacts of at least some of the more identifiable racialised inequities embedded within the coach recruitment process. This was notably the case amongst senior staff at club academies situated in more urban locales with larger numbers of BAME coaches and young players and for whom the everyday lived and occupational experience of multiculturalism was the norm. This cohort of *'racial progressives'* (Bonilla-Silva, 2010: 143) were more likely to recognise the value of cultural diversity in the youth coaching workplace and to view it pragmatically as a positive resource through which to aid the social, psychological and technical development of young players (Bradbury, 2016; Jowett & Frost, 2007). However, whilst such dual conceptualisations of the technical abilities and cultural relatability of BAME coaches were considered by these senior staff (and by some BAME coaches) as a plus factor in accessing and delivering coaching in multi-cultural academy settings, they also constituted a process of racialisation which positioned BAME coaches as 'differently abled' to and 'other than' some White coaches whose own racial identities remained invisible, unacknowledged and unremarked (Frankenburg, 1999; Hylton, 2009). In this respect, it is argued here that whilst such well-meaning *'race-conscious'* approaches might have located some BAME coaches favourably in terms of accessing coaching positions which include a strong developmental and mentoring focus, they might also have had unintentional consequences in limiting opportunities for BAME coaches to access more performance-based coaching roles with older elite level youth players. Such racialised patterns of recruitment and role allocation in which racial minority coaches have been recruited *'principally for their ability to relate to and help recruit racial minority athletes'* (Cunningham, 2010: 172) are relatively commonplace in US sporting contexts and have contributed to patterns of occupational segregation in the coaching workforce (Braddock et al., 2012; Cunningham, 2010; Day, 2015; Singer et al., 2010). Nonetheless, amongst these more *'race-conscious'* senior staff there was more broadly at least some recognition that *'inequity, inopportunity and oppression are historical artefacts that will not be easily remedied by ignoring "race" in contemporary society'* (DeCuir & Dixson, 2004: 29). As a result, these senior staff were explicitly supportive of the interventionist intentions and redistributive outcomes of the mandatory code and exhibited a strongly conjunctive operational and attitudinal adherence to its implementation.

In contrast, amongst senior staff operating *'race-neutral'* philosophies and approaches there was a strong tendency to downplay the salience of 'race' and to deny the existence and impacts of racialised inequities in the coach recruitment process. Such perceptions are relatively commonplace within the senior organisational tiers of elite level sports more broadly and tend to overlook the extent to which sporting contexts are reflective of and reflect back on the deeply racialised power relations embedded in the societies in which they take place and the subsequent myriad manifestation of racisms and racialised disadvantage in such settings (Carrington, 2010; Hylton, 2009). These senior staff were also likely to draw heavily on dominant liberal discourses of objectivity, meritocracy and race-neutrality and to conceptualise the existing coach recruitment landscape at academies as inherently fair and devoid of racial bias. These discourses drew on a series of 'colour-blind' ideologies to present a highly individualised and largely deracialised account of upward occupational mobility in football coaching as resulting from talent, ability and hard work and to consequently strip the realities of success or failure from the deeply racialised contexts in which they occur (Bonilla-Silva, 2010). From a CRT perspective, such narratives also tend to normalise evidenced patterns of racialised inequalities as resulting from individual and cultural deficit rather than from the everyday routinised practices of dominant individuals and institutions, and as such provide a culturally unreflexive rationale through which to *'justifiably dismiss racial phenomena by reasoning which suggests natural occurrences'* (Bimper, 2015: 225). These perceptions are relatively commonplace in sports more broadly and are indicative of the tendency of powerful White groups to universalise their own racially unencumbered experiences of upward occupational mobility and the related unearned benefits afforded by White privilege as the cultural norm (Carrington, 2010; Hylton, 2009). In this respect, the findings presented in this chapter allude to the power of Whiteness as an embedded structural and cultural practice to unproblematically frame the equality and diversity landscape of academy coaching in distinctly non-discriminatory terms. Whilst, simultaneously, sustaining the invisible knapsack of White privilege (McIntosh, 1990) in such ways as to ensure that members of dominant racial groups remain *'beneficiaries of a host of seemingly neutral arrangements and institutional operations, all of which seem to them to have no racial basis'* (Hartigan, 1997: 496). In such circumstances, it is perhaps unsurprising that senior staff subscribing to notions of 'race-neutrality' and 'colour-blindness' were also likely to display a marked attitudinal resistance to the reformatory goals of the mandatory code and to exhibit a largely gestural and symbolic rather than meaningful and substantive operational adherence to its implementation.

Conclusions and recommendations

In conclusion, it is argued here that the principles of the mandatory code of coach recruitment square firmly with the claims of Critical Race Theory that liberalism alone is not enough to address deeply embedded forms of institutional racism and that colour-blind ideologies and the application of neutral-criteria approaches in recruitment tend to sustain rather than redress patterns of racialised disadvantage. In this respect, the code can be understood as a distinctly interventionist and politically progressive positive action measure which aims to ensure that a full consideration of equality of opportunities *and* equality of outcomes becomes a central and prioritised feature of recruitment practices at club academies. However, for the initial operational adherence to and effectiveness of the mandatory code to be advanced and expanded over time, more holistic efforts are needed on the part of the EFL to encourage a shift in attitudes and a stronger level of organisational 'buy-in' at club academies to the central values of racial inclusivity on which the code is premised. This should include the delivery of relevant cultural awareness training for senior staff at club academies with a strong focus on contextualising the relevance and applicability of the code to academy settings, increasing understanding of the social and economic value and beneficial impacts of cultural diversity in the coaching workplace, and encouraging and enabling greater individual and organisational reflexivity in relation to processes and practices of unconscious bias. This pedagogical work should be supported by the production of a uniform guidance document and checklist of good practice in relation to each of the four inter-related and processual components of the code: *advertising, applications, interviews* and *appointments*. This guidance could be extended further to ensure that the demographic make-up of selection and interview panels are more culturally diverse and that appropriate feedback is provided to unsuccessful candidates to help them reflect on the interview process and better prepare for future applications. Taken together, it is argued here that the adoption of these procedurally adaptive and culturally reflexive measures will help club academies to develop and embed a more inclusive and equitable operational approach to coach recruitment than has been the case in the past and ensure that initial statistical advances in the representation of BAME coaches has continued longevity over time. Finally, successful efforts on this score are likely to have significant transferability as a 'game changer' model of best equality practice with direct relevance for other football and sporting contexts in the UK and beyond and for the benefit of BAME coaches, professional clubs and national governing bodies of sports more broadly.

Note

1 Black, Asian and Minority Ethnic and the acronym BAME is presently the most recognisable term of self-identification used in British social and political discourse to refer to generationally settled and newly established in-migrant Non-White communities in the UK (previously commonly referred to as ethnic minorities or minority ethnic). Whilst categorisations of this kind are conceptually limited and subject to contestation, the use of the term BAME in this chapter is done so in the context of recognising the myriad racial, ethnic, cultural and religious diversity within BAME groupings in the UK *and* the simultaneous existence of shared experiences of racial inequality and disadvantage across a range of national societal and sporting settings.

References

Ahmed, S. (2006) The non-performativity of antiracism. *Meridians*, 7(1), 104–126.

Bimper, A. (2015) Lifting the veil: Exploring colorblind racism in Black student athlete experiences. *Journal of Sport and Social Issues*, 39(3), 225–243.

Bonilla-Silva, E. (2010) *Racism without Racists: Color-blind Racism and the Persistence of Racial Inequality in America*. Maryland: Rowman & Littlefield.

Bradbury, S. (2013) Institutional racism, whiteness and the under-representation of minorities in leadership positions in football in Europe. *Soccer and Society*, 14(3), 296–314.

Bradbury, S. (2016) The progression of Black and Minority Ethnic footballers into coaching in professional football: A case study analysis of the COACH bursary programme. In Allison, W., Abraham, A. & Cale, A. (eds) *Advances in Coach Education and Development: From Research to Practice*. London and New York: Routledge. pp. 137–148.

Bradbury, S. (2018) The under-representation and racialised experiences of minority coaches in high level coach education in professional football in England. In Hassan, D. & Acton, C. (eds) *Sport and Contested Identities*. London: Routledge. pp. 11–29.

Bradbury, S. (2019) *Evaluation of the FA Coach Inclusion and Diversity Programme*. Loughborough University.

Bradbury, S. & Conricode, D. (forthcoming 2020) Addressing the under-representation of BAME coaches in professional football club youth academies: an examination of the mandatory code of coach recruitment. In Wallis, J. (ed.) *Sport Coaching in Diverse Populations: Theory and Practice*. London: Routledge.

Bradbury, S., Amara, M., Garcia, B. & Bairner, A. (2011) *Representation and Structural Discrimination in Football in Europe: The Case of Minorities and Women*. Loughborough University and the FARE Network.

Bradbury, S., Van Sterkenburg, J. & Mignon, P. (2014) *Cracking the Glass Ceiling? Levels of Representation of 'Visible' Minorities and Women in Leadership and Coaching in Football in Europe and the Experiences of Elite Level 'Visible' Minority Coaches*. London: FARE/UEFA.

Bradbury, S., Van Sterkenburg, J. & Mignon, P. (2018) The under-representation and experiences of elite level minority coaches in professional football in England, France and the Netherlands. *International Review of the Sociology of Sport*, 53(3), 313–334.

Braddock, J., Smith, E. & Dawkins, M. (2012) Race and pathways to power in the National Football League. *American Behavioural Scientist*, 56(5), 711–727.

Burdsey, D. (2007) *British Asians and Football: Culture, Identity and Exclusion*. London: Routledge.

Carrington, B. (2010) *Race, Sport and Politics: The Sporting Black Diaspora*. London: Sage.

Cashmore, E. & Clelland, J. (2011) Why aren't there more black managers. *Ethnic and Racial Studies*, 34(9), 1594–1607.

Cunningham, G. B. (2010) Understanding the under-representation of African American coaches: A multilevel perspective. *Sport Management Review*, 13(4), 395–406.

Day, J. C. (2015) Transitions to the top: Race, segregation, and promotions to executive positions in the college football coaching profession. *Work and Occupations*, 42(4), 408–446.

DeCuir, J. & Dixson, A. (2004) 'So when it comes out, they aren't that surprised that it is there': Using critical race theory as a tool of analysis of race and racism in education. *Educational Researcher*, 33(5), 26–31.

Delgado, R. & Stefancic, J. (2001) *Critical Race Theory: An Introduction*. London: NYU Press.

Duru, J. N. (2011) *Advancing the Ball: Race, Reformation and the Quest for Equal Coaching Opportunities in the NFL*. Oxford University Press.

Essed, P. & Trienekens, S. (2008) 'Who wants to feel white?' Race, Dutch culture and contested identities. *Ethnic and Racial Studies*, 31(1), 52–72.

Frankenburg, R. (1999) *Displacing Whiteness*. Durham and London: Duke University Press.

Frankenberg, R. (2004) On unsteady ground: Crafting and engaging in the critical study of whiteness. In Bulmer, M. and Solomos, J. (eds) *Researching Race and Racism*. London: Routledge. pp. 104–118.

Fletcher, T. (2014) 'Does he look like a Paki?' An exploration of 'whiteness', positionality and reflexivity in inter-racial sports research. *Qualitative Research in Sport, Exercise and Health*, 6(2), 244–260.

Football Association (2018) *In Pursuit of Progress: The FA's Equality, Diversity and Inclusion plan 2018–21*. London: The FA.

Government Equalities Office (2010) *Equality Act 2010*. Government Equalities Office.

Hartigan Jr, J. (1997) Establishing the fact of whiteness. *American Anthropologist*, 99(3), 495–505.

Hylton, K. (2005) 'Race', sport and leisure: Lessons from critical race theory. *Leisure Studies*, 24(1), 81–98.

Hylton, K. (2009) *Race and Sport: Critical Race Theory*. London: Routledge.

Hylton, K. (2010) How a turn to critical race theory can contribute to our understanding of 'race', racism and anti-racism in sport. *International Review for the Sociology of Sport*, 45(3), 335–354.

Hylton, K. (2018) *Contesting 'Race' and Sport*. London: Routledge.

Johns, N., MacBride-Stewart, S., Powell, M. & Green, A. (2014) When is positive action not positive action? Exploring the conceptual meaning and implications of the tie-break criterion in the UK Equality Act 2010. *Equality, Diversity and Inclusion: An International Journal*, 33(1), 97–113.

Jowett, S. & Frost, T. (2007) Race/Ethnicity in the all-male coach-athlete relationship: Black footballers' narratives. *International Journal of Sport and Exercise Psychology*, 5(3), 255–269,

Kilvington, D. (2017) Two decades and little change: British Asians, football, and calls for action. *Soccer and Society*, 20(4), 584–601.

King, C. (2004) 'Race' and cultural identity: Playing the race game inside football. *Leisure Studies*, 23(1), 19–30.

League Managers Association (LMA) (2018) *Black, Asian and Minority Ethnic (BAME) Football Managers*. League Managers Association.

Long, J. & Hylton, K. (2002) Shades of white: An examination of whiteness in sport. *Leisure Studies*, 21(2), 87–103.

Long, J., Robinson, P. & Spracklen, K. (2011) Promoting racial equality within sports organizations. *Journal of Sport & Social Issues*, 29(1), 41–59.

López, G. R. (2003) The (racially neutral) politics of education: A critical race theory perspective. *Educational Administration Quarterly*, 39(1), 68–94.

Lusted, J. (2014) Equality policies in sport: Carrots, sticks and a retreat from the radical. *Journal of Policy Research in Tourism, Leisure and Events*, 6(1), 85–90.

McDonald, M. G. (2005) Mapping whiteness and sport: An introduction. *Sociology of Sport Journal*, 22(3), 245–255.

McIntosh, P. (1990) *White Privilege: Unpacking the Invisible Knapsack*. Independent School, Winter, pp. 31–36.

Rankin-Wright, A. J., Hylton, K. & Norman, L. (2016) Off-colour landscape: Framing race equality in sport coaching. *Sociology of Sport Journal*, 33(4), 357–368.

Rankin-Wright, A. J., Hylton, K. & Norman, L. (2017) The policy and provision landscape for racial and gender equality in sport coaching. In Long, J., Fletcher, T. and Watson, B. (eds) *Sport, Leisure and Social Justice*. London: Routledge. pp. 194–208.

Sartore, M. L. & Cunningham, G. B. (2006) Stereotypes, race, and coaching. *Journal of African American Studies*, 10(2), 69–83.

Shaw, S. (2007) Touching the intangible? An analysis of the equality standard: A framework for sport. *Equal Opportunities International*, 26(5), 420–434.

Sin, H. S. (2007) Ethnic matching in qualitative research: Reversing the gaze on 'white others' and 'white' as 'other'. *Qualitative Research*, 7(4): 477–499.

Singer, J., Harrison, K. & Buksten, S. (2010) A critical race analysis of the hiring process for head coaches in NCAA college football. *Journal of Intercollegiate Sport*, 3, 270–296.

Solórzano, D. G. & Yosso, T. J. (2001) Critical race and LatCrit theory and method: Counter-storytelling. *International Journal of Qualitative Studies in Education*, 14(4), 471–495.

Sports People's Think Tank (SPTT) (2017) *Levels of BAME Coaches in Professional Football in England: 3rd Annual Follow Report*. Sports People's Think Tank, FARE Network and Loughborough University.

Spracklen, K., Hylton, K. & Long, J. (2006) Managing and monitoring equality and diversity in UK sport: An evaluation of the sporting equals racial equality standard and its impact on organizational change. *Journal of Sport and Social Issues*, 30(3), 289–305.

Part IV

Conclusions

Chapter 14

Priorities for researching 'race', ethnicity and racism in sports coaching and recommendations for future practice

Jim Lusted, Steven Bradbury and Jacco van Sterkenburg

Introduction

This book is the first comprehensive collection of academic work focusing specifically on the ways in which 'race', ethnicity and racism operate and are experienced in the field of sports coaching. The chapters featured in this collection reflect the research of established and emerging scholars drawn from a range of national contexts across three continents. These scholars have utilised quantitative and qualitative methodologies to generate original empirical data and/or have drawn on and applied a range of distinct but overlapping theoretical and conceptual approaches in their analysis. These efforts have helped to fulfil the original intention to bring together a series of insightful scholarly contributions to this relatively marginalised field of study into one volume. This collection is also well-timed. There is increasingly popular interest in the topic and in recent years some high-profile policy developments and targeted positive action interventions designed to diversify the sports coaching workforce in some sports across the globe have emerged. In this respect, it is hoped that this collection will encourage and empower other scholars, practitioners and students to engage in and with further critical research of this kind in order to extend the diversity of empirical focus and the breadth of theoretical understanding of racialised inequalities in sports coaching.

This concluding chapter begins by presenting some of the editors' observations as to the potential priorities for future research in this important field of enquiry. In doing so, it focuses on issues of consideration at the macro (societal), meso (organisational) and micro (individual) level of the analysis of racialised relations in sports coaching. The chapter also brings together and develops further some of the key recommendations offered by contributing authors in each of the chapters in this collection. In doing so, the editors outline some prospective priorities for key stakeholders in addressing racialised inequalities and establishing a more diverse and equitable environment in sports coaching.

Priorities for researching 'race', ethnicity and racism in sports coaching

Our chapters represent an increasing breadth and complexity of the types of research questions being asked about the influence and impacts of ideas around 'race', ethnicity and racism in sports coaching contexts. The collection is themed around three key areas of investigation; (i) representation and racialised barriers in sports coaching, (ii) racialised identities, diversity and intersectionality in sports coaching, (iii) and formalised racial equality interventions in sports coaching. This impressive scope of subjects highlights the growing scholarly attention that the field of 'race', ethnicity and racism in sports coaching is now receiving and the variety of issues being considered and examined. So what might be the priorities for future research of this kind? We take a lead in this respect from Cunningham's call in Chapter 1 for a multi-level approach to the examination of racialised inequalities in sports coaching which incorporates scholarly analysis at the macro (societal), meso (organisational) and micro (individual) level. As Cunningham states, there are important insights to be gained from adopting such a multi-level approach:

> Multilevel models make explicit the societal (macro-level), organizational and group influences (meso-level), and individual factors (micro-level) that can shape access to and experiences in sport. When scholars and practitioners fail to consider factors at multiple levels of analysis, they necessarily take for granted elements that could influence the phenomenon of interest.
>
> (Cunningham 2020: 5)

To elaborate, at the macro level, we are broadly referring to the structural conditions that underpin social arrangements; the meso level refers to the organisational and institutionalised manifestations of these structural conditions, whilst at the micro level the empirical focus is on the individual, or groups of individuals and their own lived experiences and embodiment of such structural and institutionalised arrangements. This multi-layered way of thinking about social analysis was also drawn on by Bradbury in this collection (Chapter 2) in his succinct overview of previous studies on 'race', ethnicity, racism and sports coaching:

> At the macro level, scholars have alluded to constraints engendered by the broader political and legislative climate and the role of powerful internal and external stakeholders in the coach hiring process. At the meso level, they have identified dominant monocultural processes and cultures and the existence of conscious and unconscious bias within the senior decision-making tiers of sports organisations. Further, at the

micro level, they have drawn attention to the impact of structural and institutional constraints on inhibiting opportunities for minoritised groups to develop the requisite network capital to engender upward social mobility as coaches.

(Bradbury 2020: 23)

We offer below some possible priorities to guide future research in this field across all three of these proposed levels of analysis.

Macro- (societal) level analysis: the racialised social conditions of sports coaching

The majority of previous research in this field – including that which is featured in this collection – has acknowledged the influence of the broader social conditions in which sports coaching operates, to help make sense of the past, current and future picture of racial diversity amongst the coaching workforce. For example, in this collection, the work of Bradbury (Chapter 2), Heim, Corthouts & Scheerder (Chapter 3), Van Sterkenburg (Chapter 4) and Kilvington (Chapter 5) has each drawn attention to the deeply racialised socio-historical and contemporary national political contexts in Europe in which the experiences of minoritised[1] football coaches have been 'played out'. Similarly, drawing on the US context, the contributions of Cunningham (Chapter 1) and Olushola-Ogunrinde & Carter-Francique (Chapter 9) have alluded to a series of embedded structural, representational and political barriers at the macro (societal) level and their deleterious impacts in constraining the career progression of minoritised coaches across a range of professional and college sports settings.

Our authors have also drawn on a range of distinct but overlapping theoretical and conceptual approaches to help articulate the nature and formation of these racialised structural conditions and their significance in shaping organisational arrangements and individual behaviours. In particular, many authors have drawn on the theoretical insights of Critical Race Theory (CRT) to illustrate the exclusionary impact of dominant liberal ideologies of colour-blindness, race neutrality and meritocracy – the latter being particularly influential in sporting cultures. Indeed, these authors owe a debt of gratitude to pioneer advocates of CRT and its application to sport – notably through the work of Hylton (2005, 2009, 2010) – to the extent that CRT has now arguably become the dominant theoretical lens to examine issues of 'race', ethnicity and racism in sport (and sports coaching).

However, at the same time, we also see room to examine more closely the specific nature and influence of the racialised structural conditions proposed by the CRT approach. Amongst others, Cole (2017) and Cabrera (2018) have pointed to some of the limitations of CRT explanations that we might reasonably seek to problematise in future studies in sports coaching and encourage a more eclectic mix of macro-level explanations. The former claims that CRT approaches can underplay the influence of capitalism and social class in shaping the racialised conditions of our times, favouring instead neo-Marxist ideas and concepts (Cole, 2017). Cabrera on the other hand argues that the broad CRT framework contains some theoretical 'holes' that require a more explicit racial theory to be articulated, making the case for a critical theory of racism centred on hegemonic whiteness (Cabrera, 2018).

A more dynamic approach to macro-level analysis might also help provide new insights into the relative rigidity or permeability of the societal structures that underpin racism and racialised exclusion in sports coaching. This may also open up the extent to which there exists commonalities and differences across national contexts with broadly comparative or markedly different racial histories. Further, a more detailed focus on this score might also elicit useful scholarly insights as to the extent to which such conditions have been altered and what factors have contributed to such change. We may then be in a stronger position to assess the impact these changes have had in enabling a space for progressive movements and interventions such as the adoption of the 'Rooney Rule' to emerge. Looking forward, what might these structural conditions need to consist of and how can they reasonably be modified at the macro societal level to open up a space within which to better facilitate more inclusive coaching environments and a more equitable coaching workforce? Similarly, to what extent are these structural conditions changeable by local interventions within sport? As we discuss later, one of the key recommendations that emerge from our chapters is the need for future interventions to address these structural arrangements. The challenge for future research is to further our understanding of how such conditions emerge and are sustained so we can propose suitable ways of re-shaping them.

Whilst there is a need to further our understanding of the specific conditions that shape our sports, we must also remind ourselves that we cannot separate the sporting experience from its wider societal context. Indeed, there is much more we can do to make analytical connections between the structures of sport and wider macro social, political, economic and cultural processes. In current times we are witnessing extremely rapid changes that are significantly challenging our previous assumptions about the world. Fukuyama's claim of the 'end of history' (2006) – an enduring victory for liberal democracy – seems significantly wide of the mark following recent global political events. The US election victory of Donald Trump in 2016, the referendum vote in the UK to leave the European Union in the same year, and electoral gains for right-wing political groups across many parts of the world such as Hungary, the Netherlands, Brazil and India have changed the geo-political landscape considerably in recent years. For a longer period of time, the hegemonic control of neoliberal free-market capitalist ideology across large parts of the world has also significantly shaped the structural conditions within which sports operate. The term 'racial neoliberalism' has been used by a range of authors (for example Goldberg, 2009; Kapoor, 2013; Burdsey, 2014) to explore how this broader neoliberal project is also one of 'hidden' racialisation; one that claims on the one hand that ideas of 'race' are meaningless, whilst on the other hand relying upon more subtle, nuanced forms of racialised exclusion to maintain White privilege.

The emerging technological revolution and the rise of the information age (Castells 1997) and increasing dominance of social media are shifting these conditions further. It is clearly evident that these macro-level changes have influenced sport more broadly; the #blacklivesmatter movement in the US, overtly supported by now-ostracised Black NFL quarterback Colin Kaepernick (Boykoff & Carrington, 2019), the rising racist abuse on social media of Black professional footballers in England (Farrington et al., 2015), and the increasing confidence of the far-right (re)emerging among sport fan groups across countries including Russia (Glathe, 2016) and Italy (Testa & Armstrong, 2010). These incidents remind us of the influence that macro sociopolitical changes can have on the nature of racism and racialised exclusion in sport, and will continue to have in debates around the racial diversity of sports coaches in years to come.

Meso- (organisational) level analysis: the institutionalised racialisation of sports coaching

All of the chapters featured in this collection focus their attention in one form or another at the meso organisational level of sports coaching. For example, the contributions of Cunningham (Chapter 1), Bradbury (Chapter 2), Van Sterkenburg (Chapter 4), Kilvington (Chapter 5) and Olushola-Ogunrinde & Carter-Francique (Chapter 9) all allude to the tendencies of sports organisations across a range of national contexts to operate a series of racially closed networks-based approaches to coach recruitment. These organisational processes are argued to constitute a form of institutionalised access discrimination which has restricted opportunities for minoritised coaches and contributed to sustaining patterns of homologous reproduction in the sports coaching workforce. Further, the contributions of Duru (Chapter 11), Cowell (Chapter 12) and Conricode & Bradbury (Chapter 13) have focused directly on specific institutions such as National Governing Bodies of sports in their discussions, and have sought to outline and evaluate the legislative development, operational effectiveness and measurable impacts of policy interventions designed to address racialised inequalities in sports coaching.

Whilst the work in the aforementioned chapters has helped us to assess the ways in which ideas around 'race' and processes of racialisation are institutionalised within sports organisations, particularly in relation to the recruitment and development of coaches, there is much more to be explored here. A deeper critical examination of organisational responses to the lack of diversity in sports coaching is needed to help further our understanding of how such responses have come about, the nature of such responses and the likely impact that they may (or may not) have. What are the key drivers in the formation of these policies and interventions aiming to diversify the coaching workforce? How exactly have they been developed? To what extent do they reflect the wider 'liberal' discourse of equal opportunities or seek to challenge and disrupt the dominant organisational structures and cultures of whiteness and White privilege that have been discussed by many authors in this collection? By interrogating more fully the motivations and drivers behind such initiatives we can help create a better picture of how they are likely to be received by the wide range of stakeholders involved including minoritised coaches themselves, as well as increasing our understanding of the shape and scope of barriers that might be encountered during their implementation.

This critical interrogation of organisational responses to the under-representation and racialised experiences of minoritised coaches can also help to make sense of the evident resistance that exists towards the need for and implementation of equality policies in sport (Spaaij et al., 2018, 2019). Moreover, such policies have been criticised by some scholars as adopting a bureaucratic audit or 'tick box' approach to promoting equality which focuses primarily on the formalisation of statements and providing paper evidence of compliance over meaningful action and change (Dwight & Biscomb, 2018; Lusted, 2014; Shaw, 2007; Spracklen et al., 2006). We should therefore caution our acceptance of the often celebratory rhetoric of these types of policy initiatives, along with what can be quite ambitious claims made about the likely impact they may have. This call for a more critically cautious approach is borne out by the now relatively mature policy history of equality initiatives in sport (over 30 years in some parts of the world such as the UK, Australia and Canada) that has, in many respects, failed to significantly alter the diversity of the sports coaching workforce (and leadership positions more broadly) or establish more inclusive organisational structures, processes and cultures (Doherty et al., 2010).

Elsewhere, more attention is beginning to be paid to the influence of these meso-level processes in shaping such policies and also the potential role that organisational cultures can have in perpetuating inequalities, often as a direct result of their 'display' of work around inclusion. This phenomenon has been termed 'non-performing inclusion' by Ahmed (2012), whose influential work more broadly on diversity work in organisations has begun to be taken up by other sport scholars (Bury, 2015; Hylton, 2015; Spaaij et al., 2018, 2019; see also Conricode & Bradbury in Chapter 13 in this collection). In her analysis of equality and diversity activities in Higher Education institutions in the UK and Australia, Ahmed highlights the ways that such activities often lead to very little output in the way of institutional change. Actions such as the writing of race equality plans, policies and charters take up a large part of this 'diversity work' but actually require very little action on the part of organisational actors, hence the concept of 'non-performing'. Similarly, Bury's (2015) review of anti-homophobia campaigns led by The English Football Association points to the use of strongly-worded policies and statements rarely being complemented by actions, particularly those that require internal organisational change.

Relatedly, Ahmed (2007) has also pointed to the adoption of the term 'diversity' as not simply a matter of semantics but representing a more considered shift away from ideas of social equality, equity and justice. The latter, arguably more 'radical', focus had characterised previous policies in the field that were seen to have failed or had minimal impact. The concept 'diversity' represents more of a liberal approach whereby the goal is to acknowledge and celebrate difference – such as racialised or ethnic differences – rather than explicitly scrutinise or challenge existing organisational cultures or seek internal change (Lusted, 2017). Diversity is also seen to represent the business case for equality, i.e. that claims are made about an increasingly diverse workforce aligning with wider business goals related to efficiency, competitiveness or corporate social responsibility (Lusted, 2013; Noon, 2007). This organisational tension between interpretations of social equality, and the language used to represent the preferred approach, needs closer examination within sport settings, and within the interventions formed by sports organisations that claim to tackle racialised inequalities in coaching. Taken together, this body of critical work highlights the scholarly and practical value in examining more closely the organisational responses to the under-representation and racialised experiences of minoritised sport coaches. This will allow us to reflect in a more critical way the underlying reasons for their adoption, the ideas behind the approaches they are advocating and enable a better understanding of their impact and the reasons behind their successes – limited or otherwise.

Micro- (individual) level analysis: testimonies from the racialised side-lines

Many of the chapters in this collection offer vivid accounts of the direct experiences and effects of racism and racialised exclusions and the ways in which ideas of 'race' gain credence in sports coaching settings. For example, the contributions of Bradbury (Chapter 2), Van Sterkenburg (Chapter 4), Kilvington (Chapter 5), McDonald & Spaaij (Chapter 6), Light & Evans (Chapter 7), Rankin-Wright & Hylton (Chapter 8), Olushola-Ogunrinde & Carter-Francique (Chapter 9), Knoppers & De Haan (Chapter 10) and Conricode & Bradbury (Chapter 13) all draw on the first-hand or secondary accounts of minoritised coaches and players as a means of moving beyond majoritarian stories and master narratives (Solórzano & Yosso, 2002) to illuminate and render visible the historically subjugated testimonies and experiential narratives of minoritised groups in sports coaching contexts. We should recognise here the generous time and energy given by all of the participants from the studies featured in this collection. This type of evidence remains crucial to examining the lived experiences of processes of racialisation.

In order to interrogate the underlying mechanisms behind the racialised exclusions expressed by participants in this collection, many of the authors have connected the lived experiences of minoritised coaches to the range of concepts, theories and explanations that operate more broadly at the meso and macro level of analysis. Further examination in that direction is necessary to tie everyday practice and experience to wider racialised structures and to better understand how wider discourses which circulate in sport and sports coaching contribute to regulating conduct and constructing identities and subjectivities in the field. This is important in helping to develop a more layered understanding of the ways in which ideas around 'race' are played out within the interactional spaces of sports coaching and with regard to the manifestation, negotiation and impacts of racism and racialised microaggressions on minoritised coaches in these settings (Gearity & Henderson Metzger, 2017).

In addition, in unpacking some of the more problematic assumptions embedded in debates around cultural diversity and organisational effectiveness in sports coaching (and in leadership more broadly), which in laudably seeking to promote the value and benefits of multi-culturalism might also draw unconsciously on broader racialised narratives which essentialise the skills and abilities of minoritised coaches and have unintended consequences in sustaining patterns of occupational segregation in the sports coaching workplace. It also means that a dual research focus is important in which analysis at the individual level is combined with a scrutiny of those in positions of power and control who play a central role in creating and/or reproducing a sports coaching culture where – as many chapters in the book have shown – White people are privileged whilst minoritised people generally find themselves in a disadvantaged position. We need to know much more about how such systemic discriminatory practices are internalised, reproduced and protected if we are to come up with ways of dismantling the stranglehold of these racialised power relationships in sports coaching contexts. Further, as has been argued by Rankin-Wright & Hylton (Chapter 8), Olushola-Ogunrinde & Carter-Francique (Chapter 9) and Knoppers & De Haan (Chapter 10) in this collection, much more research is needed (and needs to be supported) which draws on and foregrounds the silenced voices and marginalised experiences of black women sports coaches and which seeks to locate these intersectional oppressions within the context of institutionally embedded power relations at the organisational and societal level.

One key concept to better grasp the interplay between the individual micro level and wider structures is whiteness. In particular how the processes and discourses of whiteness strengthen and (re)produce inclusion and exclusion at the individual level along racial and ethnic lines. As some authors have already stated (Cabrera et al., 2017), whiteness is a complex concept; it is context-specific and quite hard to define in precise terms. This difficulty to pinpoint whiteness, and to identify precisely how it operates, may actually be an important reason why it is so effective in continuing to structure a range of societal and sporting contexts (Omi et al., 1994 in Cabrera et al., 2017). The core of our understanding of whiteness in this edited collection (shared explicitly by many authors in this book) is of whiteness as a powerful structural and cultural practice through which hierarchical systems of racial domination have become effortlessly created, sustained and reproduced over time (Delgado & Stefancic, 2012; Giroux, 1997). Further, whiteness can be understood as a powerful discourse which privileges White people whilst simultaneously marginalising minoritised groups on a structural basis (Hylton, 2009). As has been argued by Bradbury (Chapter 2), Van Sterkenburg (Chapter 4) and McDonald & Spaaij (Chapter 6) in this collection, the discourse of whiteness is evident within the sports coaching context through the promulgation of powerful racialised ideologies and meanings which have enabled the signification of human characteristics in such ways as to problematise the assumed attributes of minoritised coaches (and players). For example, when key decision makers consider members of the White majority ethnic group 'by default' as the 'norm' and as possessing desirable traits for positions of coaching/management (e.g. leadership, perseverance, intellect), whilst associating members of minoritised groups with athletic performance-based roles through an emphasis on physicality rather than mentality, and emotionality rather than rationality.

For future critical research and related anti-racist action in the field of sports coaching, there is a real challenge in intervening in this discourse. Whiteness usually remains hidden below the surface as those who use and benefit from it often draw on a rhetoric of colour-blindness that safely accommodates the ideals of equality and diversity. Colour-blindness can be seen as an ideology that frames situations of racism and racial inequality as completely unrelated to 'race', *'providing raceless explanations for all sort of race-related affairs'* (Bonilla-Silva, 2015: 1364). In this respect, colour-blind ideologies fail to recognise racism unless manifest in its most egregious forms and actively seek to naturalise the consequences of racialised inequalities as resulting from individual and cultural deficit rather than as being created and sustained by the practices of dominant individuals and institutions (Bonilla-Silva, 2010). In doing so, colour-blind ideologies tend to strip the realities of success or failure from the deeply racialised contexts in which they occur and consequently legitimate opposition to race-conscious equality policies designed to redress historical racialised imbalances at a societal and sporting level. This is reflected in the contributions of Van Sterkenburg (Chapter 4) and Conricode & Bradbury (Chapter 13) in this collection when minoritised football coaches in the Netherlands and senior staff in English football club academies adhered to (neo)liberal notions of meritocracy, race neutrality and colour-blindness in justifying their explicit resistance towards positive action measures such as the 'Rooney Rule' or mandatory code of coach recruitment. Given the interplay between wider exclusionary discourses on the one hand and individual experiences of minoritised coaches on the other, future research in this field might seek to provide more insights into and challenge the self-evident character of whiteness and colour-blindness in the domain of sports coaching.

Priorities for addressing racialised inequalities in sports coaching

Having laid out some suggested priorities for future research in this field, this section turns to some of the key recommendations offered by contributing authors in each of the chapters in this collection. In doing so, it is designed to offer a general account of what our authors feel needs to be prioritised in order for future policies and interventions to be effective in addressing racialised inequalities in sports coaching and in establishing a more diverse coaching workforce. The various recommendations have been collated into four key themes: (i) establishing a multi-level and holistic approach to tackling racialised inequalities in sports coaching, (ii) developing and implementing robust policy interventions, (iii) developing and implementing education and training programmes, (iv) and enhancing networks, social capital and opportunities for minoritised coaches.

(i) Establishing a multi-level and holistic approach to tackling racialised inequalities in sports coaching

A number of authors in this collection have alluded to the limitations of previous and current policies and interventions aimed at diversifying the sports coaching workforce. In the main, the critique here has been that all too often such initiatives have failed to consider and appreciate the different levels at which racial discrimination operates and the multi-layered complexity of the sources of racialised inequalities. For example, Cunningham (Chapter 1) suggests that 'single-level' interventions such as those designed to effectuate individual behaviour change have failed to fully appreciate the complex and interconnected ways in which structural, organisational and individual factors play a role in perpetuating exclusionary practices. Similarly, other authors such as Heim, Corthouts & Scheerder (Chapter 3), Kilvington (Chapter 5) and McDonald & Spaaij (Chapter 6) have suggested that previous interventions have had little impact in challenging the structural arrangements of sporting cultures and organisations. Rankin-Wright & Hylton (Chapter 8) and Conricode & Bradbury (Chapter 13) extend this point further and argue that many interventions have been informed by 'liberal equal opportunities' approaches, which focus on increasing opportunities for under-represented minoritised groups whilst simultaneously leaving the conditions which perpetuate racialised inequalities relatively unchanged. As a result, there is a strong consensus amongst the authors featured in this collection that key stakeholders should broaden their focus and efforts to adopt a more broad ranging multi-level approach to addressing racialised inequalities in sports coaching. We provide concrete examples of recommended areas of focus and how these efforts might be undertaken in practice in each of the following three sections. Further, as has been argued by Rankin-Wright & Hylton (Chapter 8), Olushola-Ogunrinde & Carter-Francique (Chapter 9) and Knoppers & De Haan (Chapter 10) such an approach should also recognise, centralise and seek to redress the often overlooked intersectional forms of oppression and double burden of racialised and gendered discrimination experienced by minoritised women in sports coaching contexts.

In this respect, any meaningful efforts to address racialised inequalities in sports coaching need to remain cognisant of the existence and expression of multiple intersectional forms of racism and discrimination, and the normative power of whiteness (and maleness) embedded in societal and sports coaching contexts. As has been argued by Bradbury (Chapter 2), Van Sterkenburg (Chapter 4) and Rankin-Wright & Hylton (Chapter 8), the tendency for key decision makers in sports to adhere to notions of meritocracy, race neutrality and colour-blindness has tended to sustain rather than redress racialised inequalities in these settings. Further, Conricode & Bradbury (Chapter 13) suggest that liberalism alone is not enough to disrupt and dismantle these powerful processes and discourses, and a more strongly interventionist and transformational approach is needed to challenge and reconfigure the long-standing structures and cultures that are regularly reproduced by those in positions of power within sports organisations. There is a strong consensus amongst the authors in this collection that a range of key stakeholders in sports – including, national governments, national sports federations, member sports organisations and clubs, equality bodies and campaign groups and minoritised coaches – should work collaboratively to develop and implement a more unified and holistic approach to addressing racialised inequalities in sports coaching. Such an approach should be appropriately resourced and engender a strong operational and attitudinal commitment to the principles and practice of diversity and inclusion at the structural, organisational and individual level. It should also utilise a range of contextually considered and targeted positive action measures to ensure equality of opportunities and experiences for minoritised coaches and to forcefully stimulate conditions under which equality of outcomes are more likely to be realised. We identify in more detail below three key areas of action that, when combined, can begin to provide this more holistic approach we have articulated above.

(ii) Developing and implementing robust policy interventions

Almost all of the authors in this collection have been explicit in their calls for key stakeholders and related bodies to work in consultation with minoritised coaches to develop and implement robust policy interventions designed to increase the representation of minoritised coaches and address racialised inequalities in sports coaching. In doing so, a number of authors such as Bradbury (Chapter 2) Heim, Corthouts & Scheerder (Chapter 3), and Van Sterkenburg (Chapter 4) have suggested that in the first instance this should include the establishment of clear policy goals and actions which incorporate the collection of baseline data, target setting, and the monitoring and evaluation of progress over time against clearly defined timescales. The allocation of roles and responsibilities for work of this kind should also reflect the organisational capacities, expertise and legal jurisdiction of key stakeholders and other bodies involved in this process.

As part of the aforementioned emphasis on policy development and implementation, there was a strong consensus amongst authors that key stakeholders and related bodies should undertake a more strongly regulated and interventionist approach to coach recruitment. Central to this discussion was the contribution of Duru (Chapter 11) which examined in detail the legislative development, operational implementation, and representational effectiveness of the 'Rooney Rule' in the US NFL. This positive action measure was championed by a number of authors (especially those examining racialised inequalities in football in Europe) as having significant transferability as an important consideration forcing mechanism through which to establish a more transparent and equitable approach to coach recruitment across a range of national and sporting contexts. In particular, in mandating that sports clubs must interview at least one suitably qualified candidate from a minoritised background for vacant senior coaching positions or incur a significant financial penalty. Further, some authors also alluded to the ways in which its operational focus, scope and effectiveness might be extended further. For example, both Bradbury (Chapter 2) and Cowell (Chapter 12) alluded to the importance of ensuring that measures of this kind adhere to and utilise creatively the opportunities embedded in national equalities legislation with regard to employment practices. Cowell (Chapter 12) also referenced the importance of consultation with local-level stakeholders and minoritised coaches at the design stage of such policy interventions, in order that their aims and intentions are better understood by those with direct responsibility for their enactment. Conricode & Bradbury (Chapter 13) argue further that such approaches are more likely to yield stronger operational and attitudinal buy-in to the principles and practice of racial inclusivity and engender more meaningful and sustainable organisational change. They continue that the provision of a uniform guidance document in relation to key components of newly formulated processes of coach recruitment might also help key decision makers to adhere to good equality practice in this respect. These points are extended further by Cunningham (Chapter 1) and Olushola-Ogunrinde & Carter-Francique (Chapter 9) who stress the importance of ensuring that the demographic make-up of selection and interview panels is culturally diverse and that appropriate feedback is provided to unsuccessful candidates to help them reflect on the interview process and better prepare for future applications. Further, Rankin-Wright & Hylton (Chapter 8), Olushola-Ogunrinde & Carter-Francique (Chapter 9), and Knoppers & De Haan (Chapter 10) suggest that positive action measures designed to diversify the sports coaching workforce should also pay attention to and seek to alleviate intersectional experiences of racialised and gendered exclusions and incorporate actions which consider multiple and multi-dimensional rather than binary forms of oppression. Finally, Duru (Chapter 11) draws attention to the likely increased representational impacts of extending the scope of the 'Rooney Rule' and related interventions to include a minimum of two candidates from under-represented groups. Such an approach is likely to increase opportunities for minoritised coaches from a broader range of racial, cultural, ethnic and gendered backgrounds to gain a foothold in the sports coaching industry.

A number of authors also called for regulatory and interventionist approaches to be extended beyond the coach recruitment process and into the field of coach education. For example, Conricode & Bradbury (Chapter 13) referenced positively the work of the English Football Association's Coach Inclusion and Diversity programme which provides financial and other resource support to empower minoritised coaches to achieve coaching qualifications and enhance their employability within the professional game. Other authors such as Heim, Corthouts & Scheerder (Chapter 3) argue that programmes of this kind should be rolled out in other national and sports coaching contexts (such as professional football in Belgium) and should include the provision of subsidised coach education and training programmes for aspiring minoritised coaches from socially and economically disadvantaged backgrounds. Van Sterkenburg (Chapter 4) extends this point further by suggesting that key stakeholder bodies should amend and broaden the selection criteria for elite level coaching courses such as the UEFA Pro-Licence in professional football in order to increase the appeal and accessibility of courses of this kind for talented minoritised coaches. Taken together, these and other authors in this collection suggested that the development and implementation of positive action interventions of this kind were necessary to unblock the early educational phase of the pipeline of progression in sports coaching and to empower minoritised coaches with the requisite skill sets and confidence to proceed into the professional coaching environs of sports.

(iii) Developing and implementing education and training programmes

A large proportion of the authors in this collection have suggested the need for the delivery of education programmes targeted at influential stakeholders in sports coaching, particularly those involved in the process of coach education and coach recruitment. For many authors, these personnel have acted as key gatekeepers with the powers to grant or withhold access to the developmental and occupational marketplace of sports coaching and have played a pivotal role in sustaining patterns of homologous reproduction within this realm. Further, as Conricode & Bradbury (Chapter 13) have indicated, these personnel often display a strong adherence to notions of meritocracy, race neutrality and colour-blind ideologies and consequently their understanding of processes of racialisation and racialised inequalities in sports coaching remains limited. In this respect, authors such as Bradbury (Chapter 2), Heim, Corthouts & Scheerder (Chapter 3), and Kilvington (Chapter 5) have argued that educational activities should pay particular attention to the ways in which overt, culturally coded and more institutional forms of racism and discrimination can work at a conscious and unconscious level to constrain the opportunities of and engender negative experiences for minoritised coaches. Rankin-Wright & Hylton (Chapter 8) and Olushola-Ogunrinde & Carter-Francique (Chapter 9) extend this point further and suggest that a much greater awareness of the interconnections between systems of oppression is needed to enable key stakeholders to understand and address racialised and gendered exclusions in sports coaching settings.

For authors such as McDonald & Spaaij (Chapter 6) pedagogical approaches of this kind should also seek to challenge and debunk stereotypical ideas and practices around the racialised black body and related deficit discourses which unproblematically position black athletes and coaches as lacking the requisite psychological characteristics to succeed in decision-making roles in sports. Similarly, Light & Evans (Chapter 7) suggest that coaches should think more strongly and reflexively as to the racialised nature of dominant anti-dialogic coaching practices and exhibit greater cultural sensitivity and understanding in their dealings with minoritised athletes. Taken together, these authors suggest that coaches and sports science professionals should engage in formalised educational activities and informal pedagogical reflection in order to challenge the everyday racialised assumptions and patterns and processes of White privilege embedded within such environs. Van Sterkenburg (Chapter 4) extends this discussion further to suggest that more educational work is needed to challenge racial stereotyping within the sport media given the powerful role they play in constructing and reproducing racialised narratives and discourse and framing popular debates around the suitability of minoritised coaches for appointments in elite level sports settings.

Conricode & Bradbury (Chapter 13) have argued that educational programmes targeting senior power brokers at professional sports clubs should also be utilised as a mechanism through which to engender stronger operational and attitudinal 'buy-in' to emerging policy interventions designed to increase the representation of minoritised coaches. This assertion chimes strongly with the points made previously about the need for a holistically considered multi-level approach to addressing racialised inequalities in sports coaching. In this respect, such programmes should contextualise the relevance and applicability of policy interventions to the sports coaching settings in which they are being implemented. They should also encourage a perceptual shift in conceptualising cultural diversity less as a problem to be 'fixed' or 'dealt with', and more as a positive individual and organisational resource to be nurtured and developed. In doing so, the authors argue that pedagogical work of this kind should feature a strong emphasis on increasing understanding of the potential and realised benefits of cultural diversity as means through which to enhance organisational effectiveness in the coaching workplace. Taken together, the calls for the development of education and training programmes by authors in this collection share a common theme in engendering an analytical shift away from a singular (albeit important) focus on 'upskilling' excluded participants, towards a more transformational approach which seeks to challenge and change the institutionally closed structures and cultures of sports organisations and the processes and discourses of whiteness which underpin them.

(iv) Enhancing networks, social capital and opportunities for minoritised coaches

Finally, a number of authors in this collection have argued that establishing, maintaining and utilising contacts and relationships with key 'insider' figures is an important source of social capital that has been shown to have significant influence on the development, recruitment and promotion of sports coaches. This is especially the case in relation to the elite level environs of coach education and coach employment where the over-reliance on networks-based approaches to identification, selection and recruitment has traditionally favoured White coaches drawn from within the dominant social and cultural insider networks of the sport industry. As a result, one of the most common recommendations for practice from authors was the need to strengthen and broaden the networks available to coaches from minoritised backgrounds. In this respect, Kilvington (Chapter 5) has called for more efforts to develop networks that encourage both 'bonding' forms of social capital where those from similar backgrounds can strengthen ties and share experiences, and 'bridging' social capital where networks are created to bring together people and groups who might otherwise rarely connect (Putnam, 2000). Kilvington (Chapter 5) continues that more needs to be done by sporting authorities to facilitate and expand upon existing but poorly resourced physical and online networks which bring together minoritised coaches and key stakeholders. Such networks are argued to provide a useful interactional space for minoritised coaches to learn about and access support to meet key developmental and organisational requirements and for key stakeholders to increase their understanding of key cultural considerations which might impact on the pace and scope of career progression.

Olushola-Ogunrinde & Carter-Francique (Chapter 9) extend this latter discussion further in drawing attention to the potential benefits of establishing formal and informal mentoring and advocacy programmes which can support the growth and development and raise the profile of minoritised coaches in sports coaching contexts. Relatedly, Van Sterkenburg (Chapter 4) has suggested that national football associations (and by proxy, sports organisations more broadly) should establish a national database of all minoritised coaches in receipt of elite level coaching qualifications. This 'ready list' of highly qualified minoritised coaches could be circulated to professional clubs as well as being used as a mechanism through which to alert minoritised coaches to emergent coaching positions in their respective sports. Such an approach would increase the awareness of and applications for coaching opportunities in sports, and increase the visibility of minoritised coaches within the eyeline and consciousness of power brokers within sports clubs. Taken together, efforts of this kind are likely to yield some success in increasing the network capital of minoritised coaches, broadening the previously closed processes of coach recruitment at sports clubs, and diversifying the sports coaching workforce.

Concluding remarks

Whilst in this final chapter we have discussed quite separately three key areas of future research priority – macro, meso and micro – and then four sets of recommendations, they should not be seen in isolation from one another. The point has been made several times that a holistic and multilevel approach is called for to be able to research and then design interventions that have the potential to create meaningful and long lasting change. The example of how we might go about changing recruitment practices illustrates this holistic and multi-level approach well. Taken together, the chapters featured in this collection point to the need for a multi-pronged approach that requires interventions across several layers. The historic recruitment practices that have dominated sports organisations need dismantling through structural interventions such as the 'Rooney Rule' and other forms of mandatory positive action schemes that have the potential to disrupt the reproduction of enduring forms of racialised privilege. Enforced changes to the membership of recruitment panels may also help encourage more equitable outcomes in the hiring of coaches. More deeply considered, contextually relevant and pedagogically effective education/training for those with responsibility for coach recruitment is also needed. This should be accompanied by activities that will develop networks to enable minoritised coaches to access the existing structures and cultures of coaching and become 'legitimate' candidates for recruitment.

The adoption of a somewhat 'radical' policy such as the 'Rooney Rule' illustrates not only how a field such as sport can be disrupted by anti-racist politics and critical academic thought, but that sport can play a central role in raising the anti-racist agenda across other spheres of social life. In this respect, sport, and specifically sports coaching, offers us a crucial site from which to embed the message of racial equality and find new ways of disrupting racialised forms of discrimination across a range of contemporary national contexts. The weight of empirical evidence backs up the casual observations of sports enthusiasts in that many minoritised athletes are not transitioning into elite coaching positions. This gives us legitimacy to continue to document such disparities, publicise them to both sports organisations and the mainstream media, and to critically evaluate the strengths and limitations of initiatives designed to address racialised inequalities in sports coaching.

Many of us probably feel that in recent times we have gone significantly backwards in the fight for racial equality across sport and wider society. Some of the 'gains' we might have reasonably claimed to have made over the last 20 years of anti-racist politics and critical scholarly endeavour seem to be increasingly under threat from a new hostile political environment. In this rapidly changing social context, the popular appeal of sport has arguably never been a more important site to challenge racialised and other forms of discrimination and exclusion. We hope this collection inspires readers to continue to pursue research and implement interventions that aim to diversify the coaching workforce, finding creative ways to dismantle the racialised inequalities and barriers that still inform people's opportunities, experiences and outcomes in sports coaching.

Note

1 As outlined in the Introduction of this collection, the term 'minoritised' is used in this chapter to reflect an understanding of 'minority status' as a socially constructed process (rather than as an entity) which takes place in specific social, economic and political contexts over time and which has resulted in 'minoritised groups' having less power or representation compared to other (White) groups in society.

References

Ahmed, S. (2012) *On Being Included: Racism and Diversity in Institutional Life*. Durham, NC: Duke University Press.

Ahmed, S. (2007) The language of diversity. *Ethnic and Racial Studies*, 30(2), 235–256.

Bonilla-Silva, E. (2015) The structure of racism in color-blind, 'post-racial' America. *American Behavioral Scientist*, 59(11), 1358–1376.

Bonilla-Silva, E. (2010) *Racism Without Racists: Colour-blind Racism and the Persistence of Racial Equality in the United States (Third Edition)*. Oxford: Rowman and Littlefield.

Boykoff, J. & Carrington, B. (2019) Sporting dissent: Colin Kaepernick, NFL activism, and media framing contests. *International Review for the Sociology of Sport* [online]. doi:1012690219861594.

Burdsey, D. (2014) One week in October: Luis Suárez, John Terry and the turn to racial neoliberalism in English men's professional football. *Identities*, 21(5), 429–447.

Bury, J. (2015) Non-performing inclusion: A critique of the English Football Association's Action Plan on homophobia in football. *International Review for the Sociology of Sport*, 50(2), 211–226.

Cabrera, N. L. (2018) Where is the Racial Theory in Critical Race Theory? A constructive criticism of the Crits. *The Review of Higher Education*, 42(1), 209–233.

Cabrera, N. L., Franklin, J. D. & Watson, J. S. (2017) *Whiteness in Higher Education: The Invisible Missing Link in Diversity and Racial Analyses*. Association for the Study of Higher Education monograph series. San Francisco, CA: Jossey-Bass.

Castells, M. (1997) An introduction to the information age. *City*, 2(7), 6–16.

Cole, M. (2017) *Critical Race Theory and Education: A Marxist Response*. London: Springer.

Delgado, R. & Stefancic, J. (2012) *Critical Race Theory: An Introduction (Second Edition)*. London: NYU Press.

Doherty, A., Fink, J. & Inglis, S. (2010) Understanding a culture of diversity through frameworks of power and change. *Sport Management Review*, 13, 368–381.

Dwight, A. & Biscomb, K. (2018) Ten years of the UK's Equality Standard for Sport. *European Journal for Sport and Society*, 15(2), 171–188.

Fukuyama, F. (2006) *The End of History and the Last Man*. London: Simon and Schuster.

Gearity, B. & Henderson Metzger, L. (2017) Intersectionality, micro-aggressions and micro-affirmations: Towards a cultural praxis of sports coaching. *Sociology of Sport Journal*. 34(2), 160–175.

Giroux, H. (1997) *Pedagogy and the Politics of Hope: Theory, Culture and Schooling: A Critical Reader*. Boulder: Westview.

Glathe, J. (2016) Football fan subculture in Russia: Aggressive support, readiness to fight, and far right links. *Europe-Asia Studies*, 68(9), 1506–1525.

Goldberg, D. T. (2009) *The Threat of Race: Reflections on Racial Neoliberalism*. Chichester: Wiley Press.

Hylton, K. (2005) 'Race', sport and leisure: Lessons from critical race theory. *Leisure Studies*, 24(1), 81–98.

Hylton, K. (2009) *'Race' and Sport: Critical Race Theory*. London: Routledge.

Hylton, K. (2010) How a turn to critical race theory can contribute to our understanding of 'race', racism and anti-racism in sport. *International Review for the Sociology of Sport*, 45(3), 335–354.

Hylton, K. (2015) 'Race' talk! Tensions and contradictions in sport and PE. *Physical Education and Sport Pedagogy*, 20(5), 503–516.

Kapoor, N. (2013) The advancement of racial neoliberalism in Britain. *Ethnic and Racial Studies*, 36(6), 1028–1046.

Farrington, N., Hall, L., Kilvington, D., Price, J., & Saeed, A. (2015) *Sport, Racism and Social Media*. London: Routledge.

Lusted, J. (2017) Understanding the varied responses to calls for a 'Rooney rule' in English football. In D. Kilvington & J. Price (eds.) *Sport and Discrimination*. London: Routledge, 44–57.

Lusted, J. (2013) Selling race equality to sport organisations: Challenges and limitations. In D. Hassan & J. Lusted (eds), *Managing Sport: Social and Cultural Perspectives*. London: Routledge, 90–107.

Lusted, J. (2014) Equality policies in sport: carrots, sticks and a retreat from the radical. *Journal of Policy Research in Tourism, Leisure and Events*, 6(1), 85–90, doi:10.1080/19407963.2013.822461

Noon, M. (2007) The fatal flaws of diversity and the business case for ethnic minorities. *Work, Employment and Society*, 21(4), 773–784.

Putnam, R. D. (2000) *Bowling Alone: The Collapse and Revival of American Community*. London: Simon and Schuster.

Solórzano, D. G. & Yosso, T. J. (2002) Critical race methodology: Counter-storytelling as an analytical framework for education research. *Qualitative Inquiry*, 8(1), 23–44.

Shaw, S. (2007) Touching the intangible? An analysis of the equality standard: A framework for sport. *Equal Opportunities International*, 26(5), 420–434.

Spaaij, R., Knoppers, A. & Jeanes, R. (2019) 'We want more diversity but...': Resisting diversity in recreational sports clubs. *Sport Management Review* [online] – available at https://doi.org/10.1016/j.smr.2019.05.007

Spaaij, R., Magee, J., Farquharson, K., Gorman, S., Jeanes, R., Lusher, D. & Storr, R. (2018) Diversity work in community sport organizations: Commitment, resistance and institutional change. *International Review for the Sociology of Sport*, 53(3), 278–295.

Spracklen, K., Hylton, K. & Long, J. (2006) Managing and monitoring equality and diversity in UK sport: An evaluation of the sporting equals racial equality standard and its impact on organizational change. *Journal of Sport and Social Issues*, 30(3), 289–305.

Testa, A. & Armstrong, G. (2010) *Football, Fascism and Fandom: The Ultras of Italian Football*. London: A&C Black.

Index

Page numbers in italics refer to figures.

Aboriginal Australians *see* Indigenous Australians
aboriginal ethics 125
academic disciplines xix
access discrimination 4, 147, 239
actor-network theory 164
advertisements, coaching positions 216–217, 229
African Americans 5; athletes 166; health, affect on 11–12; women 9, 115
African pathways programmes 104
Aguilar, Luis 190
Aluko, Eniola 132
American Football 22, 76n3, 147, 188, 192n1; *see also* professional football in Europe, minoritised coaches in
Anderson, B. 167
Anderson, Viv 197
Anthias, F. 167
anti-dialogic coaching pedagogy 122, 125
anti-dialogic pedagogy 112–113, 114; of professional sport 120–122
anti-discrimination laws 196, 203
anti-immigrant sentiment 28
Antilles/Antillean 76n2
antiracism policies 46
applications, coaching positions 217–218, 229
appointments, coaching positions 220–221, 229
Aruba 76n2
Assari, S. 11
athlete-centred coaching 116
athletes of Anglo-Celtic origin 101–102
athletic coaches 8; *see also* Australian sport, talent identification and coaching; black college coaches; Black women coaches in the UK; British Asian football coaches; coaching and racial minorities; coach recruitment; United Kingdom (UK), Black women coaches in
athletic labour 104
attitudinal implementation 215
Australia, multiculturalism in 98
Australian football 113, 118
Australian Football League (AFL) 97, 98, 99, 104, 116, 119, 120–121, 125
Australian Institute of Sport (AIS) 102
Australian Multicultural Commission 97
Australian Research Council (ARC) 99, 112
Australian sport, talent identification and coaching 97–99; biological racism 99–102; Black athletes 107; CRT 99–102; cultural transitioning 112; discourse 102–103; embodied level, racialised athletic ability 105–107; interpersonal relations within sports systems 104–105; Majak Daw 97; 'natural,' 103–107; 'preferred worker' 107; scientific and cultural discourses 100; sport organisations and clubs 104; *see also* Indigenous Australians
'authentic' racial truth 27
authoritative scientific language 106

Back, L. 79, 80, 85, 87, 88
Bairner, A. 164
BAME *see* Black, Asian and Minority Ethnic (BAME)

banking *versus* problem-posing education (coaching) 112, 113, 114–116
Barbour, D. 164
Basch, L. 160
basketball 118
Beabout, B. 115
Belgian football: African ethnicity 54; coaches 45; CSR-related policies and initiatives 53; cultural agent 52; discrimination 44, 46; Football Unit 53; non-white footballers and coaches 48; non-white racial background 54; racial and ethnic divisions 44; racial backgrounds of players and coaches 48; sub-Saharan African ethnicity 54, 55n4
Belgian football, leadership positions in 43–45; African ethnic backgrounds 52; Community Manager 55n6; data collection and analysis 49–53; ethnicity 48–50, 50, 54n1; European men 52; policy recommendations 53–54; presence and interconnection of race 47; race and ethnicity, conceptualising 47–48; racial and ethnic backgrounds 49; theoretical framework 45–47
Belgian Football Coaches Association (BFC) 53
Belgian Football Law 53
Belgian Ministry of Home Affairs 53
Belgian Pro League 44, 45, 47, 49
Belgian trade unions 46
Belgium 22; Brussels-capital region 43; citizenship 51; cultural diversity 43; Flanders 43; mining industry 50; Wallonia 43
Bell, D. 133
Bell Curve 100
bias in decision making 8–9
biological determinism 100
biological race 98, 100, 107; in education 101
Birrell, Susan 130
Black, Asian and Minority Ethnic (BAME): British Asians 78–79; within British context 91n3, 211, 229n1; coach career progression 198; coaches 80, 81, 211, 216–225; managers xvi, 196–200; role models 89; senior coaching positions 211
Black African migration to Australia 102

Black and Asian Coaches Association (BACA) 89
black athleticism 98, 100; in American college sports 101; appreciation of 105
black coaching opportunities 85
black college coaches 143–144; financial compensation 154; intersectional challenges 146; intersectionality theory 145–146; intersectional remedies for 152–154; "Othered" experience 143, 145; overrepresentation of 147; physical positions 147; political challenges 151–152; representational challenges 149–151; sport discriminatory challenges 143; structural challenges 146–149; subordination 153; systemic barriers to entry 146; under-representation 144
Black (ex-)footballers 75
Black feminism xix, 128, 129, 133, 134, 139
Black head coaches 144
Black male college athletes' abilities 150
blackness 79
Black student-athletes 144
Black women coaches in the UK 128–129, 139n1; power, privilege and resistance 132–134; 'race,' gender and intersections 128; research 134–138; 'silenced' voices in sport sociology and sport coaching 130–132
"blame the victim" approach 11
Bonilla-Silva, E. 80
Borges, M. 163
Borland, J. F. 9
Bourdieu, P. 81
Bradbury, Steven xv, xxi, xxii, xxv, 5, 10, 22, 64, 66, 80–81, 89, 211, 235, 244
British Asian football coaches 78–79, 90n1; anti-Asian and anti-Muslim football chants 79; BAME exclusion 80–81; banter 83; barriers 83–89; common-sense assumptions 87–88; CRT to examine racism 79, 81–83; doubly marginalised 81; 'foreign sounding' names 84; institutional racism 79; interviews 83, 85; methodology 81–83; oral testimonies 79, 83–89; racism 79–81; reform, recommendations for 89–90; role models 88; stealth racism 79

British Asians 89; BAME experiences 78–79; CRT to examine racism 79, 81–83; exclusion of football players 78; inferential racism 79; racialised disparity 78
British National Football Museum 128
Brooks, S. 107
Brown, G. 49
Bruening, J E. 9, 131–132, 155
Brussels-capital region 43
Buddhism 114
Burdsey, D. 79, 84

Campbell, Sol 198
capital investments 12–13
capitalist economic model 6
captaincy duties to White players 29
career progression xviii
Carter, Jimmy 80
Carter-Francique, Akilah R. 131, 143, 147–148, 155, 245
Celotex Corp. v. Catrett 183
Centre for Multicultural Youth 99
Cervin, G. 165
Chinese race/ethnicity 168
civil rights 46, 145
Civil Rights Act of 1964 7, 151, 182
Clarke, Greg 133
Clarkson, M. E. 7
Club Brugge K.V. 44
COACH Bursary Programme 198
The Coaches' Voice 129
Coach Inclusion and Diversity Programme 90
coaching and racial minorities 4; discrimination 4, 5; networks-based methods of recruitment 24, 31–35
coaching certificates 64
coaching pedagogy 112–113, 113–114
coach recruitment 213; advertisements 216–217, 229; applications 217–218, 229; appointments 220–221, 229; interviews 219–220, 229; operational implementation 225–226; race-conscious approaches 214, 221–223; race-neutral approaches 214, 223–225; *see also specific entries*
Coca-Cola Company 180, 186
Cochran, Johnnie 179, 180, 186
Cohen, P. 86
collective bargaining agreement (CBA) 181
college athletes 143

College coaching 146
Collins, P. H. 115, 128, 199
'colour-blind' ideologies 25, 36, 228
'colour-line' 86
commitment to social justice 145
competitive games 118
complaints-based approach 203
Conricode, Dominic 211, 244
constructivist grounded theory 83
Contesting 'Race' and Sport: Shaming the Colour Line (Hylton) 132
corporate social responsibility (CSR) 53
Corthouts, Joris 43, 244
court footy 118
Cowell, Sophie 196
Coyle, D. 89
Creating and Developing Coaches 89
Crenshaw, Kimberle 128, 145, 150
cricket 118
criminalization of Blackness 155
critical pedagogy xix
critical race theory (CRT) xix, 6, 24, 36, 61–62, 79, 99–102, 128, 129, 133, 139, 145, 214
critical sociological scholarship 131
Crooks, Garth 199
cross-cultural psychology 163
Crow, Jim 182
CRT *see* critical race theory (CRT)
cultural awareness deficit 29
cultural elitism 46
cultural studies xix
cultures within sports organisations xvii
Cummings, J. 163
Cunningham, G. B. 3, 9, 10, 12, 14, 147

dadirri 116
Darby, P. 51
Daw, Majak 97
decision makers 8
de Eredivisie 59
De Haan, Donna 160
Demetriou, Andrew 97, 98
Democratic Republic of the Congo 51
de-racialised sporting idealism xv
deterministic thinking 107
Detroit Free Press 7
Dewey, J. 115
dialogic learning 114
dialogic pedagogy 117, 125
discrimination 8; access and treatment 4, 23, 147–148; in behavioral domain 8;

coaching and racial minorities 4–5, 5; employment 181–182, 184; and exclusion 251; in football 46; gendered 245; institutionalised access 239; notion of treatment 12; positive 201; racial/ethnic exclusion and 66–68, 183; racisms and 23–25, 143, 248; in society 15n1
diversity: in coaching 59; education 151; patterns of 22; shortfall xx
dominant ideology 145
dominant (White) social and cultural 'old boys' club 37
double marginalisation of minoritised women xviii
DuBois, C. 11
Dungy, Tony 180
Duru, N. Jeremi 179
Dutch-Antilles 76n2
Dutch Central Office for Statistics (CBS) 60
Dutch football, under-representation of minority coaches 59–61, 65–66; alternative career paths. 69; Critical Race Theory 61; cultural studies 61; data and sample 63–65; exclusion and marginalization 73; face-to-face interviews 75; general design 63; inclusivity/exclusivity of networks 68–69; network building 68; oppositional racial/ethnic identities 71–72; qualitative findings 64; racial/ethnic exclusion and discrimination 66–68; racial/ethnic positionedness 62; role models of 70–71; stereotypes 70–71; theoretical perspectives 61–62; whiteness and racial/ethnic stereotypes 74; whiteness studies 61; White-situated perception 74
Dutch football media 59
Dutch football players: racial/ethnic diversity 61, 63
Dutch national (men's) team 60
Dutch society 22; Antillean-Dutch 60; decolonization 60; Moroccan decent 60; Moroccan-Dutch 60; multi-ethnic society 59–60; non-White minority ethnic groups 60; race and ethnicity 60; Surinamese-Dutch 60; Turkish-Dutch 60

Education Amendments of 1972 152
Edwards, Harry 152
Edwards, Herm 180
egalitarianism 79, 114
elite sporting success 160
embedded normativity 31
embedded racialised barriers xvii, 23
employment discrimination 181–182, 184
enforced self-regulation 196, 202, 203
England, race, ethnicity and football coaching in 22, 211–214; advertisements 216–217; applications 217–218; appointments 220–221; findings 216; interviews 219–220; mandatory code 216; race-conscious approaches to coach recruitment 221–223; race-neutral approaches to coach recruitment 223–225; study and methods 215–216; theoretical framework 214–215
English Football League (EFL) voluntary code of recruitment xxv, 37, 190, 196–197, 205, 206n2; BAME managers and coaches 197–200; positive action 200–202; reflexive regulation 202–205
English Premier League 190
English Rooney Rule 198; see also Rooney Rule
'English' sounding names 84–85
Equality Act 2010 207n4
Equality Standards for football clubs 198
Essed, P. 60
ethnic cross-pollination 43
ethnic prejudice 46
European colonisation 51
European Commission against Racism and Intolerance (ECRI) xvi
European football association UEFA 63
European Network Against Racism 44
European professional football coaching 33
European Union (EU) 202
Evans, John 112
exercise scientists 160
experiential knowledge 145

Facebook 190
face discrimination in society 15n1
fairness 79
FA Licensed Coaches Club 216
Fanon, F. 84
FARE (Football Against Racism in Europe) Network 26, 39n3, 63

FA UEFA B licence 213
Feagin, J. R. 6, 75, 80, 87
Fechter, A. M. 170
Fenton, S. 166
Filak, V. F. 149
financial supporters of athletic departments 8
Fitzclarence, L. 81
Flanders 43
Fletcher, T. 88
Folau, Israel 105–106
Football Bowl Subdivision (FBS) 147
football coach 90n2
Football Unit 53
'footy' 113, 114, 120, 123
foreign coaches 160, 164, 165
'foreign sounding' names 84
Foucauldian framework 163
France 22
Frederic, G. 100
Fredman, S. 203
Freire, Paulo 112–113, 114, 115, 116, 124, 125

game-based approaches 116
game sense 116, 118
gay male educators 169
gender and nationality of athletes 168
Germany 22
Giggs, Ryan 164
Gillborn, D. 101, 133
Giroux, H. A. 113
Goodwill Games 149
Greater Western Sydney 105
Green, Dennis 180
Greenhaus, J. H. 4
group-based hierarchies 45, 52
group inequality 46
Gullit, Ruud 167

Hage, Ghassan 98
Harris, T. 133
Hawkins, B. 101
'head-hunting' approaches, for senior coaches 31
health disparities 3, 6–7
hegemonic Whiteness in the sport xviii, 24, 25
Heim, Chris 43, 244
Henry, Tony 197
Hepple, B. 203, 204
Heppolette, Ricky 80

heteronormative masculinity 162
heteronormativity 161–162, 169, 171
hierarchical society 46
Higher Level Coach Education (HLCE) courses 81
Hill, F. 85
Hill Collins' matrix 131
Hokowhitu, Brendan 101
homogenous reproduction 151
homologous reproduction xvii, 219
Hughton, Chris xv–xvi
human capital investments 12
humanitarian crises 51
Hunt, Karmichael 105
Hylton, Kevin xvi, 73, 82, 101, 128, 129, 132, 166, 244, 245

identity symmetry 27
immigrant coaches 163
incarceration, high rates 3
Ince, Paul 198
Indigenous Australians 100, 112–113; anti-dialogic pedagogy of professional sport 120–122; banking *versus* problem-posing education (coaching) 114–116; contrasting coaching pedagogy 113–114; data generation and analysis 117; dialogic learning 114; dialogic pedagogy 117; informal games, learning through 118–119; methodology 116–117; *see also* Australian sport, talent identification and coaching
individuated self 13
inferential racism 79, 104
informal games, learning through 118–119
informal self-managed games 123
'inform anti-racist agendas and action' 89
institutional/structural racism 6, 44, 79, 88
Intel 190
intellectual inferiority 147
intentional racial discrimination 182
Interfederal Centre for Equal Opportunities 44
International Olympic Committee 168
intersectionality xix; scholarship 128, 129; theory 146
interviews, coaching positions 219–220, 229
Italy 22

Index

Jackson, James C. 184
Jackson v. University of New Haven 184, 185
Johnson, Lyndon 7
Johnson, R. 146
Jones, K. P. 9

KBVB/URBSFA 53, 54
Kendall, Lee 133
Kennis Centrum Sport (Knowledge Center Sport) 63
Kerr, James 104, 169
Kerr, R. 163, 164, 165
Kerwin, S. 14
Khomutova, A. 166
Kick It Out 89, 90
Kilvington, Daniel 78, 79, 80, 244
King, Martin Luther, Jr. 7
Kirby, M. 123
knock up games 124
Knoppers, Annelies 160
KNVB (national football federation) 66
Kowal, E. 100
K.S.C. Lokeren 44
Kumar, Akhil 164

labour market 46
Ladson-Billing, G. 133
Langer, A. 49
Lapchick, Richard 8, 144
Latino coach 179
Lave, J. 123
LaVoi, N. 136
Lawrence, S. xvi, 88
leadership positions in professional Belgian football 43–45; data collection and analysis 49–53; policy recommendations 53–54; presence and interconnection of race 47; race and ethnicity, conceptualising 47–48; theoretical framework 45–47
League Managers Association (LMA) 81, 89, 197, 211
Leer v. Washington Educ. Asn 181
Leonard, P. 162
lesbian coaches 169
Leverhulme Trust 215
liberal equal opportunities approaches 245
liberal ideologies of objectivity 25
liberal political leadership 7
Light, Richard 112

limited housing opportunities 3
Lorde, A. 128, 130
Lusted, Jim xv, 235

macro-level factors and racial minorities in sports 6; institutional racism 6; political climate 6–7; stakeholder expectations 7–8
macro- (societal) level analysis, sports coaching 237–239
Madden, Janice 180
management training 151
Mandatory code of coach recruitment 215
Mandatory Recruitment Code 199
Marchwinski v. Oliver Tyrone Corp. 181
marginalisation 29, 145
Marshall, A. M. 7
masculinity 161–162, 171
McDonald, Brent 97, 101, 244
McDonnell Douglas Corp. v. Green 183
McDonnell Douglass framework 183
McDowell, Jacqueline 155
McIntosh, P. 85
McKail, M. 107
McKay, P. F. 10
mediated (re)presentation 149
Mehri, Cyrus 179, 180, 186, 198
melting pot idealism xv
men's professional football in England, coaching in 22, 211–214; advertisements 216–217; applications 217–218; appointments 220–221; findings 216; interviews 219–220; mandatory code 216; over-reliance on networks-based methods 211; race-conscious approaches to coach recruitment 221–223; race-neutral approaches to coach recruitment 223–225; study and methods 215–216; theoretical framework 214–215
mentoring relationships 154
Mercurio, E. 150
meritocracy 25, 79, 139
meso-level analysis 163
meso-level factors and racial minorities in sports 8; bias in decision making 8–9; organizational culture 9–10; organizational policies 11
meso-(organisational) level analysis, sports coaching 241
micro-aggressions 29

micro-(individual) level analysis, sports coaching 241–244
micro-level factors and racial minorities 11–12; capital investments 12–13; personal identity 13; self-limiting behaviors 14
micro-level football actors 44
Microsoft 190
migration of skilled sport labor 166
Miller, Cheryl 149
Minnesota Vikings 180
minoritised coaches in professional football in Europe 22–24, 36, 39n1, 251n1; networks-based methods of recruitment 31–35; racisms and racial stereotypes 28–31; study and methods 26–27; theoretical framework 24–25
minoritised groups 39n1
minoritised sports coaches xix–xxv, xxvin1; incremental growth in 22
minority ethnic coaches, in Dutch football 59–61, 65–66; data and sample 63–65; general design 63; Inclusivity/exclusivity of networks 68–69; oppositional racial/ethnic identities 71–72; racial/ethnic exclusion and discrimination 66–68; racial/ethnic positionedness 62; stereotypes 70–71; theoretical perspectives 61–62
minority ethnic groups 15n1, 75, 76n1
'minority status' 39n1
mixed-race networks 12
monocultural processes xvii
mono-ethnic coaching networks 85
Moore, K. 163
Morocco 48
motherhood wage penalty 151
M'Poku, Paul-Jose 44
multi-cultural basketball teams 166
multiculturalism and social inclusion 33, 97
multi-cultural trespass 28
multi-ethnic practice 62
multi-level models of analysis xix, 11
'Muslim' sounding name 85
mutual acquaintance 25

NAACP v. Town of E. Haven 184
Naismith College Player of the Year 149
Nakata, M. 123

National Collegiate Athletic Association (NCAA) 3, 9, 11, 143
National Collegiate Athletic Association (NCAA) Leadership Institute 149
National Football League (NFL) xviii, 11; disparate impact 184–186; disparate treatment 182–184; diverse candidate slate concept 186–188; diversity gains 188–189; legal remedy, absence of 181–182; racial inequity among coaches 179–181, 189; Rooney Rule 189–191; Rooney Rule 2.0 191; Title VII 182
National Football League (NFL) Coaches Academy 149
nationalism and meritocracy 46
nationalistic ideologies 28
national racial population demographics xv
National Rugby League (NRL) 116, 121, 125
'natural' ability 98, 101; effects of search for 103; sentiment of 105
NCAA Division IA 85
NCAA Inclusion Forum 153
negative social value 46
networks-based methods of coach recruitment 31–35, 203
N'Ganaga, Francis 44
Nix v. WLCY Radio/Rahall Commc'ns 183
'non-black' minoritised groups 33
non-European heritage resident 39n1
non-Indigenous 'footy' 120
non-White minority ethnic coaches in Dutch professional league 59
Norman, L. 135, 160
normativity of Whiteness 25
nutritionists 160

Obel, C. 164, 169
'Old Boy' networks 199
Olushola-Ogunrinde, Joyce 131, 143, 245
Olympic Games 149
Omi, M. 87, 88
on-the-field racial diversity 33, 196, 197
oppression, multiplicative layering of 146, 153, 155
organizational cultures 9–10, 221
organizational performance 10
organizational policies 11
Ortega, F. J. 75
ostracism and racism 5

overplay xv
overseas coach 167

Pan American Games 149
Pasifika communities 104–105
Peachey, Welty 9
Pedagogy of the Oppressed (Freire) 113
personal identity 13
Peter, A. 198
physical superiority 147
physiotherapists 160
Pinterest 190
players of Suriname 60
political intersectionality 146, 151
positive pedagogy for sport coaching 114, 115, 116
post structuralism xix, 161
Powell, Hope 128–129
power relations 171
prejudice, bias 8, 9
problem-based learning (PBL) 115
problem-posing approach knowledge 115–116
pro-diversity workplace culture 10
professional club youth academy coaches 211
Professional Footballers Association and League Managers Association 212
Professional Footballers' Association (PFA) 191, 198
professional football in Europe, minoritised coaches in 22–24; networks-based methods of recruitment 31–35; normativity of Whiteness 27; over-reliance of racially closed networks-based approaches 24; racisms and racial stereotypes 24, 28–31; study and methods 26–27; theoretical framework 24–25
psychologists 160

R. Charleroi S.C. 44
Rabbatts, Dame Heather 129
race 100; neutrality 25, 82, 139; role in shaping sporting opportunities xvi
Race, Gender and Sport: The Politics of Ethnic 'Other' Girls and Women (Ratna and Samie) 130
race(ial): abuse 28; 'banter' 83; bias 46; categorisation 47; discrimination 180; diversity and sports coaching xvii, xx; domination 25; elite 80; ethnic inclusion/exclusion 72; and ethnic oppression 46; ethnic stereotyping 72; formation xvi; inequalities xv, xvi, 179
race-neutral approaches 214
racialisation 99, 101–104, 136, 227, 239–241
racialised discrimination xvi
racialised microaggressions xvii
racialised 'othering' 29
racialised power relations 35
racialised science 100, 101
racialised scientific knowledge 103
racialised society 103
racial minorities in sports 3–5, 9, 15n1; in coaching, under-representation 3–5, 22; macro-level factors 6–8; meso-level factors 8–11; micro-level factors 11–14
racial minority: access to jobs 7; athletes 5; soccer coaches 5
racial projects 35
racism: banter, justified as 83; character of xvi; defined 80; and discrimination 23; endemic 6; within institutions 80; minoritised coaches in professional football in Europe 28–31; and sexism 115
'Raise Your Game' programme 89
Ramdane, Abder 44
Rankin-Wright, Alexandra J. 128, 135, 244, 245
Ratna, A. 79, 130
reflexive regulation 196, 202, 205
Regan, M. 80
representational disparities in sports coaching 23
representational intersectionality 146, 151
Rigney, L.-I. 123
Roberts, Jason 198
Rooney, Dan 199
Rooney Rule xviii, xxvi, 11, 54, 90, 179, 188–191, 197, 198, 199, 206, 213
Rosenberg, Michael 7
Rosette, A. S. 9
routinised racisms 25
Royal Belgian Football Association 53
Royal Union Saint-Gilles 44
rugby league 113, 118
rugby union 104

Sagas, M. 147
Samie, S. 130
Sarra, C. 123

262 Index

Sartore, M. L. 9
Sasaba, I. 163
Savage, S. V. 148
Scheerder, Jeroen 43, 244
Schein, E. H. 9
Schneider, B. 169
Scraton, S. 130
Seebruck, R. 148
self-limiting behaviors 14
self-perceived identity 167
semi-formal coaching 118
semi-professional football clubs 91n5
senior coaching positions 207n3
sense of belonging 163
Sheedy, Kevin 98
Simpson, O. J. 180
Singer, J. N. 80, 153
single-axis race-based perspective 151
'single-level' interventions 244
Smith, Roy 80
Smith v. Xerox Corp. 185
social alienation 85
social capital investments 12
social categorizations 146
social cloning 88
social cohesiveness of Belgian society 53
social dominance theory (SDT) xix, 45
social hierarchies 61
social inclusion strategy 55n5
social inequalities 46, 145
social integration 46
social networks, exclusion from 5
social power relations 161
social rituals xvi
sociocultural differences 88
socio-historical exclusions 25
sovereignty of whiteness 132
Spaaij, Ramón 97, 244
Spain 22
'speed gene' 103
sports: genomics 102; labour market 98; management xix; organizations 6; pedagogy xix; performers xv; psychology xix; science 98; socio-cultural aspects xvii
sporting: equals 88, 89, 90; modernity xv
sports coaching 235; discrimination in xviii; education and training programmes 248–249; enhancing networks 249–250; institutionalised racialisation 239–241; multi-level and holistic approach 244–245; priorities for researching 'race,' ethnicity and racism 236–237; racial equality interventions xxiv–xxv; racialised identities, diversity and intersectionality xxiii–xxiv; racialised inequalities xviii, 244–250; racialised social conditions 237–239; representation and racialised barriers in xxi–xxii; robust policy interventions 246–247; testimonies from the racialised side-lines 241–244
sports talent identification practices 104
stakeholder expectations 7–8
Stangor, C. 79
stealth racism 79
Steelers, Pittsburgh 189
stereotypes, utilization of 150
stereotypes bias 8
Sterling, Raheem 197
Stringer, C. Vivian 143
Strong, Charlie 143
structural inequalities 151, 203
structural intersectionality 146, 151
structural racisms xvi
student-athletes 149
Studio Voetbal [Studio Football] 59, 75
sub-Saharan African ethnicities 48
substantial diversity 197
Super Bowl 189
Surinamese or Caribbean descent 65

Tampa Bay Buccaneers 180
Taylor, Gordon 199
Texaco 180, 186–187
The Football Association (The FA) 128
The Institute for Diversity and Ethics in Sport (TIDES) 144
the Netherlands *see* Dutch society
Thornley v. Penton Pub., Inc. 185
Tinning, R. 81
tokenism 151
Tomlin, Mike 189
Torres Strait Islanders 100
transdisciplinary perspective 145
translocational positionality 171–172
transnational coaches 160–161; appointment, preference for 165; empirical research 162–165; gender 168–170; intersectionality and translocational positionality 170–172; mobility of 168; post-colonial

approach 170; race and ethnicity 165–168; Spanish coaches 164; theoretical framework 161–162; whiteness and masculinity 162
transnational Spanish coaches 164
treatment discrimination 4–5, 148; pay, differences in 5
Trienekens, S. 60
Tudor, A. 171
Turkish heritage populations 39n1
Tweede Divisie 61

UEFA B Licence 91n4
UEFA Pro license qualified coaches 64, 82, 83, 86, 89
UEFA (Union of European Football Associations) 26, 39n2
UK Equality Act 2010 201, 213
United Kingdom (UK), Black women coaches in 128–129, 139n1; power, privilege and resistance 132–134; 'race,' gender and intersections 128; research 134–138; 'silenced' voices in sport sociology and sport coaching 130–132
University of New Hampshire (UNH) 184
University of Southern California (USC) Trojans 149
unqualified white coaches 85

Vanderbiest, Frederik 44
van Dijk, Virgil 60
Van Sterkenburg, Jacco xv, 59, 60, 235
Victorian Health Promotion Foundation 99
Vlaams Belang 44
Voluntary Code 196
Voluntary Recruitment Code 199–200
Voting Rights Act of 1965 7

Wade Trophy recipient 149
Wallonia 43
Walsh, K. 170
Ward, J. 169
Wells, J. E. 14
Wenger, E. 123
white coaches 31, 32, 212
white cultural spaces 28
'white' dream about 'blackness' 98
white habitus 80
white maleness 155
'white mask' 84
whiteness 73, 161–162
white racial frame 80
whites, privileges to 8–9
white-situated discourses 62
white-situated frames of meaning making 62
white social and cultural networks 32
'white-to-white' networks 86
white Western European hegemonic discourses 27
Wicker, P. 163
Winant, H. 87, 88
Wolverhampton Wanderers FC 199–200
women of color 131; *see also* black women coaches in the UK
Women's National Basketball Association (WNBA) 149
Workplace Diversity Committee 199
world-class coaches 160

Xerox 190

Yunkaporta, T. 123

Zamudio, M. M. 82
Zarate, M. A. 79–80
Zenga, Walter 200
Ziyech, Hakim 60

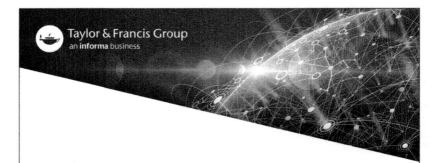